Teacher Preparation Classroom

W9-BHT-861

YOUR CLASS. THEIR CAREERS. OUR FUTURE. WILL YOUR STUDENTS BE PREPARED?

We invite you to explore our new, innovative, and engaging website and all that it has to offer you, your course, and tomorrow's educators! Preview this site today at www.prenhall.com/teacherprep/demo. Just click on "go" on the login page to begin your exploration.

Organized around the major courses pre-service teachers take, the Teacher Preparation site provides media, student/teacher artifacts, strategies, research articles, and other resources to equip your students with the quality tools needed to excel in their courses and prepare them for their first classroom.

This ultimate online education resource will provide you and your students access to:

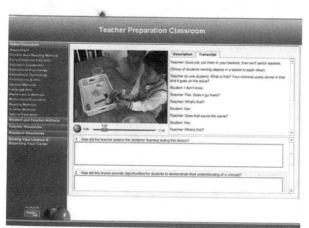

ONLINE VIDEO LIBRARY More than 250 video clips—each tied to a course topic and framed by learning goals and Praxis-type questions—capture real teachers and students working in real classrooms.

STUDENT AND TEACHER ARTIFACTS More than 200 student and teacher classroom artifacts—each tied to a course topic and framed by learning goals and application questions—provide a wealth of materials and experiences to help your students observe children's developmental learning.

LESSON PLAN BUILDER Step-by-step guidelines and lesson plan examples support students as they learn to build high-quality lesson plans.

ARTICLES AND READINGS Over 500 articles from ASCD's renowned journal *Educational Leadership* are available. The site also includes Research Navigator, a searchable database of additional educational journals.

STRATEGIES AND LESSONS Over 500 research-supported instructional strategies appropriate for a wide range of grade levels and content areas.

LICENSURE AND CAREER TOOLS Resources devoted to helping your students pass their licensure exam; learn standards, law, and public policies; plan a teaching portfolio; and succeed in their first year of teaching.

HOW TO ORDER *TEACHER PREP* FOR YOU AND YOUR STUDENTS:

For students to receive a *Teacher Prep* Access Code with this text, instructors must provide a special value pack ISBN number on their textbook order form. To receive this special ISBN, please email *Merrill.marketing@pearsoned.com* and provide the following information:

- Name and Affiliation
- Author/Title/Edition of Merrill text

Upon ordering *Teacher Prep* for their students, instructors will be given a lifetime Teacher Prep Access Code.

FOURTH EDITION

Children's Literature, Briefly

Michael O. Tunnell
Brigham Young University

James S. Jacobs
Brigham Young University

PEARSON

Merrill
Prentice Hall

Upper Saddle River, New Jersey
Columbus, Ohio

Library of Congress Cataloging in Publication Data
Tunnell, Michael O.
  Children's literature, briefly / Michael O. Tunnell, James S. Jacobs. — 4th ed.
      p. cm.
  Rev. ed. of: Children's literature, briefly / James S. Jacobs, Michael O.
Tunnell. 3rd ed. c2004.
  Includes bibliographical references and index.
  ISBN-13: 978-0-13-173490-6
  ISBN-10: 0-13-173490-3
  1. Children's literature—Study and teaching. 2. Children's literature—
History and criticism. 3. Children—Books and reading. I. Jacobs, James S.,
1945- II. Title.
  PN1008.8.J33 2008
  809'.89282—dc22

                                                          2007001844

Vice President and Executive Publisher: Jeffery W. Johnston
Senior Editor: Linda Ashe Bishop
Development Editor: Laura Weaver
Senior Production Editor: Mary M. Irvin
Design Coordinator: Diane C. Lorenzo
Cover Designer: Ali Mohrman
Cover image: Illustration from *Jabuti the Tortoise: A Trickster Tale from the Amazon*, © 2001 by Gerald
McDermott. Reproduced by permission of Harcourt Children's Books.
Production Manager: Pamela D. Bennett
Director of Marketing: David Gesell
Marketing Manager: Darcy Betts Prybella
Marketing Coordinator: Brian Mounts

This book was set in Galliard by Carlisle Publishing Services. It was printed and bound by R. R. Donnelley &
Sons Company. The cover was printed by Phoenix Color Corp.

Pearson Education Ltd.   Pearson Education Australia Pty. Limited
Pearson Education Singapore Pte. Ltd.   Pearson Education North Asia Ltd.
Pearson Education Canada, Ltd.   Pearson Educación de Mexico, S.A. de C.V.
Pearson Education—Japan   Pearson Education Malaysia Pte. Ltd.

10 9 8 7 6 5 4 3
ISBN-13: 978-0-13-173490-6
ISBN-10: 0-13-173490-3

PREFACE

The subtitle for this text should be "A children's literature textbook for people who don't like children's literature textbooks." Between us, we taught children's literature a total of 35 years without using a textbook because the ones available were too expensive and too extensive for an introductory course. We owned and regularly consulted the available texts, but they seemed more like reference books. Our biggest concern, though, was neither the cost nor the length, but the hours stolen from students when they could be reading actual children's books. The focus of a children's literature course should be on those marvelous children's titles. They are more important than any text, including this one, and we wrote this book on that assumption.

Children's Literature, Briefly is written as an overview to shed light on children's literature and its use with young readers. Our job as teachers, whether university or elementary, is to introduce children's books and illuminate them for our students. These books can offer insight and pleasure without having to be explained, analyzed, or used as objects of study. Yet appropriate commentary, if it is secondary to the books and does not become too self-important, can help both teachers and children find their own ways to the rewards of reading.

The goal of this text, then, is to provide a practical overview of children's books, offering a framework and background information while keeping the spotlight on the books themselves. That's why we kept the textbook itself and each chapter short.

And that's why we limited the book lists. The world of children's literature offers only one completely dependable book list—your own. Throughout the following chapters, we present ours, absolutely trustworthy in every way—to us. You are allowed to harbor serious doubts about our choices, but their value is that our titles may save you time wandering up and down library aisles. We organized our book lists at the end of the chapters under four different headings.

1. *Ten of Our Favorites*. The 10 books listed after each chapter in Part 2 (15 favorites, in the case of picture books) are terrific reading. These lists are very short, the result of much negotiating, often emotional, but largely friendly. The purpose of the 10 is to provide solid suggestions for those who wonder where to find a good book. Each title is annotated to give a brief idea of the content.
2. *Others We Like*. These titles (generally around 30) are not annotated. Although they are the second level of recommendations, each is a book we

like very much. Don't be surprised if you find some of them more appealing than the 10 of our favorites.

3. *Easier to Read.* Next we have added 10–15 titles of shorter, generally popular books. These help the teacher find nonthreatening titles for children who are struggling to make reading a rewarding pasttime.

4. *Picture Books.* In most genre chapters, we have included 15–20 picture books we consider representative and outstanding. Not all of these titles are for use exclusively in the lower grades; many are appropriate for the upper grades, as well.

The Children's Literature Database CD-ROM

Beyond these chapter-ending booklists we provide you with a megalist—a database with more than 20,000 titles—on a CD-ROM that accompanies this text. A four-color insert located in the back of this text walks you through the main features of the database and explains how these features function. In addition, Tech Notes throughout in the margins of the text provide you opportunities to practice using the database. Our goal is to help you become efficient at navigating the Children's Literature Database so that it might prove to be a valuable resource for creating book lists for unit planning purposes or finding books that are appropriate to meet individual children's needs.

Begin using the database by saving it to your hard drive. The navigation bar menu directs you to buttons that will allow you to move about the database quickly; run searches for books by certain authors or illustrators; locate books by genre, topic, and/or grade level; or find books that have won particular book awards. Use the Search Query Builder to create your own book lists, extend or trim a book list, and print or save those lists. You can also add to the master list and comment on any and all books you read. The database also allows you to add any new award-winning books, including such annual awards as the new Caldecott and Newbery winners, always announced in late January. This database is designed to be a teaching tool to help ensure that you and your students can find quality children's literature to read now and for years to come.

Acknowledgments

We would like to thank the reviewers of our manuscript for their valuable insights and comments: Mary Warner, San Jose State University; Ann Bullion-Mears, Angelo State University; Carolyn Brodie, Kent State University; Patricia DeMay, University of West Alabama; Louise Stearns, Southern Illinois University; Kathy R. Fox, University of North Carolina-Wilmington; Margaret T. Sacco, Miami University; and Diane E. Steiner, Chestnut Hill College.

Thanks also go to our research assistants: Michelle Groesbeck, Rosemary Groesbeck, Rebecca Maxfield, Nicole Swain, Megan Tanner, and Catharine Verhaaren for their help with the textbook and particularly with assembling and entering the data for the Children's Literature Database CD-ROM. To you, we are especially grateful.

CONTENTS

PART ONE
The Magic of Books

CHAPTER ONE
Why Read? 1

CHAPTER TWO
What Is a Good Book? 10

CHAPTER THREE
How to Recognize a Well-Written Book 18

CHAPTER EIGHT
Poetry   80

CHAPTER NINE
Traditional Fantasy   101

CHAPTER TEN
Modern Fantasy   116

CHAPTER ELEVEN
Contemporary Realistic Fiction   128

PART THREE

Books in the Classroom

CREDITS

COLOR INSERTS

1. From *The Fortune-Tellers* by Lloyd Alexander, illustrated by Trina Schart Hyman, copyright © 1992 by Trina Schart Hyman, illustrations. Used by permission of Dutton Children's Books, A Division of Penguin Young Readers Group, A Member of Penguin Group (USA) Inc., 345 Hudson Street, New York, NY 10014. All rights reserved.

2. From *Frog Goes to Dinner* by Mercer Mayer, copyright © 1974 by Mercer Mayer. Used by permission of Dial Books for Young Readers, A Division of Penguin Young Readers Group, A Member of Penguin Group (USA) Inc., 345 Hudson Street, New York, NY 10014. All rights reserved.

3. Reprinted with the permission of Simon & Schuster Books for Young Readers, an imprint of Simon & Schuster Children's Publishing Division from *Rosie's Walk* by Pat Hutchins. Copyright © 1968 Patricia Hutchins.

4. Reprinted with the permission of Atheneum Books for Young Readers, an imprint of Simon & Schuster Children's Publishing Division from *The Relatives Came* by Cynthia Rylant, illustrated by Stephen Gammell. Illustrations copyright © 1985 Stephen Gammell.

5. Illustration from *The Polar Express* by Chris Van Allsburg. Copyright © 1985 by Chris Van Allsburg. Reprinted by permission of Houghton Mifflin Company. All rights reserved.

6. From *Rapunzel* retold and illustrated by Paul O. Zelinsky, copyright © 1997 by Paul O. Zelinsky. Used by permission of Dutton Children's Books, A Division of Penguin Young Readers Group, A Member of Penguin Group (USA) Inc., 345 Hudson Street, New York, NY 10014. All rights reserved.

7. From *The Voice of the Wood* by Claude Clement, illustrated by Frederic Clement, translated by Lenny Hort. Illustrations copyright © 1988 by l'école des loisirs. Used by permission of Dial Books for Young Readers, A Division of Penguin Young Readers Group, A Member of Penguin Group (USA) Inc., 345 Hudson Street, New York, NY 10014. All rights reserved.

8. From *A Chair for My Mother*. Copyright © 1982 by Vera B. Williams. Used by permission of HarperCollins Publishers.

9. Reprinted with the permission of Atheneum Books for Young Readers, an imprint of Simon & Schuster Children's Publishing Division from *Freedom Summer* by Deborah Wiles, illustrated by Jerome Lagarrigue. Illustrations copyright © 2001 Jerome Lagarrigue.

10. From *Ox-Cart Man* by Donald Hall, illustrated by Barbara Cooney. Illustrations copyright © 1979 by Barbara Cooney Porter. Used by permission of Viking Penguin, A Division of Penguin Young Readers Group, A Member of Penguin Group (USA) Inc., 345 Hudson Street, New York, NY 10014. All rights reserved.

11. From *Flying Feet: A Mud Flat Story*. Illustrations © 2004 by James Stevenson. Used by permission of HarperCollins Publishers.

12. Illustration from *Zathura: A Space Adventure* by Chris Van Allsburg. Copyright © 2002 by Chris Van Allsburg. Reprinted by permission of Houghton Mifflin Company. All rights reserved.

13. From *Ben's Trumpet*. Copyright © 1979 by Rachel Isadora Majorano. Used by permission of HarperCollins Publishers.

14. Reprinted with the permission of Atheneum Books for Young Readers, an imprint of Simon & Schuster Children's Publishing Division from *Once a Mouse . . .* by Marcia Brown. Copyright © 1961 Marcia Brown; copyright renewed 1989 Marcia Brown.

15. Illustration from *Bernard the Angry Rooster* by Mary Wormell. Farrar, Straus & Giroux. 2001.

16. From *One Night in the Coral Sea*. Text and illustrations copyright © 2006 by Sneed B. Collard III. Illustrations copyright © 2006 by Robin Brickman. Used with permission of Charlesbridge Publishing, Inc. All rights reserved.

17. From *Abraham Lincoln* by Ingri & Edgar d'Aulaire, copyright 1939, 1957 by Doubleday, a division of Random House, Inc. Used by permission of Random House Children's Books, a division of Random House, Inc.

18. Illustration from *Ella Fitzgerald: The Tale of a Vocal Virtuoso* by Brian Pinkney. Hyperion (Jump at the Sun). 2002.

19. Illustration copyright © 1993 by Bruce McMillan from *Mouse Views: What the Class Pet Saw*. All rights reserved. Used by permission of Holiday House, Inc.

20. From *The Paper Crane*. Copyright © 1985 by Molly Bang. Used with the permission of Greenwillow Books. Used by permission of HarperCollins Publishers.

21. From *Deep in the Forest* by Brinton Turkle, copyright © 1976 by Brinton Turkle. Used by permission of Dutton Children's Books, A Division of Penguin Young Readers Group, A Member of Penguin Group (USA) Inc., 345 Hudson Street, New York, NY 10014. All rights reserved.

22. Illustration from *Tuesday* by David Wiesner. Copyright © 1991 by David Wiesner. Reprinted by permission of Clarion Books, an imprint of Houghton Mifflin Company. All rights reserved.

23. Illustration copyright © 1992 by Glen Rounds from *Three Little Pigs and the Big Bad Wolf*. All rights reserved. Used by permission of Holiday House, Inc.

24. Reprinted with the permission of Simon & Schuster Books for Young Readers, an imprint of Simon & Schuster Children's Publishing Division from

Thorn Rose by The Brothers Grimm, illustrated by Errol Le Cain. Copyright © 1975 Errol Le Cain.

25. Reprinted with the permission of Simon & Schuster Books for Young Readers, an imprint of Simon & Schuster Children's Publishing Division from *Thorn Rose* by The Brothers Grimm, illustrated by Errol Le Cain. Copyright © 1975 Errol Le Cain.

26. Reprinted with the permission of Simon & Schuster Books for Young Readers, an imprint of Simon & Schuster Children's Publishing Division from *Thorn Rose* by The Brothers Grimm, illustrated by Errol Le Cain. Copyright © 1975 Errol Le Cain.

27. One two-page illustration from *Snow-White and the Seven Dwarfs* by The Brothers Grimm, translated by Randall Jarrell, pictures by Nancy Ekholm Burkert.

28. From *Round Trip*. Illustrations © 1983 by Ann Jonas. Used by permission of HarperCollins Publishers.

29. From *Saint George and the Dragon* by Margaret Hodges. Copyright © 1984 by Margaret Hodges (Text); Copyright © 1984 by Trina Schart Human (Illustrations). By permission of Little, Brown and Co., Inc.

30. Illustration from *Golem* by David Wisniewski. Copyright © 1996 by David Wisniewski. Reprinted by permission of Clarion Books, an imprint of Houghton Mifflin Company. All rights reserved.

31. From *Heartland*, by Diane Siebert. Illustrations copyright © 1989 by Wendell Minor. Used by permission of HarperCollins Publishers. This selection may not be re-illustrated without written permission of HarperCollins.

32. From *Blueberries for Sal* by Robert McCloskey, copyright 1948, renewed © 1976 by Robert McCloskey. Used by permission of Viking Penguin, A Division of Penguin Young Readers Group, A Member of Penguin Group (USA) Inc., 345 Hudson Street, New York, NY 10014. All rights reserved.

POEMS

p. 81 "Take the Butterfly" from *One at a Time* by David McCord. Copyright © 1965, 1966 by David McCord. By permission of Little, Brown and Co., Inc.

p. 83 *The New Kid on the Block* by Jack Prelutsky. Text copyright © 1984 by Jack Prelutsky. Used by permission of HarperCollins Publishers.

p. 84 From *Overheard on a Salt Marsh* by Harold Munro. Preprinted by permission of Gerald Duckworth and Co. Ltd.

p. 85 "Editing the Chrysalis" from *Fly With Poetry: An ABC of Poetry* by Avis Harley (Wordsong, an imprint of Boyds Mills Press, 2000). Reprinted with the permission of Boyds Mills Press, Inc. Text copyright © 2000 by Avis Harley.

pp. 85–86 "Song of the Train" from *One at a Time* by David McCord. Copyright © 1965, 1966 by David McCord. By permission of Little, Brown and Co., Inc.

p. 86 "I Like It When It's Mizzly" from *I Like the Weather* by Aileen Fisher. Copyright © 1963, © renewed 1991 by Aileen Fisher. Used by permission of Marian Reiner on behalf of the Boulder Public Library Foundation, Inc.

Chapter 1

Why Read?

Like most important questions, "Why read?" seems embarrassingly obvious. Reading simply *is* important. Period. We know that, and we assume everyone else knows that. Even in today's climate of constant controversy and limitless lawsuits, where no one appears to agree with anyone on anything, reading receives unanimous support. An antireading position has no voice, claims no champion, and gets no press. No magazine or newspaper prints an article about the evils of the reading act or how time spent with print is wasted. The push is always toward more reading. So why is reading universally acclaimed?

 THE REWARDS OF READING

Like eating, reading is one of life's activities that simultaneously yields both pleasure and benefit. When we chomp down on a three-way chimichanga, the sensations of texture, temperature, and taste reward us right then. No one needs to confirm the results; from our own personal taste buds, we know immediately that the bite is satisfying. Any attempt to change our mind is a waste of words. In addition to the obvious pleasure, our digestive system now turns the agreeable mixture of beans, beef, lettuce, onions, and tortilla into nutrients that keep us going. Benefits automatically follow the pleasing meal—energy and good health—but the primary reason for lifting a fork is the immediate reward of tasting.

Similarly, immediate reward is the one dependable criterion for determining why people choose to read. Beyond that, it is impossible to predict how a particular reader will be affected by print, as illustrated by the following actual incidents:

- Conventional wisdom says that a reader must comprehend a certain percentage of written material for reading to be successful, yet 3-year-old Bobby Morgan, whose parents read to him regularly, got up early to spend time with issues of *National Geographic,* which he preferred to picture books. His parents knew

1

that he was comprehending only a fraction of the material, but he continued to spend hour after hour with the magazine.

- Common sense indicates that we seek comfortable surroundings when engaging in a long activity such as extended reading, yet Sean, a college student, drove to the bookstore on a snowy day to buy a new book and decided to spend a few minutes looking it over in his car before heading home. Time passed, and the sun set. To continue reading, Sean had to hold the book to the window so the lights from the parking lot would shine onto the page. Four hours later, he started his chilled car for the drive to his apartment.

- Educational practice says that the difficulty of a text should be matched to individual reading abilities, yet Bill, a junior high student with second-grade reading skills, chose a book far beyond his tested level. A part of his school day was spent in intensified reading instruction in a lab setting, with the last half-hour devoted to uninterrupted individual reading. Educator Dan Fader watched Bill during his 30 minutes of reading time until the bell sounded. "Still absorbed in his reading, Bill closed the book, glanced at the cover, placed the book in his bag, and started for the door. Intrigued by this 13-year-old second-grade reader, I crossed his path at the door and walked with him as I asked, 'What are you reading?' '*Jaws.*' 'Is it good?' 'Yeah!' 'But isn't it hard?' 'Sure it's hard, but it's worth it!'" (Fader, 1976, p. 236).

When we read words that have meaning for us, we know "it's worth it." No one needs to confirm the results. We, ourselves, have proven their value. Beyond the immediate satisfaction, a number of benefits come our way: expanded vocabulary, increased world knowledge, improved reading skills, better communication skills, strengthened knowledge of language, new insights, power to compete in an information-driven age, and perhaps a certain amount of additional confidence. Engaging in the act of reading leads us down the sure path to becoming educated, but the primary reason for turning pages is always the immediate reward. Some novels provide that appeal from the first paragraph, as does *The Ruby in the Smoke* by Philip Pullman (1985).

> On a cold, fretful afternoon in early October, 1872, a hansom cab drew up outside the offices of Lockhart and Selby, Shipping Agents, in the financial heart of London, and a young girl got out and paid the driver.
>
> She was a person of sixteen or so—alone, and uncommonly pretty. She was slender and pale, and dressed in mourning, with a black bonnet under which she tucked back a straying twist of blond hair that the wind had teased loose. She had unusually dark brown eyes for one so fair. Her name was Sally Lockhart; and within fifteen minutes, she was going to kill a man. (p. 3)

Nonfiction can have the same immediate appeal. In *The Human Body: And How It Works* by Steve Parker, a double-page spread focuses on the skin. The first paragraph reads:

> On the outside, you are dead. Your hair and the surface of your skin are made of dead cells. But less than a millimeter away under the surface of your skin are some of the busiest cells in your body. They are continually dividing to make new layers of skin cells which harden and die, to replace the top layer of skin as it is worn away. Every

day millions of dead skin cells rub off as you wash, dry yourself with a towel, get dressed and move about. Much of the "dust" in a house is dead skin which has rubbed off the bodies of people. (1998, p. 10)

Real reading, then, offers us two rewards. The first is immediate. The text pulls us into images and ideas at the very moment we travel through the words: Suddenly we realize that dust particles illuminated by a shaft of sunlight are bits of our own skin! We find ourselves intrigued with this new thought. The second reward of reading is long term. Over time, the accumulated benefits—increased language and thinking skills plus additional knowledge, experience, and insight—add up to the reader becoming an educated person.

Jim Trelease identifies some of the powerful benefits of reading (2001, p. xxiv):

One can arguably state: reading is the single most important social factor in American life today. Here's a formula to support that. It sounds simplistic, but all its parts can be documented, and while not 100 percent universal, it holds true far more often than not.

1. The more you read, the more you know. (Foertsch, 1992)
2. The more you know, the smarter you grow. (Anderson, Hiebert, Scott, & Wilkinson, 1985)
3. The smarter you are, the longer you stay in school. (Associated Press, 1994)
4. The longer you stay in school, the more diplomas you earn and the longer you are employed—thus the more money you earn in a lifetime. (Lee, 1994)
5. The more diplomas you earn, the higher your children's grades will be in school. (de Vinck, 1991)
6. The more diplomas you earn, the longer you live. (Rogot, Sorlie, & Johnson, 1992)

The rewards of reading also can be viewed through the lens of bibliotherapy. In its broadest definition, bibliotherapy is any kind of emotional healing that comes from reading books. Therapy derived from books falls into at least three different categories: (1) the broad therapeutic feelings of recreation and gratification experienced by an individual reader, (2) the sense of connectedness felt by members of a group who read and share books together, and (3) the particular information and insight books can provide in dealing with specific personal problems (Chatton, 1988).

The first two categories, recreation and connectedness, result naturally from reading. Those who have found compelling titles experience the first category as they discover the deep satisfaction, stimulation, and comfort that books can bring. The second category—connectedness—occurs when readers experience a book along with others, a new dimension to the group relationship. A teacher and classroom of children who read a book together are able to connect with one another in new ways when laughing, crying, or simply talking about their mutual experience.

The third category—dealing with specific and often deep-seated personal problems—is, of course, best reserved for trained psychologists and psychotherapists, who can and do use books successfully in their practices. Other adults can serve children simply by reading and recommending good books and allowing personal insight, comfort, and the answering of troubling questions to come in their own natural and timely ways.

Bibliotherapy, whatever the level, promises parents, teachers, and children personal rewards as a result of time spent with books.

UNENGAGED AND ENGAGED READING

If we all agree that reading is so rewarding and beneficial, why don't more people spend more time at it? To understand why we choose to read and why we don't, it is helpful to recognize that reading tends to fall into two categories: unengaged and engaged. Unengaged reading is the reading of necessity, the reading required by others or forced on us. A certain amount of engagement can result from reading of necessity, but most often reading imposed by work or school remains unengaged, speaking neither to our heads nor to our hearts. Even novels can be misused by well-intentioned teachers who unwittingly prevent their students from experiencing the power of a book in a variety of ways. In an effort to improve vocabulary, for example, teachers ask students to find the nine examples of onomatopoeia in the first chapter of *Island of the Blue Dolphins* (O'Dell, 1960). Or, before having students read a chapter, teachers introduce the difficult vocabulary and ask students to locate the words, define them, and use them in sentences. When students know that a traditional book report (plot, setting, theme, characterization, style, point of view) is expected, they tend to read books from a less personal perspective.

Few immediate or lasting benefits come from unengaged reading. If the reader is not involved with the text—not engaged in the information or experience—the reading is often empty and unproductive.

Why Do So Few People Read?

One reason so few people read a book after leaving school is that they have seldom gone beyond assigned reading. Despite having completed the required reading that marks the path to a diploma, a surprising number of supposedly educated graduates have rarely, if ever, known the sustaining thrill of reading a book that speaks directly and personally to them. The reading they did was for someone else, according to someone else's rules and expectations, thus life was never breathed into the books they completed for their classes. In short, the books never happened.

These unengaged readers, the ones who can read but don't, are sometimes called aliterate. The aliterate person has all the necessary know-how to unlock the meaning in print but chooses not to pick up books. And, as the sign over a small school library reminds us, "The person who can read, and doesn't, is no better off than the one who can't read."

Reading Is Personally Motivating

Engaged reading is personally motivated. Those who read for personal reasons know the satisfying feeling of finding pleasure in print and are rewarded in two areas: locating information and gaining experience.

People who want certain information seek it out. We read for information when we check the sodium content in frozen dinners, plan the drive from Poughkeepsie to Pittsburgh, look in the dictionary for the meaning of *obfuscate*, scan the newspaper ads for a furniture sale, follow the so-called directions for assembling a barbecue grill, or scan the note from Harold's teacher. No one makes us do those things. We choose to do them because the messages locked in those passages of print are interesting to us. Yet in each of these cases, someone else could read and summarize the content, and we would be satisfied. In her transactional theory of literature and reading, Louise Rosenblatt (1978) calls this reading for facts "efferent" reading. We are motivated by getting basic information. In these cases, if someone else could do the reading and supply us with the facts, we would be as content as if we had read the words ourselves.

"Esthetic" reading is different from efferent reading because the goal is not to acquire facts but to participate in an experience. In esthetic reading, readers focus on what they are experiencing as their eyes pass over the words. This kind of reading cannot be summarized by another, but must be done personally because it is not centered on data. The facts are not the most important part; engagement with the experience is. Knowing the plot of *Tuck Everlasting* (Babbitt, 1975) is not the same as experiencing with Winnie Foster her difficult choice between following a natural life span or living forever as a young girl. Being told that the protagonist in *Stargirl* (Spinelli, 2000) shakes up the social structure at school with her honest but unorthodox views of life comes nowhere close to being with her as she brings her ukulele and white rat to class. Reading for experience—esthetic reading—can no more be done by someone else and then reported to us than our eating can be done by another. We don't want information on food flavors; we want those flavors to flow over our own taste buds. When we read for experience, we aren't satisfied simply by knowing where the book ends up. We want to make that journey to the final page ourselves. When we participate in the experience of a good book, our lives are never quite the same again.

For reading to make a difference, it has to be personal. People generally do not turn to books because they want to study the author's use of vocabulary or have a desire to describe the major and minor characters any more than people attend movies to examine the cinematographer's use of the long shot or analyze the use of background music. We read fiction and go to the movies to get lost in the story, to see through eyes other than our own. Almost magically, participating in these vicarious experiences sheds light on our own lives. We compare, test, experience, and come away with new thoughts and visions, wondering how we ourselves would have responded in similar situations. The same idea of engagement holds true for nonfiction as well as fiction. When we are engaged in reading informational books, it is largely not the facts that rivet us, but the thoughts and insights that come as we read. In *Shipwreck at the Bottom of the World* (Armstrong, 1998), we marvel at Shackleton's courage in leading his men across Antarctica after their ship was crushed by ice. We also ponder the achievements of those visionaries who defied convention in *Seven Wonders of the Ancient World* (Curlee, 2002).

If someone forces us to shift all our concentration from the experience to the externals—the form, the theme, the use of language, or the mere facts in nonfiction—the focus on these elements may make reading the book or attending the movie no more than tedious labor. For example, would our experience with a good movie be enhanced if the manager of the theater passed out mandatory study guides to be completed while we watched the film? We would look over the questions, and our purpose for viewing the movie would shift from living the film to ferreting out the correct responses. At the end, we would not have seen the movie at all. We would have witnessed a collection of facts we needed to identify and isolate. If such were the case, we would likely stop going to movie theaters and wait for films to be released on DVD.

Like the movie example just given, the act of reading can't serve two masters—we read either for ourselves or for some other purpose. When anything comes between the reader and the printed page—such as a teacher's expectation or an assignment—the reading tends to be unengaged and remains artificial, even if eyes continue to march across the rows of words. For example, how many of us have completed several pages of assigned reading in a textbook, only to discover that we have not registered one morsel of meaning? Yet we have also experienced being so consumed by a novel or biography that we do not notice when the chapters begin or end.

Engaged and Unengaged Reading

A reader can respond differently even to the same book. Lloyd Alexander, an author who attributes his writing success to childhood reading, discovered *Treasure Island* at home as a child and loved it—pure engaged reading. He lived with Jim, he pondered the story when he was away from the book, and he longed to return to the people and events of the tale. Years later he was assigned the same novel in a high school English class. This time the reading did not produce the same involvement. Class discussion centered on elements he found uninteresting, assignments interfered with his experience, and he failed the final test "because I couldn't remember the construction of that damned blockhouse" (Alexander, 1993). The teacher held "discussions" with the class but asked only factual questions, gave assignments that did not include Lloyd's focus, and based success on a test of specific and unimportant details. Instead of helping Lloyd get deeper into the story, the teacher's approach actually kept him from the book, turning an earlier engaged reading experience into an unengaged one.

Classic unengaged reading often comes during traditional reading instruction time at school. There the focus is not on the text as a purveyor of meaning but on the text as underbrush, where the secret skills of reading hide out. The sentences and paragraphs serve as camouflage for initial consonant blends, prediction questions, comprehension checks, vocabulary words, and the objects of a multitude of other skills lessons. This is not to say that the skills of reading are unimportant. The skills need to be learned, and students need the confidence that comes from understanding how language works and from an awareness that they are skilled and competent readers. The problem comes when students are given a good story to read with the primary goal of identifying skill components in it. This emphasis is a bit like sitting down to Thanksgiving dinner and seeing only vitamins and minerals on your plate or, worse yet, being served a pile of pills instead of the steaming turkey and trimmings because, after all, those nutritional elements are what is important for fueling our bodily furnaces.

Does this mean that any book assigned in school automatically suffers the kiss of death? Of course not. An assigned book may begin as unengaged, uninteresting reading and yet become important, even invaluable, to the reader. For that to occur, however, it must receive the reader's personal stamp of approval. Somewhere between the covers, even with the full knowledge that the book is required reading and a part of the final grade, the reader must become personally involved in the text. At that point, the book moves from assigned reading to personal reading—from unengaged to engaged. If it never makes the switch, it never develops the power to influence or affect that one reader. (See Figure 1–1.)

Some readers have spent so many years reading for others that they have difficulty identifying their own responses to a book. Even some good students respond automatically to "What did you think about the book?" with thoughts like, "What should I have thought about the book?" "What am I supposed to think about the book?"

When we already have an interest in what we read, engaged reading comes naturally. No one wonders if the instructions to assemble a swing set for a much-loved but impatient three-year-old will make good reading. The purpose is determined, and the reading engages immediately. Before the first word is read, we know the instructions are worth it. At a bookstore sale table, a Civil War buff picks up a book on Stonewall Jackson and is likely to buy it. A child with an interest in dinosaurs is drawn to a book on the subject. Even when a book is not particularly well written, the person who is interested in the topic becomes an engaged reader without persuasion or effort.

How do we determine if a reader is engaged or unengaged? An engaged reader is not aware of the reading process. Engaged readers don't even see words after the first sentence or two. In a story, they see scenes, people, action. In nonfiction, they test theories or think of applications or chew on the facts. But in neither instance do they focus on the skills of reading. They are unaware of how many pages they have read or how long they have been at the book. They pace themselves accordingly,

FIGURE 1–1
Unengaged and engaged reading.

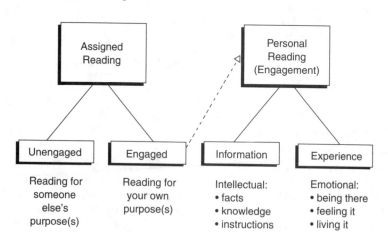

gulping down great whacking passages quickly or dawdling over a line that gives them particular delight. They never say, "Look at me. I have chosen the correct sound of *y* at the end of *happy*—long *e*. I didn't confuse it with the long *i* sound, like at the end of *fly*. I am comprehending this paragraph with 80 percent accuracy and can pick out the topic sentence." During engaged reading there is no focus on skill, decoding, or vocabulary. When engaged readers come to a word they can't pronounce or define, they skip right over it without hesitation or guilt. A real reader engaged in a book is no more aware of reading skills than a running back threading his way through the defensive team is aware of his ability to run. He is not saying, "Right foot, then left foot, now pivot 45 degrees on the next step." His focus is on the game, and he simply uses his body to get where he wants to go. When something gets in the way, both the athlete and the reader improvise—self-correct—so the goal is still in sight and the action is uninterrupted.

So, why do we read? For personal and immediate reward. We read what already interests us. We learn new interests through reading a skillfully written account that takes us places we have never before been. And we can experience the genuine pleasure of having an assigned book work its way under our skin and become part of us. Author Gary Paulsen, whose early years in Minnesota were largely spent in the library, suggests we should "read like a wolf eats" (1987)—in great hulking bites, with vigor, as often and much as possible. In the middle of this enthusiastic sampling of print, we will find those things that personally are worth it, while allowing the rest to slough off naturally. All the while, we increase our range of reading skills and strengthen our education without being aware of either. The very real benefits come predictably and automatically.

Occasionally, we even stumble onto a benefit beyond expectation. For instance, actor Walter Matthau may have discovered the ultimate bonus of engaged reading. In response to the question, "What book made the greatest difference in your life?" he wrote:

> The book that made the greatest difference in my life was *The Secret in the Daisy,* by Carol Grace, Random House, published 1955.
>
> The difference it made was enormous. It took me from a miserable, unhappy wretch to a joyful, glad-to-be-alive human. I fell so in love with the book that I searched out and married the girl who wrote it.
>
> Most sincerely,
> Walter Matthau (Sabine & Sabine, 1983, p. 29)

REFERENCES

Alexander, Lloyd. (1993). Telephone conversation with James S. Jacobs, 2 March.

Anderson, Richard C., Hiebert, Elfrieda H., Scott, Judith A., & Wilkinson, Ian A. G. (1985). *Becoming a nation of readers: The report of the Commission on Reading.* Champaign-Urbana, IL: Center for the Study of Reading.

Armstrong, Jennifer. (1998). *Shipwreck at the bottom of the world: The extraordinary true story of Shackleton and the Endurance.* New York: Crown.

Associated Press. (1994). Students cite pregnancies as a reason to drop out. *New York Times*, September 14, p. B7.

Babbitt, Natalie. (1975). *Tuck everlasting*. New York: Farrar, Straus & Giroux.

Chatton, Barbara. (1988, Spring). Apply with caution: Bibliotherapy in the library. *Journal of Youth Services in Libraries, 1*(3), 334–338.

Curlee, Lynn. (2002). *The seven wonders of the ancient world*. New York: Atheneum.

de Vinck, Christopher. (1991, Spring). An open book. *The College Board Review, 159*, 9–12.

Fader, Daniel. (1976). *Hooked on books*. New York: Berkley Books.

Foertsch, Mary. (1992, May). *Reading in and out of school*. Educational Testing Service/Education Information Office. Washington, DC: U.S. Department of Education.

Lee, Melissa. (1994). When it comes to salary, it's academic. *Washington Post*, July 22, p. D1.

O'Dell, Scott. (1960). *Island of the blue dolphins*. Boston: Houghton Mifflin.

Parker, Steve. (1998). *The human body: And how it works*. Illustrated by Giovanni Caselli. New York: Dorling Kindersley.

Paulsen, Gary. (1987). Books and early reading. Speech given to Clarke County Library Association, Las Vegas, Nevada, 29 January.

Pullman, Philip. (1985). *The ruby in the smoke*. New York: Putnam.

Rogot, Eugene, Sorlie, Paul D., & Johnson, Norman J. (1992, July/August). Life expectancy by employment status, income, and education in the National Longitudinal Mortality Study. *Public Health Reports, 107*, 457–461.

Rosenblatt, Louise. (1978). *The reader, the text, the poem*. Carbondale: Southern Illinois University Press.

Sabine, Gordon, & Sabine, Patricia. (1983). *Books that made the difference*. Hamden, CT: Shoe String Press.

Spinelli, Jerry. (2000). *Stargirl*. New York: Knopf.

Trelease, Jim. (2001). *The read-aloud handbook*. New York: Penguin.

Chapter 2

What Is a Good Book?

When we select books for children, we want to pick good ones. The trouble is, we're not always sure what "good book" means. Left to our own choosing, we thumb through titles, trying to find something that seems beneficial and desirable for young readers. We forge ahead, sometimes oblivious of the criteria we use to determine what is good. But criteria we have.

 ## CHOOSING CHILDREN'S BOOKS

All adults choose children's books according to some kind of standard, even though we may be unaware of exactly why we pick one book over another. Our first responsibility when selecting books, then, is to determine what guides our choices. For instance:

1. The lessons they teach. We want children to learn the correct lessons about life. If a book teaches what we want taught, we call it a good book.
2. Large, colorful illustrations. Young eyes need stimulation, and color provides it better than black and white. Also, the pictures need to be large enough for children to see clearly.
3. Absence of harshness. Children will run into difficulty soon enough. Let them enjoy childhood. Protect them from the tough side of life as long as possible.
4. Absence of scariness. We don't want to invite fears or nightmares.
5. Absence of swearing. We don't want books to model inappropriate behavior.
6. Short. Keep the reading easy.
7. Simple vocabulary. We don't want to frustrate or overpower children.
8. Familiar content. We think our child will respond to a book about zoos because we go to one often. If a book connects with a child's experience, it will be a better book.
9. Personal and/or social preference. We want the values and social views represented in the book to be what we consider appropriate.

A problem with the reasons just listed is that they are narrow and sometimes misguided; they focus on only a tree and miss the forest. If we want to help create life-long readers by choosing books that appeal to the greatest range and number of children, we need to view the book as a whole instead of focusing on only a small element. And the most trustworthy standard for viewing the whole book is to look at the experience it offers. Titles of lasting value can almost be defined as experiences that re-create the very texture of life.

Problems can arise, however, in trying to convince others of the power of that experience. Generally, when we like a book—or don't like it—we assume the book deserves our response. When books please us, we think they are well written or have other measurable literary value. Works that leave us cold are somehow lacking in merit. It is largely human nature to think others will respond the way we do. The following two cases illustrate the extremes.

Case 1: "*The Wind in the Willows* (Grahame, 1908) is a classic," he said. "It has received critical acclaim for a century, and I loved it. If you want a wonderful experience, take it now and read it." So she did. Her response was different, however: total boredom. How do we explain that a book of acknowledged literary merit can excite one person while the friend he recommends it to finds the title definitely ho-hum?

Case 2: The librarian held up a book between thumb and forefinger like a five-day-old fish. "The Nancy Drew books lack quality and merit. This series is predictable and weak." Maria, fifth grade, reads the beginning of a newly released Nancy Drew mystery and can't put it down until she finishes. A trained educator judges a title to be substandard literature, and yet Maria considers it a good book. How can this be?

People often don't see eye-to-eye when it comes to judging whether a book is worthwhile because *good book* is a common phrase with two different definitions, one based on quality and the other on taste.

JUDGING A BOOK: LITERARY QUALITY VERSUS PERSONAL TASTE

Quality

A good book is one created by a knowledgeable and skilled author in which the elements of literature measure up under critical analysis. Quality is recognized by evaluating different elements of the book, including style and language, character, plot, illustrations, pacing, setting, tension, design and layout, mood, accuracy, tone, point of view, and theme.

Style and Language. How a story is told is as important as the story itself. Style is the way a writer manipulates all the facets of language—such as word choice, syntax, and sentence length—to tell that story (see Chapter 3). The author's style can even reinforce a part of the story, as in Spinelli's (1990) *Maniac Magee*, where the short chapters and short sentences mirror the constant running and rapid movements of the main character.

Character. Good books must have characters that are unique and believable. People who live between the covers of a book must be as real as people who live across the street. It is impossible to identify with or have feelings for a person unless we know the individual, and it is the author's job to show us the character's personality in such a way that we can become involved with that life.

Plot. A good plot shows what happens to the characters in such a way that the reader cares about the outcome. Every plot must have a conflict, and how that conflict is resolved carries the book to its conclusion. Well-defined plots, according to author Pam Conrad, introduce a question early on that will be answered yes or no by the end of the story. She calls this the "major dramatic question" (MDQ) and cautions that the MDQ is not asked outright but is clearly evident. The plot, then, is the series of events that lead to the yes or no answer. In *Hatchet* (Paulsen, 1987), for instance, the major dramatic question is, "Will Brian be rescued from the Canadian wilderness where he survived a plane crash?" In *Make Way for Ducklings* (McCloskey, 1941), the MDQ is, "Will the ducks make the trip safely from the Charles River to the Boston Public Garden?"

Illustrations. The art or photography in a book can strengthen and extend the content beyond the words. The marriage of illustration and text can yield an experience more powerful than either alone. (See Chapter 4.)

Pacing. How quickly or slowly a story moves is pacing. While most books tell their stories at a relatively constant rate, pacing can vary according to the author's desire to linger over the content or move the story along.

Setting. Where the book takes place is the setting, which can be as vast as a planet or as small as one room. When detailed and fleshed out, the physical surroundings add credibility and depth to the story.

Tension. Fiction without tension is bland. Tension makes the reader want to read on to see how the conflict is resolved and what happens to the people involved in the problem. Even in picture books, tension—a close relative of suspense—is what piques and sustains interest.

Design and Layout. All visual elements of a book—such as the cover, the colors, the margins, the spacing, the font style and size, and the positions of page numbers—are a part of the design and layout. Although word order is not affected by the design and layout, word placement on the page is—particularly in picture books. The visual appeal of a book can determine if a potential reader will pick it up or march right on by, and the look of a page can affect the reader's desire to get into the content.

Mood. The atmosphere evoked in the writing is the mood: spooky, hilarious, innocent, understated, exaggerated, caustic, and the like.

Accuracy. Whenever books deal with real facts, whether centering on them in nonfiction or using them as background in fiction, they must be true. Writers need to do their homework in order to gain and keep readers' trust.

Tone. The tone is the author's attitude toward the subject or audience in a particular book. Tone can reflect the range of human emotion: reverential, sarcastic, condescending, enthusiastic, and so on.

Point of View. The point of view is the position taken by the narrator. Most stories are told in first person ("I") or third person ("he/she").

Theme. The central idea of the story is the theme: friendship, coming-of-age, sibling rivalry, coping with the death of a pet, and adjusting to a new town, to name a few.

Of the 13 elements listed, 3 provide most of the information for judging the quality of fiction: style and language, character, and plot. When a book reveals its story in powerful language, contains memorable characters, and follows a compelling plot, the fiction generally can be said to have quality.

One additional characteristic is worth noting: believability. The key to creating a good book is to make everything believable. We know that fiction is the product of an imagination. The people never lived. The story is made up. The setting often is invented. So why do we care about these people who never were, doing things that never happened, in a place that may not exist? Because the emotional reality is absolutely true. Because their imagined lives reflect the actual lives of living, breathing people. Because we can get genuine experience through living side by side with fictional characters while they endure their own trials and enjoy their successes. We participate, we enjoy, and we learn—all simultaneously. Yet if anything in the book reminds us that what we read is invented, the story loses its power, much in the same way that the spell of a movie is broken when we notice a boom microphone hanging over the head of the police chief. All the elements in a story must be logical, sensible, and consistent. Authors are obligated to keep their techniques and manipulations out of sight when putting the book together. The actions, motives, responses, and facts must be credible in a book of quality.

Yet an author can pay careful attention to all the elements of fiction, skillfully weaving together a praiseworthy book, and still not win the reader's heart. Why?

Taste

The second definition of a good book is simply "a book the reader likes," quality or not. For instance, *The Wind in the Willows* is judged to be quality literature for children. This prototype of modern animal fantasy skillfully delineates the four main characters, contains satisfying action sequences, and is told in rich and varied language. But some children do not become engrossed in the story when they try to read it, nor do they particularly like to have it read aloud to them. The book has definite literary merit—it is critically a good book—yet for those who are not taken by the story, it has no appeal. Conversely, the Nancy Drew books win no literary awards. Yet they continue to be read by many who find pleasure in reading these tales of a young, independent woman who can always solve the mystery. Thousands of children sail through the series, reporting that each Nancy Drew title is a good book. Some adults may think that children who read such formulaic, shallow stories should feel shame for doing so,

but so far no guilt has been detected in those who move quickly from one volume to the next.

So, when determining which books are good, a problem surfaces: The positive feelings a reader has about a book are the same whether they come from a quality book or one of low literary merit. As long as a reader likes a book, quality or not, it is called "good." Were we able to identify precisely the sources of our positive responses, we would more accurately say, "I like this book because the author's skill took me places and showed me things I have not previously thought about or experienced." If the book is well crafted, believable, and supplies all the elements needed for a rewarding new experience, the author should take a bow. What the writer of the book brought to the work creates this "good" response. On the other hand, if we like a book because it serves as a link to something already a part of us, we might say, "I like this book because it connects me with something important in my life." When the book presents us with a view or situation we are hardwired to like—reliving my summer with Grandma, supporting my view that society undervalues females, or illustrating how a selfish child learns kindness—credit for positive feelings toward the book belongs largely to the reader. When we like a book, we usually don't examine the source of our responses. We don't ask if the book takes us new places or connects us with the old. We just say it is a "good" book. We gain some insight by asking ourselves, "Does the 'good' feeling come because of the author's skill, or does it come because of my background and expectations?" Figure 2–1 depicts the roles and meaning of "good" in book quality and reader response.

A book can be written well or badly, and a reader can respond well or badly to both strong and weak books. Quadrant 1 of Figure 2–1 shows that an author has written a book with literary merit, and the reader likes it. We have no problem with a reader who responds positively to quality writing. A well-crafted book deserves no less. Similarly, quadrant 4 presents no difficulty. The author displays little skill in

FIGURE 2–1
Evaluating books: Four possible outcomes.

	Literary Merit of Book	Reader Response		Literary Merit of Book	Reader Response	
1	+	+		+	—	2
3	—	+		—	—	4

producing a book of minimal merit, and the reader does not respond well to this flawed product. These two unshaded quadrants pose little problem for the teacher and student.

But problems may occur when a quality book is not well received. Quadrant 2 shows that an author has written a good book, but the reader doesn't care for it. Teachers who recognize quality may have a tendency to feel they are shirking their duty if children don't respond favorably to a quality book. Teachers who redouble their efforts to convince the unbeliever that something wonderful is being missed usually drive the unbelieving student further from the book. In quadrant 3, the reader accepts a weak book with open arms. This scenario is often played out as a teacher tries to show the young reader just how poor the book really is. These sincere efforts are generally as successful as trying to dam the Mississippi River using a teaspoon. Attempting to convince enthusiastic young readers that a book is not worthy of devotion is foolish and often counterproductive. They have tried it and liked it. All we can do, and should do, is continue to mention and offer different titles that may appeal to those readers. Allowing individual response is wisest in the long run. After all, if children read nothing, then our opportunity to broaden their taste and judgment about books is nonexistent.

In both quadrants 2 and 3, the teacher needs to accept the honest feelings of the reader, misguided as they might be in the adult eye, and continue to provide and introduce better books. Doing so carries no guarantee that young readers will like them, but it does increase the chances that this may happen. Direct attacks on positive responses to poor-quality books, however, almost guarantee that a rift will develop between teacher and student and, in the case of quadrant 2, between a student and a genuinely good book.

Understanding that a positive response can be a result of either the author's skill or the reader's individual taste can help in solving some mysteries about how readers respond to books. A British reviewer of children's books was surprised when her daughter, Alison, chose as her favorite book one that was far inferior to the many quality titles in their home. The story tells of Peppermint, a pale kitten, who is last in a litter and alone after the others are matched with new families. Eventually, she is given to a girl who loves her, fusses over her, and prepares her so well for the cat show that Peppermint wins first prize. Alison's mother finally realized the appeal of Peppermint's story.

> Alison is an adopted child; her hair is pale straw, her eyes are blue; she was taken home, like Peppermint, to be loved and cared for and treasured. It was a matter of identification not just for the duration of the story, but at a deep, warm, comforting and enduring level. . . . The artistically worthless book—hack-written and poorly illustrated—may, if the emotional content is sound, hold a message of supreme significance for a particular child. (Moss 1977, pp. 141–142)

When a class of 30 college students read a not-very-good biography about Maria Tallchief, an Osage ballerina who captured the attention of the dancing world in the early 20th century, all the students, except for five women, pronounced the book mediocre. That enthusiastic handful loved the book and couldn't understand why the others were not impressed by this story that had meant so much to them. During the short discussion, the fact surfaced that all of the five young women had taken and loved ballet as children. When they read about Maria Tallchief, they were reading their own stories. For them, the book served as a link to a meaningful personal experience. The others, without ballet backgrounds, did not find enough to interest them in the shallow way the author presented the story.

As adults working with children, we spend our time more productively in quadrants 1 and 2 in Figure 2–1 for two reasons. First, the more a book has to offer readers, the greater the chance the reader will respond. In *Julius, the Baby of the World*, Kevin Henkes (1990) identifies precisely an only child's reaction to the arrival of a new sibling. The reader participates in Lilly's jealousy, as well as shares her outrage when Cousin Garland dares to criticize her baby brother. The author's range of emotion and humor is so broad that readers at a variety of age levels are able to respond. The second reason is that judging literary merit is easier than identifying specific reader idiosyncrasies that result in positive responses to books. We can identify a good plot and pick out a compelling character. But we have no way of knowing that Alison will find comfort in Peppermint or that five students will be linked by their ballet lessons to Maria Tallchief.

This whole evaluative process is somewhat like examining two new couches in Danish modern style. From a distance, they appear identical, but one reflects the true value of $2,200 while the other carries an honest price tag of $500. However, if allowed to inspect the couches at close range, even the nonprofessional should be able to determine which couch is of real quality and which is of lesser worth. We can determine the more expensive by examining the stitching, which should be close and even; the fabric, which should be tight and finely woven; the wood, which should be heavy, joined perfectly, well stained, and flawlessly finished; the padding, which should be thick and firm; the weight, which should be heavy; and the comfort, which should be evident upon sitting. Once identified, however, the quality piece will not necessarily be welcomed into every living room. If Danish modern style does not appeal to me, it is of no importance that I now have the $1,800 couch. I can recognize its fine craftsmanship and can see that its less expensive counterpart is lacking in quality, but that does not make me want to own the fine couch if my taste runs counter to its appearance. Ultimately, the piece must please me before it gets my stamp of approval.

George Woods, the late and longtime children's book critic for the *New York Times*, addressed the topic of evaluating children's books in a speech to an auditorium of college students. "How do we know a good book?" he asked his audience. Pens came to the ready for the scholar's definition. "We know a good book . . . (pause) . . . because it hits us in the gut" (Woods, 1977).

Taste and personal response often determine an individual's decision about the worth of a book. However, there are some generally accepted guidelines about quality writing. Some books simply are better constructed than others, offering a clearer understanding of the human experience and a deeper sense of pleasure. These quality books are the ones we need to introduce to children because they generally have more power to stir up interest where none is apparent and, over time, will provide readers with a more enlarging experience than will mediocre books. Yet we can't force these quality titles on children; we can only offer by enthusiastically sharing them. To become truly engaged readers, children must have the freedom to accept or reject a title. Just as we can't insist on a positive response to a book of quality, we can't erase a positive response to a poorly written book.

In the end, the question of "good book" is one of respect: respect for the truly fine work of authors who pay their dues and create works of lasting value, and also respect for the response of individual readers who cast the deciding vote on a book's personal appeal. There is, after all, only one list of good books that is completely dependable— your own. However, though your list may have books of both lower and higher literary merit, the quality titles will end up taking you further.

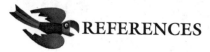

REFERENCES

Grahame, Kenneth. (1908). *The wind in the willows*. London: Methuen.

Henkes, Kevin. (1990). *Julius, the baby of the world*. New York: Greenwillow.

McCloskey, Robert. (1941). *Make way for ducklings*. New York: Viking.

Moss, Elaine. (1977). What is a good book? In Margaret Meek, Aiden Warlow, & Griselda Barton, Eds., *The cool web*. London: Bodley Head.

Paulsen, Gary. (1987). *Hatchet*. New York: Bradbury.

Spinelli, Jerry. (1990). *Maniac Magee*. Boston: Little, Brown.

Woods, George. (1977). Evaluating children's books. Speech given at Brigham Young University, Provo, Utah, 17 September.

Chapter 3

How to Recognize
a Well-Written Book

To evaluate the literary merit of a book is to make a judgment about how well the author uses words. "This book is well written" is a common badge of praise. What does *well written* mean? Often it is nothing more than the speaker's way of saying the book is pleasing. If it pleases me, it must be well written. As evidence supporting a positive response to a book, the phrase "well written" has become a generalized catchall.

CHOOSING THE RIGHT WORDS

If a book is truly well written, the words between its covers are arranged in almost magical patterns that stir deep emotional responses in readers. The words do far more than relate the events of the story. The words make the book by defining character, moving the plot along, identifying the setting, isolating the theme, creating the tone, identifying the point of view, developing the mood, establishing the pace, making the story believable, and reporting information accurately. Identifying how words create each literary element, however, does not give us a clear picture of exactly what makes a book so memorable. Certainly plot must be well structured, but it cannot be separated from the major characters who are living the story. Conversely, well-defined characters lose their appeal if they are not involved in a compelling plot. The elements of writing are integrated, worked into a well-orchestrated whole, by a talented writer.

Talented writers create works that are clear, believable, and interesting. A story is not good because it is about a particular topic or peopled with certain characters; it is good because of the way it is presented. A work of nonfiction is not good because of the subject matter; it is good because of the way it views and reveals the subject. For example, note the difference in the following reports of the same event:

Case 1: The college football coach finished his 20th successful season and was honored at a banquet where his praises were sung loudly and long. As dishes were being cleared and tables taken down after the festivities, the coach talked with his friend, the college president. At one point, the coach paused and then asked, "President, I appreciate this evening more than you'll ever know. Yet sometimes I find a nagging question in my mind: Would all of you still love me if I lost football games instead of won them?"

"Oh, Coach, we'd love you just as much," the president said as he reached out his arm, pulled the coach in close, and looked him right in the eye. "And we'd miss you."

Case 2:   A college student said to his classmate, "Did you hear that last night after the banquet honoring the football coach, the president said he'd be fired if he started losing?"

In case 2, the reader gets all the pertinent information: the banquet in the coach's honor, the president and coach's conversation afterward, and the gist of their exchange. In the first example, the reader gets to participate in the event, discovering the point of the story and its subtle humor simultaneously with the characters.

Human beings can't draw conclusions without information, and we gain information only through the five senses. If data can't enter through one of the holes in the head (sight, sound, taste, or smell) or through the skin (touch), they can't be processed. Good writers know readers need specific information—details that enter through the senses—and take the trouble to provide it. Lesser writers generalize. The difference between providing sensory detail and generalizing is the difference between showing and telling. Where lesser writing *tells* by summarizing (as in case 2), quality writing *shows* the reader what is going on by providing enough sensory detail to allow the reader to make personal discoveries and come to personal conclusions (as in case 1). Consider, for instance, the opening paragraph of *The Illyrian Adventure:*

> Miss Vesper Holly has the digestive talents of a goat and the mind of a chess master. She is familiar with half a dozen languages and can swear fluently in all of them. She understands the use of a slide rule but prefers doing calculations in her head. She does not hesitate to risk life and limb—mine as well as her own. No doubt she has other qualities as yet undiscovered. I hope not. (Alexander, 1986, p. 3)

The reader is solidly introduced to Vesper Holly. Alexander reveals Vesper's particular personality by *showing* her skills, accomplishments, abilities, and interests. Had Alexander begun by *telling* us about Vesper, he may have summarized her character by saying, "Miss Vesper Holly is courageous, intelligent, daring, a skilled linguist, delightfully irreverent, and headstrong." We would then know what to expect of her, but we wouldn't know her as well.

The "showing" we need from the printed page comes to us in various forms: precise vocabulary, figurative language, dialogue, music in language, understatement, and surprise observations. Though not a comprehensive list, these six characteristics identify some of the ways words create interest and personalize content.

Precise Vocabulary

By age 4, children have acquired most of the elements of fully developed language, including sentence structure, word order, subject-verb agreement, verb tenses, and so on

(Morrow, 2005). The only additional refinements take place in acquiring more complex structures and in semantics—learning new words and their meanings. Semantic development continues for the rest of their lives. With more than 800,000 words (including 300,000 technical terms), English has the richest vocabulary of the 5,000-plus languages on the planet. One of the great pleasures of language is to find in this fertile and varied vocabulary precisely the right word to use in exactly the right place. Mark Twain described the difference between the right word and the almost right word as being like the difference between lightning and the lightning bug. And the only way to learn the fine differences between words and develop a broad personal vocabulary is to be surrounded by precise words used accurately. When Newbery-winning author Elaine Konigsburg writes for children, she tries "to expand the perimeter of their language, to set a wider limit to it, to give them a vocabulary for alternatives" (1970, pp. 731–732).

William Steig is a master of providing those wider limits, largely by using precise vocabulary. In *The Amazing Bone* (1976), Pearl the pig, wearing her flowered dress and sunbonnet, takes her time coming home from school: "On Cobble Road she stopped at Maltby's barn and stood gawking as the old gaffers pitched their ringing horseshoes and spat tobacco juice." (Someone afraid this sentence would not be accessible to the younger reader would write something like: "She stopped at the barn and watched the old men play horseshoes.") Naming the road and the barn gives the story depth and credibility—the place seems to exist. "Gawking" identifies exactly the kind of looking she did—wide-eyed, unabashed staring. "Ringing horseshoes" provides a dimension of sound to the game, adding an additional layer to the picture. And "spat tobacco juice" presents a side of the men and their activities that rounds them out. But the genius on this page is the selection of the word *gaffers*. English has a number of specific words for the phrase *old man:* patriarch, ancient, graybeard, Nestor, grandfather, gaffer, geezer, codger, dotard, Methuselah, antediluvian, preadamite, veteran, old-timer, old soldier, old stager, dean, doyen, senior, elder, oldest, first-born, seniority, primogeniture (*The New Roget's Thesaurus in Dictionary Form*, 1991, s.v. "old men"). The only ones general enough to be considered for this setting are codger, dotard, gaffer, geezer, and old-timer. *The Compact Edition of the Oxford English Dictionary* (1991) reports that each carries a specific view of old men:

> *Codger:* "A mean, stingy, or miserly (old) fellow; a testy or crusty (old) man"
>
> *Dotard:* "One whose intellect is impaired by age; one whose dotage is in his second childhood"
>
> *Gaffer:* "A term applied originally by country people to an elderly man or one whose position entitled him to respect"
>
> *Geezer:* "A term of derision applied to elderly persons"
>
> *Old-timer:* "[O]ne whose experience goes back to old times"

Gaffer is the only term that is neither negative nor neutral. Its positive connotation complements the pleasant, unhurried scene while reflecting a strong image of the elderly.

The right words do not have to be fancy or complex. Even ordinary words can be right. In *Julius, the Baby of the World* (Henkes, 1990), the birth of Julius brings misery to his sister, Lilly. To her friends, and even strangers, this former only child dutifully gives warnings about the perils of newborns. Approaching a very pregnant woman on the sidewalk, Lilly offers this dire prediction: "You will live to regret that bump under your dress!" "Will live to regret" does not mince words. It carries no waffling and allows no possibility that the situation could end well. Calling the baby a "bump" makes it less than human—reduces it to an inanimate, shapeless mass—which reveals the depth of Lilly's negative feelings more powerfully than had she said, "You will be sorry you're pregnant."

In *Temporary Times, Temporary Places* (Robinson, 1972), teenaged Marilyn is stunned when she comes out of the church after an evening social to see her friend Janet walking away with the boy of their dreams, the one they have spent endless hours discussing. He has never spoken to either of them, and here he is leaving with Janet. Carrying her sweater in her hand, Marilyn can only stare: "She was standing on the steps of the church, mouth open, eyes wide, sweater dragging." With those six words—"mouth open, eyes wide, sweater dragging"—astonishment is *shown*. Robinson has thought about what astonishment looks like in this situation and presented it precisely. A lesser writer, who tells instead of shows, would have written something like, "She was standing on the steps of the church, a look of astonishment on her face." This sentence tells readers they should feel astonishment, but it does not create the image or the experience. In Robinson's hands, the scene is more specific, more complete, and more believable.

Figurative Language

Simile, metaphor, personification, and imagery are examples of figurative language. All can strengthen language by adding specificity, clarity, power, and layers of meaning. In addition, figurative language is economical. It conveys meaning quickly and with emotional intensity. For example, in *Maniac Magee* we are shown that March, supposedly the month of spring and hope, can also be a brute: "During the night, March doubled back and grabbed April by the scruff of the neck and flung it another week or two down the road" (Spinelli, 1990, p. 149). Spinelli's personification of March reminds us vividly that this unpredictable month of spring can also present a sudden nastiness.

From *Tuck Everlasting* comes the lingering image of Mae Tuck, described as a "great potato of a woman" (Babbitt, 1975, p. 7). In five words Babbitt creates a feeling for Mae's lumpy shape, her absence of pretense, her plainness, her lack of color, her solidity, her accessibility, and other earthy and dependable traits associated with a vegetable that is not spectacular, fragile, or rare but is a nutritional staple.

Figurative language can add power and insight to whole paragraphs. It is one thing to say that Winnie Foster was made to do housework continually, but in *Tuck Everlasting*, the author underscores the seriousness of cleaning in Winnie's household by loading the description with images of war.

> Winnie had grown up with order. She was used to it. Under the pitiless double assaults of her mother and grandmother, the cottage where she lived was always squeaking

clean, mopped and swept and scoured into limp submission. There was no room for carelessness, no putting things off until later. The Foster women had made a fortress out of duty. Within it, they were indomitable. And Winnie was in training. (Babbitt, 1975, p. 44)

When we read the paragraph, we get the solid impression that housecleaning in the Foster cottage is the focal point of life. Only when we go back and pick out the military terms Babbitt has chosen—"double assaults," "fortress," "duty," "in training"—do we see the image of soldiers in battle that has helped persuade us of the Foster obsession with cleanliness.

Dialogue

Speech reveals character. When a person's mouth opens, truth emerges about personality, motives, desires, prejudices, and feelings. Bernard Waber has an ear for real speech that reveals the nuances, challenges, and bluffing responses of sibling conversation. In *Ira Sleeps Over,* Ira has been invited to spend the night at a friend's house—his first sleepover. When his older sister learns of his plans, she asks:

> "Are you taking your teddy bear along?"
> "Taking my teddy bear along!" I said. "To my friend's house? Are you kidding? That's the silliest thing I ever heard! Of course, I'm not taking my teddy bear."
> And then she said: "But you never slept without your teddy bear before. How will you feel, sleeping without your teddy bear for the very first time? Hmmmm-mmm?" (Waber, 1972, pp. 5–7)*

In this brief exchange between brother and sister, Waber shows the older sister's need and ability to control her younger brother with what appears to be an innocent question: "Are you taking your teddy bear along?" What difference does it make to her if he takes it? None, but her job is to make his life miserable, and she performs it well. His reply, a little too quick and laced with false bravado, shows his insecurity. And her final statement is a knockout punch that leaves him no chance to get to his feet, reminding him that he has never slept alone, asking how that would feel, and ending with that taunting, "Hmmmmmmm?"

If speech is not natural and not as individual as a particular personality, it depicts the characters as shallow and stiff, distracting from the story and consequently weakening it. Unnatural dialogue appears in Cari Meister's (2006) *My Pony Jack at the Horse Show.* Lacy is to compete in a horse show, but she is suddenly frightened by the prospect of riding her horse Jack in front of the crowd and the judges. But her riding teacher calms her.

> "Lacy!" calls Annie.
> "We are over here.
> Take a deep breath.
> Now wipe your tears.

> Just do like your lessons.
> You will be fine
> Put on a smile,
> and get in that line." (pp. 12–16)

Later, after Lacy wins second place, she says,

> "Into the trailer, Jack.
> You know the way.
> It is time to go home.
> What a fun day!" (pp. 28–31)

Real little girls and real adults simply do not talk that way. This dialogue is written with the primary goal of providing simplified reading rather than engaging storytelling.

Music in Language

The sounds of words increase the appeal and strength of a story as they blend together, create emphasis, repeat tones, establish patterns, provide a cadence, and add variety. After 80 years, the rhythm in *Millions of Cats* (Gág, 1928) still rings in the ear and burrows into the mind: "Hundreds of cats, Thousands of cats, Millions and billions and trillions of cats." The rhyme in *Goodnight Moon* (Brown, 1947) does the same: "Goodnight stars. Goodnight air. Goodnight noises everywhere."

Buford in *Buford the Little Bighorn* (Peet, 1967) is a small mountain sheep whose horns have grown enormously, way out of proportion to his body. They cause him balancing problems, and he falls from craggy heights but is saved when his horns hook onto a small tree. From then on, his friends have to help him over the rough spots in their high, rocky world. To help him climb a steep ledge, two sheep from above grab his horns in their teeth and pull, while one butts him skyward, giving "Buford a big boost from below" (Peet, 1967, p. 3). Those explosive *b*'s echo the heavy sounds and sudden movements of butting and boosting as well as link the phrase together by repeating the sound.

Because the eye does not detect the fine points of language as accurately as the ear, it is common for authors to submit their writing to a final check by reading it aloud. In two versions of "Snow White," the queen questions the mirror in language that is subtly yet powerfully different. Submit the following two passages to the read-aloud test:

> Mirror, mirror on the wall. Who is the fairest one of all? (Walt Disney Productions, 1973, p. 2)

> Mirror, mirror on the wall, Who is fairest of us all? (Grimm Brothers, 1972, p. 2)

Uneven meter in the first passage makes it more difficult to read aloud; the cadence is rougher and the sound choppier. The language in the second example flows, falling smoothly and effortlessly from the mouth. The result is a more musical reading. The second also echoes an archaic form of speech that matches the "once upon a time" setting of the fairy tale.

Varied sentence length is another feature of language that appeals to the ear. In natural speech patterns, sentences are of differing length. These diverse sentences add

variety to the language, creating balance, interest, and appeal. Read aloud the opening passages from the Disney and Grimm versions of "Snow White," paying attention to how they feel coming from the mouth and how they fall upon the ear.

> Long ago there lived a princess named Snow White. She was a beautiful princess. And like all princesses she lived in a castle.
> Her stepmother, the queen, also lived in the castle. The queen had a magic mirror. Every day she looked into the mirror and asked the same thing.
> "Mirror, mirror on the wall. Who is the fairest one of all?"
> The mirror always gave her the same answer. "Oh, queen, YOU are the fairest one of all." (Walt Disney Productions, 1973, p. 2)

> Once it was the middle of winter, and the snowflakes fell from the sky like feathers. At a window with a frame of ebony a queen sat and sewed. And as she sewed and looked out at the snow, she pricked her finger with the needle, and three drops of blood fell in the snow. And in the white snow the red looked so beautiful that she thought to herself: "If only I had a child as white as snow, as red as blood, and as black as the wood in the window frame!" (Grimm Brothers, 1972, pp. 1–2)

For most readers, the many short sentences in the first example interrupt the flow of the story, creating a degree of choppiness. The varied sentence construction in the second helps produce a smooth and flowing narrative that reads with a musical quality. The first has 10 sentences, the second 4. The first has an average of 7.9 words per sentence, the second 23.5. Having more words per sentence is not necessarily an earmark of good writing, but in this case the longer sentences help paint stronger, more emotion-laden images.

Understatement

When facts and feelings are presented clearly in writing, readers draw their own conclusions without being told precisely what to think. Readers then participate in the experience instead of being led through it. Part of this participatory process is understatement, which presents minimal but carefully chosen facts and details without any explanatory comment. Understatement is simply very brief "showing." The opposites of understatement are overexplanation and sensationalism.

The power of understatement is evident in *Tuck Everlasting* (Babbitt, 1975). Angus Tuck tries to convince young Winnie Foster, whom he has grown to love like his own child, not to drink from the same magical spring that has transformed the Tucks into people who cannot age or die. When the Tuck family is forced to move away, Angus is uncertain of what Winnie will do—let her life follow its natural course, as he counseled, or submit to the enticements of living forever. In the epilogue, Angus and Mae Tuck return to Winnie's town 60 years later and visit the cemetery. When he discovers her tombstone, Angus's throat closes and he briefly salutes the monument, saying, "Good girl." No long discourses with his wife about Winnie's wise decision. No fits of crying or sentimental remembrances. Just "good girl."

A second example of understatement comes from Ann Martin's *A Corner of the Universe*, when 12-year-old Hattie is in the front yard with her childlike Uncle Adam, who, despite his age, is very naïve and lacks social skills. It is Sunday, and two of her friends pass by the house on their way home from church when Adam spots them and in a loud voice invites the pair to come and have a glass of lemonade. Hattie sees the two girls poke each other, then "put their hands to their mouths, which does absolutely nothing to hide their giggles. It occurs to me," she observes, "that they must not be getting much out of their churchgoing. They turn and run. I hear their laughter all the way to the corner" (Martin, 2002, p. 53). Martin includes all that is necessary for the reader to deduce that lessons about kindness and valuing others associated with church attendance did not take with the two girls, but she does not summarize or explain. She allows readers to draw those conclusions on their own.

In *A Summer to Die* (Lowry, 1977), the family is going through a period of mourning as it becomes clear that teenage Molly is going to die. On the way home from a particularly good hospital visit, the family sings childhood songs, capturing the comforting feelings of what life used to be like before Molly became so ill. After that scene, the next words are, "Two weeks later, she was gone" (Lowry, 1977, p. 108). No jarring telephone brings news of the inevitable. No heap of details describes her last moments. We have lived through the disease, joined in the family's efforts to understand and draw together, and now the inescapable has arrived. That's all we need to know. Understatement gives power to writing because of what is not said and shows that an author trusts readers to make important, personal connections with the story.

Unexpected Insights

Like life, good stories contain occasional small surprises. We live with characters as they work their way through problems, but may be delighted suddenly by an eye-opening insight about the human experience that comes from their struggles. For instance, Maniac Magee wonders why the people in East End call themselves black. "He kept looking and looking, and the colors he found were gingersnap and light fudge and dark fudge and acorn and butter rum and cinnamon and burnt orange. But never licorice, which, to him, was real black" (Spinelli, 1990, p. 51). "That's absolutely right," we find ourselves saying. We were aware that differences exist within races but did not see the general truth with such fresh precision until we looked through Maniac's eyes.

Lloyd Alexander is famous for such insights. In the five-book series, *The Prydain Chronicles,* the elderly Dwyvach Weaver-Woman presents a beautiful cloak to the girl Eilonwy. "Take this as a gift from a crone to a maiden," says Dwyvach, "and know there is not so much difference between the two. For even a tottering granddam keeps a portion of girlish heart, and the youngest maid a thread of old woman's wisdom" (1968, p. 115). And in counsel to Taran, who is disappointed that he did not accomplish more while away on his quest, the enchanter Dallben points out, "There are times when the seeking counts more than the finding" (Alexander, 1964, p. 215). These discoveries are not proverbs or maxims tacked onto the story; they surface naturally and appropriately as the characters learn about their own situations.

In *Charlotte's Rose* (Cannon, 2002), a 19th-century Welsh woman has lost four children as babies and is saddened because they died unbaptized and are therefore damned. With another couple and some family members, she agrees to meet with a pair of traveling missionaries, one thin as a pole and the other looking like a mountain with a beard. She starts the conversation.

> "I was told you . . . don't baptize your babies. Is this true?"
> The mountain with the beard nodded.
> "Why not?"
> "Why should we?"
> "So they won't go to hell."
> "Why would babies go to hell?"
> "Because they have not been cleansed of sin."
> Mountain smiled. So did Pole.
> "God deliver us from sinful babies," said Pole.
> "Gambling babies," said Mountain.
> "Drinking babies."
> "Cussing babies."
> "Lying babies."
> "Cheating babies."
> "Thieving babies."
> I laughed, and so did Papa and the Bowens. (pp. 71–72)

And so does the reader. The new perspective—the unexpected insight—simply brings a smile to the lips.

Skilled writers, who pay attention to small details and keep looking until they discover truth, help us to find a freshness and more precise understanding even in familiar things. When Beric, the youthful slave and protagonist in *Outcast*, accidentally cut his hand while in ancient Rome, he instinctively lifted the wound to his mouth. Instantly he tasted the blood, "both salty and sweet" (Sutcliff, 1995, p. 118). Those of us who also have raised a nicked finger to our lips recognize that Sutcliff's "both salty and sweet" describes accurately the unusual taste of our own blood, and we automatically say, "That's it. That's exactly what blood tastes like." Unexpected insights add depth and credibility to the story while providing the reader with recognition and connections.

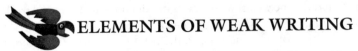 ## ELEMENTS OF WEAK WRITING

The easiest definition of weak writing is to say it is the opposite of good writing: not clear but fuzzy, not believable but implausible, not interesting but dull. Particularly in children's books, however, some weak elements stand out: didacticism, condescension, and controlled vocabulary.

Didacticism, discussed more fully in Chapter 5, is writing that pretends to be a story but actually is a lesson. Good books can and do provide lessons, but in good books, the story is primary and the lessons are secondary. They are secrets to be discovered rather than sermons to be suffered. The learning and insights—the lessons—arrive as additional gifts, by-products of experiencing a good story. When the main purpose of fiction is to promote the message instead of to provide an experience, the book has been weakened.

Condescension may be slightly harder to pin down than didacticism. Condescension often results when the author underestimates the reader's abilities, as in labeling the esophagus a "food tube" in a nonfiction book aimed at fourth graders. "Food tube" is an uncommon and babyish term, and 10-year-old children are perfectly capable of saying and reading "esophagus." Condescension doesn't trust the reader to get the point and overexplains the obvious. Evident mostly in books for very young readers, a condescending tone also treats children with a certain wide-eyed amazement bordering on phoniness. In *The Boat Alphabet Book*, for instance, the general straightforward description of different kinds of boats occasionally slips into a condescending tone. Accompanying a realistic drawing of an ocean-going tanker is this text: "Tankers are ships that carry liquids. Most tankers carry oil products such as crude oil, kerosene, grease, and gasoline." The entry then concludes with, "What else could a tanker be carrying? Maybe chocolate milk?" (Palotta, 2001, p. 22). This question talks down to the reader and is hard to take seriously.

Controlled vocabulary is based on the idea that children learn to read easy words first, then graduate slowly to more difficult ones to avoid frustration. However, so-called dumbed-down text, which overly controls vocabulary and arranges words in unnatural patterns ("I see the mat. The mat is tan. It is a tan mat."), often has proven to be more difficult for children to read and understand than text with interesting words and language patterns. The dumbed-down text does not correspond with what they have learned through the ear (Goodman, 1988). Children can sometimes learn difficult words more easily than seemingly simple ones. If first graders are shown the words *surprise, was,* and *elephant,* the one they will learn to sight read first is *elephant.* Although it is longer and more difficult, it is also more specific. Try drawing a picture of a *surprise* or a *was.* The hardest of the three—the one that takes the most exposures to become included in children's sight vocabulary—is *was.*

In the 1980s, basal companies recognized the power of natural text and began to include excerpts from authentic literature as a part of their reading programs. However, in the 1990s, schools began buying and using sets of controlled-vocabulary paperback books instead of basal textbooks. Therefore, to meet demand, basal companies also began to include with their literature-based reading series sets of controlled-vocabulary paperbacks. Today, teachers must choose wisely because, once again, reading materials available in the elementary schools may focus on particular word patterns, largely ignoring the appeal of natural language and cohesive stories.

In short, the standards for a well-written children's book are no different from the standards for any well-written book. The author treats the audience with respect and writes so that the text is honest and interesting. The literary devices employed to achieve that honesty and interest operate so smoothly they remain virtually invisible. The story (fiction) and the information (nonfiction) are so compelling that the reader sails along, engaged in the insights and precise language and unaware of the talent and time necessary for making the final product appear so effortless.

REFERENCES

Alexander, Lloyd. (1964). *The book of three*. New York: Holt.

Alexander, Lloyd. (1968). *The high king*. New York: Holt.

Alexander, Lloyd. (1986). *The Illyrian adventure*. New York: Dutton.

Babbitt, Natalie. (1975). *Tuck everlasting*. New York: Farrar, Straus & Giroux.

Brown, Margaret Wise. (1947). *Goodnight moon*. Illustrated by Clement Hurd. New York: Harper & Row.

Cannon, A. E. (2002). *Charlotte's rose*. New York: Wendy Lamb Books/Random House.

Gág, Wanda. (1928). *Millions of cats*. New York: Coward McCann.

Goodman, Kenneth. (1988, fall). Look what they've done to Judy Blume!: The basalization of children's literature. *The New Advocate, 1*(1), 29–41.

Grimm Brothers. (1972). *Snow-White and the seven dwarfs*. Translated by Randall Jarrell. Illustrated by Nancy Eckholm Burkert. New York: Farrar, Straus & Giroux.

Henkes, Kevin. (1990). *Julius, the baby of the world*. New York: Greenwillow.

Konigsburg, E. L. (1970, February 15). Double image. *Library Journal, 95,* 731–734.

Lowry, Lois. (1977). *A summer to die*. Boston: Houghton Mifflin.

Martin, Ann. (2002). *A corner of the universe*. New York: Scholastic.

Meister, Cari. (2006). *My pony Jack at the horse show*. New York: Viking.

Morrow, Leslie M. (2005). *Literacy development in the early years: Helping children read and write*. Boston: Allyn and Bacon.

Palotta, Jerry. 2001. *The boat alphabet book*. Watertown, MA: Charlesbridge.

Peet, Bill. (1967). *Buford the little bighorn*. Boston: Houghton Mifflin.

Robinson, Barbara. (1972). *Temporary times, temporary places*. New York: Harper & Row.

Spinelli, Jerry. (1990). *Maniac Magee*. Boston: Little, Brown.

Steig, William. (1976). *The amazing bone*. New York: Farrar, Straus & Giroux.

Sutcliff, Rosemary. (1995). *Outcast*. New York: Farrar, Straus & Giroux.

Waber, Bernard. (1972). *Ira sleeps over*. Boston: Houghton Mifflin.

Walt Disney Productions. (1973). *Snow White and the seven dwarfs*. New York: Random House.

Chapter 4

How to Recognize a Well-Illustrated Book

In this age of visual bombardment—daily overloads of images on computer screens, in magazines, on television, at the movies, and along the roadside—do children need even more images in picture books? The answer is a resounding "Yes!" The problem is not that children have too much to see, but that they must learn to be discriminating about what they see. We use the term *visual literacy* to describe this sort of discrimination. More than any other generation, today's children need to develop discretion about what they view. Picture books are a perfect vehicle for opening a child's eyes to the beauty and power of art, because they do not function like other books, where words alone tell a story or convey information.

Illustrations in the better picture books share the function of storytelling or concept teaching. In fact, in wordless picture books the illustrations do the whole job. So the pictures beg for active participation in their viewing, unlike so many of the random images that are flashed daily in front of us. Text and illustration weave together to communicate. To get the full measure of meaning and fulfillment from a good picture book, the reader must attend carefully to both (Kiefer, 1995). Through the beautifully crafted picture books available today, young readers not only may become aware of the variety of artistic styles, media, and techniques that artists employ, but also may develop a sense for judging quality.

VISUAL LITERACY: DEVELOPING THE ABILITY TO "SEE"

Adults tend to sell children short when it comes to their abilities to perceive the world visually. Both of us have heard our university students, who are, of course, adults, say such things as, "This artwork is too sophisticated for children. Won't they OD on this?" One woman actually asked, "Why do they waste such great art on kids?" Truth be known, children are generally more visually aware and alert than most adults (McDermott, 1974b). The older we get, the more our visual awareness is likely to be dulled by overload or by the real or imagined expectations our educational systems have

imposed on us that alter the way we view images. Honest responses to art and other visual stimuli are programmed out of most children over time. They begin to ignore their own personal reactions and the fascinating detail in the art in order to second-guess their teachers' agendas, thus becoming basically less aware. This process is not much different from analyzing poetry with children until the beauty is beaten out of it.

As we have read to children over the years, they have shown us detail in picture book illustrations that our supposedly sophisticated adult eyes overlooked. For example, we had read *On Market Street* (Lobel, 1981) many times, but had not noticed that the figure representing *T* for toys in this alphabet book had on her hands puppets of the immensely popular Frog and Toad characters. That is, we did not notice them until a child pointed them out. Frog and Toad were made famous in Newbery and Caldecott Honor books created by Arnold Lobel—husband of Anita Lobel, who illustrated *On Market Street*. Children have shown us that the church tower clock in each illustration in *Anno's Counting Book* (Anno, 1977) always points to the hour that corresponds with the number being presented. Gerald McDermott has observed that younger children, when reading *Arrow to the Sun* (McDermott, 1974a), notice the sun symbol on the chest of the Sun God's Pueblo Indian child, an obvious visual link between father and son. However, McDermott (1974b) points out that older children tend not to see the boy's emblem.

Illustration in picture books is meant to delight, to capture attention, to tell a story or teach a concept, and to develop appreciation and awareness in children. Of course, appreciation is developed in part by consistent exposure to the wonderful varieties of art that are coupled with pleasing stories in today's picture books. Young children begin to sense something special in good art when they see lots of it. For example, Quincy had seen many fine picture books in his short six years. When he was listening to a new book, *17 Kings and 42 Elephants* (Mahy, 1987), which has jewel-like paintings by Patricia McCarthy, he suddenly interrupted to say, "Dad, these pictures are marvelous!" "Marvelous" was a bit unexpected coming from such a little body, but more amazing was his evaluative response to the illustrations. Quincy didn't have the understanding or the words to analyze McCarthy's batik-on-silk artwork, but he simply knew it was good stuff. How did he know? Because he'd seen so many picture books that he'd developed a level of appreciation that governed his taste in illustrations. Taste and appreciation come by experience, by comparing a variety of examples. Taste is broadened and cultivated by exposure; it is narrowed or allowed to lay fallow by restricting experience. Indeed, if all that children see in the world of art are Saturday morning cartoons, then such will be the standard of art for them.

FUNCTIONS OF ILLUSTRATIONS IN PICTURE BOOKS

"The function of art is to clarify, intensify, or otherwise enlarge our experience of life" (Canaday, 1980). This statement is as true for picture book illustrations as it is for gallery paintings, but picture book artwork also must operate in a manner unique to its special format. Because picture books are made up of a series of illustrations that typically tell a story, the art may function in one or more of the following ways.

ESTABLISH SETTING. Art is a natural for creating the setting in an illustrated book. Time periods in historical stories or far-flung cultural settings can be brought to life through illustrations in ways words cannot do. Look at *The Fortune-Tellers* (Alexander, 1992) as an example. This is a universal story that could have been set in any number of places and times, but Trina Schart Hyman's illustrations allow the story to spring suddenly into a certain place and time—the west African country of Cameroon in what Hyman called "the fantastical present" (Hyman, 1995). The handsome people in rainbow-colored costume and the crisp, highly detailed surroundings create an idyllic, slightly larger-than-life backdrop for Alexander's literary folktale. (See Illustration 1 in the color insert.)

DEFINE AND DEVELOP CHARACTERS. Artists can give characters an extra fleshing-out through illustrations. David Small's artwork in *The Friend* (Stewart, 2004) intensifies the loving relationship between little Belle and her family's African American housekeeper, Bea, by showing the girl's emotionally distant mother and father. Belle's wealthy parents are departing on an extended trip, and yet her lavishly dressed mother only leans down to extend a powdered cheek to accept her daughter's good-bye kiss—no hugs and certainly no tears. Her father, in his driving gloves and camel-hair coat, is impatiently checking his watch, and as they motor away from the mansion, he doesn't look back. Another illustration shows Belle clinging to Bea as the automobile recedes in the distance. The text does not describe this aspect of Mr. and Mrs. Dodd's personalities.

Frog Goes to Dinner (Mayer, 1974), a wordless picture book, relies completely on illustrations to define and develop the characters. Mayer is a marvel when it comes to using facial expressions to communicate what his characters are feeling. Note the double-page illustration of the angry family driving home after they have been thrown out of Fancy Restaurant. Each family member harbors an individual response to the disaster. (See Illustration 2.)

REINFORCE TEXT. The primary function of some picture book illustrations is to reinforce the text. Nonfiction picture books often fall into this category, with the illustrations and diagrams restating visually what the words say. For instance, Steven Kellogg's illustrations for *How Much Is a Million?* (Schwartz, 1985) reinforce the concept of large numbers. For text that reads, "If a billion kids made a human tower . . . they would stand up past the moon," the accompanying illustration shows the top of a stack of happy children with the lunar landscape in the background. The topmost children are holding a banner that reads "1,000,000,000 KIDS."

Illustrations in a picture storybook also may function primarily to reinforce the story. In the ever popular *Blueberries for Sal* (McCloskey, 1948), for example, readers see what the text describes—the countryside in Maine as well as the characters who are out picking blueberries—but no major extensions to the text are evident. (See Illustration 32.)

PROVIDE A DIFFERING VIEWPOINT.   One of the most enjoyable ways in which illustrations may function in a picture book is that of telling a story different from the text or even being in opposition to the words. In *Rosie's Walk* (Hutchins, 1968), the text says that Rosie the hen takes a peaceful stroll around the farm and gets "back in time for dinner." However, the illustrations tell another tale: A fox, never mentioned in the narrative, lurks behind Rosie every step of the way, but is somehow frustrated each time it pounces forward to make Rosie its dinner. (See Illustration 3.) Peter Spier's *Oh, Were They Ever Happy* (1978) is an example of words and text that are humorously in opposition to one another. Children inadvertently left alone for the day (the babysitter has her days confused and doesn't show) decide to do something nice for their parents—paint the house. The words say "Neat job" and "Pretty color!" while the illustrations show what a horrible mess the kids are making. They paint the bricks and windowpanes; they finish one color of paint and take up another.

EXTEND OR DEVELOP THE PLOT.   The plot of a story may be advanced by illustrations. In wordless picture books, the whole plot is unfolded through pictures. Sometimes the plot is merely extended or rounded a little by the illustrations, as in Stephen Gammell's art in *The Relatives Came* (Rylant, 1985). Gammell shows that one family's journey to a family reunion is a bit perilous because Dad isn't such a good driver. Although Rylant's words say nothing about the driving, Dad levels the mailbox on the way out, loses suitcases, careens around mountain curves, and destroys their relatives' fence upon arrival. (See Illustration 4.)

PROVIDE INTERESTING ASIDES.   Sometimes picture book illustrations are filled with interesting asides—subplots or details not necessarily related to the main story line. In Denys Cazet's (1990) *Never Spit on Your Shoes,* the little dog Arnie tells his mother about his tiring first day at school. Though the illustrations show the events he mentions, each picture reveals other humorous vignettes taking place concurrently. For example, as Arnie tells about Raymond, who can write his name backwards, we see this new kid demonstrating his talent on the chalkboard. However, in a corner of the classroom, several animal children are using glue for an art project. A piglet is eating the glue, the sight of which sickens his classmates. In another area of the room, a child approaches the teacher and says, "Thank you very much for inviting me, but I'll be going home now." On another double-page spread, while Arnie describes having lunch in the cafeteria, a hippo is sticking drinking straws in his nose, pretending to be a centipede. His antics awe some at his table and disgust others.

ESTABLISH MOOD.   Illustrations are extremely effective in determining the mood of a picture storybook. *The Polar Express* (Van Allsburg, 1985) is a Christmas story, and Christmas stories typically use a bright and cheery palette. The mood in Van Allsburg's story, however, is mysterious, and he uses dark colors to establish that mood. With muted reds and blues and even muted yellows along with plenty of black and brown, the artist creates an eerie atmosphere as a young boy watches a magical train steam its way into his front yard late Christmas Eve. The mood is maintained as the train whisks

1. From *The Fortune-Tellers* by Lloyd Alexander, illustrated by Trina Schart Hyman.

2. From *Frog Goes to Dinner* by Mercer Mayer.

3. From *Rosie's Walk* by Pat Hutchins.

4. From *The Relatives Came* by Cynthia Rylant, illustrated by Stephen Gammell.

5. From *The Polar Express* by Chris Van Allsburg.

7. From *The Voice of the Wood* by Claude Clément, translated by Lenny Hort, illustrated by Frédéric Clément.

6. From *Rapunzel* by Paul O. Zelinsky.

8. From *A Chair for My Mother* by Vera B. Williams.

9. From *Freedom Summer* by Deborah Wiles, illustrated by Jerome Lagarrigue.

10. From *Ox-Cart Man* by Donald Hall, illustrated by Barbara Cooney.

11. From *Flying Feet: A Mud Flat Story* by James Stevenson.

13. From *Ben's Trumpet* by Rachel Isadora.

12. From *Zathura* by Chris Van Allsburg.

14. From *Once a Mouse* by Marcia Brown.

15. From *Barnard the Angry Rooster* by Mary Wormell.

16. From *One Night in the Coral Sea* by Sneed B. Collard, illustrated by Robin Brickman.

17. From *Abraham Lincoln* by Ingri and Edgar Parin d'Aulaire.

18. From *Ella Fitzgerald: The Tale of a Vocal Virtuoso* by Brian Pinkney.

19. From *Mouse Views: What the Class Pet Saw* by Bruce McMillan.

It happened just as the stranger had said. The owner had only to clap his hands and the paper crane became a living bird, flew down to the floor, and danced.

20. From *The Paper Crane* by Molly Bang.

21. From *Deep in the Forest* by Brinton Turkle.

22. From *Tuesday* by David Wiesner.

23. From *Three Little Pigs and the Big Bad Wolf* by Glen Rounds.

24. From *Thorn Rose* by the Brothers Grimm, illustrated by Errol Le Cain.

25. From *Thorn Rose* by the Brothers Grimm, illustrated by Errol Le Cain.

26. From *Thorn Rose* by the Brothers Grimm, illustrated by Errol Le Cain.

27. From *Snow White and the Seven Dwarfs* by the Brothers Grimm, translated by Randall Jarrell, illustrated by Nancy Ekholm Burkert.

28. From *Round Trip* by Ann Jonas.

29. From *Saint George and the Dragon* by Margaret Hodges, illustrated by Trina Schart Hyman.

30. From *Golem* by David Wisniewski.

31. From *Heartland* by Diane Siebert, illustrated by Wendell Minor.

32. From *Blueberries for Sal* by Robert McCloskey.

him and other children toward the North Pole, zipping past dark forests filled with wolves. (See Illustration 5.)

STYLE AND MEDIA IN PICTURE BOOK ILLUSTRATIONS

Artists use a vast array of styles and media to create the illustrations in children's books. In fact, some of the best and most varied art being done today appears in picture books. We know a professional artist who regularly checks the children's section at the public library to see what's new because he believes the best contemporary artwork is to be found there.

Excellent illustrations can, of course, be rendered in various styles, ranging from extremely realistic to abstract. *Realism*, or *representational* style, is a faithful reproduction of nature, people, and objects as they actually appear. The illustrations in Zelinsky's *Rapunzel* (1997) are representational. (See Illustration 6.) *Surrealism* is realism skewed. It is an attempt to represent the workings of the unconscious mind by creating a dreamlike state, as in Clément's *The Voice of the Wood* (1989). (See Illustration 7.) *Expressionism*, which is an attempt to give objective expression to inner experience, often makes use of bright colors and figures that are a bit disproportionate. This stylized form is evident in Williams's *A Chair for My Mother* (1982). (See Illustration 8.) Another popular style is *impressionism*, which emphasizes light, movement, and color over detail. A fine example of impressionism is Lagarrigue's art for Wiles's *Freedom Summer* (2001). (See Illustration 9.) *Naive* is a style that gives the appearance of being childlike, perhaps lacking perspective or a sense of proportion. Barbara Cooney used a naive style in her paintings for Hall's *Ox-Cart Man* (1979). (See Illustration 10.) There are, of course, other artistic styles, including *cartoon art*, as found in James Stevenson's *Flying Feet* (2004). (See Illustration 11.)

The various styles artists use to create their artwork may be rendered in a variety of artistic media. There are basically two categories of media: painterly and graphic.

Painterly media include the most common art materials, such as paint, pencil, and ink. In *Rapunzel*, Zelinsky used *oil paints*, an opaque layering of colors. (See Illustration 6.) Watercolors, which are translucent, were the medium for Stevenson's paintings in *Flying Feet*. (See Illustration 11.) Van Allsburg used *graphite*, or *pencil*, another painterly medium, in *Zathura* (2002). (See Illustration 12.) Also in this category is *pen and ink*, which Isadora used in *Ben's Trumpet* (1979). (See Illustration 13.) Other painterly media include *colored pencils*, *pastels* (chalk), *charcoal*, *crayons*, *felt-tip markers*, *gouache* (opaque water-based paints), *tempera* (opaque water-based or egg-yolk-based paints), and *acrylics* (plastic paints).

Artists apply painterly media directly to canvas, paper, or some other surface. But when artists use *graphic media*, they generally create the artwork elsewhere before applying it to the final surface. With *woodcuts*, for instance, the artist carves images in relief into a block of wood. Then inks or paints are applied to the wood and transferred to a surface, such as paper. Marcia Brown's illustrations for *Once a Mouse . . .* (1961) are woodcuts. (See Illustration 14; notice the wood grain.) *Linoleum cuts* are similar in technique to woodcuts, but they produce a cleaner line, as in Mary Wormell's *Barnard the Angry Rooster* (2001). (See Illustration 15.) *Collage,* another popular graphic technique, involves cutting and tearing shapes from paper or fabric and arranging them on the page, as in *One Night in the Coral Sea* (Collard, 2005). (See Illustration 16.) Collage may also include other objects that are attached to the surface, like the breakfast cereal and wire hangers in Diaz's illustrations for Bunting's *Smoky Night* (1994). David Wisniewski's dramatic illustrations in *Golem* (1996), created by overlaying intricate paper cutouts, are a sophisticated form of collage. (See Illustration 30.) *Stone lithography* is an engraving on stone that is printed on paper, such as the illustrations for the 1939 edition of *Abraham Lincoln* by Ingri and Edgar d'Aulaire. (See Illustration 17.) A graphic medium that looks a bit like pen-and-ink drawings is called *scratchboard.* A black ink coating is scratched away to show the white surface beneath; color may be added after the "drawing" is complete, as in *Ella Fitzgerald: The Tale of a Vocal Virtuoso* (Pinkney, 2002). (See Illustration 18.) Even *photography* can be considered a graphic technique. Bruce McMillan's *Mouse Views: What the Class Pet Saw* (1993) uses color photography to give children a fresh look at their world. (See Illustration 19.) Also, artists will often mix media, using both graphic and painterly techniques together. A prime example is Molly Bang's *The Paper Crane* (1985), which uses three-dimensional paper cutouts, traditional collage, and painterly techniques. Each page was then photographed to retain its three-dimensional quality. (See Illustration 20.)

VISUAL ELEMENTS

Like all artists, picture book illustrators incorporate several visual elements into the creation of their pictures that subtly affect the way we respond to the art. These elements are line, shape, color, texture, and composition.

LINES.   Lines in illustrations are either curved or straight. These lines may vary in thickness or length. They may run horizontally, diagonally, or vertically. They may be solid or broken. How line is used often plays an important role in what a picture communicates. For instance, diagonal lines suggest movement (slant of the road in Illustration 4 and of the keyboard in Illustration 13). The dominant vertical lines of the trees in Illustration 5, from Van Allsburg's *The Polar Express,* create a static look, as if this scene were a photograph capturing and arresting a moment in the flow of action. On the other hand, horizontal lines may suggest order or tranquillity, such as the prairie horizon and straight fence lines in Minor's illustration from *Heartland* (Siebert, 1989). (See Illustration 31.)

Artists also use line to direct the viewer's eye. Le Cain's use of line in *Thorn Rose* (1975), the Grimm Brothers' version of "Sleeping Beauty," focuses the eye upon the ominous tower holding the only remaining spinning wheel. The lines created by a balustrade, wall, row of windows, and roof line lead to the upper right-hand corner and seem to converge at the tower that harbors Thorn Rose's fate. Even the fountain and the horizon point the way. In this manner, Le Cain guides our viewing of his painting. (See Illustration 26.)

SHAPE.   Shape is the two-dimensional form representing an object. Shapes may be simple or complex. The objects may be readily identifiable or so abstract as to be difficult to recognize. Curved shapes generally suggest things found in nature, and angular shapes depict objects built by humans. For example, the illustration from *Round Trip* by Ann Jonas (1983) shows from one perspective people sitting in a movie theater. Neither the theater nor the humans are clearly recognizable; they are only suggested by the shapes. The human-made items (seats, lights, screen) are angular forms, while the people are suggested by rounded forms representing heads. (See Illustration 28.)

COLOR.   Color is a visual element with the traits hue, value, and saturation. Hue is simply the color itself (red, blue, yellow), and these hues are often categorized as being either cool (blue, green, violet) or warm (red, yellow, orange). The scene by Le Cain (Illustration 24) predominately uses reds, yellows, and oranges to create the impression of a hot, bustling kitchen. Value is the lightness or darkness of the color (dark blue, light green), achieved by adding black or white to the hue. As discussed earlier in this chapter, the mood of a picture may be manipulated by value, as in the mysterious mood achieved by the dark palette Van Allsburg used in *The Polar Express* (Illustration 5). Finally, saturation, or chroma, is the brightness or dullness of a color. For example, the brightness of the colors in the picture from *The Fortune-Tellers* (Illustration 1) creates a festive atmosphere, while the muted hues in Illustration 29 add an appropriately ancient feeling to the story of *Saint George and the Dragon* (Hodges, 1984). Illustrations also may be achromatic, rendered in only black, white, and the various shades of gray in between. (See Illustrations 2 and 13.) Monochromatic illustrations use only one hue, such as the all-blue pictures in McCloskey's (1948) *Blueberries for Sal*. (See Illustration 32.)

TEXTURE.   Texture is a tactile sensation communicated by the artist: rough, smooth, hard, soft, and so on. Collage, as discussed earlier, is the most obvious way of creating texture in illustrations because of its three-dimensional qualities. The cutout crane in Illustration 20, for instance, clearly has the sharp edges of a folded paper bird. However, illustrators most often create a sense of texture on a two-dimensional surface, as with the fabric of the automobile seats in Illustration 2. Mercer Mayer used cross-hatching (the crossing of lines) to produce the coarse texture of the material in both the seats and the boy's suit.

COMPOSITION.   Composition serves to unify all of the elements in an illustration.

> In arranging the elements on each page, including the printed type, the artist tries to obtain an effective balance between unity and variety and creates visual patterns that may be carried on from page to page. (Kiefer 1995, p. 129)

For example, an artist may balance objects in an illustration, either by distributing them evenly (symmetrically) or irregularly (asymmetrically). In Illustration 22, David Wiesner splits the picture evenly down the center from top to bottom. The backgrounds of both sides are balanced asymmetrically by the careful yet irregular placement of vehicles and people, yet the clouds in the sky (which look like frogs) are symmetric. Another facet of composition concerns object dominance. Artists can

ensure that certain shapes are dominant by making them larger or brighter in order to attract the eye. In Illustration 22, the police detective in the foreground is larger than any other individual and thus is the dominant figure. In this way, Wiesner directs the viewer's attention to the detective's actions.

ADDITIONAL ILLUSTRATION CRITERIA: ACTION AND DETAIL

According to Cianciolo (1976, p. 9), in quality picture book art "something of significance is said." In inferior picture books, the art all begins to look the same—flat line and color washes, as in books like the Sponge Bob titles and most things from Disney. In other words, quality picture book art is individual and unique. Stereotypical artwork denies individuality, both in the artistic rendering and in the characters and settings represented. It is more difficult to relate to the human experience and to get involved with the story when the art depicts generic or stereotypical people and places. In better picture book illustrations, two basic elements tend to give individuality to the illustrations: action and detail.

Depicting Action

Action is important in picture storybooks in particular because the artwork moves the story along. Note the illustration from *Deep in the Forest* (Turkle, 1976), a role-reversal version of "Goldilocks and the Three Bears." (See Illustration 21.) This scene freezes the action at the climax, but the illustration is by no means static. The tilt of the human forms as they barrel forward in pursuit and the wild-eyed little bear with fully outstretched body and churning legs create for us a true sense of the chaotic, frenzied chase. Sometimes action in illustrations is subtle but suggests a great deal of activity. For example, in *Tuesday* (Wiesner, 1991), the police detective examines a lily pad suspended from a pencil, his quizzical look suggesting his mental activity. "Why and how?" he seems to ask himself, unable to fathom the hundreds of frogs who invaded the nighttime sanctity of his town on flying lily pads. (See Illustration 22.) One of the ways picture book artists create tension in their work is by using illustrations to anticipate or foreshadow action. Look at the illustration from *Rosie's Walk* (Hutchins, 1968). (See Illustration 3.) Rosie, still unaware her life is in danger, is about to inadvertently foil another of the fox's attempts to capture her. The rope coiled about her leg shows us what is to come.

Creating Depth with Detail

Certainly it is not difficult to see that details in illustrations tend to give the artwork depth and allow artists to assert their individuality. Even the power of a carefully placed line can make loosely drawn pictures say volumes. Consider the illustration from Glen Rounds's *Three Little Pigs and the Big Bad Wolf* (1992). (See Illustration 23.) Although the wolf is rather scratchily drawn, his raggedy appearance makes him look as if he's fallen on hard times. The flowing lines give the wolf a fluid, slinky sense of movement, which seems to say "vagabond."

Detail also may be evident in the use of perspective in many quality picture books. In Le Cain's *Thorn Rose* (1975), the artist shows a single scene from two very different perspectives. When everyone in the castle falls asleep, one illustration looks past the cook (who is about to box the kitchen boy's ears), out the kitchen door, and beyond the horses sleeping in a stall. Later, when the prince finally arrives on the castle grounds, we are allowed to look past him, past the horses, and back into the kitchen to where the cook is slumped over a table. (See Illustrations 24 and 25.) This may seem a small thing, but such detail provides the setting with depth and makes it a believable place. Obviously, Le Cain envisioned this world carefully and translated his vision into illustrations that give us a sense of being there.

Le Cain also uses his illustrations in *Thorn Rose* to foreshadow most subtly the impending doom connected with the last spinning wheel to be found in the kingdom. (See Illustration 26.) In one painting, the artist shows Thorn Rose, now an adolescent, standing on a balcony walkway with a castle tower in the distance. The left side of the illustration is verdant; Thorn Rose is surrounded by flowering plants and peacocks, and the sky is bright. However, as one's eyes move across the painting toward the tower, the sky darkens ominously. The gardenlike surroundings of the castle give way to a craggy, foreboding appearance. A great serpent, a symbol of evil, is wound about the parapet leading to the tower, which has a rather dragonlike look. Of course, the tower holds the accursed spinning wheel. This visual foreshadowing creates an unconscious feeling of tension in the reader.

Careful attention to detail often requires extensive research before an artist begins work on the illustrations. Depending on the book, illustrators may spend untold hours investigating details of Ming Dynasty culture, the anatomy of wolves, or rain forest botany, for example. In Jarrell's retelling of *Snow-White and the Seven Dwarfs* (Grimm Brothers, 1972), the artist, Nancy Ekholm Burkert, re-created the time period and cultural setting of the tale with accuracy. Even the illustration showing the evil queen's laboratory is stunning in its detail. The accoutrements of black magic are displayed on a workbench; each herb and root is authentic and poisonous. (See Illustration 27.) Trina Schart Hyman's illustrations for *Saint George and the Dragon* (Hodges, 1984) include drawings, primarily in borders surrounding the text, of plants and flowers indigenous to Britain during those magical times. In researching his book *Make Way for Ducklings*, Robert McCloskey (1941) filled notebooks with artistic studies of ducks—sketches of wing extensions and so on (Schmidt, 1990). He even had ducks swimming in his bathtub and walking about his apartment to use as ready references. McCloskey (1965) pointed out that when he spent time visualizing all the elements of a tree from leaf to twig to branch to trunk to root, the effort may not be apparent to the viewer of the artistically rendered tree, but the tree is better for his having thought of it in such detail.

Indeed, detail is often subtle. In fact, most artistic devices are like cosmetics; they must not be too noticeable, or they are not doing their job. Makeup, for instance, must enhance so that we say, "What a gorgeous face," not "What great eye shadow." A device that Maurice Sendak (1963) used in *Where the Wild Things Are* is so subtle that most readers don't notice they are being influenced by it. As Max's anger grows, so do

the illustrations, getting larger and larger until they fill a full double-page spread. Then as Max's anger cools, the illustrations begin to shrink.

Care Given to Bookmaking

Finally, the process of fine bookmaking gives us a few other evaluative considerations. The size and shape of books may match the story line, as in Stevens's (1995) *Tops and Bottoms*. The book is formatted so that it must be turned sideways to read, offering taller double-page spreads that accommodate the extended view of what parts of a plant grow above ground and what parts grow below. Other book design elements can set quality publications apart. For example, the rainbow trail, a significant recurring design on Pueblo Native American pottery and other art forms, becomes a unifying factor as it leads the reader through *Arrow to the Sun* (McDermott, 1974a). Ann Jonas's *Round Trip* (1983) is designed to be read as a round trip. The illustrations are ingeniously created so that when we reach the end of the book, we flip it upside down and read it backward. All the illustrations suddenly transform into new pictures, an optical illusion of sorts. (See Illustration 28; a movie theater becomes a restaurant.) At the same time, the round-trip theme is a part of the story—a trip into the city and then home again.

Even small details such as decorated endpapers enhance the visual appeal of a picture book. The endpapers inside the cover of a book actually bind book to cover and are traditionally white. However, not only are endpapers often brightly colored in many of today's books, but they often are illustrated, sometimes with original pieces not found inside. Good examples are the two original paintings by Helen Oxenbury on the endpapers of Rosen's retelling of *We're Going on a Bear Hunt* (1989). A deserted, daytime seashore scene appears on the front endpaper, and a nighttime seashore scene with a bear lumbering along in the surf is on the back.

Other illustrative techniques extend art beyond the traditional designs. Hyman's borders in *Saint George and the Dragon* (Hodges, 1984) give the look of observing the story through an old-fashioned window. (See Illustration 29.) In Christopher Bing's illustrations for Ernest Lawrence Thayer's *Casey at the Bat* (2000), real and created reproductions of artifacts, newspaper clippings, photographs, and other late-19th-century memorabilia (ticket stubs, coins, medals, baseball cards) are superimposed on bold pen-and-ink drawings resembling the sort appearing in old newspapers. Even the front and back matter, such as the acknowledgments and Library of Congress cataloging information, are hidden away within these reproductions. In fact, the whole book is carefully designed to look as if it is a scrapbook from the year 1888.

All these elements of picture book creation and production are what make the visual storytelling and concept-teaching process so successful. Children have available to them some of the best current artwork. As teachers and parents, we have the opportunity to help our children become visually literate through fine picture books, and to curb the numbing effects of mindless television viewing. Our charge is to offer our children the best in picture and in word, to give them an arsenal for making artistic and literary judgments and developing taste.

For more on picture books, see Chapter 7.

REFERENCES

Alexander, Lloyd. (1992). *The fortune-tellers.* Illustrated by Trina Schart Hyman. New York: Dutton.

Anno, Mitsumasa. (1977). *Anno's counting book.* New York: Crowell.

Bang, Molly. (1985). *The paper crane.* New York: Greenwillow.

Collard, Sneed B. (2005). *One night in the Coral Sea.* Illustrated by Robin Brickman. Watertown, MA: Charlesbridge.

Brown, Marcia. (1961). *Once a mouse. . . .* New York: Scribner's.

Bunting, Eve. (1994). *Smoky night.* Illustrated by David Diaz. New York: Harcourt.

Canaday, John. (1980). *What is art?* New York: Knopf.

Cazet, Denys. (1990). *Never spit on your shoes.* Orchard.

Cianciolo, Patricia. (1976). *Illustrations in children's books.* Dubuque, IA: W. C. Brown.

Clément, Claude. (1989). *The voice of the wood.* Illustrated by Frédéric Clément. New York: Dial.

d'Aulaire, Ingri, & d'Aulaire, Edgar. (1939). *Abraham Lincoln.* New York: Doubleday.

Grimm Brothers. (1972). *Snow-White and the seven dwarfs.* Translated by Randall Jarrell. Illustrated by Nancy Ekholm Burkert. New York: Farrar, Straus & Giroux.

Grimm Brothers. (1975). *Thorn Rose.* Illustrated by Errol Le Cain. New York: Bradbury.

Hall, Donald. (1979). *Ox-cart man.* Illustrated by Barbara Cooney. New York: Viking.

Hodges, Margaret. (1984). *Saint George and the dragon.* Illustrated by Trina Schart Hyman. Boston: Little, Brown.

Hutchins, Pat. (1968). *Rosie's walk.* New York: Macmillan.

Hyman, Trina Schart. (1995). Telephone interview with Elena Rockman, 27 January.

Isadora, Rachel. (1979). *Ben's trumpet.* New York: Greenwillow.

Jonas, Ann. (1983). *Round trip.* New York: Greenwillow.

Kiefer, Barbara Z. (1995). *The potential of picture-books: From visual literacy to aesthetic understanding.* Upper Saddle River, NJ: Merrill/Prentice Hall.

Lobel, Arnold. (1981). *On Market Street.* Illustrated by Anita Lobel. New York: Greenwillow.

Mahy, Margaret. (1987). *17 kings and 42 elephants.* Illustrated by Patricia McCarthy. New York: Dial.

Mayer, Mercer. (1974). *Frog goes to dinner.* New York: Dial.

McCloskey, Robert. (1941). *Make way for ducklings.* New York: Viking.

McCloskey, Robert. (1948). *Blueberries for Sal.* New York: Viking.

McCloskey, Robert. (1965). *The lively art of picture Books.* [Videocassette]. Weston, CT.: Weston Woods.

McDermott, Gerald. (1974a). *Arrow to the sun.* New York: Viking.

McDermott, Gerald. (1974b). Image in film and picture book. Speech given at the University of Georgia, Athens, 26 September.

McMillan, Bruce. (1993). *Mouse views: What the class pet saw.* New York: Holiday House.

Pinkney, Andrea. (2002). *Ella Fitzgerald: The tale of a vocal virtuoso.* Illustrated by Brian Pinkney. New York: Jump at the Sun/Hyperion.

Rosen, Michael. (1989). *We're going on a bear hunt.* Illustrated by Helen Oxenbury. New York: Macmillan.

Rounds, Glen. (1992). *Three little pigs and the big bad wolf.* New York: Holiday House.

Rylant, Cynthia. (1985). *The relatives came.* Illustrated by Stephen Gammell. New York: Bradbury.

Schmidt, Gary D. (1990). *Robert McCloskey.* Boston: Twayne.

Schwartz, David M. (1985). *How much is a million?* Illustrated by Steven Kellogg. New York: Lothrop, Lee, & Shepard.

Sendak, Maurice. (1963). *Where the wild things are.* New York: Harper.

Siebert, Diane. (1989). *Heartland.* Illustrated by Wendell Minor. New York: Crowell.

Spier, Peter. (1978). *Oh, were they ever happy.* New York: Doubleday.

Stevens, Janet. (1995). *Tops and bottoms.* New York: Harcourt.

Stevenson, James. (2004). *Flying feet: A mud flat story.* New York: Greenwillow.

Stewart, Sarah. (2004). *The friend*. Illustrated by David Small. New York: Farrar, Straus & Giroux.

Thayer, Ernest Lawrence. (2000). *Casey at the bat: A ballad of the republic sung in the year 1888*. Illustrated by Christopher Bing. Brooklyn, NY: Handprint.

Turkle, Brinton. (1976). *Deep in the forest*. New York: Dutton.

Van Allsburg, Chris. (1985). *The Polar Express*. Boston: Houghton Mifflin.

Van Allsburg, Chris. (2002.) *Zathura*. Boston: Houghton Mifflin.

Wiesner, David. (1991). *Tuesday*. New York: Clarion.

Wiles, Deborah. (2001). *Freedom summer*. Illustrated by Jerome Lagarrigue. New York: Atheneum.

Williams, Vera B. (1982). *A chair for my mother*. New York: Greenwillow.

Wisniewski, David. (1996). *Golem*. New York: Clarion.

Wormell, Mary. (2001). *Bernard the angry rooster*. New York: Farrar, Straus & Giroux.

Zelinsky, Paul. (1997). *Rapunzel*. New York: Dutton.

Chapter 5

Children's Books: History and Trends

The notion of childhood dawned late in the history of our Western world, not until the 17th century. The English philosopher John Locke influenced the prevailing attitudes about children as much as anyone in his time. Locke's book *Some Thoughts Concerning Education,* published in 1693, suggested gentler ways of raising children. He even proposed that children's books be made available, books that were easy and pleasant to read. However, *childhood* was a concept only among the affluent until well into the 20th century. As in the days before Locke, many children in both England and the United States continued to be treated as if they were small adults. Consider that child labor laws were not legislated until the early 20th century in both countries. Kids dressed, worked, and lived like their adult counterparts, if that well. Therefore, for the general populace, the idea of special books for children was slow in coming.

EARLY BOOKS FOR CHILDREN

As far back as the Middle Ages, books intended for youngsters existed in very limited numbers in the form of handwritten texts for the extremely wealthy. However, because literature aimed at young readers has always reflected society's attitudes about children, the stories in these early books were meant to indoctrinate, to provide lessons in proper behavior. The best stories children were exposed to came from storytellers—fairy tales, myths, ballads, epics, and other tales from our oral tradition. Yet these stories were not really meant for children, although they were allowed to listen. Nevertheless, over time these magical tales have become the property of childhood.

By the same token, books published in the early days of the printing press, books meant for adults, were also enjoyed and adopted by children. William Caxton, an English businessman and printer, produced several such books, including *Aesop's Fables* (1484), which was decorated with woodcut illustrations. From that time forward, children have claimed many books meant for adult audiences, including such well-known titles as Daniel Defoe's *Robinson Crusoe* (1719), Jonathan Swift's *Gulliver's Travels* (1726), Johann Wyss's *The Swiss Family Robinson* (1814), Walter Scott's *Ivanhoe* (1820), and J. R. R. Tolkien's *The Hobbit* (1937). (See Figure 5–1.)

FIGURE 5–1
A chronology of history and trends in children's literature.

1440	Introduction of hornbooks
1484	*Aesop's Fables* published by William Caxton
1580	Introduction of chapbooks
1646	*Spiritual Milk for Boston Babes in Either England, Drawn from the Breasts of Both Testaments for Their Soul's Nourishment* by John Cotton
1657	*Orbis Pictus* by Johann Amos Comenius
1697	*Tales of Mother Goose* retold by Charles Perrault
1719	*Robinson Crusoe* by Daniel Defoe
1726	*Gulliver's Travels* by Jonathan Swift
1744	*A Pretty Little Pocket-Book* published by John Newbery
1765	*The History of Little Goody Two Shoes* published by John Newbery
1812	*Household Tales* retold by Jacob and Wilhelm Grimm
1814	*The Swiss Family Robinson* by Johann Wyss
1820	*Ivanhoe* by Walter Scott
1823	*Grimm's Fairy Tales* illustrated by George Cruikshank
1835	*Fairy Tales Told for Children* by Hans Christian Andersen
1846	*A Book of Nonsense* by Edward Lear
1863	*The Water Babies* by Charles Kingsley
1864	*Journey to the Center of the Earth* by Jules Verne
1865	*Alice's Adventures in Wonderland* by Lewis Carroll (Charles Dodgson), illustrated by John Tenniel
1865	*Hans Brinker, or the Silver Skates* by Mary Mapes Dodge
1868	*Little Women* by Louisa May Alcott
1871	*At the Back of the North Wind* by George MacDonald
1873	*St. Nicholas Magazine* begins publication
1876	*The Adventures of Tom Sawyer* by Mark Twain (Samuel Clemens)
1878	*The Diverting History of John Gilpin* illustrated by Randolph Caldecott
1878	*Under the Window* illustrated by Kate Greenaway
1881	*The Adventures of Pinocchio* by Carlo Collodi
1883	*Treasure Island* by Robert Louis Stevenson
1883	*The Merry Adventures of Robin Hood of Great Reknown* written and illustrated by Howard Pyle
1885	*A Child's Garden of Verses* by Robert Louis Stevenson
1894–95	*The Jungle Books* by Rudyard Kipling
1900	*The Wonderful Wizard of Oz* by L. Frank Baum
1902	*The Tale of Peter Rabbit* written and illustrated by Beatrix Potter
1906	*Peter Pan in Kensington Gardens* by J. M. Barrie, illustrated by Arthur Rackham
1908	*Anne of Green Gables* by Lucy Maud Montgomery
1908	*The Wind in the Willows* by Kenneth Grahame

FIGURE 5–1
Continued

1911	*The Secret Garden* by Frances Hodgson Burnett
1913	*Mother Goose* illustrated by Arthur Rackham
1922	John Newbery Medal established
1926	*Winnie-the-Pooh* by A. A. Milne, illustrated by Ernest Shepard
1928	*Millions of Cats* written and illustrated by Wanda Gag
1937	*The Hobbit* by J. R. R. Tolkien
1937	*And to Think that I Saw It on Mulberry Street* written and illustrated by Dr. Seuss (Theodor Geisel)
1938	Randolph Caldecott Medal established
1939	*Goodnight Moon* by Margaret Wise Brown, illustrated by Clement Hurd
1939	*Madeline* written and illustrated by Ludwig Bemelmans
1941	*Make Way for Ducklings* written and illustrated by Robert McCloskey
1950	*The Lion, the Witch and the Wardrobe* by C. S. Lewis
1952	*Charlotte's Web* by E. B. White, illustrated by Garth Williams
1956	Hans Christian Andersen Prize established
1957	*Little Bear* by Else Minarik, illustrated by Maurice Sendak
1957	*The Cat in the Hat* by Dr. Seuss
1959	*The Lantern Bearers* by Rosemary Sutcliff
1962	*The Snowy Day* written and illustrated by Ezra Jack Keats
1963	*Where the Wild Things Are* written and illustrated by Maurice Sendak
1964	*Harriet the Spy* by Louise Fitzhugh
1964	*The Book of Three* by Lloyd Alexander
1966	Mildred L. Batchelder Award established
1967	*A Boy, a Dog, and a Frog* by Mercer Mayer
1969	Coretta Scott King Award established
1970	*Are You There God? It's Me, Margaret* by Judy Blume
1971	*Journey to Topaz* by Yoshiko Uchida
1972	*Push-Pull, Empty-Full: A Book of Opposites* by Tana Hoban
1974	*My Brother Sam is Dead* by James Lincoln and Christopher Collier
1975	*M. C. Higgins, the Great* by Virginia Hamilton
1976	*Why Mosquitoes Buzz in People's Ears* retold by Verna Aardema, illustrated by Leo and Diane Dillon
1977	NCTE Excellence in Poetry for Children Award established
1981	*A Visit to William Blake's Inn: Poems for Innocent and Experienced Travelers* by Nancy Willard, illustrated by Alice and Martin Provensen
1983	*Sugaring Time* by Kathryn Lasky, photographs by Christopher Knight
1985	*The Polar Express* written and illustrated by Chris Van Allsburg
1987	*Lincoln: A Photobiography* by Russell Freedman
1988	*Joyful Noise: Poems for Two Voices* by Paul Fleischman
1989	*Color Zoo* by Lois Ehlert
1990	*Orbis Pictus* Award established
1996	Pura Belpré Award established
1998	*Harry Potter and the Sorcerer's Stone* by J. K. Rowling
2000	Michael L. Printz Award established
2001	Robert F. Sibert Informational Book Award established
2004	Theodor Seuss Geisel Award established

Literature intended specifically for children and published from the 15th through the 17th centuries still was designed to indoctrinate. The so-called hornbooks, or lesson paddles, existed as reading material for children for more than two centuries, beginning in the 1440s. Generally made of wood, these small rectangular paddles (about 3 by 5 inches) had pasted to them pieces of parchment on which were printed the alphabet, verses from the Bible, or the like. The term *hornbook* comes from the thin, transparent sheet of cow horn that covered and protected the parchment. Hornbooks were particularly popular among the Puritans in colonial America, who believed that children were basically wicked, like adults, and therefore in need of saving. This pious attitude is clearly evident in the first book published for American children, John Cotton's catechism called *Spiritual Milk for Boston Babes in Either England, Drawn from the Breasts of Both Testaments for Their Souls' Nourishment*. First published in England in 1646, it was revised and published in America in 1656.

Despite the preachy, often unpleasant nature of children's literature in the early days of printing, one especially bright spot appeared in 1657. Johann Amos Comenius, a Moravian teacher and bishop, wrote *Orbis Pictus* (The World in Pictures), which is often called the first children's picture book. *Orbis Pictus* is filled with woodcut illustrations that work in harmony with the simple text to describe the wonders of the natural world.

In 1697, Charles Perrault, who had set about collecting the French fairy tales, published his enduring collection, *Tales of Mother Goose*, which included such old favorites as "The Sleeping Beauty" and "Cinderella." Here we find the first mention of Mother Goose, a figure popularized in many subsequent books and stories. Although Perrault's stories were popular with adults in the court of King Louis XIV, his fairy tale collection contains a frontispiece showing an old woman (presumably Mother Goose) telling stories to a group of children.

Even as early as the 16th century, a form of underground reading became popular. Called *chapbooks*, these crudely printed booklets were often sold by peddlers for pennies. Chapbooks became extremely popular in the 17th and 18th centuries and provided the first real break from the oppressive, overly didactic, you-are-a-sinner books for children. The Puritans, of course, decried these tales of Robin Hood, King Arthur, and even an early rendition of "Froggie Went a-Courting." Yet, children and adults reveled in them, though often on the sly.

Chapbooks may have been indirectly responsible for what is arguably the most important development in the history of children's literature—John Newbery's children's book publishing house. Certainly Newbery was influenced by John Locke, who dared suggest that youngsters should enjoy reading, so it seems likely that he observed the popularity of chapbooks among children and decided there was a market for true children's books. In any case, Newbery ushered in the age of children's books by beginning to publish exclusively for young readers. He released his first title for children in 1744. *A Pretty Little Pocket-Book* taught the alphabet not with catechism, but with entertaining games, rhymes, and fables. Newbery published hundreds of books (some of which he may have written himself), the most famous and enduring of which was *The History of Little Goody Two Shoes* (1765). So great was Newbery's contribution to children's publishing that the oldest of the world's children's book prizes bears his name, America's John Newbery Medal, first given in 1922. Still, the moralistic tale continued to dominate much of children's literature, even in many of Newbery's books. Didacticism—emphasizing lesson more than story—ruled well into the 19th century.

CHILDREN'S BOOKS COME OF AGE

The 1800s

The onset of the 19th century brought some of the most influential, honest, and lasting children's stories into print. Jacob and Wilhelm Grimm collected from oral sources the German variants of the folk and fairy tales and retold them in their *Household Tales,* which appeared in 1812 and included "Snow White" and "Rumpelstiltskin." Some of Hans Christian Andersen's original fairy tales were published in 1835 in a volume titled *Fairy Tales Told for Children.* The stories of this Danish author, such as "The Ugly Duckling" and "The Emperor's New Clothes," remain popular to this day.

One of the century's greatest contributions to verse for children came from England. Edward Lear's *A Book of Nonsense* (1846), a collection of outrageous limericks, became an immediate bestseller. Lear made the limerick famous, and it remains a favorite verse form among today's children. Robert Louis Stevenson's *A Child's Garden of Verses* (1885) is another poetry collection that children still love.

A number of noteworthy books surfaced during the second half of the 19th century. Fantasy novels emerged with the publication of such greats as *The Water Babies* by Charles Kingsley in 1863 and, of course, Lewis Carroll's (Charles Dodgson) *Alice's Adventures in Wonderland* in 1865. Other noteworthy titles include *At the Back of the North Wind* by George MacDonald (1871), *The Adventures of Pinocchio* by Carlo Collodi (1881), and the novels of Jules Verne, which mark the advent of the science fiction genre. Beginning with *Journey to the Center of the Earth* in 1864, Jules Verne created stories meant for adults but happily embraced by young readers.

Stories about contemporary life were especially preachy and pious until a monumental children's novel made its debut in 1868. *Little Women* by Louisa May Alcott was like a breath of fresh air with its lively characters whose actions, words, and feelings reflected honest human experiences. The character of Jo March, for example, deviated radically from female characters of the past who were docile and certainly inferior to their male counterparts. In fact, Jo was something of a rebel (an early feminist), who railed constantly against what she considered the false set of standards dictated by the Victorian code of behavior. *Little Women* set the course for many realistic novels that immediately followed its publication, including several more from Alcott herself. A few years later came Mark Twain's (Samuel Clemens) *The Adventures of Tom Sawyer* (1876) and Robert Louis Stevenson's *Treasure Island* (first serialized in the magazine *Young Folks,* then published as a book in 1883). The last

USING THE CHILDREN'S LITERATURE DATABASE

Be sure the CD database is installed on your hard drive. On the Home page of the CD, click on Book List in the left navigation bar. Click on the Year column to sort by year. The books in the database are now sorted chronologically by year published. What authors or titles do you recognize from the 1800s?

decade of the 19th century gave us Rudyard Kipling's masterpiece, *The Jungle Books* (1894–1895).

A number of magazines for children began publication during the 19th century. *St. Nicholas Magazine,* published in the United States starting in 1873, set standards of excellence in the world of children's literature. Edited by Mary Mapes Dodge, who wrote *Hans Brinker, or the Silver Skates* (1865), the best-known children's authors and illustrators contributed to *St. Nicholas.* Several novels first appeared in the magazine in serialized form, including *Jo's Boys* by Louisa May Alcott, *Sara Crewe* by Frances Hodgson Burnett, and *The Jungle Books* by Rudyard Kipling.

Children's book illustration also came of age during the 19th century. Illustrators gained status as printing techniques improved and color illustrations became more common. Publishers enticed well-known artists, such as George Cruikshank, who illustrated *Grimm's Fairy Tales* in 1823, to produce work for children's books. The artwork by the immortal Victorian-age illustrators in Great Britain, such as Randolph Caldecott, Kate Greenaway, and Walter Crane, rival the fine work being done today, in spite of comparatively primitive color printing methods. So influential were these artists that two major awards for children's book illustration today bear their names: The Randolph Caldecott Medal established in 1938 in the United States and the Kate Greenaway Medal in the United Kingdom, first given in 1956. Randolph Caldecott is often noted as the first illustrator to show action in pictures, as evidenced in *The Diverting History of John Gilpin* (1878), which has perhaps his best-remembered illustrations. In fact, the Caldecott Medal affixed to winning picture books is embossed with the most famous scene, John Gilpin's wild ride. American Howard Pyle also created stunning illustrations for classics like *The Merry Adventures of Robin Hood of Great Reknown* (1883), which he also wrote.

1900–1950

And so the domain of children's books was firmly established by the dawning of the 20th century, which began with the birth of the modern picture storybook. Illustrations in books for children, beautiful as they were, functioned primarily as decorations until Beatrix Potter wrote and illustrated her enduring story, *The Tale of Peter Rabbit* (1902). Potter incorporated colored illustration with text, page for page, becoming the first to use pictures as well as words to tell the story. Beatrix Potter was thus the mother of the modern picture storybook, and *Peter Rabbit* the firstborn.

Another first that occurred early in the 20th century was marked by the publication of L. Frank Baum's *The Wonderful Wizard of Oz* in 1900. Modern fantasy had been primarily the domain of the Europeans, especially the British. *The Wonderful Wizard of Oz* was the first classic modern fantasy written by an American.

Many other enduring classics emerged in the first part of the century, such as J. M. Barrie's magical *Peter Pan in Kensington Gardens,* adapted in 1906 into a book from its original form as a play, and Lucy Maud Montgomery's Canadian classic *Anne of Green Gables* (1908), featuring the spunky, red-headed Anne Shirley. Also in 1908, the granddaddy of animal fantasies appeared. Kenneth Grahame's *The Wind in the Willows* became the standard for all subsequent animal fantasy stories. Another trend-setting fantasy, A. A. Milne's gentle story of *Winnie-the-Pooh,* was published in 1926.

While talented illustrators such as Arthur Rackham (*Mother Goose,* 1913) were at work in the United Kingdom, the United States produced its counterpart to Beatrix Potter—Wanda Gág. Her *Millions of Cats* (1928) is credited as the first American picture storybook. Its descriptive pictures and rhythmic text have remained unforgettable: "Hundreds of cats, Thousands of cats, Millions and billions and trillions of cats." Other landmark picture books from the first half of the 20th century include American favorites such as *Goodnight Moon* (1939), a classic bedtime story by Margaret Wise Brown, and *Madeline,* Ludwig Bemelmans's 1939 tale of the little, irrepressible Parisian girl who lived in a boarding school. Dr. Seuss (Theodor Geisel), who became the most widely known of American children's book authors and illustrators, released his first book, *And to Think That I Saw It on Mulberry Street,* in 1937. Another immortal name in the history of children's picture books, Robert McCloskey, published *Make Way for Ducklings* in 1941. Today as much as ever, children love this endearing tale of a spunky mother duck and her eight ducklings' dangerous trek through Boston to reach the Public Garden.

Along with the many noteworthy books during the first half of the 20th century, a number of popular but lesser-quality books appeared. The books published by the Stratemeyer Syndicate created a publishing phenomenon that has extended into current times. Beginning in the late 19th century, Edward Stratemeyer saw the potential profit in publishing a quickly produced fiction series for young readers. Certainly series books had been published and done well before Stratemeyer, but he created a machine that pumped out thousands of titles over the years. Typically, Stratemeyer would outline plots and then turn the writing over to a host of ghostwriters. He published his series books under various pseudonyms, which many children still believe belong to real authors. Some of the Stratemeyer series titles include The Rover Boys, The Bobbsey Twins, Tom Swift, The Hardy Boys, and Nancy Drew. Today series books, such as the Animorphs, the Secrets of Droon books, the Katie Kazoo titles, the Dragon Slayers' Academy, and the Hoofbeats series, are commonly the best-selling children's books, despite their sometimes less-than-sterling literary quality (Brooks, Waterman, & Allington, 2003; Chevannes, McEvoy, & Simson, 1997; Greenlee, Monson, & Taylor, 1996; Saltman 1997; Roback, 2001).

1950–Present

In the latter half of the 20th century, a revolution in the world of children's books occurred. The decade of the 1950s was a stable time for children's publishing. Books still had predictable plots and contained the basic decency and restrained good fun that most adults expected. Some enduring modern classics were born during this period, such as E. B. White's *Charlotte's Web* (1952) and C. S. Lewis's *The Lion, the Witch and the Wardrobe* (1950), not to mention the fine historical fiction of Rosemary Sutcliff (*The Lantern Bearers,* 1959). Another step forward in the world of children's books occurred in 1956, when the International Board on Books for Young People established the major international award for children's writing, the Hans Christian Andersen Prize.

The financial boom of the 1960s, which included large government grants to school libraries, helped make children's publishing big business. More books began to be published and sold, which is reflected by an increase in the number of books chosen as "Notables" each year by the American Library Association. There were 19 Notable titles in 1956 and 62 Notables in 1964.

New Realism

Along with an increase in sales, the 1960s brought a revolution in writing and illustrating: the age of new realism. Long-standing taboos imposed on authors and illustrators began to break down as the social revolution of the 1960s began to boil. Few books before this time dealt with topics such as death, divorce, alcoholism, and child abuse. In fact, books did not even show children and parents at odds with one another. And there were almost no quality books for children written by and about minorities. Then, in the early 1960s, daring new books began to emerge. A picture book, *Where the Wild Things Are* (1963) by Maurice Sendak, and a novel, *Harriet the Spy* (1964) by Louise Fitzhugh, are often credited with ushering in this age of new realism. Both were mildly controversial, partly because they showed children at odds with their parents. Max's mother in *Wild Things* loses her temper at his unruly behavior and sends him "to bed without eating anything." And Harriet's parents are aloof and too busy to be concerned with her day-to-day activities. Max's psychological fantasy, a vent for his frustration and for the anger he feels toward his mother, and Harriet's eventual need for psychotherapy were unsettling story elements for some adults.

As the 1970s progressed, new realism spread its wings. Shockingly realistic novels and picture books became the mode as authors addressed serious taboos. For example, the novels of Judy Blume, such as her controversial yet extremely popular *Are You There God? It's Me, Margaret* (1970) and her even more explicit *Forever* (1975), treated physical maturation and sex candidly. Authors of historical novels also dared present to young readers varied and often unpopular viewpoints about our past. Books began to look at the American Revolution from perspectives other than that of a righteous rebellion, such as James Lincoln Collier and Christopher Collier's *My Brother Sam Is Dead* (1974). Some regarded these efforts to represent history more accurately as unpatriotic. Embarrassing annals from American history also began to appear more frequently in books for young readers, such as Yoshiko Uchida's book *Journey to Topaz* (1971), a fictionalized autobiographical account of life in the Japanese-American internment camps during World War II.

Minority Books

The Snowy Day by Ezra Jack Keats, published in 1962, was the first picture book to show a black child as a protagonist with no vestiges of negative stereotyping. The book won the Caldecott Medal in 1963 and remains a favorite of children.

In spite of *The Snowy Day*, there were few books with African American characters in the early 1960s (Larrick, 1965), and books written by African Americans about themselves were even scarcer. However, an emphasis in the United States both on international books—many about various races and cultures—and on books written and illustrated by African Americans was encouraged by the establishment of two awards in the 1960s: the Mildred L. Batchelder Award for translated books and the Coretta Scott King Award for African American writers and illustrators. Today, the American Library Association administers both awards.

Still, it was more than a decade before African Americans won Newbery and Caldecott Awards. Finally in 1975, Virginia Hamilton received the Newbery Medal for *M. C. Higgins, the Great*, and in 1976, Leo Dillon won the Caldecott Medal (along with his wife, Diane, who is not African American) for *Why Mosquitoes Buzz in People's Ears*. This was indicative of an increase in the number and quality of books created by American minority populations during the rest of that decade.

Although the overall number of books being published steadily increased year-by-year, titles about minorities in the United States decreased during the 1980s. Between the early 1970s and early 1980s, the number dropped by more than half, according to a list released by the New York Public Library (Rollock, 1989). However, in the 1990s, the negative trend reversed (Micklos, 1996). The establishment in 1996 of the Pura Belpré Award, a new American Library Association prize for books by Latino/Latina authors and illustrators, reflected a renewed interest in books about minority cultures.

The Changing Trends in Genres and Formats of Children's Books

Strong American high fantasy, rivaling the work of C. S. Lewis, also appeared in the 1960s, most notably the five books of The Prydain Chronicles by Lloyd Alexander, beginning with *The Book of Three* (1964).

Historical novels, which waned during the 1970s, began a comeback in the 1980s, and informational books (nonfiction) flourished. Although good informational books were available in earlier decades, an explosion of engaging, well-illustrated, and well-written nonfiction occurred. Informational books, which seldom appeared on Newbery Award lists, began to show up more frequently. Books winning Newbery Honors in the last 25 years include *Sugaring Time* by Kathryn Lasky (1983); *Commodore Perry in the Land of the Shogun* by Rhoda Blumberg (1985); *Volcano* by Patricia Lauber (1986); *The Wright Brothers* (1991), *Eleanor Roosevelt: A Life of Discovery* (1993), and *The Voice That Challenged a Nation: Marion Anderson and the Struggle for Equal Rights* (2004) by Russell Freedman; *The Great Fire* (1995) and *An American Plague: The True and Terrifying Story of the Yellow Fever Epidemic of 1793* (2003) by Jim Murphy; and *Hitler Youth: Growing Up in Hitler's Shadow* (2005) by Susan Campbell Bartoletti. *Lincoln: A Photobiography* by Russell Freedman, published in 1987, was awarded the Newbery Medal. One of the most exciting trends of the 1980s and 1990s undoubtedly was the increase in and emphasis on quality nonfiction for all age levels. Informational books now are better as a

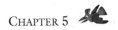

whole than ever. (See Chapter 14.) The first national award strictly for nonfiction writing was established by the National Council of Teachers of English in 1990 and appropriately named the *Orbis Pictus* Award in honor of the first nonfiction book published for children. In 2001, the American Library Association also established a nonfiction prize, the Robert F. Sibert Informational Book Award.

Expanding the emphasis placed on books for the very young in the 1970s, an increased number of quality "I can read," or beginning reader, picture books appeared in the 1980s and 1990s. The trendsetters in this area had emerged decades earlier with the 1957 publications of *Little Bear* by Else Minarik and *The Cat in the Hat* by Dr. Seuss. But large numbers of well-written books for fledgling readers were not available until the 1980s. For example, HarperCollins publishes a series called I Can Read Books, of which Minarik's *Little Bear* is a part. Fine authors who often have made a name by writing for older children have contributed to the series, which now offers parents, teachers, and children an exciting array of worthwhile beginning reader books. In 2004, the American Library Association established an award acknowledging excellence in writing for very young readers, the Theodor Seuss Geisel Award. It was first presented in 2006 to Cynthia Rylant (2005) for *Henry and Mudge and the Great Grandpas.*

Poetry also received more attention during the 1980s and 1990s. Two books of poetry won Newbery Medals during this time: *A Visit to William Blake's Inn: Poems for Innocent and Experienced Travelers* by Nancy Willard (1981) and *Joyful Noise: Poems for Two Voices* by Paul Fleischman (1988). In 1977, the National Council of Teachers of English established the Excellence in Poetry for Children Award, a lifetime achievement award honoring poets who write for young readers.

A Changing Marketplace

Federal monies for school libraries in the United States dwindled in the 1970s, and the market for children's books shifted toward a consumer, or bookstore, market. According to Melanie Donovan (2006) of HarperCollins Publishers, today retail sales command more than half the children's book market, a significant rise over the 5 to 10 percent common before 1970. For companies that publish top-selling series paperbacks, 70 percent or more of sales may derive from retail markets (Donovan, 2006).

This change in marketplace brought about a change in books. In an effort to attract adult retail consumers of children's books, editors shifted some of their emphasis to more lavishly illustrated books as well as to titles for younger audiences. New printing technologies allowed for more affordable yet extremely sophisticated, full-color, camera-separated reproductions (picture book art is now scanned and manipulated with computers). As a result, picture books became more colorful and the renderings increasingly showy, a draw for bookstore patrons. For example, *The Polar Express* by Chris Van Allsburg (1985), with its stunning, Caldecott-winning illustrations, became a popular Christmas gift for adults to give not only to children, but also to other adults. Sales skyrocketed, and 500,000 copies were printed within the first two years.

Nonfiction concept picture books and wordless picture books also became popular with consumers. Illustrated with photographs, Tana Hoban's concept books, such as

Push-Pull, Empty-Full: A Book of Opposites (1972), led the way in this category. Mercer Mayer (1967) popularized the wordless picture book beginning with *A Boy, a Dog, and a Frog*. Baby/board books, virtually indestructible little books for babies and toddlers, invaded bookstores as well. So-called toy (engineered) books also proliferated—pop-up, scratch-and-sniff, texture (touchy/feely) books—which are typically too fragile for library and school markets. Toy books in the 1990s often emphasized the toy more than the book. A book might be packaged with a stuffed animal, an inflatable globe, or even a full-blown kit for building a pyramid or planting a terrarium. An engineered/toy book, Lois Ehlert's *Color Zoo* (1989), was the first of its type to win a Caldecott Honor Medal.

In the 1970s, picture books first became available in paperback, making them cheaper for young readers to own. Publishers further realized that the cheaper series chapter books, published only in paperback, would sell quickly in bookstores. Books like the Hardy Boys made a mammoth resurgence in the 1970s, and other paperback series, such as teenage romance books, began to appear on store shelves. The 1990s brought a proliferation of new paperback series titles—Goosebumps, Fear Street, Animorphs, Saddle Club, American Girls, Bailey School Kids, and so on—as well as the repackaging of older series such as the Boxcar Children and the Nancy Drew mysteries. Also, starting in the 1990s, consumers began to find these books and other children's titles in stores not traditionally connected with bookselling: Walmart, Target, T. J. Maxx, Sam's Club, Costco, and supermarket chains such as Stop & Shop (Rosen, 1997).

In the 1980s and 1990s, children's publishers were doing well financially. Even Wall Street had to pay attention when illustrator Chris Van Allsburg negotiated an $800,000 advance for the book *Swan Lake* (Helprin, 1989). Though this sort of remuneration is not the rule, $1 million advances, especially for multiple-book contracts, are not unheard of today. For example, Putnam paid Michael Hoeye $1.8 million for the rights to publish his previously self-published novel, *Time Stops for No Mouse* (2002), and two other titles (Baker, 2001).

The 1980s saw the formation of publishing conglomerates. Larger corporations, often businesses having no relation to books, began purchasing publishing houses. Many long-standing U.S. publishers became imprints of so-called umbrella companies or disappeared altogether. For example, the Macmillan Publishing Company purchased Atheneum, along with other publishing houses, until its children's book division comprised 11 hardcover imprints. Then Macmillan was purchased by Simon & Schuster, which was then acquired by Paramount. Soon Paramount was snapped up by the media conglomerate Viacom. So children's book publishing became even bigger business. At this writing, Simon & Schuster's many hardcover children's book imprints have been consolidated under three names: Simon & Schuster Books for Young Readers, Atheneum Books for Young Readers, and Margaret K. McElderry Books—though Simon Pulse, a teen paperback imprint, has begun publishing a limited number of hardcover titles.

The number of children's trade books published annually in the United States rose from approximately 2,500 in 1975 (Miele & Prakkan, 1975, p. 163) to about 4,500 in the mid-1990s (Bogart, 1997) and then up to 5,000 in 1999 (Bogart, 2001). Though retail sales were mostly responsible for such growth, a rise in institutional purchases of

books had some effect as well. As teachers began to embrace literature-based reading philosophies and methodologies, schools began to purchase more and more trade books (books other than textbooks or reference books) for use in the classroom. Some school systems began to allot a percentage of the textbook budget for the acquisition of children's books, and sales from school paperback book clubs (e.g., Trumpet Club, Scholastic, Troll, Weekly Reader) leaped into the hundreds of millions of dollars.

THE 21st CENTURY

As the new millennium dawned, the number of children's trade books published in the United States grew to 6,600 by 2004 (Bowker, 2006). Interesting trends and events also occurred, such as the industry's love of old titles. Books from 25, 50, even 100 years ago (often long out of print) were being resurrected and rereleased, such as the delightful Freddy the Pig books from the 1930s, 1940s, and 1950s, written by Walter R. Brooks (*Freddy the Detective,* 1932). Other examples include picture books by Newbery-winning author Lois Lenski (*The Little Fire Engine,* 1946) and the Newbery Honor book *Enchantress from the Stars* (1970) by Sylvia Louise Engdahl.

In 2000, young adult literature was finally recognized with its own American Library Association award, the Michael L. Printz Award. Newbery committee members had long wondered whether to include young adult books with mature themes and older protagonists in their award deliberations. The Printz Award could have alleviated this dilemma, but since the award's inception, the same title has appeared on both award lists more than once.

The biggest news as the 20th century ended had to be the stunning success of the Harry Potter books. *Harry Potter and the Sorcerer's Stone* by J. K. Rowling (1998) traveled from the United Kingdom to the United States, taking the country by storm. Not only kids, but adults, too, were hooked on Harry, and it was not unusual to see air travelers in business suits reading the book. The Harry Potter books are the first children's titles to appear on both the adult and children's bestseller lists, and as of this writing, they have sold 300 million copies worldwide (Raincoast Books, 2006).

Authors and illustrators of children's books continue to experiment with form and content. The rewards of this experimentation outweigh the obvious risks; many fine books are being published as a result. The risk requires that we accept the fact that many more weak books are being published, too. For instance, since the 1990s we have been in an age of politically correct standards for evaluating books. Children's literature watchdogs—of which there are many from all walks of adult life—are today scrutinizing books for what they deem to be material inappropriate for young readers. However, former school librarian Cynthia DeFelice (2002, p. 21), now a well-known children's book author, points out that "political correctness is the antithesis of honesty and truth, and writing is about nothing so much as trying to capture what is true in words. And the truth, unfortunately, includes some 'upsetting parts.'"

This new sort of didacticism goes beyond the preaching of morality, as in decades past, and often focuses on politically correct attitudes and/or causes. A novel can be strengthened by its insights into issues and problems, but not when the book's major purpose is to promote an agenda. Then the message becomes more important than the story, and the book suffers.

Using a story as a soapbox interferes with the impact of the reading experience. Chris Van Allsburg's *Just a Dream* (1990), for instance, is an obvious, rather preachy lesson on ecology. In *Growing Up Is Hard*, kindergartner Sammy feels that his life is awful—his teacher wants him to do better, his friend plays with another boy, and he forgot to take out the trash and now can't watch his favorite TV show. His dad, seeing that Sammy is discouraged, talks with him about his problems. After their discussion, Sammy says, "Daddy, I think I get it. I was looking at everything as bad. You made those things look like they could also be good. Let me try now" (Schlessinger, 2001, p. 28). Sammy then puts his life neatly together. The lesson is preached at the reader instead of emerging naturally from the story. Another example is John Lithgow's *Marsupial Sue* (2000), which in greeting-card style sacrifices story to hammer home its message: You should be happy being yourself.

In many books today it is often politically expedient to be artificially evenhanded, as in Rosemary Wells's (2000) *Emily's First 100 Days of School*. Emily is baking cookies with her grandmother when she exclaims joyfully that they are making 72 cookies for Christmas, Hanukkah, Solstice, and Kwanza—exactly the words that would come out of a normal kindergartener! Instead of keeping the story believable, Wells diminishes her usual fine writing style by making certain, at all cost, that every group celebrating a December holiday is included.

Many books receiving stellar reviews suffer from these types of didacticism, which often means that, from a literary standpoint, weaker books receive acclaim because of subject matter. Weaker books may also receive attention because of celebrity authorship. For instance, publishers have attempted to cash in on name recognition by releasing a wave of picture books by celebrities such as Will Smith, Katie Couric, Jamie Lee Curtis, John Lithgow, Maria Shriver, Bill Cosby, Dr. Laura (Laura Schlessinger), Madonna, Billy Joel, Billy Crystal, Leann Rimes, Jerry Seinfeld, Jay Leno, and so on. One of the great storytellers of our age, Nobel Prize–winner Isaac Bashevis Singer (1992), warned us about the emphasis on message or name recognition rather than story: "In our epoch, when storytelling has become a forgotten art and has been replaced by amateurish sociology and hackneyed psychology, the child is still the independent reader who relies on nothing but his own taste. Names and authorities mean nothing to him."

In some instances, children's literature watchdogs demand that books address in a uncompromising manner any number of "hot" issues: child abuse, sexual orientation, abortion, and so on. Of course, each critic expects the topic to be handled in the certain way they believe it should be addressed. In this vein, an unsettling trend in young adult fiction is the idea that being "edgy" is desirable. Edginess means pushing the limits of the age of new realism to extremes, and so it is not uncommon to see well-reviewed young adult books focusing on blatant sex and using the foulest of language. Many reviewers and critics believe that edgy means "real," and "real" means the book is better. However, a book's worth cannot be determined by the presence, or absence, of edginess.

Considering the changes in books and publishing, including some of the current problematic trends, children's literature is still a testament to John Newbery's vision.

REFERENCES

Alexander, Lloyd. (1964). *The book of three*. New York: Holt, Rinehart and Winston.

Baker, John F. (2001, August 20). Big money for kids' mouse book. *Publishers Weekly, 248*(34), 17.

Bartoletti, Susan Campbell. (2005). *Hitler youth: Growing up in Hitler's shadow*. New York: Scholastic.

Blumberg, Rhoda. (1985). *Commodore Perry in the land of the Shogun*. New York: Lothrop.

Blume, Judy. (1970). *Are you there God? It's me, Margaret*. Englewood Cliffs, NJ: Bradbury.

Blume, Judy. (1975). *Forever*. New York: Bradbury.

Bogart, Dave. (Ed.) (1997). *The Bowker annual: Library and book trade almanac* (42nd ed). New Providence, NJ: R. R. Bowker.

Bogart, Dave. (Ed.) (2001). *The Bowker annual: Library and book trade almanac* (46th ed). New Providence, NJ: R. R. Bowker.

Bowker. R. R. (2006, May 18). U.S. Trade Book Production (All Hardback and Paper back). Available online at *http://www.bookwire.com/trade.html*.

Brooks, G., Waterman, R., & Allington, R. (2003, Spring). A national survey of teachers' reports of children's favorite series books. *The Dragon Lode, 21*(2), 8–14.

Brooks, Walter R. (1932). *Freddy the detective*. New York: Walck. (Rereleased in 1997 by Overlook Press.)

Chevannes, Ingrid, McEvoy, Dermot, & Simson, Maria. (1997, April 4). Big names top the charts. *Publishers Weekly, 244*(14), 58–64.

DeFelice, Cynthia. (2002). Untitled, unpublished speech presented at the Brigham Young University Symposium on Books for Young Readers, Provo, Utah, 19 July.

Donovan, Melanie. (2006). Telephone interview with Michael O. Tunnell, 18 May.

Ehlert, Lois. (1989). *Color zoo*. New York: Lippincott.

Engdahl, Sylvia Louise. (1970). *Enchantress from the stars*. New York: Atheneum.

Fleischman, Paul. (1988). *Joyful noise: Poems for two voices*. New York: Harper.

Freedman, Russell. (1987). *Lincoln: A photobiography*. New York: Clarion.

Freedman, Russell. (1991). *The Wright brothers*. New York: Holiday House.

Freedman, Russell. (1993). *Eleanor Roosevelt: A life of discovery*. New York: Clarion.

Freedman, Russell. (2004). *The voice that challenged a nation: Marion Anderson and the struggle for equal rights*. New York: Clarion.

Greenlee, Adele A., Monson, Dianne L., & Taylor, Barbara M. (1996, November). The lure of series books: Does it affect appreciation for recommended literature? *The Reading Teacher, 50*(3), 216–225.

Helprin, Mark. (1989). *Swan Lake*. Boston: Houghton Mifflin.

Hoban, Tana. (1972). *Push-pull, empty-full: A book of opposites*. New York: Macmillan.

Hoeye, Michael. (2002). *Time stops for no mouse*. New York: Putnam.

Larrick, Nancy. (1965, September 11). The all white world of children's books. *Saturday Review*, pp. 63–65, 84–85.

Lasky, Kathryn. (1983). *Sugaring time*. New York: Macmillan.

Lauber, Patricia. (1986). *Volcano*. New York: Bradbury.

Lenski, Lois. (1946). *The little fire engine*. New York: Random House. (Rereleased in 2000.)

Lithgow, John. (2000). *Marsupial Sue*. New York: Simon & Schuster.

Locke, John. (1693). *Some thoughts concerning education*. (1709 ed.). London: A. and J. Churchill.

Mayer, Mercer. (1967). *A boy, a dog, and a frog*. New York: Dial.

Meile, Madeline, & Prakkan, Sarah. (Eds.). (1975). *The Bowker annual of library and book trade information* (20th ed.). New York: R. R. Bowker.

Micklos, John, Jr. (1996, September). 30 years of minorities in children's books. *The Education Digest, 62*(1), 61–64.

Minarik, Else. (1957). *Little bear*. Illustrated by Maurice Sendak. New York: Harper.

Murphy, Jim. (1995). *The great fire*. New York: Scholastic.

Murphy, Jim. (2003). *An American plague: The true and terrifying story of the yellow fever epidemic of 1793*. New York: Clarion.

Raincoast Books. (2006). *Harry Potter*. Available online at *http://www.raincoast.com/harrypotter/faq.html*.

Roback, Diane. (2001, March 19). A year of big numbers. *Publishers Weekly, 248*(12), 43–50.

Rollock, Barbara. (1989). *Black experience in children's books.* New York: New York Public Library.

Rosen, Judith. (1997, July 21). They're everywhere you look. *Publishers Weekly, 244*(29), 120–123.

Rowling, J. K. (1998). *Harry Potter and the sorcerer's stone.* New York: Scholastic.

Rylant, Cynthia. (2005). *Henry and Mudge and the great grandpas.* New York: Simon and Schuster.

Saltman, Judith. (1997, May/June). Groaning under the weight of series books. *Emergency Librarian, 24*(5), 23–25.

Schlessinger, Laura. (2001). *Growing up is hard.* New York: HarperCollins.

Seuss, Dr. (1957). *The cat in the hat.* New York: Random House.

Singer, Isaac Bashevis. (1992). *A day of pleasure and other stories for children.* New York: Galahad Books.

Sutcliff, Rosemary. (1959). *The lantern bearers.* New York: Walck.

Van Allsburg, Chris. (1985). *The Polar Express.* New York: Houghton Mifflin.

Van Allsburg, Chris. (1990). *Just a dream.* Boston: Houghton Mifflin.

Wells, Rosemary. (2000). *Emily's first 100 days of school.* New York: Hyperion.

Willard, Nancy. (1981). *A visit to William Blake's inn: Poems for innocent and experienced travelers.* New York: Harcourt Brace and Jovanovich.

Chapter 6

Organizing Children's Literature by Genre

The difficulty in covering the field of children's literature in one course is perhaps best understood by looking at a common undergraduate class for English majors, Shakespeare's Tragedies. The course focuses on one author, and only on a part of what he wrote at that. On the other hand, the content of an introductory course in children's literature comprises all authors of children's books and all the titles they have written. Considering the content, a solitary children's literature course makes only the briefest of introductions to the subject matter—one thread in the whole cloth.

Naturally, the teacher of children's literature must find an organized and digestible way of presenting such massive subject matter—more than 385,000 children's books in print in the United States (Bowker, 2006a, p. vii) and about 5,000 new titles each year (Bowker, 2006b). The most common method of cutting children's literature into small bites is to group books by *genre*, a French word meaning "type" or "kind." Genre is a familiar term in many artistic areas: the genre of motion pictures (film noir, westerns, comedy, horror, and so on), or the genre of adult literature (novel, novella, short story, play, and poem).

THE GENRES

In children's literature, genre identifies books according to content (see Figure 6–1). Beginning at the left of the genre tree, we see that all literature is either *prose or poetry*. To define poetry, the initial impulse might be to identify it as rhyming, or condensed, or rhythmic. Yet these obvious elements of poetry are not true distinctions. Some poetry does not rhyme. Some poetry is longer than some prose. Some poetry is less rhythmic than some prose. With all the forms poetry can take—haiku, sonnet, couplet, blank verse, limerick, narrative, cinquain, and free verse, to name a few— finding a definition that both identifies them all and distinguishes them from prose is next to impossible. It is easier and more practical to define poetry by saying what it is not. The most obvious "not" is that poetry is not written in paragraphs.

FIGURE 6–1

Genres of children's literature.

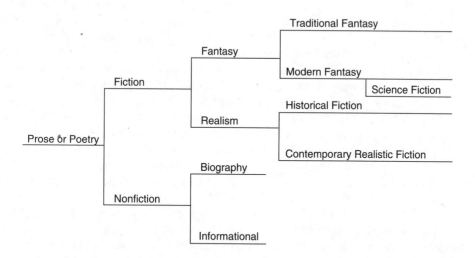

Poetry may appear on the page as a single line, a thin column, or in the shape of a tree, but not in a paragraph. Prose, on the other hand, is always written in paragraphs. Beyond that difference in format, the function of the two literary forms is identical: Both poetry and prose thoughtfully explore the world, give insight into the human condition and experience, and bring pleasure to the reader.

The difference between fiction and nonfiction is verifiability. *Fiction* springs largely from the author's imagination. An idea, question, or incident from the real world may give rise to a work of fiction, and the setting and even many details may be verifiable, but the plot comes from the workings of the mind. In Staple's (2005) *Under the Persimmon Tree,* the setting and story involve the actual events in and cultural trappings of Afghanistan in the days after the attack on the World Trade Center in New York City, including the American counterstrike, the Taliban's repression of women, and the careful descriptions of Afghani cities and villages. However, the plot revolves around two *fictional* characters who eventually meet in a refugee camp. If this book were nonfiction, however, it would be wholly factual— no fictional elements. *All* the evidence and facts presented in nonfiction books can be verified. The distinction between fiction and nonfiction is similar to determining which answer is correct on a true-false test: If any part of the statement is false, the answer is false. If any part of the book is fiction, the whole book is categorized as fiction.

Nonfiction books are classified as biography and informational. *Biography* (and *autobiography*) tells the story, or at least part of the story, of an actual person's life. As with all nonfiction, reliable sources and documentation are imperative.

Informational books are called nonfiction in adult publishing. Children's libraries classify all books in one of ten categories (ranging by 100s from 000 to 900) in the Dewey Decimal System. All except the 800s (literature—fiction and poetry) are informational

books. Anything in the world is grist for the nonfiction mill: building a violin, life in China, the history of the ball bearing, animals that hibernate, how governments work, and so on. In the last 25 years, no area of children's literature has changed so dramatically. Although some excellent informational books were written decades ago, in recent times subject matter has broadened, the quality of writing and illustration has improved, and the number of books published has increased.

Realistic fiction and *fantastic fiction* have much in common. Both are invented stories, often with invented characters, and they may take place in invented settings. Even when the setting is real, such as Boston or Berlin, the exact neighborhood is often imagined. The difference between realism and fantasy lies in the laws of our universe. If an invented story takes place in the world exactly as we know it—where dogs bark, trees are green, and gravity is everywhere—it is realistic fiction. If a story has one or more elements not found in our world—if animals speak, magic is present, or time travel is involved—it is called fantasy. The rest of the story might be absolutely realistic, but it is called fantasy if it contains any deviation from natural physical law.

The aim of both *contemporary realistic fiction* and *historical fiction* is to tell an interesting story about people in our world. The definitions are clear in the names of the genres. *Contemporary* identifies a story that takes place in today's world; *historical* indicates a tale that happened earlier, as in pioneer America or medieval England. At times, though, the difference between the two genres depends on the age of the reader. Some people classify a story that happened during the collapse of the communist government in Eastern Europe as contemporary; to others, it is clearly historical.

Like historical and contemporary fiction, the division between *traditional fantasy* and *modern fantasy* relates to antiquity. Some stories are as old as humanity. These ancient stories are called traditional because they are part of our human tradition. Their origin is oral; their authors are unknown. Although they are now preserved in print, those who first wrote them down, such as the Brothers Grimm, were not authors, but collectors. If a fantasy story has an identifiable author, and therefore originated in print, it is called modern fantasy. Thus, the tales of Hans Christian Andersen are classified as modern fantasy because we know he created them, even though the tales read like traditional stories.

Science fiction, included under the modern fantasy heading, deals with scientific possibilities. Both modern fantasy and science fiction contain story elements not found in the known universe, such as being able to change shapes or read another character's thoughts. In fantasy, those abilities just *are* or come about by magic—no questions asked. In science fiction, they result from an injection of distilled fluids discovered in the mucous membranes of a poisonous tree frog or from altering a person's brain chemistry using microlaser bursts. The otherworldly elements in science fiction are based on extrapolated scientific fact pushed into logical but unproven possibilities, such as creating a bionic being that is a perfect reproduction of an existing woman. Modern fantasy needs no such justifications: The character's double appears by magic.

While knowing the different genres can offer understanding in the field of children's literature, none of the definitions is watertight. The categories are not to be slavishly followed. It is possible to make a solid case that some books belong in more than one genre. For example, Livia Bitton-Jackson's *I Have Lived a Thousand Years: Growing Up in the Holocaust* (1997), a compelling tale of young Livia and her Jewish family being taken from their native Hungary to Auschwitz during World War II, can be classified as both biography and historical fiction. Ruth Heller's series of informational books about the parts of speech, including *Mine, All Mine: A Book About Pronouns* (1997) and *Fantastic! Wow! And Unreal!: A Book About Interjections* (1998), are, at the same time, also books of poetry. The correct category for some titles depends not on immutable definition, but on personal decision.

Although genre lines at times may blur, these designations are used most often by adults to organize the field of children's literature. These categories are less important to children, however. Young readers usually do not care if a book belongs to a certain genre. What they want is a good book, regardless of the classification. But adults can use the six genres to help understand the field of children's literature more clearly, to draw on a framework for discussing books, and to provide a yardstick for determining what holes exist in their own particular reading backgrounds. If a teacher has never read modern fantasy or science fiction, for instance, that becomes immediately apparent when considering each of the genres. A self-check of our reading backgrounds can help us realize where we need more exposure, can provide direction to broaden our personal reading, and ultimately can help us serve students better. However used, the genres of children's literature (Chapters 9–14) provide a road map for those interested in finding their way about.

Before exploring the six genres, separate chapters address two formats also important in children's literature. The two formats are so closely associated with categorizing books for children they have become pseudo-genres and, indeed, have their own headings in this book and the accompanying database: the *picture book* and *poetry*. The picture book (Chapter 7), still a mainstay of beginning reading and the primary-grade classroom, has extended its appeal to include older children and also to offer expanded information in nonfiction picture books. Because this format is so distinctive and is important to many teachers, we list it as a genre in the accompanying CD-ROM Children's Literature Database, so picture book titles may easily be identified and located. Poetry (Chapter 8), like prose, includes all the genres of literature. However, we choose to treat poetry as a separate genre because too few poems are available to study them under the same classifications we use for prose. If we were absolutely accurate, we would study "biographical prose" and also "biographical poetry," "modern fantasy prose" as well as "modern fantasy poetry," and so on. Because of the relatively small number of published poems, we look at poetry as a whole and at the various forms of poetry instead of concentrating on the content.

An additional topic follows the genre chapters: multicultural and international books. Multicultural and international books (Chapter 15) currently receive close attention because of their importance in helping us build human bridges among groups and nations.

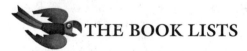 THE BOOK LISTS

The world of children's literature offers only one completely dependable book list— your own. Throughout the following chapters, we present ours, absolutely trustworthy in every way—to us. You are allowed to be skeptical about our choices, but their value lies in saving you time wandering up and down library aisles. Please note that we have included a mix of titles from several decades—listing only brand-new books makes no more sense than ignoring Shakespeare because it's "old." Many of the best books have been around for years. John Brunner, science fiction author, points out that only a fool says, "This is new, and therefore better" (Talwar, 2005). And so, we list our favorite titles without regard to publication date.

We organized our book lists at the end of the chapters under four different headings and offer another list on the CD-ROM accompanying this text.

1. *Ten of Our Favorites.* The 10 books listed after each genre chapter in Part 2 (15 in the case of picture books) are terrific reading. These lists are very short, the result of much negotiating between us, often emotional but largely friendly. The purpose of the 10 is to provide solid suggestions for those who wonder where to find a good book. Each title is annotated to give a brief idea of the content.

2. *Others We Like.* These titles (generally around 30) are not annotated. Although they are the second level of recommendations, each is a book we like very much. Don't be surprised if you find some of them more appealing than the 10 of our favorites.

3. *Easier to Read.* Next we have added 10 to 15 titles of shorter, generally popular books. These help the teacher find nonthreatening titles for children struggling to make reading a rewarding pastime.

4. *Picture Books.* In most genre chapters, we have included 15 to 20 picture books we consider representative and outstanding. Not all of these titles are for use exclusively in the lower grades; many are appropriate for the upper grades as well.

The biggest list we offer you is on the Children's Literature Database, located on the accompanying CD-ROM—over 20,000 titles.

USING THE CHILDREN'S LITERATURE DATABASE

For user instructions and more information, see guidelines for using the database in the four-color insert in the back of this text.

REFERENCES

Bitton-Jackson, Livia. (1997). *I have lived a thousand years: Growing up in the Holocaust.* New York: Simon & Schuster.

Bowker, R. R. (2006a). *Children's books in print 2006,* volume I. New Providence, NJ: Bowker.

Bowker, R. R. (2006b, May 18). U.S. Trade Book Production (All Hardback and Paperback). Available online at *http://www.bookwire.com/trade.html.*

Heller, Ruth. (1997). *Mine, all mine: A book about pronouns.* New York: Grosset & Dunlap.

Heller, Ruth. (1998). *Fantastic! Wow! And unreal!: A book about interjections.* New York: Grosset & Dunlap.

Staples, Suzaane Fisher. (2005). *Under the persimmon tree.* New York: Farrar, Straus & Giroux.

Talwar, Kunal. (2005). Quotations. Available online at *http://stat.www.berkeley.edu/users/shanky/quotations.html.*

Chapter 7

Picture Books

The picture book is a format of children's literature rather than a genre. Picture books may be of any genre, including poetry. They are unique because illustrations and text share the job of telling the story or teaching content. No other type of literature works in the same manner.

Picture books often are considered to be only for the very young. Yet picture books—from rugged board books for babies to the mysterious tales of Chris Van Allsburg, which adults appreciate wholeheartedly—exist for a wide a range of readers. In today's publishing world, the picture book has ascended to a true art form. As full-color printing processes have improved and the demand for quality picture books has increased, some of our best artists and authors spend at least part of their creative lives expressing themselves in the picture book form. (See Chapters 4 and 5 for details about picture book art and about the history and trends in picture book publishing.)

CATEGORIES OF PICTURE BOOKS

Several basic categories may serve as a vehicle for discussing the variety of picture books available. Once again, it is important to remember that these divisions are not mutually exclusive. A single book may fall into several categories.

ABC Books

Alphabet books were one of the earliest varieties of illustrated books for children, and artists and authors continue to devise inventive ways of introducing the ABCs to children. In Suse MacDonald's Caldecott Honor Book *Alphabatics* (1986), for example, MacDonald shows each letter going through an amazing acrobatic metamorphosis: *E* tips and turns and mutates until it becomes the legs of an elephant. Stephen Johnson's *Alphabet City* (1995) is a series of 26 paintings, so realistic that they are sometimes mistaken for photographs, wherein letters of the alphabet are formed by objects found in

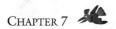

a townscape. For example, the letter *G* is located within the wrought iron decorations on a lamppost.

The alphabet may also be used as a vehicle to introduce or categorize information or concepts for older children. For example, *Beastiary: An Illuminated Alphabet of Medieval Beasts* by Jonathan Hunt (1998) is an ABC introduction to the mythical creatures people feared during the Middle Ages: *A* is for amphisbaena, *B* is for basilisk, *C* is for catoblepas, and so on (with a paragraph of explanation for each animal).

One of the most inventive ABC books in recent years is Cathi Hepworth's *Antics! An Alphabetical Anthology* (1992). Hepworth paints humanlike ants, whose personality traits represent words that begin with each letter of the alphabet and have the letters *ant* embedded in them. For the letter *B,* Hepworth shows an Albert Einstein-type ant labeled "Brilli**ant**," and for *I,* the illustration shows forlorn, turn-of-the-century "Immig**rant**s" huddled nervously on the deck of a ship.

Another example of a creative approach to the ABC book is *Tomorrow's Alphabet* by George Shannon (1996; illustrated by Donald Crews). It works this way: "A is for seed—tomorrow's apple. B is for eggs—tomorrow's birds. C is for milk—tomorrow's cheese."

For the most part, alphabet books are not well suited to teaching the ABCs along with their phonic generalizations and are not intended to serve such a purpose. However, if a teacher or parent insists on using an ABC book as a medium for teaching the alphabet and its sounds, then care must be exercised to find some of the extremely rare books that conform to this task. Three criteria help define this type of ABC book (Criscoe, 1988, p. 233).

1. Words used to represent each letter must begin with the common sound generally associated with that letter. In other words, blends, digraphs, and silent letters should be avoided. MacDonald's *Alphabatics* violates this principle in its use of *ark* for *A, elephant* for *E,* and *owl* for *O.*

2. Illustrations must represent each letter using only one or two objects that are easily identifiable by and meaningful to young children. Once again, *Alphabatics* often violates this rule. For instance, the word *insect* is used for the letter *I,* and the illustration shows an insect along with a large, bright yellow flower. A young child's attention may be drawn to the flower, thus *I* is for "flower."

3. Illustrations must represent objects that do not have several correct names, thus confusing young readers. *Alphabatics* uses *quail* for *Q,* which would certainly be identified as "bird" by a child. Even the insect in the preceding example would likely be called a bee, a fly, or a bug.

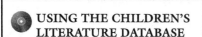

USING THE CHILDREN'S LITERATURE DATABASE

Be sure the CD database is installed on your hard drive. Click on Book List in the left navigation bar on the Home screen. You can identify the Library of Congress terms used for ABC books by looking at the Topics field for each specific book record. Perform a search for ABC books. Select New Search at the top left of the book list. Then click Run Search to generate a list of ABC books. Type "ABC" in the Keyword Search field in the Search Query Builder screen, and then click on the Title, Topics, and Description checkboxes. Run Search. You now have a list of ABC books that you can save for future reference.

Alphabet books are meant to introduce fascinating words and interesting concepts and to entertain. Clever ABC books appeal to adults as well as children, and almost any subject can be the focus. For example, *An Alphabet of Dinosaurs* (Dodson, 1995) identifies 26 dinosaurs, each beginning with a different letter. *M is for Music* (Krull, 2003) introduces musical terms from allegro to zarzuela. Some titles are self-explanatory: *My First Buddhist Alphabet* (Bates & Bates 2004), *The Gardner's Alphabet* (Azarian, 2000), *Jazz A·B·Z: An A to Z Collection of Jazz Portraits* (Marsalis, 2005), *C is for Cowboy: A Wyoming Alphabet* (Gagliano, 2003), and *26 Ways to Say "I Love You"* (Jarrell, 2000). Alphabet books can also introduce the unusual. *Candle Time ABC* (Gillis, 2002) features various holidays that use candles as a part of their celebration, and *The Butterfly Alphabet* (Sandved, 1996) shows each letter appearing naturally on the wing design of a butterfly or moth, a task that took the author 25 years to complete.

Counting Books

Counting books were also one of the earlier types of picture books for children. Numbers and letters have always been considered the rudiments of early education. However, unlike ABC books, counting books usually do help children learn basic numbers and give them practice counting, typically from 1 to 10.

The simplest form of the counting book provides a printed Arabic number accompanied by the same number of like objects:

$$5 = 🍎🍎🍎🍎🍎$$

However, the better counting books allow for personal discovery and are beautifully illustrated. *Anno's Counting Book* by Mitsumasa Anno (1982) is a classic example.

Anno begins with an important concept generally ignored in counting books: zero. Teachers who work with older elementary children can attest that many of them do not understand how zero works and therefore have problems with place value. So, Anno wisely introduces the idea of zero to children just beginning to learn numbers. The first double-page spread shows a barren, snow-covered landscape. The Arabic number 0 is on the right side of the book, and an empty counting stick partitioned into 10 squares is on the left.

Each succeeding double-page spread shows the same scene, only buildings, people, trees, animals, and other objects are added. For example, on the spread for seven, Anno has the Arabic numeral on the right and seven different-colored cubes stacked in front of the counting stick on the left. Also, the once-barren landscape now has sets of seven of a variety of objects: seven buildings, seven children, seven adults, seven evergreen trees, seven deciduous trees, seven colors in the rainbow, seven windows in one of the houses, seven pieces of laundry on the line, and so on. So much can be discovered in each scene that older children who have mastered counting long ago still search the pictures to find all the sets of one, two, three, and so on. Even the clock in the church tower always shows the hour of the number in question!

Besides variety and opportunity for discovery, Anno also offers fledgling mathematicians one final boon: He does not stop at 10. Anno wisely chooses to go on to 11 and 12, two transitional numbers that do not conform to the usual pattern (oneteen and twoteen?). Anno also has applied the 12 numbers to other concepts. The seasons change throughout the scenes and correspond to the 12 months of the year. Twelve hours are, of course, on the face of the clock. As a whole package, *Anno's Counting Book* is a marvel: beautiful, naive-style paintings, sound-teaching processes, and pure entertainment.

Concept Books

Concept books introduce single, focused concepts to young children. Some typical topics include colors, the idea of opposites (over, under; outside, inside), and basic geometric shapes. ABC and counting books are usually considered concept books as well.

Tana Hoban is well known for her classic concept books that are usually wordless and are illustrated with crisp, clear photographs. *Is It Red? Is It Yellow? Is It Blue?* (1978) has become a concept book classic that reinforces a child's knowledge of colors. Quality concept books tend to help children think about ideas, and Hoban accomplishes this by providing a brilliant color photograph of a city or home scene and then placing colored circles below each photo. The young reader is drawn back and forth between circles and photographs to find the matching colors. Other Hoban titles include *Exactly the Opposite* (1990) and *Cubes, Cones, Cylinders & Spheres* (2000). Other well-known creators of concept books include Anne Rockwell (*Four Seasons Make a Year*, 2004), Lois Ehlert (*Waiting for Wings*, 2001), Donald Crews (*Cloudy Day, Sunny Day*, 1999), Ellen Stoll Walsh (*Mouse Magic*, 2000), and Byron Barton (*My Car*, 2001).

Picture books that deal with concepts in greater depth are sometimes called *informational picture books* (see Chapter 14), although the lines between concept and informational picture books may blur. For instance, *How Much Is a Million?* by David Schwartz (1985; illustrated by Steven Kellogg) deals with the concept of large numbers, but this more complex idea may not be ideal for younger children. Another Schwartz book, *If You Hopped Like a Frog* (1999), introduces the concept of ratio by comparing what humans could do if they had particular animal bodies: "If you hopped like a frog . . . you could jump from home plate to first base in one mighty leap!"

Participation Books

A number of picture books are designed to involve children in a physical activity that goes beyond the reading of the text, such as finding hidden objects in an illustration (*Where's Waldo?* by Martin Handford, 1987), manipulating the flaps and tabs of a pop-up book (*The Wheels on the Bus* by Paul Zelinsky, 1990), or chiming in with a refrain ("Hundreds of cats, Thousands of cats, Millions and billions and trillions of cats" from *Millions of Cats* by Wanda Gág, 1928). *Anno's Counting Book* (Anno, 1982) becomes a participation book when children search for and discover the sets of objects representing each number. Another classic participation book is Janet and Allan Ahlberg's *Each Peach Pear Plum* (1979), a marvelous romp through the land of fairy tales and nursery rhymes. It is an "I Spy" book wherein small children search for a familiar character hidden in each illustration: "Cinderella on the stairs, I spy the Three Bears." Cinderella, partially hidden in the previous picture, is now in full view, while the Three Bears are difficult to spot as they peek into the cottage through a window. Tana Hoban's *Just Look* (1996) invites participation in the form of a guessing game. Children peer through a page with a die-cut hole that allows them to see only part of a familiar object. After guessing what it is, they lift the page to discover whether they are correct.

Of course, participation books also typically fall into other categories. Counting books, for instance, usually demand a child's physical participation, and refrains that invite listeners to chime in often appear in picture storybooks.

Wordless Picture Books

Books without words may seem a contradiction in terms to some parents and teachers. "How can kids learn to read by just looking at pictures?" they ask. But young children discover much of what they know about books as they "read" by themselves (left-to-right/top-to-bottom orientations, the grammar of story, personal pleasure of reading). Also, teachers may find that wordless picture books are a vehicle for practicing the language experience approach. For example, children may create their own text for an action-packed wordless book, such as *Frog Goes to Dinner* by Mercer Mayer (1974) or *Sector 7* by David Wiesner (1999). The teacher records the students' dictated text, and the children then read and reread their new, worded version of the picture book. Older children may try their hand at writing the words for a wordless picture book as a creative and meaningful writing experience.

Wordless picture books are meant, above all, to be enjoyed like any other book. They may tell stories or teach concepts, and many of today's offerings are stunning lessons in art. Mercer Mayer is credited with popularizing the wordless picture book, beginning in 1967 with the publication of *A Boy, a Dog, and a Frog.* Mayer's skill at telling a story and creating characters through illustrations is remarkable: Facial expressions speak with the power of words, visual actions foreshadow events, and the story line flows seamlessly. On the other hand, the wordless concept books of Tana Hoban (*Is It Red? Is It Yellow? Is It Blue?* 1978; *Exactly the Opposite*, 1990; *Shapes, Shapes, Shapes,* 1986) teach with economy and clarity. David Wiesner's work has been awarded the most prestigious U.S. prize for picture book art: Caldecott Honor Medals in 1989 for *Free Fall* (1988) and 2000 for *Sector 7* (1999) and the Caldecott Medal in 1992 for *Tuesday* (1991) and 2007 for *Flotsam* (2006). Indeed, wordless picture books have much to offer.

Predictable Books

As young children begin to read, predictable books, sometimes called pattern books, often can be their bridge into the world of independent reading. These picture books are characterized by repeated language patterns, story patterns, or other familiar sequences. However, creating a lifeless, stilted, and uninteresting predictable book is an easy trap to fall into if an author focuses on pattern at the expense of good writing and good story. The best of the predictable books are lively, use interesting words, and invite children to chime in. Bill Martin's classic *Brown Bear, Brown Bear, What Do You See?* (1967) is still a favorite in kindergartens everywhere:

> Brown Bear, Brown Bear, what do you see?
> I see a redbird looking at me.

> Redbird, redbird, what do you see?
> I see a yellow duck looking at me.
> Yellow duck . . .*

Predictable books may use a repeated story pattern, often found in fairy tales and folktales such as "The Three Billy Goats Gruff" or "The Little Red Hen." Cumulative tales provide even greater repetition, as in "The House That Jack Built." Sometimes a song or verse is predictable because of its familiarity as well as its repetitive language patterns, such as "There Was an Old Lady Who Swallowed a Fly," which has appeared variously in picture book form (see Simms Taback's 1998 Caldecott Honor Book version: Taback, 1997). Even familiar sequences, such as numbers or days of the week, can make for easily recognized patterns. Eric Carle's *The Very Hungry Caterpillar* (1969) follows an unconventional caterpillar through each day of the week as he eats one, then two, then three of certain foods not meant for caterpillar consumption. The familiarity of numbers and days helps children "read" this well-loved predictable picture book. Nancy Shaw's "Sheep" books (*Sheep in a Jeep,* 1986; *Sheep Out to Eat,* 1992; *Sheep Trick or Treat,* 1997; and others) make use of rhyming words to create a predictable text.

Beginning Reader Picture Books

The beginning reader picture book is designed to give fledgling independent readers well-written yet easy-to-read materials. Both Dr. Seuss (Theodor Geisel) and Else Minarik put the beginning reader picture book on the map in 1957 with the publication of Seuss's *The Cat in the Hat* and Minarik's *Little Bear.* Minarik's several Little Bear titles became part of HarperCollins's I Can Read Book series, which continues to be one of the best collections of beginning reader picture books. The series represents all genres, including poetry, and often the books are written and illustrated by some of the best-known names in children's publishing, such as Arnold Lobel, who created the Frog and Toad books. In fact, *Frog and Toad Are Friends* (1970) was chosen as a Caldecott Honor Book, and *Frog and Toad Together* (1972) as a Newbery Honor Book. HarperCollins also publishes the My First I Can Read Book series, with books that have few words, yet tell compelling stories. Usually the HarperCollins I Can Read Books are divided into three to five short chapters to give young readers an early introduction to the format of longer books. However, each page is illustrated so that the look of a picture book is maintained. During the last few years, HarperCollins has begun assigning a difficulty level to these easier readers (Level 1, Level 2, Level 3).

Many other beginning reader series have been developed by other publishers in recent years, such as Simon & Schuster's Ready-to-Read series, Dial's Easy-to-Read books, Scholastic's Hello Reader! series, Harcourt's Green Light Readers, DK Publishing's Eyewitness Readers, and the Holiday House Readers. Newbery-winner Cynthia

---

*From *Brown Bear, Brown Bear, What Do You See?* by Bill Martin, Jr., © 1967, 1970 by Harcourt Brace & Company, © 1995 by Bill Martin, Jr. Reprinted by permission of Henry Holt and Company, LLC.

Rylant has created a series of easy-to-read picture books featuring Henry and his dog, Mudge (such as *Henry and Mudge and the Happy Cat*, 1990; *Henry and Mudge and Annie's Perfect Pet*, 2000; and *Henry and Mudge and the Great Grandpas*, 2005). Rylant has written several other easy reader series, including stories about Poppleton the pig, Mr. Putter and Tabby, and the guinea pig, Little Whistle. Another popular series of easy readers is Marjorie Sharmat's Nate the Great mysteries (*Nate the Great*, 1972; *Nate the Great and the Monster Mess*, 1999; *Nate the Great and the Big Sniff*, 2001; *Nate the Great on the Owl Express*, 2003; and others). However, not all beginning reader picture books are part of a series. Excellent individual titles pop up on many publishers' lists.

Adults often will choose any controlled-vocabulary picture book for their children merely because the words are overly simplified and seem easy to read. However, many of these titles offer little more than vocabulary practice and are of limited interest to children (see Chapter 3). A strong story and a fresh and lively writing style coupled with a wise control of vocabulary make for easier reading. Beginning-reader picture books that are stilted and contrived—that follow the unnatural language patterns evident in basal readers with overly controlled vocabulary—are actually more difficult for young readers (Goodman, 1988).

Picture Storybooks

The origin of the picture storybook goes back to the publication in 1902 of Beatrix Potter's *The Tale of Peter Rabbit* (see Chapter 5). What set Potter's book apart from other illustrated books of the time, including books illustrated by Randolph Caldecott and Kate Greenaway, was the true marriage of illustration and story (see Chapter 4). The hallmark of the picture storybook is that text and illustrations work together on each page to tell a story.

Picture storybooks are the most plentiful and the most popular variety of picture book. Most of the Caldecott winners are picture storybooks, and picture storybooks are the most likely choice for parents and children who read together before bedtime. Such books are read to young children long before they are able to read them on their own and are often the best-loved stories from childhood, such as *Where the Wild Things Are* (Sendak, 1963), *Make Way for Ducklings* (McCloskey, 1941), and *The Polar Express* (Van Allsburg, 1985). Picture storybooks are the foundation of our literacy training. Children typically learn their favorite books by heart, thus beginning a process that eventually becomes full-fledged reading. The rich vocabulary and sparkling illustrations help broaden language horizons and develop taste in art.

Engineered Books

The category of engineered books is one of physical structure. Paper engineering involves the cutting, folding, or otherwise restructuring of the normal printed or illustrated page. Pop-up books are likely the best-known variety of the engineered book. Jan Piénkowski has a long-standing reputation for unique pop-up books, such as *Dinnertime* (Carter, 1981), *Haunted House* (1979), *ABC Dinosaurs* (1993), and *The First Noël* (2004).

FIGURE 7–1

Notable authors and illustrators of picture books.

Anno, Mitsumasa: Wordless concept books.

Brown, Marcia: Appears on the Caldecott list nine times; illustrates in a variety of artistic styles.

Bunting, Eve: Writes picture book texts about social issues.

Cooney, Barbara: Varied subject matter, including picture book biographies, folktales, realistic and historical fiction.

Crews, Donald: Concept books rendered in graphic-arts style.

dePaola, Tomie: Prolific illustrator of more than 200 books; trademark style using pastel colors.

Dillon, Leo, and Diane Dillon: Many books on African themes.

Ehlert, Lois: Engineered concept books.

Gammel, Stephen: Airy illustration style created with colored pencil and graphite.

Henkes, Kevin: Family and school stories with talking animals as characters.

Hoban, Russell: Family and school stories with talking animals as characters.

Hyman, Trina Schart: Lavish illustrations accompanying classic fairy tale retellings.

Jeffers, Susan: Best known for illustrated folktales.

Keats, Ezra Jack: Stories of the inner city for primary grades.

Kellogg, Steven: Humorous stories often involving animals; tall-tale retellings.

Lobel, Arnold: Popularized beginning reader picture books with the Frog and Toad series.

Lynch, P. J.: British illustrator, folk/fairy tales and historical stories.

McCloskey, Robert: Picture books set in New England, mostly on the coast of Maine.

McDermott, Gerald: Folktales and myths rendered in an abstract artistic style.

Peet, Bill: Animal fantasies written in lively prose and verse; former Disney animator.

Pinkney, Brian: Scratchboard specialist, mostly African American themes.

Pinkney, Jerry: Watercolor specialist; mostly African American themes.

Polacco, Patricia: Historical and contemporary fiction, often drawn from her own family.

Potter, Beatrix: Mother of the modern picture storybook in English, *The Tale of Peter Rabbit*.

Say, Allen: Asian American stories reflecting family themes.

Sendak, Maurice: Fantasy stories, most notably *Where the Wild Things Are*.

Seuss, Dr.: Pioneered the beginning reader picture book with his zany, nonsensical stories.

Small, David: A variety of topics, including zany stories and historical subjects.

Steig, William: Sketchy artistic style and Newbery Award–winning picture book prose.

Stevens, Janet: Animal fantasy.

Van Allsburg, Chris: Fantasy stories for older readers.

Wells, Rosemary: Family and school stories with talking animals as characters.

Wiesner, David: Wordless fantasy stories.

Wisniewski, David: Folktales illustrated with intricate paper cutouts.

Young, Ed: Mostly Chinese folktale variants.

Zelinsky, Paul O.: Traditional tales in classical artistic style.

Robert Sabuda's pop-up books (*The Christmas Alphabet*, 1994; *The Wonderful Wizard of Oz: A Commemorative Pop-Up* [Baum, 2000]; Dinosaurs: *Encyclopedia Prehistorica*, 2005), are also noteworthy.

Often pop-ups include pull-tabs, cardboard wheels to be turned, or flaps to be lifted, thus allowing children to manipulate the pages. In *Haunted House*, for example, pull-tabs cause a skeleton to jump from a wardrobe and ducks in a wallpaper pattern to come to life and flap their wings. Paul Zelinsky's *The Wheels on the Bus* (1990) animates the familiar song with the use of similar manipulatives: Bus doors swing open and a rider steps out, riders bounce as the bus goes over bumps, windshield wipers swish back and forth, and babies' mouths open and close as they bawl. Sabuda's pop-up illustrations for Baum's *The Wonderful Wizard of Oz: A Commemorative Pop-Up* (2000) include a tornado that leaps from the page, spinning as you open the book, and green-colored glasses through which to view the Emerald City.

Some engineered books rely completely on lifting flaps to reveal concept or story elements. Others provide a tactile experience, such as the classic *Pat the Bunny* by Dorothy Kunhardt (1940), which allows children to pet a fuzzy little rabbit, and *Fuzzy Yellow Ducklings* by Van Fleet (1995), which offers children a variety of textures to feel. The die-cut book, with pages that have shapes cut away, became the first type of engineered book to be recognized by a Caldecott committee, when *Color Zoo* by Lois Ehlert (1989) received a Caldecott Honor Medal in 1990. Ehlert incorporates die-cuts to teach geometric shapes while creating the figures of animals (see Chapter 14). Later, in 2000, another die-cut book, *Joseph Had a Little Overcoat* (Taback, 1999) won the Caldecott Award.

A comparatively new variety of engineered book is the electronic book. By embedding a microchip in thicker cardboard pages or covers, readers can make a book play music, make animal noises, create the sounds of a flushing toilet, flash lights, and so on. For example, Eric Carle's *The Very Quiet Cricket* (1997) tells the story of a mute cricket who finally, as the reader turns the last page, finds his "voice." The authentic-sounding chirp is powered by a watch battery that can be replaced through a small door on the back cover.

Engineered books—and the baby/board books discussed next—are distinctions of physical structure, not content. When considering the content, every engineered and baby/board book belongs also in at least one of the picture book categories previously listed.

Baby/Board Books

Baby books, especially the board book variety, were firmly established as a distinct type of picture book in 1981 with the publication of Helen Oxenbury's titles *(Dressing; Family; Friends; Playing; Working)*. These comparatively armor-clad books are made from thick cardboard with clear plasticized coatings. They are meant to withstand the buffetings, dunkings, and suckings of babies and toddlers. Some of these baby books are wordless, each page depicting a single object, such as a shoe or a spoon, that is common in a baby's environment. Sometimes single words or short phrases accompany illustrations. Rosemary Wells's Max books, however, are a bit more sophisticated. For example, in *Max's First Word* (1979), big sister Ruby is trying to teach her little bunny brother how to talk, but Max's only word is "BANG!" No matter how she prompts him, "bang" is his only response—that is, until Ruby gives him an apple and says, "APPLE, Max. Say, APPLE." Max's final response: "Delicious." Other noteworthy examples of board books include Rosemary Wells's Bunny Reads Back series (*Bingo*, 1999), Tony Ross's Little Princess books (*Shapes*, 1995), Janet and Allan Ahlberg's

Baby's Catalogue books (*See the Rabbit*, 1998), and Jane Simmons's First Daisy Books (*Quack, Daisy, Quack!*, 2002).

A picture book trend evident in the last decade is releasing regular-format picture books in smaller, board book form. Examples include *Prayer for a Child* (Field, 1944), *The Snowy Day* (Keats, 1962), and *Freight Train* (Crews, 1978)—all Caldecott or Caldecott Honor titles. Other examples include David McPhail's *Fix-it* (1984), Rick Walton's *One More Bunny* (2000), Mark and Caralyn Buehner's *Snowmen at Night* (2002), and Eric Carle's electronic book, *The Very Lonely Firefly* (1995).

Picture books are an abundant resource for initiating children into the worlds of literacy and image. Parents, teachers, and librarians must make a dedicated effort to share with children the best picture books, whether new titles or old, for it is the best books that make the most profound impressions on young minds.

PICTURE BOOKS AVAILABLE IN AUDIOVISUAL FORMATS

Many picture books are available in nonprint media. Two companies that produce excellent DVDs, videotapes, and audiotapes are Live Oak Media (*http:// www.liveoakmedia.com*) and Weston Woods (*http://teacher.scholastic.com/products/ westonwoods*). Consult their websites for the latest catalogs and offerings.

The American Library Association honors the most distinguished American video for children with an annual award, the Carnegie Medal for Excellence in Children's Video. Most of the winners are based on children's books. The winners, since its inception in 1991, are:

1991	*Ralph S. Mouse* by George McQuilkin and John Matthews (Churchill Films)
1992	*Harry Comes Home* by Peter Matulavich (Barr Films)
1993	*The Pool Party* by John Kelly and Gary Soto (Distributed by Gary Soto)
1994	*Eric Carle: Picture Writer* by Rawn Fulton (Searchlight Films)
1995	*Whitewash* by Michael Sporn (Churchill Media)
1996	*Owen* by Paul R. Gagne (Weston Woods)
1997	*Notes Alive! On the Day You Were Born* by Tacy Mangan (What a Gal Productions)
1998	*Willa: An American Snow White* by Tom Davenport (Davenport Films)
1999	*The First Christmas* by Frank Moynihan (Billy Budd Films)
2000	*Miss Nelson Has a Field Day* by Paul R. Gagne (Weston Woods Studio)
2001	*Antarctic Antics* by Paul R. Gagne (Weston Woods Studios)
2002	*My Louisiana Sky* by Dante Di Loreto and Anthony Edwards (Aviator Films) and Willard Carroll and Tom Wilhite (Hyperion Studio)
2003	*So You Want to Be President* by Paul Gagne and Melissa Reilly (Weston Woods Studios)
2004	*Giggle, Giggle, Quack* by Paul Gagne and Melissa Reilly (Weston Woods Studios)
2005	*The Dot* by Paul Gagne and Melissa Reilly (Weston Woods Studios)
2006	*The Man Who Walked Between the Towers* by Michael Sporn, Paul Gagne, and Melissa Reilly (Weston Woods Studios)
2007	*Knuffle Bunny* by Mo Willems (Weston Woods Studios)

PICTURE BOOK READING LISTS

FIFTEEN OF OUR FAVORITES

Alexander, Lloyd. 1992. *The Fortune-Tellers*. Illustrated by Trina Schart Hyman. Dutton. (Picture story.) A carpenter goes to a fortune-teller and finds that the predictions about his future come true in an unusual way.

Anno, Mitsumasa. 1977. *Anno's Counting Book*. Crowell. (Counting.) A counting book depicting the growth in a village and surrounding countryside during 12 months.

Crews, Donald. 1978. *Freight Train*. Greenwillow. (Concept.) Colors and the names of the cars on a freight train are introduced with sparse but rhythmic text and brilliantly colored illustrations. A Caldecott Honor Book.

Henkes, Kevin. 1990. *Julius, the Baby of the World*. Greenwillow. (Picture story.) Lilly is convinced that the arrival of her new baby brother is the worst thing that has happened in their house, until Cousin Garland comes to visit.

Hepworth, Cathi. 1992. *Antics! An Alphabetical Anthology*. Putnam. (ABC.) Alphabet entries from A to Z all have an "ant" somewhere in the word, such as *E* for Ench*ant*er, *P* for P*ant*aloons, *S* for S*ant*a Claus, and *Y* for Your *Ant* Yetta.

Mayer, Mercer. 1974. *Frog Goes to Dinner*. Dial. (Wordless.) Having stowed away in a pocket, Frog wreaks havoc and disgraces his human family at the posh restaurant where they are having dinner.

Parish, Peggy. 1963. *Amelia Bedelia*. Illustrated by Fritz Siebel. Harper. (Beginning reader.) A literal-minded housekeeper causes a ruckus in the household when she attempts to make sense of some instructions.

Peet, Bill. 1982. *Big Bad Bruce*. Houghton Mifflin. (Picture story.) Bruce, a bear bully, never picks on anyone his own size until he is diminished in more ways than one by a small but very independent witch.

Sendak, Maurice. 1963. *Where the Wild Things Are*. Harper. (Picture story.) A naughty little boy, sent to bed without his supper, sails to the land of the Wild Things, where he becomes their king. Winner of the Caldecott Medal.

Steig, William. 1982. *Doctor DeSoto*. Farrar. (Picture story.) A clever mouse dentist outwits his wicked fox patient. A Newbery Honor Book.

Turkle, Brinton. 1981. *Do Not Open*. Dutton. (Picture story.) Following a storm, Miss Moody and her cat find an intriguing bottle washed up on the beach. Should they ignore its "Do not open" warning?

Van Allsburg, Chris. 1981. *Jumanji*. Houghton Mifflin. (Picture story.) Left on their own for an afternoon, two bored and restless children find more excitement than they bargain for in a mysterious and mystical jungle adventure board game. Winner of the Caldecott Medal.

Waber, Bernard. 1972. *Ira Sleeps Over*. Houghton Mifflin. (Picture story.) A little boy is excited at the prospect of spending the night at his friend's house, but worries about how he'll get along without his teddy bear.

Wells, Rosemary. 1979. *Max's First Word*. Dial. (Baby/board.) It seems Max can say only one word, no matter how hard his older sister tries to teach him others.

Wiesner, David. 2006. *Flotsam*. (Wordless.) A boy spots a mysterious, old camera that washes up on the beach and discovers a fantasy-filled mystery waiting for him on the roll of film inside.

OTHERS WE LIKE

ABC

Aylesworth, Jim. 1992. *Old Black Fly*. Illustrated by Stephen Gammell. Holt.

Dodson, Peter. 1995. *An Alphabet of Dinosaurs*. Illustrated by Wayne D. Barlowe. Scholastic.

Ehlert, Lois. 1989. *Eating the Alphabet*. Harcourt.

Ernst, Lisa Campbell. 2004. *The Turn-Around, Upside-Down Alphabet Book*. Simon and Schuster.

Garten, Jan. 1994. (1964). *Alphabet Tale*. Illustrated by Muriel Batherman. Greenwillow.

Howell, Will C. 2002. *Zoo Flakes ABC*. Walker.

Johnson, Stephen T. 1995. *Alphabet City*. Viking.

Jonas, Ann. 1990. *Aardvarks, Disembark!* Greenwillow.

Lester, Mike. 2000. *A Is for Salad*. Putnam.

Lobel, Arnold. 1981. *On Market Street*. Illustrated by Anita Lobel. Greenwillow.

MacDonald, Suse. 1986. *Alphabatics*. Bradbury.

Martin, Bill, Jr., and John Archambault. 1989. *Chicka Chicka Boom Boom*. Illustrated by Lois Ehlert. Holt.

Melmed, Laura Krauss. 2005. *New York, New York! The Big Apple from A to Z*. Illustrated by Frané Lessac. Harper.

Minor, Wendell. 2006. *Yankee Doodle America*. Putnam.

Rohmann, Eric. 2005. *Clara and Asha*. Roaring Brook Press.

Sandved, Kjell. 1995. *The Butterfly Alphabet*. Scholastic.

Schnur, Steven. 2002. *Winter: An Alphabet Acrostic*. Illustrated by Leslie Evans. Clarion.

Shannon, George. 1996. *Tomorrow's Alphabet*. Illustrated by Donald Crews. Greenwillow.

Spirin, Gennady. 2005. *A: Apple Pie*. Philomel.

Van Allsburg, Chris. 1987. *The Z Was Zapped: A Play in Twenty-Six Acts*. Houghton Mifflin.

COUNTING

Anno, Mitsumasa. 1982. *Anno's Counting House*. Philomel.

Base, Graeme. 2001. *The Water Hole*. Abrams.

Bourke, Linda. 1995. *Eye Count: A Book of Counting Puzzles*. Chronicle.

Cronin, Doreen. 2005. *Click, Clack, Splish, Splash*. Illustrated by Betsy Lewin. Atheneum.

Dobson, Christina. 2003. *Pizza Counting*. Illustratrated by Matthew Holmes. Charlesbridge.

Fleming, Denise. 1992. *Count!* Holt.

Geisert, Arthur. 1992. *Pigs from 1 to 10*. Houghton Mifflin.

Giganti, Paul, Jr. 2005. *How Many Blue Birds Flew Away: A Counting Book with a Difference*. Illustrated by Donald Crews. Greenwillow.

Hoban, Tana. 1985. *1, 2, 3*. Greenwillow.

Hutchins, Pat. 1982. *1 Hunter*. Greenwillow.

Johnson, Stephen T. 1998. *City by Numbers*. Viking.

Kaufman, Karen. 2006. *If Mom Had Three Arms*. Illustrated by Pete Whitehead. Sterling.

Martin, Bill, Jr., Michael Sampson, and Lois Ehlert. 2004. *Chicka Chicka 1,2,3*. Simon & Schuster.

Merriam, Eve. 1993. *12 Ways to Get to 11*. Illustrated by Bernie Karlin. Simon & Schuster.

Reiser, Lynn. 2006. *Hardworking Puppies*. Harcourt.

Sloat, Teri. 1991. *From One to One Hundred*. Dutton.

Walsh, Ellen Stoll. 1991. *Mouse Count*. Harcourt.

CONCEPT

Barton, Byron. 1986. *Trains*. Crowell.

Davis, Lee. 1994. *The Lifesize Animal Opposites Book*. Dorling Kindersley.

Ehlert, Lois. 1989. *Color Zoo*. Lippincott.

Fisher, Valerie. 2006. *How High Can a Dinosaur Count? And Other Math Mysteries*. Schwartz & Wade.

Hoban, Tana. 1978. *Is It Red? Is It Yellow? Is It Blue?* Greenwillow.

Hoban, Tana. 1997. *Look Book*. Greenwillow.

Krebs, Laurie. 2005. *We're Sailing to Galapagos*. Illustrated by Grazia Restelli. Barefoot Books.

McMillan, Bruce. 1991. *Eating Fractions*. Scholastic.

Micklethwait, Lucy. 2004. *I Spy Shapes in Art*. Greenwillow.

Park, Linda Sue. 2005. *What Does Bunny See: A Book of Colors and Flowers*. Illustrated by Maggie Smith. Clarion.

Payne, Nina. 2001. *Four in All*. Illustrated by Adam Payne. Front Street.

Schwartz, David M. 1999. *If You Hopped Like a Frog*. Illustrated by James Warhola. Scholastic.

Serfozo, Mary. 1988. *Who Said Red?* Illustrated by Keiko Narahashi. McElderry.

Walsh, Ellen Stoll. 2007. *Mouse Shapes*. Harcourt. (See also *Mouse Paint* [1995] and *Mouse Magic* [2000].)

PARTICIPATION

Ahlberg, Janet, and Allan Ahlberg. 1979. *Each Peach Pear Plum*. Viking.

Anno, Mitsumasa. 1983. *Anno's U.S.A.* Philomel.

Boynton, Sandra. 2005. *Dog Train: A Wild Ride on the Rock-and-Roll Side*. Michael Ford, Collaborator. Workman.

Carlstrom, Nancy. 1986. *Jesse Bear, What Will You Wear?* Illustrated by Bruce Degen. Macmillan.

Cressy, Judith. 2004. *Can You Find It, Too?* The Metropolitan Museum of Art/Abrams.

Gág, Wanda. 1928. *Millions of Cats*. Putnam.

Handford, Martin. 1987. *Where's Waldo?* Little, Brown.

Hill, Eric. 2005 (1980). *Where's Spot?* Putnam.

Hook, Jason. 2004. *Where's the Dragon?* Illustrated by Richard Hook. Sterling.

Ljungkvist, Laura. 2006. *Follow the Line*. Viking.

Martin, Bill, Jr. 1993. *Old Devil Wind*. Illustrated by Barry Root. Harcourt.

Marzollo, Jean. 2005. *I Spy a Pumpkin*. Photographs by Walter Wick. Scholastic.

Munro, Roxie. 2005. *Amazement Park: 12 Wild Mazes*. Chronicle.

Yolen, Jane. 2000. *How Do Dinosaurs Say Goodnight?* Illustrated by Mark Teague. Blue Sky/Scholastic.

WORDLESS

Baker, Jeannie. 2004. *Belonging*. Walker.

Briggs, Raymond. 1978. *The Snowman*. Random.

Day, Alexandra. 2005. *Carl's Sleepy Afternoon*. Farrar.

Faller, Régis. 2002. *The Adventures of Polo*. Roaring Brook.

Geisert, Arthur. 2005. *Lights Out*. Houghton Mifflin.

Goodall, John. 1988. *Little Red Riding Hood*. McElderry.

Hutchins, Pat. 1971. *Changes, Changes*. Macmillan.

Lehman, Barbara. 2006. *Museum Trip*. Houghton Mifflin. (See also *The Red Book* [2004].)

Mayer, Mercer. 1976. *Ah-choo*. Dial.

McCully, Emily Arnold. 2004. *First Snow*. Harper.

Rohmann, Eric. 1994. *Time Flies*. Crown.

Schories, Pat. 2006. *Jack and the Night Visitors*. Front Street.

Spier, Peter. 1977. *Noah's Ark*. Doubleday.

Spier, Peter. 1982. *Rain*. Doubleday.

Varon, Sharon. 2006. *Chicken and Cat*. Scholastic.

Wiesner, David. 1991. *Tuesday*. Clarion.

Wiesner, David. 1999. *Sector 7*. Clarion.

PREDICTABLE

Brown, Margaret Wise. 1947. *Goodnight Moon*. Harper.

Carle, Eric. 1969. *The Very Hungry Caterpillar*. Philomel.

Carle, Eric. 1997. *The Very Quiet Cricket*. Philomel.

Christelow, Eileen. 2004. *Five Little Monkeys Play Hide-and-Seek*. Clarion.

Cowley, Joy. 2003. *Mrs. Wishy-Washy's Farm*. Illustrated by Elizabeth Fuller. Puffin.

Emberley, Barbara. 1967. *Drummer Hoff*. Illustrated by Ed Emberley. Prentice Hall.

Hoberman, Mary Ann. 2002. *Bill Grogan's Goat*. Illustrated by Nadine Bernard Westcott. Little, Brown.

Martin, Bill, Jr. 1964. *Brown Bear, Brown Bear, What Do You See?* Illustrated by Eric Carle. Holt.

Numeroff, Laura Joffe. 1985. *If You Give a Mouse a Cookie*. Illustrated by Felicia Bond. Harper. (See other books in the "If You Give . . ." series.)

Rosen, Michael. 2005. (1989). *We're Going on a Bear Hunt*. Illustrated by Helen Oxenbury. Walker.

Sendak, Maurice. 1991. (1962). *Chicken Soup with Rice*. Harper.

Shaw, Nancy. 1986. *Sheep in a Jeep*. Illustrated by Margot Apple. Houghton Mifflin. (See the other books in the "Sheep in a . . ." series.)

Slobodkina, Esphyr. 1947. *Caps for Sale*. Addison-Wesley.

Taback, Simms. 2002. *This Is the House That Jack Built*. Putnam.

Waddell, Martin. 1992. *Farmer Duck*. Illustrated by Helen Oxenbury. Candlewick.

Wood, Audrey. 1984. *The Napping House*. Illustrated by Don Wood. Harcourt.

Yolen, Jane. 2000. *Off We Go!* Illustrated by Laura Molk. Little, Brown.

BEGINNING READER

Arnold, Tedd. 2006. *Super Fly Guy*. Scholastic.

Bulla, Clyde Robert. 1987. *The Chalk Box Kid*. Illustrated by Thomas B. Allen. Random.

Byars, Betsy. 1990. *Hooray for the Golly Sisters!* Illustrated by Sue Truesdell. Harper.

Cazet, Denys. 2005. *The Octopus*. Harper.

Cohen, Miriam. 1990. *First Grade Takes a Test*. Illustrated by Lillian Hoban. Greenwillow.

Durant, Penny. 2005. *Sniffles, Sneezes, Hiccups, and Coughs*. DK Publishing.

Howe, James. 2006. *Houndsley and Catina*. Illustrated by Marie-Louise Gay. Candlewick.

Lobel, Arnold. 1970. *Frog and Toad Are Friends*. Harper. (See others in the Frog and Toad series.)

Lobel, Arnold. 1981. *Uncle Elephant*. Harper.

Minarik, Else. 1957. *Little Bear*. Illustrated by Maurice Sendak. Harper. (See others in the Little Bear series.)

Rylant, Cynthia. 2005. *Henry and Mudge and the Great Grandpas*. Illustrated by Suçie Stevenson. Simon & Schuster. (See others in the Henry and Mudge series.)

Rylant, Cynthia. 2006. *Mr. Putter & Tabby Spin the Yarn*. Illustrated by Arthur Howard. Harcourt. (See others in the Mr. Putter & Tabby series.)

Seuss, Dr. 1957. *The Cat in the Hat*. Random.

Sharmat, Marjorie Weinman, and Mitchell Sharmat. 2006. *Nate the Great Talks Turkey*. Illustrated by Jody Wheeler. Delacorte. (See others in the Nate the Great series.)

Van Leeuwen, Jean. 2006. *Oliver Pig and the Best Fort Ever*. Illustrated by Ann Schweninger. Dial. (See others in the Oliver Pig series.)

PICTURE STORY

Ackerman, Karen. 1988. *Song and Dance Man*. Illustrated by Stephen Gammell. Knopf.

Agee, Jon. 2001. *Milo's Hat Trick*. Hyperion.

Allard, Harry. 1977. *Miss Nelson Is Missing!* Illustrated by James Marshall. Houghton Mifflin.

Arnold, Tedd. 2004. *Even More Parts*. Dial.

Bemelmans, Ludwig. 1939. *Madeline*. Viking.

Browne, Anthony. 2004. *Into the Forest*. Candlewick.

Cooney, Barbara. 1982. *Miss Rumphius*. Viking.

Cronin, Doreen. 2000. *Click, Clack, Moo: Cows That Type*. Illustrated by Betsy Lewin. Simon & Schuster.

Crowe, Robert. 1976. *Clyde Monster*. Illustrated by Kay Chorao. Dutton.

Demi. 1997. *One Grain of Rice: A Mathematical Folktale*. Scholastic.

dePaola, Tomie. 1975. *Strega Nona*. Prentice Hall.

Falconer, Ian. 2006. *Olivia Forms a Band*. Atheneum.

Henkes, Kevin. 2005. *Lilly's Big Day*. Greenwillow.

Hoban, Russell. 1964. *Bread and Jam for Frances*. Illustrated by Lillian Hoban. Harper. (See others in the Frances series.)

Howitt, Mary. 2002. *The Spider and the Fly*. Illustrated by Tony DiTerlizzi. Simon & Schuster.

Keats, Ezra Jack. 1971. *Apt. 3*. Macmillan.

Kellogg, Steven. 1979. *Pinkerton, Behave!* Dial.

Mayer, Mercer. 1968. *There's a Nightmare in My Closet*. Dial.

McCloskey, Robert. 1948. *Blueberries for Sal*. Viking.

Meddaugh, Susan. 2004. *Perfectly Martha*. Houghton Mifflin. (See also other titles in the Martha series.)

Peet, Bill. 1983. *Buford the Little Bighorn*. Houghton Mifflin.

Pinkney, Andrea. 2006. *Peggony-Po: A Whale of a Tale*. Illustrated by Brian Pinkney. Jump at the Sun/Hyperion.

Polacco, Patricia. 1998. *Thank You, Mr. Falker*. Philomel.

Rylant, Cynthia. 1985. *The Relatives Came*. Illustrated by Stephen Gammell. Bradbury.

Salley, Coleen. 2006. *Epossumondas Saves the Day*. Illustrated by Janet Stevens. Harcourt.

Schwartz, Amy. 1988. *Anabelle Swift, Kindergartner*. Orchard.

Seuss, Dr. (Theodor Geisel). 1938. *The 500 Hats of Bartholomew Cubbins*. Vanguard.

Shulevitz, Uri. 1998. *Snow*. Farrar, Straus & Giroux.

Small, David. 1985. *Imogene's Antlers*. Crown.

Steig, William. 1976. *The Amazing Bone*. Farrar.

Van Allsburg, Chris. 1979. *The Garden of Abdul Gasazi*. Houghton Mifflin.

Viorst, Judith. 1972. *Alexander and the Terrible, Horrible, No Good, Very Bad Day*. Illustrated by Ray Cruz. Atheneum.

Wisniewski, David. 1996. *Golem*. Clarion.

Yolen, Jane. 1987. *Owl Moon*. Illustrated by John Schoenherr. Putnam.

ENGINEERED

Ahlberg, Janet, and Allan Ahlberg. 1986. *The Jolly Postman or Other People's Letters*. Little, Brown.

Carle, Eric. 1995. *The Very Lonely Firefly*. Philomel.

Ehlert, Lois. 1990. *Color Farm*. Lippincott.

Goodall, John. 1988. *Little Red Riding Hood*. McElderry.

Hill, Eric. 2005. *Who's There, Spot?* Putnam.

Lee, Jeanie. 2006. *Baby Farm Friends*. Little Simon.

Moerbeek, Kees. 2002. *The Diary of Hansel and Gretel*. Little Simon.

Pelham, Sophie, and David Pelham. 2004. *Counting Creatures: Pop-up Animals from 1 to 100*. Little Simon.

Piénkowski, Jan. 1979. *Haunted House*. Paper engineering by Tor Lokvig. Dutton.

Reinhart, Matthew. 2005. *The Ark*. Little Simon.

Sabuda, Robert. 1994. *The Christmas Alphabet*. Orchard.

Sabuda, Robert. 2005. *A Winter's Tale*. Little Simon.

Sabuda, Robert. 2006. *Sharks and Other Sea Monsters*. Candlewick.

Taback, Simms. 1999. *Joseph Had a Little Overcoat*. Viking.

Van Fleet, Matthew. 1995. *Fuzzy Yellow Ducklings*. Dial.

Van Fleet, Matthew. 2003. *Tails*. Harcourt.

Zelinsky, Paul O. 1990. *The Wheels on the Bus*. Paper engineering by Rodger Smith. Dutton.

BABY/BOARD

Alborough, Jez. 2005. *Duck in the Truck*. Kane/Miller.

Boynton, Sandra. 1995. *Blue Hat, Green Hat*. Little Simon.

Boyton, Sandra. 2005. *Belly Button Book*. Workman.

Buehner, Caralyn. 2004. *Snowmen at Night*. Illustrated by Mark Buehner. Dial.

Burton, Katherine. 2006. *One Gray Mouse*. Illustrated by Kim Fernandes. Kids Can Press.

Dickens, Lucy. 1991. *At the Beach*. Viking.

Hill, Eric. 2005. *Spot Loves His Daddy*. Putnam.

Hoban, Tana. 1985. *What Is It?* Greenwillow.

Kirschner, Tanja. 2005. *Bottoms*. North-South.

Oxenbury, Helen. 1981. *Dressing*. Simon & Schuster.

Pfister, Martin. 1996. *The Rainbow Fish*. North-South Books.

Simmons, Jane. 2000. *Daisy's Day Out*. Little, Brown.

Tafuri, Nancy. 2006. *Goodnight, My Duckling*. Scholastic.

Walton, Rick. 2001. *One More Bunny*. Illustrated by Paige Miglio. HarperFestival.

Yorke, Jane, editor. 2006. *My First Tractor Board Book*. DK Publishing.

For details about books listed here and for a more complete list of picture book titles, consult the *Children's Literature Database: A Resource for Teachers, Parents, and Media Specialists* CD that accompanies this text. Traditional fantasy picture books are, for the most part, found in Chapter 9.

REFERENCES

Ahlberg, Janet, & Ahlberg, Allan. (1979). *Each peach pear plum*. New York: Viking.

Ahlberg, Janet, & Ahlberg, Allan. (1998). *See the rabbit*. Boston: Little, Brown.

Anno, Mitsumasa. (1982). *Anno's counting book*. New York: Philomel.

Azarian, Mary. (2000). *The gardner's alphabet*. Boston: Houghton Mifflin.

Barton, Byron. (2001). *My car*. New York: Greenwillow.

Bates, John, & Bates, Natalie. (2004). *My first Buddhist alphabet*. Santa Monica, CA: Treasure Tower Press.

Baum, L. Frank. (2000). *The wonderful Wizard of Oz: A commemorative pop-up*. Illustrated by Robert Sabuda. New York: Little Simon.

Buehner, Caralyn, & Buehner, Mark. (2002). *Snowmen at night*. Illustrated by Mark Buehner. New York: CA Dial.

Carle, Eric. (1969). *The very hungry caterpillar*. New York: Philomel.

Carle, Eric. (1995). *The very lonely firefly*. New York: Philomel.

Carle, Eric. (1997). *The very quiet cricket*. New York: Philomel.

Carter, Anne. (1981). *Dinnertime*. Los Angeles: Price Stern Sloan.

Crews, Donald. (1978). *Freight train*. New York: Greenwillow.

Crews, Donald. (1999). *Cloudy day, sunny day*. New York: Harcourt.

Criscoe, Betty. (1988, Summer). A pleasant reminder: There is an established criteria for writing alphabet books. *Reading Horizons, 28*(4), 232–234.

Dodson, Peter. (1995). *An alphabet of dinosaurs*. Scholastic.

Ehlert, Lois. (1989). *Color zoo*. New York: Lippincott.

Ehlert, Lois. (2001). *Waiting for wings*. New York: Harcourt.

Field, Rachel. (1944). *Prayer for a child*. New York: Macmillan.

Gág, Wanda. (1928). *Millions of cats*. New York: Putnam.

Gagliano, Eugene M. (2003). *C is for cowboy: A Wyoming alphabet*. Chelsea, MI: Sleeping Bear Press.

Gillis, Jennifer Blizen. (2002). *Candle time ABC*. Chicago: Heinemann Library.

Goodman, Kenneth. (1988, fall). Look what they've done to Judy Blume!: The basalization of children's literature. *The New Advocate, 1*(1), 29–41.

Handford, Martin. (1987). *Where's Waldo?* Boston: Little, Brown.

Hepworth, Cathi. (1992). *Antics! An alphabetical anthology*. New York: Putnam.

Hoban, Tana. (1978). *Is it red? Is it yellow? Is it blue?* New York: Greenwillow.

Hoban, Tana. (1986). *Shapes, shapes, shapes*. New York: Greenwillow.

Hoban, Tana. (1990). *Exactly the opposite*. New York: Greenwillow.

Hoban, Tana. (1996). *Just look*. New York: Greenwillow.

Hoban, Tana. (2000). *Cubes, cones, cylinders & spheres*. New York: Greenwillow.

Hunt, Jonathan. (1998). *Bestiary: An illuminated alphabet of medieval beasts*. New York: Simon and Schuster.

Jarrell, Jane Cabaniss. (2000). *26 ways to say "I love you."* Eugene, OR: Harvest House.

Johnson, Stephen T. (1995). *Alphabet City*. New York: Viking.

Keats, Ezra Jack. (1962). *The snowy day*. New York: Viking.

Krull, Kathleen. (2003). *M is for music*. New York: Harcourt.

Kunhardt, Dorothy. (1940). *Pat the bunny*. Racine, WI: Western.

Lobel, Arnold. (1970). *Frog and Toad are friends*. New York: Harper & Row.

Lobel, Arnold. (1972). *Frog and Toad together*. New York: Harper & Row.

MacDonald, Suse. (1986). *Alphabatics*. New York: Bradbury.

Marsalis, Wynton. (2005). *Jazz A•B•Z: An A to Z collection of jazz portraits*. Cambridge, MA: Candlewick.

Martin, Bill, Jr. (1967). (reissued 1992). *Brown Bear, Brown Bear, what do you see?* Illustrated by Eric Carle. New York: Holt, Rinehart & Winston.

Mayer, Mercer. (1967). *A boy, a dog, and a frog*. New York: Dial.

Mayer, Mercer. (1974). *Frog goes to dinner*. New York: Dial.

McCloskey, Robert. (1941). *Make way for ducklings*. New York: Viking.

McPhail, David. (1984). *Fix-it*. New York: Dutton.

Minarik, Else. (1957). *Little Bear*. New York: Harper & Row.

Oxenbury, Helen. (1981). *Dressing*. New York: Wanderer Books.

Oxenbury, Helen. (1981). *Family*. New York: Wanderer Books.

Oxenbury, Helen. (1981). *Friends*. New York: Wanderer Books.

Oxenbury, Helen. (1981). *Playing*. New York: Wanderer Books.

Oxenbury, Helen. (1981). *Working*. New York: Wanderer Books.

Piénkowski, Jan. (1979). *Haunted house*. New York: Dutton.

Piénkowski, Jan. (1993). *ABC dinosaurs*. New York: Dutton.

Piénkowski, Jan. (2004). *The first noël*. Cambridge, MA: Candlewick.

Potter, Beatrix. (1902). *The tale of Peter Rabbit*. New York: Warne.

Rockwell, Anne. (2004). *Four seasons make a year*. Illustrated by Megan Halsey. New York: Walker.

Ross, Tony. (1995). *Shapes*. NewYork: Harcourt (Red Wagon Books).

Rylant, Cynthia. (1990). *Henry and Mudge and the happy cat*. Illustrated by Suçie Stevenson. New York: Bradbury.

Rylant, Cynthia. (2000). *Henry and Mudge and Annie's perfect pet*. Illustrated by Suçie Stevenson. New York: Simon & Schuster.

Rylant, Cynthia. (2005). *Henry and Mudge and the great grandpas*. Illustrated by Suçie Stevenson. New York: Simon & Schuster.

Sabuda, Robert. (1994). *The Christmas alphabet*. New York: Orchard.

Sabuda, Robert, & Reinhardt, Matthew. (2005). *Dinosaurs: Encyclopedia prehistorica*. Cambridge, MA: Candlewick.

Sandved, Kjell. (1996). *The butterfly alphabet*. New York: Scholastic.

Schwartz, David M. (1985). *How much is a million?* Illustrated by Steven Kellogg. New York: Lothrop.

Schwartz, David M. (1999). *If you hopped like a frog*. Illustrated by James Warhola. New York: Scholastic.

Sendak, Maurice. (1963). *Where the wild things are*. New York: Harper & Row.

Seuss, Dr. (1957). *The cat in the hat*. New York: Random House.

Shannon, George. (1996). *Tomorrow's alphabet*. Illustrated by Donald Crews. New York: Greenwillow.

Sharmat, Marjorie. (1972). *Nate the Great*. Illustrated by Marc Simont. New York: Coward, McCann & Geoghegan.

Sharmat, Marjorie. (1999). *Nate the Great and the monster mess*. Illustrated by Martha Weston. New York: Delacorte.

Sharmat, Marjorie. (2001). *Nate the Great and the big sniff*. Illustrated by Martha Weston. New York: Delacorte.

Sharmat, Marjorie. (2003). *Nate the Great on the Owl Express*. Illustrated by Martha Weston. New York: Delacorte.

Shaw, Nancy. (1986). *Sheep in a jeep*. Illustrated by Margot Apple. Boston: Houghton Mifflin.

Shaw, Nancy. (1992). *Sheep out to eat*. Illustrated by Margot Apple. Boston: Houghton Mifflin.

Shaw, Nancy. (1997). *Sheep trick or treat*. Illustrated by Margot Apple. Boston: Houghton Mifflin.

Simmons, Jane. (2002). *Quack, Daisy, quack!* Boston: Little, Brown.

Taback, Simms. (1997). *There was an old lady who swallowed a fly*. New York: Viking.

Taback, Simms. (1999). *Joseph had a little overcoat*. New York: Viking.

Van Allsburg, Chris. (1985). *The Polar Express*. Boston: Houghton Mifflin.

Van Fleet, Matthew. (1995). *Fuzzy yellow ducklings*. New York: Dial.

Walsh, Ellen Stoll. (2000). *Mouse magic*. New York: Harcourt.

Walton, Rick. (2000). *One more bunny*. Illustrated by Paige Miglio. New York: HarperFestival.

Wells, Rosemary. (1979). *Max's first word*. New York: Dial.

Wells, Rosemary. (1999). *Bingo*. New York: Scholastic.

Wiesner, David. (1988). *Free fall*. New York: Lothrop.

Wiesner, David. (1991). *Tuesday*. New York: Clarion.

Wiesner, David. (1999). *Sector 7*. New York: Clarion.

Wiesner, David. (2003). *The Three Pigs*. New York: Clarion.

Zelinsky, Paul O. (1990). *The wheels on the bus*. New York: Dutton.

Chapter 8

Poetry

Unfortunately, poetry does not receive the same attention in our elementary and secondary schools as do other literary forms. Several years of informal polls of our undergraduate preservice elementary teachers continue to affirm that a large percentage of these students enter teacher training with either an ambivalence toward or a distinct dislike for poetry. From one- to two-thirds of each class admit such negative attitudes. Is the alarming frequency of these attitudes due to teaching practices that alienate children from poetry or simply due to the absence of poetry in the curriculum? Whatever the reason, the fact remains that if many of our young teachers enter the field with an ambivalence toward poetry—or worse—then it is likely that a similar feeling will be passed to our children.

WHY CHILDREN MAY LEARN TO DISLIKE POETRY

Children have a natural affinity for poetry, which is exhibited before they enter school by their love for Mother Goose and other nursery rhymes, jingles, and childhood songs. Sometime during the course of their schooling, a great number of these children seem to change their minds about the appeal of poetry. Indeed, some of our teaching practices may be responsible. When asked what sorts of poetry-related school activities they found distasteful, our undergraduate students invariably listed these: memorizing and reciting, writing poetry, and heavy-duty analyzing of a poem's structure and meaning. Many students reported a distaste for playing the "I know the true meaning of this poem; it's your job to discover it" game with their teachers.

Teachers who don't appreciate poetry tend to ignore it in their daily routine. They may spend time with a poetry unit—teaching a few forms, giving practice in those forms by having the students write some poems (which are illustrated and posted on the bulletin board), memorizing and reciting some poetry—and then will move on, leaving poetry behind for good. Haiku, a Japanese poetry form, is commonly the form most abused in this manner. It is a seemingly quick and simple form to teach and write, having only 17 syllables (a line of 5 syllables, a line of 7 syllables, and another line of 5 syllables) that traditionally express something about nature:

> Take the butterfly:
> Nature works to produce him.
> Why doesn't he last?

> *David McCord*

Haiku may be short, but it is not simple. Because it is a rather abstract form, children actually require some experience and maturity to understand and appreciate haiku. Thus, as studies of children's poetry preferences indicate, generations of children have been taught to despise haiku (Fisher & Natarella, 1982; Kutiper & Wilson, 1993; Terry, 1974). With proper instructional techniques, however, children can and do learn to appreciate this elegant verse form.

Obviously, teachers who dislike poetry may have negative effects on children's poetry attitudes. However, the overzealous teacher who dearly loves poetry may cause problems, too, by rushing headlong into the sophisticated poems rendered by the traditional poets. Children may be overwhelmed by the complicated structures and intense imagery and figurative language. When pushed at an early age to analyze and discover deeply couched meanings, their excitement about poetry wanes.

Studies of children's poetry preferences reveal children's common dislikes about poetry. Kutiper and Wilson (1993) summarized the results of several of the best-known studies:

1. The narrative form of poetry [and limericks] was popular with readers of all ages, while free verse and haiku were the most disliked forms.
2. Students preferred poems that contain rhyme, rhythm, and sound.
3. Children most enjoyed poetry that contained humor, familiar experiences, and animals. [Disliked poems about nature.]
4. Younger students (elementary and middle school/junior high age) preferred contemporary poems.
5. Students disliked poems that contained visual imagery or figurative language. (p. 29)

What students like about poetry relates to their early childhood love for poems that are heavily rhymed and straightforward in meaning. What they dislike is frequently associated with teaching practices: the abuse of haiku (which also surfaces in a dislike of nature poems), a lack of connection with the more abstract form of free verse, and the distaste for figurative language. Sometimes in elementary schools and middle schools, we seem to know and teach only simile, metaphor, and personification. After innumerable exercises wherein students are asked to find, circle, and label in a poem (or story) examples of simile, metaphor, and personification, it is little wonder that figurative language seems a burden.

PEANUTS® by Charles M. Schultz

PEANUTS reprinted by permission of United Feature Syndicate, Inc.

Bernard Lonsdale and Helen Mackintosh (1973) best express how we should approach poetry in the elementary schools:

> Experiences with poetry should be pleasurable and should never be associated with work. Teachers defeat their own purpose if they attempt to analyze the structure or form of the poem other than to show whether it rhymes; what the verse pattern is; and whether it is a ballad, a limerick, a lyric poem, or perhaps haiku. Children in elementary schools should be asked questions of preference and of feeling rather than of knowing. (p. 213)

Children have less opportunity for preference and feeling when the teacher makes all the decisions about poetry and its use in the classroom. If the teacher selects one poem for the entire class to memorize, fewer children will respond positively than if each is allowed to choose a favorite poem for memorization. If the teacher presents one form of poetry and afterward insists that everyone write a poem in that style, the overall response is less enthusiastic than if the teacher waits until two or three forms have been introduced and permits students to select the type they wish to write. Or, insightful teachers can help students see that their poems may be free of form yet extremely personal and powerful. (See *A Celebration of Bees: Helping Children Write Poetry* by Barbara Juster Esbensen, 1995.) The principle of allowing children to make choices whenever possible is closely associated with success in presenting poetry in the elementary classroom.

BUILDING APPRECIATION FOR POETRY

Children who have learned a dislike for poetry can be lured back by teachers who capitalize on the winning power of light, humorous verse. No collection of light verse has done more to attract children to poetry than Shel Silverstein's *Where the Sidewalk Ends* (1974). Young readers hungrily latch onto Silverstein's lighthearted, sometimes irreverent, poems about contemporary childhood. Jack Prelutsky's poems are similar to Silverstein's, but they are more numerous and more varied in theme. Prelutsky's collection *The New Kid on the Block* (1984) actually edged out

Where the Sidewalk Ends as the most circulated poetry book in the libraries of schools selected for a poetry preference study (Kutiper & Wilson, 1993). Here is the poem that opens the collection:

THE NEW KID ON THE BLOCK

There's a new kid on the block,
and boy, that kid is tough,
that new kid punches hard,
that new kid plays real rough,
that new kid's big and strong,
with muscles everywhere,
that new kid tweaked my arm,
that new kid pulled my hair.
That new kid likes to fight,
and picks on all the guys,
that new kid scares me some,
(that new kid's twice my size),
that new kid stomped my toes,
that new kid swiped my ball,
that new kid's really bad,
I don't care for her at all.

As Kutiper and Wilson (1993) point out, the light verse that children tend to prefer must not remain their only poetry diet. Wise teachers will use the rhythmic, humorous verse to build appreciation for poetry in general and use it as a bridge to more sophisticated contemporary and traditional poetry written for children and adults. Teachers who share poems daily, with no ulterior motive other than to build appreciation, help create students (and future teachers) who will have a lifelong interest in poetry. Share a poem as children wait in the lunch line, sit down after recess, or as a way to begin each school day. One teacher simply wrote a new poem on the chalkboard each day without reading or referring to it. Soon students were commenting on the poems, and some began writing down the ones they liked. Poetry may fit nicely into a social studies or science unit—in fact, into any area of the curriculum. In language study, Ruth Heller's beautifully illustrated poems present the parts of speech (*Kites Sail High: A Book About Verbs,* 1988; *Mine, All Mine: A Book About Pronouns,* 1997; *Fantastic! Wow! and Unreal!: A Book About Interjections and Conjunctions,* 1998; and others). The key is consistent, unfettered exposure to poetry by an enthusiastic teacher who begins mixing light verse and more artistic poetry.

As poetry really is meant to be heard more than read silently, the avenue to poetry

 USING THE CHILDREN'S LITERATURE DATABASE

Be sure the CD database is installed on your hard drive. Click on Search Query Builder in the left navigation bar on the Home screen. Search for poetry about math. Type "Math" in the Keyword Search field, and check the All button. Click on the Title, Topics, and Description checkboxes. Check the P box (poetry) for Genre. Search again for additional poetry books, but with a keyword of your choice.

appreciation for many students is the oral highway. Therefore, teachers should read poems aloud—fresh selections as well as old favorites—on a regular, even daily, basis. And for older, hard-core poetry haters, music is often the road to recovery. Students tend not to associate the lyrics of songs they know and love with poetry. Teachers of older children have changed students' negative attitudes toward poetry by duplicating the lyrics of popular tunes and distributing them as poems. Often barriers will tumble down, clearing the way for sharing other sorts of poetry.

Choral speaking is another oral/aural method for sharing poetry. Through choral speaking, children get the opportunity to play with words and their sounds—to both hear and manipulate the language. For example, free verse (noted by children as one of their least favorite forms) can spring to life when performed as a choral reading. Here is a free-verse poem by Harold Munro, divided into speaking parts by a teacher, that has proven to be an icebreaker with upper elementary students:

OVERHEARD ON A SALT MARSH

BY HAROLD MUNRO

(May also be divided as light voices and dark voices, or boys as the goblins and girls as the water nymphs.)

Boys: NYMPH, NYMPH, WHAT ARE YOUR BEADS?

Girls: Green glass, goblin. Why do you stare at them?

Boys: GIVE THEM ME.

Girls: NO.

Boys: GIVE THEM ME.
GIVE THEM ME.

Girls: NO.

Boys: THEN I WILL HOWL ALL NIGHT IN THE REEDS,
LIE IN THE MUD AND HOWL FOR THEM.

Girls: Goblin, why do you love them so?

Boys: THEY ARE BETTER THAN STARS OR WATER,
BETTER THAN VOICES OF WINDS THAT SING,
BETTER THAN ANY MAN'S FAIR DAUGHTER,
YOUR GREEN GLASS BEADS ON A SILVER STRING.

Girls: Hush, I stole them out of the moon.

Boys: GIVE ME YOUR BEADS, I WANT THEM.

Girls: NO.

Boys: I WILL HOWL IN A DEEP LAGOON
FOR YOUR GREEN GLASS BEADS,
I LOVE THEM SO.
GIVE THEM ME. GIVE THEM.

Girls: NO.[*]

Sometimes teachers can be intimidated by poetry. "Poetry phobia" often results from of a lack of knowledge and usually disappears with increased understanding.

---

[*]From *Overheard on a Salt Marsh* by Harold Munro. Reprinted by permission of Gerald Duckworth and Co. Ltd.

Those with poetry phobia can develop confidence when learning about poetry from two children's books: Avis Harley's *Fly with Poetry: an ABC of Poetry* (2000) and *Leap into Poetry: More ABCs of Poetry* (2001). These simple, clever picture books illuminate poetry forms and terms with poetic examples and straightforward definitions. For instance, in *Fly with Poetry* "Acrostic" is the poetry form for the letter "A," and Harley (2000, p. 11) explains that in such a poem "the first letters of the lines form a word or sentence when read downward." Then she gives an example of her own making:

> *EDITING THE CHRYSALIS*
> "At last," cried Butterfly,
>
> Poised
> Over its
> Empty chrysalis,
> "My final draft!"

Teachers do much to convince children of the worth of poetry when they share what is personally delightful. They are always more successful when presenting poems they honestly like. A folder with readily accessible favorite poems or a shelf holding favorite poetry volumes makes the job easier. If teachers do not have a collection of personal favorites, it is only because they have not read enough poems. The pleasure of writing poetry should be modeled in a similar way. We recall a sixth-grade teacher who genuinely enjoyed writing limericks for his students, who soon became so enamored with limericks they chose to stay in during recess to write poems!

THE NCTE POETRY AWARD

To encourage the sharing of poetry with children and to raise the awareness of teachers about the quality of the poetry available, the National Council of Teachers of English (NCTE) established an award to recognize a living poet whose body of work for children ages 3 to 13 is deemed exceptional. The NCTE Award for Excellence in Poetry for Children was presented annually from 1977 until 1982, when the council began giving it every three years.

The works of the poets who have won the NCTE Poetry Award are certainly not as well known among children as the poems of Silverstein and Prelutsky, but they provide teachers a reservoir of fine poetry that is both very accessible to children and of better artistic quality than the popular lighter verse. (See *A Jar of Tiny Stars: Poems by NCTE Award–Winning Poets* edited by Bernice E. Cullinan 1996.) Here are the names of the award-winning poets, the dates of their awards, and a sample of their poetry. Try reading each selection aloud for full effect.

DAVID McCORD, 1977

SONG OF THE TRAIN
Clickety-clack,
Wheels on the track,

This is the way
They begin the attack:
Click-ety-clack,
Click-ety-clack,
Click-ety, *clack*-ety,
Click-ety
Clack.

Clickety-clack,
Over the crack,
Faster and faster
The song of the track:
Clickety-clack,
Clickety, clack
Clickety, clackety,
Clackety
Clack.

Riding in front,
Riding in back,
Everyone hears
The song of the track:
Clickety-clack,
Clickety-clack,
Clickety, *clickety*,
Clackety
Clack.

AILEEN FISHER, 1978
I LIKE IT WHEN IT'S MIZZLY
I like it when it's mizzly
and just a little drizzly
so everything looks far away
and make-believe and frizzly.

I like it when it's foggy
and sounding very froggy.
I even like it when it rains
on streets and weepy windowpanes
and catkins in the poplar tree
and *me*.

KARLA KUSKIN, 1979
FULL OF THE MOON
It's full of the moon

The dogs dance out
Through brush and bush and bramble.
They howl and yowl
And growl and prowl.
They amble, ramble, scramble.
They rush through brush.
They push through bush.
They yip and yap and hurr.
They lark around and bark around
With prickles in their fur.
They two-step in the meadow.
They polka on the lawn.
Tonight's the night
The dogs dance out
And chase their tails till dawn.

MYRA COHN LIVINGSTON, 1980

My Box

Nobody knows what's there but me,
knows where I keep my silver key
and my baseball cards
and my water gun
and my wind-up car that doesn't run,
and a stone I found with a hole clear through
and a blue-jay feather that's *mostly* blue,
and a note that I wrote to the guy next door
and never gave him—and lots, lots more
of important things that I'll never show
to anyone, *anyone* else I know.

EVE MERRIAM, 1981

Teevee

In the house
of Mr. and Mrs. Spouse
he and she
would watch TV
and never a word
between them spoken
until the day
the set was broken.

Then "How do you do?"
said he to she.
"I don't believe
that we've

met
yet.
Spouse is my name.
What's yours?" he asked.

"Why, mine's the same!"
said she to he,
"Do you suppose that we could be—?"

But the set came suddenly right about,
and so they never did find out.

JOHN CIARDI (*CHAR-DEE*), 1982

HOW TO TELL THE TOP OF A HILL

The top of a hill
Is not until
The bottom is below.
And you have to stop
When you reach the top
For there's no more UP to go.
To make it plain
Let me explain:
The one *most* reason why
You have to stop
When you reach the top—is:
The next step up is sky.

LILIAN MOORE, 1985

PIGEONS

Pigeons are city folk
content
to live with concrete
and cement.

They seldom
try
the sky.

A pigeon never sings
of hill
and flowering hedge,
but busily commutes
from sidewalk
to his ledge.

Oh pigeon, what a waste of wings!

ARNOLD ADOFF, 1988

LOVE SONG

great goblets of pudding   powder in milk
hot with marshmallows on a winter afternoon
syrup on vanilla ice cream   frosting on cake
a kind of cake   dripping to dry on warm
doughnuts fresh from the oven   candy
                                 candy bars
bars   chunks   thick and broken pieces   squares
spoons and pots   and lots
                              before brushing
fudge and milk
        and german and sour cream
light and dark and bitter sweet and
                                    even
                                    white
you are no good
                for me
you are no good

you are so good

Chocolate
Chocolate
           i
love
    you so
          i
want
         to
marry
       you
       and
live
    forever
         in the
         flavor
of your
    brown

VALERIE WORTH, 1991

STOCKINGS (FROM AT CHRISTMASTIME)

Long ago, we
Hung up my
Mother's old

Nylons, and
Woke to find
Them swollen

With beige
Unnatural bulges,
Thigh to toe.

Nowadays, there
Are velvety
Crimson boots,

Brighter, and
Shapelier—but
A lot shorter.

BARBARA ESBENSEN, 1994

PENCILS

The rooms in a pencil
are narrow
but elephants   castles and watermelons
fit in

In a pencil
noisy words yell for attention
and quiet words wait their turn

How did they slip
into such a tight place?
Who
gives them their
lunch?

From a broken pencil
an unbroken poem will come!
There is a long story living
in the shortest pencil

Every word in your
pencil
is fearless   ready to walk
the blue tightrope lines
Ready
to teeter and smile
down   Ready to come right out
and show you
thinking!

ELOISE GREENFIELD, 1997

KEEPSAKE

Before Mrs. Williams died
She told Mr. Williams
When he gets home
To get a nickel out of her
Navy blue pocketbook
And give it to her
Sweet little gingerbread girl
That's me

I ain't never going to spend it

X. J. KENNEDY, 2000

THE KITE THAT BRAVED OLD ORCHARD BEACH

The kite that braved Old Orchard Beach
    But fell and snapped its spine
Hangs in our attic out of reach,
    All tangled in its twine.

My father says, "Let's throw it out,"
    But I won't let him. No,
There has to be some quiet spot
    Where cracked-up heroes go.

MARY ANN HOBERMAN, 2003

NIGHT

The night is coming softly, slowly;
Look, it's getting hard to see.
    Through the windows,
    Through the door,
    Pussyfooting
    On the floor,
    Dragging shadows,
    Crawling,
    Creeping,
Pull down the shades.
Turn on the light.
Let's pretend it isn't night.

NIKKI GRIMES, 2006

MUSIC LESSONS

The choir paints
    the sanctuary walls
with bands of sound
    more glorious than gold

And all around
    the altar, voices raise
In matchless harmonies
    of perfect praise—

Perfect, except
    for Mom, who tonelessly
expands the meaning of
    the phrase "off-key."

She swears I'll miss
    her singing when she's gone.
Says she, "Not all folks get
    the gift of song."

That may be true,
    But miss her singing? *Wrong.*

 FORMS OF POETRY

Poetry is distinguishable from prose primarily because of its distinct patterns or forms. The variety of patterns, in turn, distinguishes one form of poetry from another. Of the many forms of poetry, here are a few teachers commonly use in elementary school.

NARRATIVE POEMS.   Narrative poems tell stories. Children usually enjoy narrative poetry because they are naturally attuned to stories, and because it is easy to understand. A classic example is Henry Wadsworth Longfellow's "The Midnight Ride of Paul Revere," available in a picture book version (2001) handsomely illustrated by Christopher Bing. Ballads are narrative poems adapted for singing or for creating a musical effect, such as the popular American ballad "On Top of Old Smoky."

LYRIC POEMS.   Lyric poetry is melodic or songlike. Generally, it is descriptive, focusing on personal moments, feelings, or image-laden scenes. John Ciardi's poem "How to Tell the Top of a Hill" (1982) is an example of a lyric poem (see p. 89).

LIMERICKS.   Limericks are humorous poems that were popularized with the publication of Edward Lear's *Book of Nonsense* in 1846 (1863 American edition). The rhyming scheme and verse pattern of limericks are familiar to most children:

A thrifty young fellow of Shoreham
Made brown paper trousers and woreham;
    He looked nice and neat
    Till he bent in the street
To pick up a pin; then he toreham.

Anonymous

HAIKU.   As described earlier in this chapter, haiku has a total of 17 syllables (a line of 5 syllables, a line of 7 syllables, and another line of 5 syllables). Refer to "Why Children May Dislike Poetry," earlier in this chapter, for an example and further description.

CONCRETE POEMS.   A concrete poem is written or printed on the page in a shape representing the poem's subject. It is a form of poetry that is meant to be seen even more than heard and often does not have a rhyming scheme or a particular rhythm:

J. Patrick Lewis

FREE VERSE.   Free verse, though relying on rhythm and cadence for its poetic form, is mostly unrhymed and lacks a consistent rhythm. Its topics are typically quite philosophical or abstract, but intriguing. The poems presented in this chapter by Harold Munro (p. 85) and Valerie Worth (pp. 90–91) are examples of free verse.

OTHER POETIC FORMS. For child-friendly information about 52 forms and/or elements of poetry, see the Avis Harley books mentioned earlier. Also, see Paul Janeczko's picture book, *A Kick in the Head: An Everyday Guide to Poetic Forms* (2005).

BUILDING A POETRY COLLECTION

A poetry collection should include poems that meet the needs of children who are in the process of developing an appreciation of poetry. This means building a collection filled with a variety of poems to match differing tastes and levels of sophistication: light and humorous verse, poems that create vivid images or express hard-to-communicate feelings, story poems, or poetry that plays with the sounds of language.

Do not rely on textbooks to supply poetry for your classroom. For one thing, basal readers simply do not have enough poetry. Also, because poems (and other literary works) are protected by copyright laws for the author's lifetime plus 70 years, textbook companies and other anthologizers find it less expensive to choose poems that are in the public domain; in other words, whose author has been dead long enough that one does not have to pay a permission fee to reprint the poem. As a result, basals and anthologies may be heavily weighted toward older poetry. Although some old poems appeal to modern children, contemporary poetry—found largely in single, thin volumes or specific collections—generally has a stronger draw for today's reader. A second reason not to rely on textbooks is that some basal readers now include little or no poetry (Roe, Cuellar, & Fickle, 2004).

The world of children's books offers teachers an almost endless supply of poetry. The reading list at the end of this chapter is representative of the excellent collections available that provide a broad range of poetry to meet every need. Many books of poetry are collections of a single poet's work (note collections by the NCTE Poetry Award winners). However, some fine general anthologies are also listed, such as *The Random House Book of Poetry* (compiled by Jack Prelutsky, 1983) and *Poetry by Heart* (compiled by Liz Attenborough, 2001). Both books have themed sections, such as a collection of scary poems or animal poems, and provide a balance of modern and traditional poets. *The Random House Book of Poetry* contains 579 poems, and although *Poetry by Heart* has considerably fewer poems, it is illustrated by a variety of talented artists. Other useful anthologies include Mary Ann Hoberman's *My Song Is Beautiful: Poems and Pictures in Many Voices* (1994), Ivan and Mal Jones's *Good Night, Sleep Tight* (2000), and Belinda Hollyer's *The King-fisher Book of Family Poems* (2003).

A number of specialized anthologies appear in the reading list as well. These collections contain poems about a particular topic, written by a variety of poets. Myra Cohn Livingston perhaps created more specialized poetry collections than anyone else. Examples of her titles include *Cat Poems* (1987a), *Poems for Mothers* (1988), *Birthday Poems* (1989a), *Halloween Poems* (1989b), *Valentine Poems* (1987b), *Poems for Jewish Holidays* (1986), *Animal, Vegetable, Mineral: Poems About Small Things* (1994), and

FIGURE 8–1

Notable children's poets.

Adoff, Arnold	Livingston, Myra Cohn
Ciardi, John	McCord, David
Esbensen, Barbara Juster	Merriam, Eve
Fisher, Aileen	Moore, Lilian
Fleischman, Paul	Nye, Naomi Shihab
Florian, Douglas	Prelutsky, Jack
Greenfield, Eloise	Schertle, Alice
Hoberman, Mary Ann	Seibert, Diana
Hopkins, Lee Bennett	Silverstein, Shel
Kennedy, X. J.	Worth, Valerie
Kuskin, Karla	Yolen, Jane
Lewis, J. Patrick	

Cricket Never Does: A Collection of Haiku and Tanka (1997). Jane Yolen, Lee Bennett Hopkins, and Jack Prelutsky also have compiled many specialized anthologies.

The single-poem picture book is another variety of poetry book that is particularly useful for giving children a taste of the more traditional and sometimes more sophisticated poet. For example, Susan Jeffers has illustrated a stunning picture book version of *Stopping by Woods on a Snowy Evening* by Robert Frost (1978), which will attract the most reluctant poetry reader. Other examples include *The Tyger* (1993) by William Blake (illustrated by Neil Waldman) and *The Rime of the Ancient Mariner* (1992) by Samuel Taylor Coleridge (illustrated by Ed Young).

Teachers who do not know the world of children's poetry have a responsibility not only to discover the bounty that awaits them but also to use it to help stem the tide of ambivalence toward poetry among their students. A well-rounded classroom and school library poetry collection will have something for everyone. By sharing and enjoying poetry frequently, teachers and children together will build a lifelong appreciation, as the following poem by Eloise Greenfield expresses.

> *THINGS*
> Went to the corner
> Walked in the store
> Bought me some candy
> Ain't got it no more
> Ain't got it no more
>
> Went to the beach
> Played on the shore
> Built me a sandhouse
> Ain't got it no more
> Ain't got it no more

Went to the kitchen
Lay down on the floor
Made me a poem
Still got it
Still got it

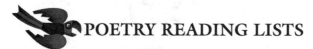

POETRY READING LISTS

TEN OF OUR FAVORITES

Ciardi, John. 1962. *You Read to Me, I'll Read to You.* Illustrated by Edward Gorey. Lippincott. Designed so that the child reads the poem on one page and the adult reads the poem on the next page. A collection mostly of humorous verse.

de Regniers, Beatrice Schenk, Eva Moore, Mary Michaels White, and Jean Carr, compilers. 1988. *Sing a Song of Popcorn.* Illustrated by nine Caldecott Award–winning artists. Scholastic. A collection of poems by a variety of well-known poets with illustrations by nine Caldecott medalists.

Esbensen, Barbara. 1992. *Who Shrank My Grandmother's House?* Illustrated by Eric Beddows. Harper. A collection of poems about childhood discoveries concerning everyday objects and things.

Fleischman, Paul. 1988. *Joyful Noise: Poems for Two Voices.* Illustrated by Eric Beddows. Harper. A collection of poems (divided into two columns to be read together by two people) describing the characteristics and activities of a variety of insects. Winner of the Newbery Medal.

Harley, Avis. 2000. *Fly with Poetry: An ABC of Poetry.* Wordsong/Boyds Mills Press. Harley defines, plus provides an example, of 26 poetry forms, one for each letter of the alphabet: acrostic, blank verse, cinquain, and so on.

Merriam, Eve. 2002. (1987). *Spooky ABC.* Illustrated by Lane Smith. Macmillan. Each letter of the alphabet introduces a different spooky aspect of Halloween.

Prelutsky, Jack. 1984. *The New Kid on the Block.* Illustrated by James Stevenson. Greenwillow. Humorous poems about such strange creatures and people as Baloney Belly Billy and the Gloopy Gloopers.

Schertle, Alice. 1996. *Keepers.* Illustrated by Ted Rand. Lothrop. A collection of poems about personal mementos that bring to mind special moments and feelings.

Siebert, Diane. 2006. *Tour America: A Journey Through Poems and Art.* Illustrated by Stephen T. Johnson. Chronicle Books. Mixed-media artwork and poems evoke familiar and unfamiliar places throughout the United States, including Kentucky's famed Derby, Florida's Everglades, and the Oregon vortex.

Thayer, Ernest Lawrence. 2000. *Casey at the Bat: A Ballad of the Republic Sung in the Year 1888.* Illustrated by Christopher Bing. Handprint. This rendition of Thayer's immortal poem about baseball hero Casey, who strikes out and loses the big game, is illustrated with reproductions of artifacts, newspaper clippings, photographs, and other late-19th-century memorabilia (ticket stubs, coins, medals, baseball cards).

OTHERS WE LIKE

Attenborough, Liz. 2001. *Poetry by Heart: A Child's Book of Poems to Remember.* Scholastic.

Cullinan, Bernice E., ed. 1996. *A Jar of Tiny Stars: Poems by NCTE Award–Winning Poets.* Illustrated by Andi MacLeod and Marc Nadel. Wordsong/Boyds Mills.

de la Mare, Walter. 2002. (1947). *Rhymes and Verse: Collected Poems for Young People.* Illustrated by Elinore Blaisdell. Holt.

Dotlich, Rebecca Kai. 2004. *Over in the Pink House: New Jump Rope Rhymes.* Illustrated by Melanie Hall. Wordsong/Boyds Mills.

Esbensen, Barbara Juster. 1995. *Dance with Me.* Illustrated by Megan Lloyd. Harper.

Fisher, Aileen. 2002. *I Heard a Bluebird Sing.* Illustrated by Jennifer Emery. Wordsong/Boyds Mills.

Florian, Douglas. 2004. *Omnibeasts.* Harcourt.

Fox, Dan, ed. 2003. *A Treasury of Children's Songs: Forty Favorites to Sings and Play.* The Metropolitan Museum of Art/Holt.

Greenfield, Eloise. 1978. *Honey, I Love and Other Poems.* Illustrated by Leo and Diane Dillon. Harper.

Holbrook, Sara. 2002. *Wham! It's a Poetry Jam: Discovering Performance Poetry.* Wordsong/Boyds Mills.

Hopkins, Lee Bennett. 2006. *Got Geography: Poems.* Illustrated by Philip Stanton. Greenwillow.

Janeczko, Paul B., ed. 2001. *A Poke in the I: A Collection of Concrete Poems.* Illustrated by Christopher Raschka. Candlewick.

Janeczko, Paul B. and J. Patrick Lewis. 2006. *Wing Nuts: Screwy Haiku.* Illustrated by Tricia Tusa. Little, Brown.

Kennedy, X. J. 1986. *Brats.* Illustrated by James Watt. Atheneum.

Kuskin, Karla. 2003. *Moon, Have You Met My Mother?* Illustrated by Sergio Ruzzier. Harper.

Larrick, Nancy, ed. 1968. *Piping Down the Valleys Wild.* Illustrated by Ellen Raskin. Delacorte.

Lewis, J. Patrick. 2005. *Monumental Verses.* National Geographic Society.

Lewis, J. Patrick. 2005. *Please Bury Me in the Library.* Illustrated by Kyle M. Stone. Harcourt.

McCord, David. 1977. *One at a Time.* Little, Brown.

Moore, Lilian. 2005. *Mural on Second Avenue and Other City Poems.* Illustrated by Roma Karas. Greenwillow.

Morrison, Lillian. 2001. *More Spice Than Sugar: Poems About Feisty Females.* Illustrated by Ann Boyajian. Houghton.

Moses, Will. 2003. *Will Moses Mother Goose.* Philomel.

Nye, Naomi Shihab, ed. 2000. *Salting the Ocean: 100 Poems by Young Poets.* Illustrated by Ashley Bryan. Greenwillow.

Prelutsky, Jack. 1976. *Nightmares: Poems to Trouble Your Sleep.* Illustrated by Arnold Lobel. Greenwillow.

Prelutsky, Jack, ed. 1983. *The Random House Book of Poetry for Children.* Illustrated by Arnold Lobel. Random House.

Prelutsky, Jack. 2005. *Read a Rhyme, Write a Rhyme.* Illustrated by Meilo So. Knopf.

Rosen, Michael, ed. 1998. *Classic Poetry: An Illustrated Collection*. Illustrated by Paul Howard. Candlewick.

Silverstein, Shel. 1974. *Where the Sidewalk Ends*. Harper.

Volavkova, H., ed. 1994. . . . *I Never Saw Another Butterfly: Children's Drawings and Poems from Terezin Concentration Camp, 1942–1944*. Random.

Worth, Valerie. 2002. *Peacock and Other Poems*. Illustrated by Natalie Babbitt. Farrar.

Yolen, Jane, ed. 2005. *This Little Piggy and Other Rhymes to Sing and Play*. Illustrated by Will Hillenbrand. Candlewick.

EASIER TO READ

Brown, Marc, ed. 1987. *Play Rhymes*. Dutton.

Dakos, Kalli. 2003. *Put Your Eyes Up Here and Other School Poems*. Illustrated by G. Brian Karas. Simon and Schuster.

Goldstein, Bobbye S., ed. 1998. *Sweets & Treats: Dessert Poems*. Illustrated by Kathy Couri. Hyperion.

Hopkins, Lee Bennett, ed. 1987. *More Surprises*. Illustrated by Megan Lloyd. Harper.

Hopkins, Lee Bennett, ed. 1999. *Sports! Sports! Sports!: A Poetry Collection*. Illustrated by Brian Floca. Harper.

Hopkins, Lee Bennett, ed. 2003. *A Pet for Me: Poems*. Illustrated by Jane Manning. Harper.

James, Simon. 2000. *Days Like This*. Candlewick.

Kuskin, Karla. 1992. *Soap Soup and Other Verses*. Harper.

Kuskin, Karla. 2004. *Under My Hood I Have a Hat*. Illustrated by Fumi Kosaka. Harper.

Livingston, Myra Cohn. 1990. *My Head Is Red and Other Riddle Rhymes*. Illustrated by Tere LoPrete. Dutton.

Prelutsky, Jack. 1980. *Rolling Harvey Down the Hill*. Illustrated by Victoria Chess. Greenwillow.

Prelutsky, Jack. 1983. *It's Valentine's Day*. Illustrated by Yossi Abolafia. Greenwillow.

Zolotow, Charlotte. 2002. *Seasons: A Book of Poems*. Illustrated by Eric Blegvad. Harper.

PICTURE BOOKS

Adoff, Arnold. 1973. *Black Is Brown Is Tan*. Illustrated by Emily Arnold McCully. Harper.

Baylor, Byrd. 1986. *I'm in Charge of Celebrations*. Illustrated by Peter Parnall. Scribner's.

Blake, William. 1993. *The Tyger*. Illustrated by Neil Waldman. Harcourt.

Frost, Robert. 1978. *Stopping by Woods on a Snowy Evening*. Illustrated by Susan Jeffers. Dutton.

Hoberman, Mary Ann. 1978. *A House Is a House for Me*. Illustrated by Betty Fraser. Viking.

Kuskin, Karla. 2002. *The Animals and the Ark*. Illustrated by Michael Grejniec. Atheneum.

Lewis, J. Patrick. 2003. *The Snowflake Sisters*. Illustrated by Lisa Desimini. Atheneum.

Longfellow, Henry Wadsworth. 1983. *Song of Hiawatha*. Illustrated by Susan Jeffers. Dial.

Longfellow, Henry Wadsworth. 2001. *The Midnight Ride of Paul Revere*. Illustrated by Christopher Bing. Handprint.

Nye, Naomi Shihab. 2003. *Baby Radar*. Illustrated by Nancy Carpenter. Greenwillow.

Prelutsky, Jack. 2001. *Awful Ogre's Awful Day*. Illustrated by Paul O. Zelinsky. Greenwillow.

Schertle, Alice. 2004. *All You Need for a Beach*. Illustrated by Barbara Lavallee. Harcourt.

Service, Robert W. 1987. *The Cremation of Sam McGee*. Illustrated by Ted Harrison. Greenwillow.

Siebert, Diane. 1989. *Heartland*. Illustrated by Wendell Minor. Crowell.

For details about books listed here and for a more complete list of poetry titles, consult the *Children's Literature Database: A Resource for Teachers, Parents, and Media Specialists* CD that accompanies this text.

REFERENCES

Attenborough, Liz. (2001). *Poetry by heart*. New York: The Chicken House (Scholastic).

Blake, William. (1993). *The tyger*. Illustrated by Neil Waldman. New York: Harcourt.

Coleridge, Samuel Taylor. (1992). *The rime of the ancient mariner*. Illustrated by Ed Young. New York: Atheneum.

Cullinan, Bernice E. (Ed.). (1996). *A jar of tiny stars: Poems by NCTE Award–winning poets*. Honesdale, PA: Wordsong/Boyds Mills.

Esbensen, Barbara Juster. (1995). *A celebration of bees: Helping children write poetry*. New York: Holt.

Fisher, Carol J., & Natarella, Margaret A. (1982). Young children's preferences in poetry: A national survey of first, second and third graders. *Research in the Teaching of English, 16*(4), 339–354.

Frost, Robert. (1978). *Stopping by woods on a snowy evening*. Illustrated by Susan Jeffers. New York: Dutton.

Harley, Avis. (2000). *Fly with poetry: An ABC of poetry*. Honesdale, PA: Wordsong/Boyds Mills Press.

Harley, Avis. (2001). *Leap into poetry: More ABCs of poetry*. Honesdale, PA: Wordsong/Boyds Mills Press.

Heller, Ruth. (1988). *Kites sail high: A Book about verbs*. New York: Grosset & Dunlap.

Heller, Ruth. (1997). *Mine, all mine: A book about pronouns*. New York: Grosset & Dunlap.

Heller, Ruth. (1998). *Fantastic! Wow! and Unreal!: A book about interjections and conjunctions*. New York: Grosset & Dunlap.

Hoberman, Mary Ann. (1994). *My song is beautiful: Poems and pictures in many voices*. Boston: Little, Brown.

Hollyer, Belinda. (2003). *The Kingfisher book of family poems*. New York: Kingfisher.

Janeczko, Paul B. (2005). *A kick in the head: An everyday guide to poetic forms*. Cambridge, MA: Candlewick.

Jones, Ivan, & Jones, Mal. (2000). *Good night, sleep tight*. New York: Scholastic.

Kutiper, Karen, & Wilson, Patricia. (1993, September). Updating poetry preferences: A look at the poetry children really like. *The Reading Teacher, 47*(1), 28–35.

Lear, Edward. (1863). *Book of nonsense*. Philadelphia: W. P. Hazard.

Livingston, Myra Cohn. (1986). *Poems for Jewish holidays*. Holiday House.

Livingston, Myra Cohn. (1987a). *Cat poems*. New York: Holiday House.

Livingston, Myra Cohn. (1987b). *Valentine poems*. New York: Holiday House.

Livingston, Myra Cohn. (1988). *Poems for mothers*. New York: Holiday House.

Livingston, Myra Cohn. (1989a). *Birthday poems.* New York: Holiday House.

Livingston, Myra Cohn. (1989b). *Halloween poems.* New York: Holiday House.

Livingston, Myra Cohn. (1994). *Animal, vegetable, mineral: Poems about small things.* New York: HarperCollins.

Livingston, Myra Cohn. (1997). *Cricket never does: A collection of haiku and tanka.* New York: McElderry.

Longfellow, Henry Wadsworth. (2001). *The midnight ride of Paul Revere.* Illustrated by Christopher Bing. New York: Handprint.

Lonsdale, Bernard J., & Mackintosh, Helen K. (1973). *Children experience literature.* New York: Random House.

Martin, Bill, Jr. (1972). *Sounds of mystery.* New York: Holt, Rinehart & Winston.

Prelutsky, Jack. (Ed). (1983). *The Random House book of poetry.* Illustrated by Arnold Lobel. New York: Random House.

Prelutsky, Jack. (1984). *The new kid on the block.* Illustrated by James Stevenson. New York: Greenwillow.

Roe, Mary F., Cuellar, Megan B., & Fickle, Michelle J. (2004). 49th Annual Meeting of the College Reading Association, Savannah, Georgia, November 5.

Silverstein, Shel. (1974). *Where the sidewalk ends.* New York: Harper.

Terry, Ann C. (1974). *Children's poetry preferences.* Urbana, IL: NCTE Research Report No. 16.

Chapter 9

Traditional Fantasy

Traditional tales had their beginnings around hearthside and campfire. The stories were almost always fantastic in nature, involving magic or talking animals. Originally, these tales provided entertainment for adults, who freely altered details as they told and retold the stories. As adults shared these stories with one another, children surely lounged about the fringes and listened. In modern times, many of the tales have shifted from their origin with adults to being identified with children.

TRADITIONAL FANTASY: A PART OF EVERY CULTURE

Because these stories were born in the oral tradition, no one knows who first told each tale and which version is the original. The definition of traditional fantasy is that the literature (1) originated orally and (2) has no author. Therefore, we often associate these tales with a collector or reteller. Jacob and Wilhelm Grimm collected, retold, and recorded in print the European variants of some of the best-known traditional tales in our Western cultures, such as "Cinderella," "Sleeping Beauty," and "Little Red Riding Hood." Other collectors include Charles Perrault, who preceded the Brothers Grimm in collecting many of the European tales. He filed off the hard edges of the tales so that they would be more acceptable to the genteel folk of the French court of Louis XIV. Joseph Jacobs collected the British tales loved by young children, such as "The Three Little Pigs" and "The Little Red Hen." Peter Asbjørnsen and Jorgen Moe gathered the Scandinavian tales into a volume titled *East of the Sun and West of the Moon,* which included "The Three Billy Goats Gruff."

Tales from the oral tradition are part of the fabric of every culture. *The 1001 Arabian Nights,* including the story of Aladdin, is a collection of the Scheherazade tales from the Middle East. Other collections of traditional tales from the Middle East include the Hodja stories from Turkey that tell of the wisdom of Nasreddin Hodja and the Jataka stories from India that are centered on the lives of Buddha. The masterful storytelling of Isaac Bashevis Singer has preserved much of the folklore of Jewish tradition. Tales of Asian, African, and Native American tradition abound and are available to children, most often in stunning picture book versions. (See the list of picture books at the conclusion of this chapter.)

Stories written by modern authors and patterned after traditional tales—such as the work of Hans Christian Andersen and Rudyard Kipling's collection of *Just-So Stories*—are often confused with traditional tales that have no authors. However, these "literary tales" are *modern fantasy* stories, for they originated in written form.

Peculiarities of Traditional Fantasy

Traditional stories differ in various ways from more modern writings, and therefore are held to a different critical standard. For example, characters must be well developed in modern stories, but in traditional tales character development is lean and spare. Think of Cinderella, for example. How rounded is her character? We know very little about her. How does she feel about her ill treatment? About her change in fortune? What are her interests? We don't even know much about her physical appearance. If listeners and readers are told about her personality or thoughts, it is only in general terms: "She wept at her mother's grave." Characters in traditional stories generally are archetypes; they are meant to be symbolic of certain basic human traits, such as good or evil. So, instead of the gradations of character in modern stories, where a character may reveal the mix of good and bad in all of us, in traditional tales we find single-faceted characters who typically do not change during the course of the story. Traditional tales, then, are stories of the human experience told in primary colors, the nuances of life stripped away to reveal the basic component parts: love, fear, greed, jealousy, mercy, and so on. Therefore, traditional stories from around the world are basically alike because fundamental human characteristics and motivations are universal.

Plots are also simple and direct in traditional fantasy. And because the tales generally were told by and among the common folk, they are often success stories that show the underdog making good—the youngest son or daughter, the little tailor, unwanted children, and so on. And success is often obtained against overwhelming odds, such as accomplishing an impossible task (spinning straw into gold, slaying invincible monsters).

These story lines are accompanied by typical themes, such as the rewards of mercy, kindness, and perseverance; justice, particularly the punishment of evil; and the power of love. Settings are quickly established and always in the distant past ("Once upon a time . . ."), and time passes quickly (Sleeping Beauty's 100 years of rest pass in a flash). Another hallmark of traditional stories is repeated patterns or elements. The magical number three appears frequently in tales: Rumpelstiltskin's three evenings of spinning straw into gold, Cinderella's three visits to the ball, Jack's three trips up the beanstalk. Or a refrain is repeated throughout the story: "Fee, fi, fo, fum. I smell the blood of an Englishman."

The Universal Nature of Traditional Fantasy

Although tales certainly vary from culture to culture, it is amazing how alike in form they are, how the basic sorts of literary elements are similar in Chinese stories, in stories from Native American tribes, and in stories from Europe (Frye, 1964). Because traditional tales deal with such basic human experiences, stories like "Cinderella" have surfaced in nearly every part of the world. The variants are different in setting and detail, but a fascinating sameness still exists. "Cinderella" variants include *Yeh-Shen* (1990; Chinese) retold by Ai-Ling Louie, *The Egyptian Cinderella* (1989; Egyptian) by Shirley Climo, *The Rough-Face Girl* (1992; Native American) by Rafe Martin, *Mufaro's Beautiful Daughters* (1987; African) by John Steptoe, *The Gift of the Crocodile* (2000; Indonesian) by Judy Sierra, and *Cinderella* (2005; French) by Barbara McClintock, to mention a few.

Another example of the pervasiveness of traditional stories in modern literature (and conversation) is the almost constant use of allusions to traditional literature. Often we speak and write using a sort of old-tale shorthand. It is a part of the cultural cement that binds us together. We nod knowingly when someone says or writes, "Misery loves company," or "You are judged by the company you keep." Both maxims come from Aesop, who either collected most of his fables from more ancient oral sources or, as some scholars believe, did not exist at all. The Greek myths and European variants of the fairy tales are alluded to continually in novels written by authors from Western cultures. Note the distinct part Red Riding Hood plays in Lois Lowry's Newbery-winning historical novel, *Number the Stars* (1989), which takes place during World War II. As Anna makes her way through the woods with a basket of food containing a hidden packet of chemicals designed to disarm the wolf's, or rather the guard dogs', ability to smell the Danish escapees, she suddenly feels as if she's walked this way before.

> The handle of the straw basket scratched her arm through her sweater. She shifted it and tried to run. She thought of a story she had often told to Kirsti as they cuddled in bed at night. "Once upon a time there was a little girl," she told herself silently, "who had a beautiful red cloak. . . . " (pp. 106–108)

In fact, we are surrounded by such allusions. We write with Venus pencils; clean with Ajax cleanser; drive on Atlas tires; use words like *volcano, furious, cereal, music;* describe the human body and mind with terms like *Achilles tendon* and *Narcissus complex;* name the planets, the days of the week, and the cities of the world (*Mars, Saturday, Atlanta*)—all from Greek and Roman myths. Perhaps one of the clearest examples of the way the old tales provide a cultural cement is evident in newspaper and magazine cartoons. The political cartoon shown in Figure 9–1 was published in the *Chicago Tribune* when a number of day-care centers in the Chicago area were charged with child abuse and molestation. Because "Hansel and Gretel" is basic to our literary culture, the cartoon needs no caption.

USING THE CHILDREN'S LITERATURE DATABASE

Be sure the CD database is installed on your hard drive. Search the database for Cinderella variants from different cultures. Click Search Query Builder in the left navigation bar on the Home screen. Type "Cinderella" in the Keyword Search field. Select the Title, Topics, and Description checkboxes. Click Run Search. Once your book list is generated, click on Constrain This List; then click Run Search. Type "Indian" in the Keyword Search field to find Native American Cinderella variants. Check the All button, and select the Title, Topics, and Description checkboxes. Click Run Search to view the revised book list.

FIGURE 9–1
Without our common knowledge of folktales, this cartoon has no meaning.

However simple and straightforward traditional fantasy may seem, it is the mother of all literature. There are literally no character types, basic plots, or themes that have not been explored in the oral tradition. Indeed, noted child psychologist Bruno Bettelheim (1977) believed that no other literature better prepares children to meet the complexities of adult life. Traditional fantasy is a wonderful metaphor for human existence, and because of its rich imagery and dreamlike quality, it speaks to us deeply. And, unless these stories have been dumbed down for printing in educational reading materials or oversimplified picture books, traditional tales are a blueprint for rich, masterful language (see the example from Randall Jarrell's translation of *Snow-White and the Seven Dwarfs* in Chapter 3).

The Values of Fantasy

Besides giving us modern readers a common ground for communicating, traditional fantasy—in fact, fantasy literature in general—offers us certain benefits that realistic fiction cannot supply with quite the same power. Lloyd Alexander (1968), who has drawn liberally from the well of ancient stories to write his modern high-fantasy books, encapsulates these benefits into four notable points:

First, on the very surface of it, the sheer delight of "let's pretend" and the eager suspension of disbelief; excitement, wonder, astonishment. There is an exuberance in good fantasy quite unlike the most exalted moments of realistic fiction. Both forms have similar goals; but realism walks where fantasy dances. . . .

[Second, fantasy has the] ability to work on our emotions with the same vividness as a dream. The fantasy adventure seems always on a larger scale, the deeds bolder, the people brighter. Reading a fantasy, we never get disinterested bystanders. To get the most from it, we have to, in the best sense of the phrase, "lose our cool. . . . "

Another value of fantasy [is its ability to develop a capacity for belief]. . . . In dealing with delinquency—I do not mean the delinquency that poverty breeds, but the kind of cold-hearted emptiness and apathy of "well-to-do," solid middle-class delinquents—one of the heart-breaking problems is interesting these young people in something. In anything. They value nothing because they have never had the experience of valuing anything. They have developed no *capacity* for believing anything to be really worthwhile.

I emphasize the word *capacity* because, in a sense, the capacity to value, to believe, is separate from the values or beliefs themselves. Our values and beliefs can change. The capacity remains.

Whether the object of value is Santa Claus or Sunday school, the Prophet Elijah or Arthur, the Once and Future King, does not make too much difference. Having once believed wholeheartedly in something, we seldom lose the ability to believe. . . .

Perhaps, finally, the ability to hope is more important than the ability to believe. . . . Hope is one of the most precious human values fantasy can offer us—and offer us in abundance. Whatever the hardships of the journey, the days of despair, fantasy implicitly promises to lead us through them. Hope is an essential thread in the fabric of all fantasies, an Ariadne's thread to guide us out of the labyrinth, the last treasure in Pandora's box. . . .*

TYPES OF TRADITIONAL FANTASY

Categories of any genre of literature are never cast in concrete. People will never agree on category names or on whether certain stories belong under certain category headings. Traditional fantasy is no different in this respect. However, we will present our view of what constitutes traditional stories, keeping in mind that this list is mostly a tool for introducing you to the stories themselves.

FOLKTALES. Quite rightly, all traditional stories could be called *folktales* or stories of the people. We will use this heading to encompass a number of stories that are the most general or universal in nature. The most common kinds of folktales follow.

- *Cumulative tales.* These stories are "added upon" as the telling unfolds. Typically, the story is told up to a certain point, then begun again from near the beginning and told until a new segment is added. Then the teller starts again and

---

*Reprinted with permission of Lloyd Alexander from "Wishful Thinking—or Hopeful Dreaming." *The Horn Book, 44* (August 1968): 387–390.

again, each time adding a new wrinkle to the story, expanding a chain of events or a list of participants. Probably the best-known examples are the reasonably simple cumulative tale "The House That Jack Built" and the folk song "I Know an Old Lady Who Swallowed a Fly."

- *Pourquoi tales.* *Pourquoi* means "why" in French. These folktales answer questions or give explanations for the way things are, particularly in nature. Examples are "Why the Bear Is Stumpy-Tailed" or *Why Mosquitoes Buzz in People's Ears* (1975), as retold by Verna Aardema.

- *Beast tales.* Their distinction is simple: Beast tales are stories with animals as the principal players. The animals typically represent humans and are therefore anthropomorphized, such as the animals in "The Three Little Pigs" and "The Three Billy Goats Gruff."

- *Trickster tales.* Often a variety of beast tale, the trickster tale features a character who outsmarts everyone else in the story. Sometimes the trickster is sly and mischievous (Br'er Rabbit from the Uncle Remus stories). In other stories, the trickster is wise and helpful, as with some of the Anansi the Spider folktales from Africa (see the Caldecott-winning *A Story, a Story* by Gail Haley, 1970). Other examples include Gerald McDermott's Native American trickster tales, such as *Raven* (1993), *Coyote* (1994), and *Jabuti the Tortoise* (2001).

- *Noodlehead, or numbskull, tales.* These humorous stories center on the escapades of characters who are not too bright. Sometimes they really make a mess of things with their incredibly stupid mistakes, as in the story "Epaminondas," in which a silly boy nearly destroys a number of items placed in his charge because he follows the wrong instructions for their care. For example, he is told to wrap butter in leaves and dip it in cool water to keep it in good shape. But then he uses those instructions with a puppy. In other stories, such as the Grimms' "Hans in Luck," the simpleton stumbles merrily through life, coming out on top only because of providence.

- *Realistic tales.* Realistic tales seem to have their basis in an actual historical event or to feature an actual figure from history. These folktales have few, if any, elements of fantasy. An example is "Dick Whittington's Cat," the story of a country boy who goes to London during the reign of King Edward III. Dick, who makes his fortune because his cat is such a fine mouser, later goes on to become the mayor of London. Though the tale is likely fictional, the real Dick Whittington did, indeed, become London's mayor, as well as the town's sheriff.

- *Fairy tales.* Of all the folktales, the fairy tale, or wonder tale, is the most magical. In fairy tales we see enchantments that go beyond talking animals to fairy godmothers, wicked witches, magical objects (mirrors, cloaks, swords, rings), and the like. (See Chapter 10 for a discussion of fantasy motifs.) Fairy tales are extremely popular with young listeners and readers. "Snow White," "Cinderella," "Sleeping Beauty," "Beauty and the Beast," and "Aladdin and His Wonderful Lamp" are a few examples of well-known fairy tales.

FIGURE 9–2
Notable retellers and illustrators of traditional stories.

The names in this list include influential retellers and illustrators of traditional stories other than the pioneers who first preserved these tales in print (Brothers Grimm, Joseph Jacobs, Charles Perrault, and others).

Aardema, Verna (reteller): *African folktales.*

Bierhorst, John (reteller): *Native American folktales.*

Brown, Marcia (reteller and illustrator): *Folktales from a variety of cultures.*

Bruchac, Joseph (reteller): *Native American folktales.*

Dillon, Leo and Diane (illustrators): *African folktales.*

Evslin, Bernard (reteller): *Greek myths.*

Fisher, Leonard Everett (reteller and illustrator): *Greek myths.*

Hamilton, Virginia (reteller): *Folktale collections, primarily African American.*

Hutton, Warwick (reteller and illustrator): *Bible stories.*

Hyman, Trina Schart (illustrator): *European fairy tales.*

Kimmel, Eric (reteller): *Folktales from around the world.*

McDermott, Gerald (reteller and illustrator): *Myths and folktales from various cultures.*

San Souci, Robert D. (reteller): *Myths and folktales from various cultures.*

Singer, Isaac Bashevis: *Jewish traditional tales.*

Sutcliff, Rosemary (reteller): *Arthurian and Greek myths and legends.*

Yolen, Jane (reteller): *Mostly European myths, legends, and fairy tales.*

Young, Ed (reteller and illustrator): *Asian folklore.*

Zelinsky, Paul O. (reteller and illustrator): *European fairy tales.*

Zwerger, Lisbeth (illustrator): *European fairy tales.*

TALL TALES.   Exaggeration is the major stylistic element in tall tales. Many tall tales grew out of the push to open the North American continent to settlement. Tall-tale characters, such as Paul Bunyan, Pecos Bill, Johnny Appleseed, John Henry, and Old Stormalong, were based either on actual people or on a composite of rough-and-tumble lumberjacks, sailors, or cowboys. Tall tales, of course, exist beyond our American culture. For instance, the Chinese tale "The Seven [or Five] Chinese Brothers," tells of several brothers who use amazing talents, such as the ability to swallow an entire sea, to ward off the conquests of an evil emperor.

FABLES.   Fables are brief stories meant to teach a lesson, and they usually conclude with a moral, such as "A bird in the hand is worth two in the bush" or "Haste makes waste." Besides the well-known collection of Aesop's fables from Greece, there are fables in ancient Egyptian culture, in the *Panchatantra* and the Jataka stories from India, plus a collection of fables by French poet Jean de La Fontaine.

MYTHS.   Myths grew out of early people's need to understand and explain the world around them and their own existence; they therefore recount the creation of the world and tell of the gods and goddesses who control the fate of humans. Many myths are

similar to pourquoi folktales because they explain nature. For example, the Greek myth of Apollo explains how and why the sun travels across the sky each day. Gerald McDermott's *Musicians of the Sun* (1997), a retelling of an Aztec myth, explains how music and color came into the world. Every culture has its myths, although the Greek myths are perhaps the best known in the Western world. The international flavor of mythology is evident in Virginia Hamilton's collection of creation myths, *In the Beginning: Creation Stories from Around the World* (1988).

One variety of myth focuses on the heroic quest rather than on the mysteries of planet Earth. The hero myth, such as the story "Jason and the Argonauts," is a grand adventure that usually involves the intervention of heavenly beings. The hero myth is related to the epic.

EPICS, BALLADS, AND LEGENDS.   The line separating epics, ballads, and legends tends to blur. The unifying feature is the hero tale, including hero myths, but epics, ballads, and legends also have distinguishing qualities.

- Epics are lengthy hero tales or even a series of tales focusing on a hero. Examples are the tales of the Trojan War (*The Iliad*) and the return of Odysseus (Ulysses) from Troy to his home in Ithaca (*The Odyssey*). Both of these epics are also steeped in the mythology of ancient Greece. *Beowulf,* the most famous piece of Old English literature, is another well-known epic.
- Ballads are typically hero stories in poetic form. Both *The Iliad* and *The Odyssey* are epic poems supposedly composed by the blind poet Homer, whose existence is doubted by some scholars, although others regard him as the recorder of a much-retold set of tales. In Europe, the bards of old traveled from stronghold to stronghold, entertaining the people by singing ballads about local mythological and legendary heroes.
- The heroes in legends are rooted a bit more firmly in history. So, *The Iliad* could be considered an epic and a legendary ballad, since the Greeks actually laid seige to Troy. King Arthur also lives in epic, ballad, and legend. There are mythic stories of Arthur as well as historical accounts that indicate that he indeed existed and unified the British tribes around 500 C.E. Robin Hood, though probably more thief than hero, is a character from ballad and legend. Of course, legendary characters also appear in the tall tales of North America (Mike Fink, Davy Crockett, Johnny Appleseed, John Henry, Casey Jones) and in realistic folktales.

RELIGIOUS STORIES.   Classifying religious stories as traditional fantasy or as myths may bother many people, but *myth* in this sense can be broadly defined as the human quest to discover and share truth concerning the spiritual aspects of existence. Stories derived from the sacred writings of Buddhism, Christianity, Hinduism, Islam, and other religions of the world contribute to this arena of traditional literature.

Books and stories in this category include parables and Old Testament stories, as well as any number of legends or apocryphal tales with religious connections, such as Ruth Robbins's *Baboushka and the Three Kings* (1960) or Tomie dePaola's *The Legend of Old Befana* (1980)—both variants of a Christmas story about an old woman too busy to follow the Three Wise Men. Other examples include *Buddha Stories* (1997), the Jataka tales retold by Demi; *And the Earth Trembled* (1996), an Islamic version of the creation of Adam and Eve by Shulamith Levey Oppenheim; *Rama: A Legend* (1994) by Jamake Highwater, a novel based on a Hindu epic; and *Creation* (2003) by Gerald McDermott.

IN DEFENSE OF TRADITIONAL FANTASY

"About once every hundred years some wiseacre gets up and tries to banish the fairy tale. Perhaps I had better say a few words in its defence, as reading for children" (Lewis, 1980, p. 213). These words by C. S. Lewis, who is known for his enduring fantasy series, the Narnia Chronicles, were written as part of his defense of traditional tales in 1952. Yet, in far less than 100 years—in fact, on a regular basis—"wiseacres" have been attempting to censor traditional stories. We have already discussed the importance of fairy and folktales but now wish to provide some responses to the major complaints voiced against traditional literature. These objections mainly fall into four categories: psychological fantasy, violence, frightening to young children, and waste of time (Tunnell, 1994).

Psychological Fantasy

Some adults fear that fantasy stories will lead children to be somehow out of touch with reality, to suffer from fantasy in the clinical, psychological sense of the word. Psychological fantasy—the inability of the mind to distinguish what is real—does not result from reading literary fantasy. In fact, children who read stories that contain "unrealistic" elements—animals that talk, magical events, time travel—are actually less at risk of losing touch with the realities of daily life. Bruno Bettelheim (1977) confirmed this position when he said that fairy stories are not only safe for children, but also necessary, and that children deprived of a rich fantasy life (which traditional tales provide) are more likely to seek a psychological escape through avenues such as black magic, drugs, or astrology. Through fairy and folktales, children may vicariously vent the frustrations of being a child controlled by an adult world, for they subconsciously identify with the heroes of the stories, who are often the youngest, smallest, least powerful characters (Hansel and Gretel, Cinderella, Aladdin). They also are given a sense of hope about their ultimate abilities to succeed in the world.

C. S. Lewis goes a step further, believing that certain realistic stories are far more likely to cause problems than good fantasy. He points to adult reading as an example:

> The dangerous fantasy is always superficially realistic. The real victim of wishful reverie . . . prefers stories about millionaires, irresistible beauties, posh hotels, palm beaches, and bedroom scenes—things that really might happen, that ought to happen, that would have happened if the reader had had a fair chance. [T]here are two kinds of longing. The one is an askesis, a spiritual exercise, and the other is a disease. (1980, p. 215)

Violence

Critics suggest that violent acts in some traditional tales will breed violence in young children. The work of psychologist Ephraim Biblow shows how wrong-minded this sort of thinking is. In his experimental study, Biblow (1973) showed that children with rich fantasy lives responded to aggressive films with a significant decrease in aggressive behavior, while "low-fantasy" children showed a tendency toward increased aggression.

> The low-fantasy child, as observed during play, presented himself as more motorically oriented, revealed much action and little thought in play activities. The high-fantasy child in contrast was more highly structured and creative and tended to be verbally rather than physically aggressive. (p. 128)

Much of the violence in fairy and folktales involves the punishment of truly evil villains. Children are concerned from an early age with the ramifications of good and bad behavior, which is represented in fundamental, archetypal ways in traditional stories. Lawrence Kohlberg's stages of moral development describe the young child as being in the "premoral stage" (up to about 8 years), which basically means that "the child believes that evil behavior is likely to be punished and good behavior is based on obedience or avoidance of evil implicit in disobedience" (Lefrancois 1986, p. 446). According to Bettelheim (1977), the evil person in fairy tales who meets a well-deserved fate satisfies a child's deep need for justice to prevail. Sometimes this requires destroying the evil altogether.

Violence in movies and many books cannot be equated with the violence in fairy and folktales. Even in the Grimms' version of "Cinderella," one of the bloodiest of fairy stories, the violent acts are surprisingly understated. Both truly wicked stepsisters mutilate themselves (a trimmed heel and a cut-off toe) to make the slipper fit and are revealed by the blood. Later, birds peck out their eyes as punishment for their treachery. Yet, the tale simply, compactly states the fact of each violent act. We don't read of viscous fluid streaming down faces or blood spurting on walls and floors. That's the stuff of slasher horror movies and violent video games, sensationalism designed to shock or titillate, but not a careful comment on justice.

Frightening for Young Children

Many adults worry that some of the traditional tales will frighten children, causing nightmares and other sorts of distress. However, because dangerous story elements, such as wicked witches or dragons, are far removed in both time and place from the lives of children, they prove much less frightening than realistic stories of danger that focus on real-life fears (Smith, 1989). Lewis felt that insulating a child completely from fear was a disservice. "Since it is so likely they will meet cruel enemies, let them at least have heard of brave knights and heroic courage. Otherwise you are making their destiny not bright but darker" (Lewis, 1980, p. 216).

Fairy and folktales provide children a message of hope. No matter how bleak the outlook or how dark the path, these stories promise children that it is possible to make it through and come out on top. In fact, children who recoil from strong images of danger in fairy tales have the most to gain from the exposure (Smith, 1989).

Some adults feel they can circumvent the problem of frightening children by choosing softened versions of fairy and folktales. This approach may have the opposite effect, causing children to become more distressed. Trousdale (1989) tells the story of a mother who used only the softened version of "The Three Little Pigs" with her young daughter. In this version the pigs are not eaten, and the wolf is not killed in boiling water. Instead, he comes down the chimney, burns his derriere, rockets up the chimney, and disappears into the sunset, never to be seen again. The little girl said, "He's gonna come back," and began to have nightmares. Trousdale (p. 77) advised the child's mother to read the Joseph Jacobs version, in which the wolf dies; Trousdale soon received a letter that said, "Well, we put the Big Bad Wolf to rest." The evil was destroyed and thus the threat eliminated. The nightmares stopped.

Waste of Time

Perhaps the most insidious complaint is that traditional fantasy is a waste of time. Some adults simply bypass fairy or folktales when making selections to use with children in favor of more "substantial" stories and books about the real world. However, no genre of literature better fosters creativity than fantasy (both modern and traditional). Recall that Biblow's study showed high-fantasy children to be "more highly structured and creative." Russian poet Kornei Chukovsky (1968) claims that fantasy is "the most valuable attribute of the human mind and should be diligently nurtured from the earliest age" (p. 17). He even points out that great scientists have acknowledged this fact and quotes eminent British physicist John Tindale:

> Without the participation of fantasy . . . all our knowledge about nature would have been limited merely to the classification of obvious facts. The relation between cause and effect and their interaction would have gone unnoticed, thus stemming the progress of science itself, because it is the main function of science to establish the link between the different manifestations of nature, since creative fantasy is the ability to perceive more and more such links. (Chukovsky, 1968, p. 124)

As the story goes, a woman with a mathematically gifted son asked Albert Einstein how she should best foster his talent. After a moment of thought, Einstein answered, "Read him the great myths of the past—stretch his imagination" (Huck, 1982, p. 316). Teachers bemoan the lack of creative and critical thinking in today's students. How can we then not promote the very books and stories that cultivate imaginative thought?

TRADITIONAL FANTASY READING LIST

TEN OF OUR FAVORITES

COLLECTIONS AND CHAPTER BOOKS

Hamilton, Virginia. 1988. *In the Beginning: Creation Stories from Around the World.* Illustrated by Barry Moser. Harcourt. An illustrated collection of 25 myths from various cultures explaining the creation of the world. A Newbery Honor Book.

Manushkin, Fran. 2001. *Daughters of Fire: Heroines of the Bible*. Illustrated by Uri Shulevitz. Silver Whistle/Harcourt. Eleven stories about women of the Hebrew Bible who influenced the course of Jewish history through their courageous actions.

Osborne, Mary Pope. 1998. *Favorite Medieval Tales*. Illustrated by Troy Howell. Scholastic. A collection of well-known tales from medieval Europe, including "Beowulf," "The Sword in the Stone," "The Song of Roland," and "Gudren and the Island of the Lost Children."

Soifer, Margaret, and Irwin Shapiro. 1957 (reissued 2003). *Golden Tales from the Arabian Nights*. Illustrated by Gustaf Tenggren. Random House. Illustrated retellings of 10 stories of Scheherazade, along with the legend of how they came to be told.

Sutcliff, Rosemary. 1996. *The Wanderings of Odysseus: The Story of the Odyssey*. Illustrated by Alan Lee. Delacorte. A retelling of the adventures of Odysseus on his long voyage home from the Trojan War.

PICTURE BOOKS

Dillon, Leo, and Diane Dillon. 1998. *To Every Thing There Is a Season: From Ecclesiastes*. New York: Scholastic. The text is taken from the King James version of the Bible (Ecclesiastes chapter 3, verses 1–8) and each verse is illustrated in the traditional artistic style of a different ancient culture.

Grimm Brothers (translated by Randall Jarrell). 1972. *Snow-White and the Seven Dwarfs*. Illustrated by Nancy Ekholm Burkert. Farrar. A beautifully illustrated rendition of the classic fairy tale. A Caldecott Honor Book.

Hasting, Selina. 1985. *Sir Gawain and the Loathly Lady*. Illustrated by Juan Wijngaard. Lothrop. After a horrible hag saves King Arthur's life by answering a riddle, Sir Gawain agrees to marry her and thus releases her from an evil enchantment.

Steptoe, John. 1987. *Mufaro's Beautiful Daughters: An African Tale*. Lothrop. Mufaro's two beautiful daughters, one bad-tempered, one kind and sweet, go before the king, who is choosing a wife. An African variant of Cinderella. A Caldecott Honor Book.

Zelinsky, Paul O. 1997. *Rapunzel*. Dutton. The author melded several versions of the Rapunzel story in creating this unique telling. Caldecott Medal.

OTHERS WE LIKE

CHAPTER BOOKS AND COLLECTIONS

Doherty, Berlie. 1998. *Tales of Wonder and Magic*. Illustrated by Juan Wijngaard. Candlewick.

Garland, Sherry. 2001. *Children of the Dragon: Selected Tales from Vietnam*. Illustrated by Trina Schart Hyman. Harcourt.

Harris, Joel Chandler (adapted by Van Dyke Parks and Malcolm Jones). 1986. *Jump! The Adventures of Brer Rabbit*. Illustrated by Barry Moser. Harcourt.

Heaney, Marie. 2000. *The Names upon the Harp*. Illustrated by P. J. Lynch. Scholastic.

Lively, Penelope. 2001. *In Search of a Homeland: The Story of the Aeneid*. Illustrated by Ian Andrew. Delacorte.

McKissack, Patricia C. 1992. *The Dark-Thirty*. Illustrated by Brian Pinkney. Knopf.

Osborne, Mary Pope. 1996. *Favorite Norse Myths*. Illustrated by Troy Howell. Scholastic.

Pinkney, Jerry. 2000. *Aesop's Fables*. SeaStar.

Sutcliff, Rosemary. 1981. *The Sword and the Circle*. Dutton. (See others in this Arthur trilogy.)

Sutcliff, Rosemary. 1981. *Tristan and Iseult*. Dutton.

Vinge, Joan D. 1999. *The Random House Book of Greek Myths*. Illustated by Oren Sherman. Random.

Yolen, Jane. 2003. *Mightier Than the Sword: World Folktales for Strong Boys*. Illustrated by Raul Colón. Harcourt.

PICTURE BOOKS

Aardema, Verna. 1975. *Why Mosquitoes Buzz in People's Ears*. Illustrated by Leo and Diane Dillon. Dial.

DeFelice, Cynthia. 2000. *Cold Feet*. Illustrated by Robert Andrew Parker. Dorling Kindersley.

Demi. 1997. *One Grain of Rice*. Scholastic.

Goble, Paul. 1985. *The Girl Who Loved Wild Horses*. Bradbury.

Grimm Brothers. 1975. *Thorn Rose*. Illustrated by Errol Le Cain. Bradbury.

Grimm Brothers. 1983. *Little Red Riding Hood*. Illustrated by Trina Schart Hyman. Holiday House.

Grimm Brothers (retold by Barbara Rogasky). 1986. *The Water of Life*. Illustrated by Trina Schart Hyman. Holiday House.

Hamilton, Virginia. 2000. *The Girl Who Spun Gold*. Illustrated by Leo and Diane Dillon. Scholastic.

Hodges, Margaret. 2004. *Merlin and the Making of a King*. Illustrated by Trina Schart Hyman. Holiday.

Hofmeyr, Dianne. 2001. *The Star Bearer: A Creation Story from Ancient Egypt*. Illustrated by Jude Daly. Farrar.

Isaacs, Anne. 1994. *Swamp Angel*. Illustrated by Paul O. Zelinsky. Dutton.

Johnson-Davies, Denys. 2005. *Goha the Wise Fool*. Illustrated by Hag Hamdy and Hany. Philomel.

Kellogg, Stephen. 1986. *Pecos Bill*. Morrow.

Kimmel, Eric. 2005. *The Hero Beowulf*. Illustrated by Leonard Everett Fisher. Farrar.

Lester, Julius. 1994. *John Henry*. Illustrated by Jerry Pinkney. Dial.

Louie, Ai-Ling. 1982. *Yeh-Shen: A Cinderella Story from China*. Illustrated by Ed Young. Philomel.

Martin, Rafe. 1992. *The Rough-Face Girl*. Illustrated by David Shannon. Putnam.

Mayer, Marianna. 1978 (reissued 2000). *Beauty and the Beast*. Illustrated by Mercer Mayer. SeaStar.

Mayer, Marianna. 1998. *Pegasus*. Illustrated by K. Y. Craft. Morrow.

McDermott, Gerald. 1974. *Arrow to the Sun*. Viking.

McDermott, Gerald. 2001. *Jabuti the Tortoise*. Harcourt.

Moser, Barry. 2001. *The Three Little Pigs*. Little, Brown.

Moses, Will. 2006. *Hansel & Gretel*. Philomel.

Perrault, Charles (translated by Malcolm Arthur). 1990. *Puss in Boots*. Illustrated by Fred Marcellino. Farrar.

Pinkney, Jerry. 2006. *The Little Red Hen*. Dial.

San Souci, Robert. 1989. *The Talking Eggs*. Illustrated by Jerry Pinkney. Dial.

San Souci, Robert. 2004. *The Well at the End of the World*. Illustrated by Rebecca Walsh. Chronicle.

Shannon, Mark. 1994. *Gawain and the Green Knight*. Illustrated by David Shannon. Putnam.

Shepard, Aaron. 2003. *The Princess and the Mouse: A Tale of Finland*. Illustrated by Leonid Gore. Atheneum.

Wiesner, David, and Kim Kahng. 2005. *The Loathsome Dragon*. Illustrated by David Wiesner. Clarion.

Wisniewski, David. 1996. *Golem*. Clarion.

For details about books listed here and for a more complete list of traditional fantasy titles, consult the Children's Literature Database: A Resource for Teachers, Parents, and Media Specialists CD *that accompanies this text.*

REFERENCES

Aardema, Verna. (1975). *Why mosquitoes buzz in people's ears*. New York: Dial.

Alexander, Lloyd. (1968, August). Wishful thinking—or hopeful dreaming. *The Horn Book, 44* 382–390.

Bettelheim, Bruno. (1977). *The uses of enchantment: The meaning and importance of fairy tales*. New York: Vintage.

Biblow, Ephraim. (1973). Imaginative play and the control of aggressive behavior. In Jerome L. Singer (Ed.), *The child's world of make-believe* (pp. 104–128). New York: Academic Press.

Chukovsky, Kornei. (1968). *From two to five*. Los Angeles: University of California Press.

Climo, Shirley. (1989). *The Egyptian Cinderella*. New York: Harper.

Demi. (1997). *Buddha stories*. New York: Holt.

dePaola, Tomie. (1980). *The legend of Old Befana*. New York: Harcourt.

Frye, Northrop. (1964). *The educated imagination*. Bloomington: University of Indiana Press.

Haley, Gail. (1970). *A story, a story*. New York: Atheneum.

Hamilton, Virginia. (1988). *In the beginning: Creation stories from around the world*. New York: Harcourt.

Highwater, Jamake. (1994). *Rama: A legend*. New York: Harper.

Huck, Charlotte. (1982, Autumn). I give you the end of a golden string. *Theory into Practice, 12*(4), 315–325.

Lefrancois, Guy R. (1986). *Of children*. Belmont, CA: Wadsworth.

Lewis, C. S. (1980). On three ways of writing for children. In Sheila Egoff, G. T. Stubbs, & L. F. Ashley (Eds.), *Only connect* (pp. 207–220). New York: Oxford University Press.

Louie, Ai-Ling. (1990). *Yeh-Shen*. New York: Philomel.

Lowry, Lois. (1989). *Number the stars*. Boston: Houghton Mifflin.

Martin, Rafe. (1992). *The rough-face girl*. New York: Putnam.

McClintock, Barbara. (2005). *Cinderella*. New York: Scholastic.

McDermott, Gerald. (1993). *Raven*. New York: Harcourt.

McDermott, Gerald. (1994). *Coyote*. New York: Harcourt.

McDermott, Gerald. (1997). *Musicians of the sun*. New York: Simon & Schuster.

McDermott, Gerald. (2001). *Jabuti the tortoise: A trickster tale from the Amazon*. New York: Harcourt.

McDermott, Gerald. (2003). *Creation*. New York: Dutton.

Oppenheim, Shulamith Levey. (1996). *And the Earth trembled: The creation of Adam and Eve.* New York: Harcourt.

Robbins, Ruth. (1960). *Baboushka and the three kings.* New York: Parnassus.

Sierra, Judy. (2000). *The gift of the crocodile: A Cinderella story.* New York: Simon & Schuster.

Smith, Charles A. (1989). *From wonder to wisdom.* New York: New American Library.

Steptoe, John. (1987). *Mufaro's beautiful daughters.* New York: Lothrop.

Trousdale, Ann. (1989, June). Who's afraid of the big bad wolf? *Children's Literature in Education, 20*(2), 68–79.

Tunnell, Michael O. (1994). The double-edged sword: Fantasy and censorship. *Language Arts, 71*(8), 606–612.

Chapter **10**

Modern Fantasy

And so they lived many happy years, and the promised tasks were accomplished. Yet long afterward, when all had passed away into distant memory, there were many who wondered whether King Taran, Queen Eilonwy, and their companions had indeed walked the earth, or whether they had been no more than dreams in a tale set down to beguile children. And, in time, only the bards knew the truth of it. (Alexander 1968a, p. 285)

Lloyd Alexander's epic five-book fantasy series called The Prydain Chronicles ends with these words in *The High King.* Those who have lived vicariously in the imaginary kingdom of Prydain and survived its trials with Taran and Eilonwy yearn to hold on to those golden, mythical times as surely as we reach out longingly to hold onto a pleasant dream. This is the legacy traditional fantasy gives to modern fantasy—a sense of the magical that extends back to our ancient roots. "Magic had its feet under the earth and its hair above the clouds. . . . [In] the beginning, Magic was everywhere and nowhere" (Colwell, 1968, p. 178).

A DEFINITION OF MODERN FANTASY

As with traditional fantasy, modern fantasy is distinguished from other genres by story elements that violate the natural, physical laws of our known world—events akin to magic. However, modern fantasy has known authors.

The application of these miraculous elements varies greatly in modern fantasy stories: talking animals, imaginary worlds, fanciful characters (hobbits, dwarves, giants), magical beings (witches, sorcerers, genies), and so on. However, quality fantasy stories do not employ fantastic elements casually. In fact, fantasy is probably the most difficult genre to write because an author must create a new set of physical laws and then conform unerringly to them. A tiny slip can destroy the credibility of a story. Lloyd Alexander recognizes the need for this sort of specialized internal consistency:

Once committed to his imaginary kingdom, the writer is not a monarch but a subject. Characters must appear plausible in their own setting, and the writer must go along with

116

the inner logic. Happenings should have logical implications. Details should be tested for consistency. Shall animals speak? If so, do *all* animals speak? If not, then which—and how? Is it essential to the story, or lamely cute? Are there enchantments? How powerful? If an enchanter can perform such-and-such, can he not also do so-and-so? (1965, pp. 143–144)

Modern fantasy stories are not merely a matter of make-believe. Critics hold this genre to the same basic critical standards as they do other genres. For instance, modern fantasy must have strong, believable characters; a strong, credible plot, and should examine issues of the human condition—the universal truths found in well-written books.

CATEGORIES OF MODERN FANTASY

Modern fantasy stories are sometimes categorized by the type of fantastic story element employed. *Animal fantasy,* for example, is the tag often given to stories that depart from reality exclusively because of talking animals, such as E. B. White's immortal *Charlotte's Web* (1952), Brian Jacques's popular Redwall series (beginning with *Redwall,* 1987), or Michael Hoeye's stories of Hermux Tantamoq, the intrepid watchmaker mouse (*No Time Like Show Time* [2004] and others). Other categories, and titles that exemplify each, include the following:

- Toys and objects imbued with life: *Pinocchio* by Carlo Collodi (1904), *The Mennyms* by Sylvia Waugh (1994)
- Tiny humans: *The Borrowers* by Mary Norton (1953), *The Various* by Steve Augarde (2004)
- Peculiar characters and situations: *Mary Poppins* by P. L. Travers (1934), *Skellig* by David Almond (1999)
- Imaginary worlds: *Alice's Adventures in Wonderland* by Lewis Carroll (1865), *The Amber Spyglass* by Philip Pullman (2000)
- Magical powers: *The Chocolate Touch* by Patrick Catling (1979), *Harry Potter and the Half-Blood Prince* by J. K. Rowling (2005)
- Supernatural tales: *Wait Till Helen Comes: A Ghost Story* by Mary Downing Hahn (1985), *Stonewords* by Pam Conrad (1990)
- Time-warp fantasies: *Tom's Midnight Garden* by Philippa Pearce (1958), *King of Shadows* by Susan Cooper (1999)
- High fantasy: *The Lion, the Witch and the Wardrobe* by C. S. Lewis (1950), *The High King* by Lloyd Alexander (1968a)

Modern fairy and folktales, or literary tales, round out this list. As discussed in the last chapter, modern fairy and folktales are written in the form of the ageless traditional

 USING THE CHILDREN'S LITERATURE DATABASE

Be sure the CD database is installed on your hard drive. Go to the Book List in the left navigation bar on the Home screen. Select New Search, and click on Run Search. Enter "Fantasy and Animals" in the Keyword Search field. Check the All button, as well as the Title, Topics, and Description boxes. Click Run Search. After your search is complete, click on the Title column to sort by title. Click on the Omit button (located to the right of each record) for titles that might not be of interest to you. When you are finished, create your final list by clicking on Save This List as Set in the top navigation bar. Give your saved set a name (in the pop-up window), and click Submit.

tales, which were passed from generation to generation by word of mouth. Although a number of authors have written modern folktales—Oscar Wilde, George MacDonald, Rudyard Kipling, and Jane Yolen, to name a few—the stories of Hans Christian Andersen are perhaps the best known, such as "The Little Mermaid" and "The Steadfast Tin Soldier." Fractured folktales and fairy tales, such as *The True Story of the 3 Little Pigs!* by Jon Scieszka (1989) or *Rumpelstiltskin's Daughter* by Diane Stanley (1997), also fall into this category.

SIX BASIC FANTASY MOTIFS

Even though all modern fantasy stories contain some sort of magical element, some stories have a higher fantasy quotient than others. Madsen (1976) identified six basic fantasy motifs; if a story contains all six, it is either a classic fairy tale or an example of modern high fantasy. However, if a story contains fantasy's one necessary ingredient, the motif of magic or the violation of our world's physical laws, it is still classified as fantasy literature. *Winnie the Pooh.*

1. *Magic.* Magic is fantasy literature's most basic element. In fact, each of the other five motifs is tinged by magic to some degree. Magic is often a part of the setting, explaining otherwise inexplicable events. In Lloyd Alexander's *The High King* (1968a), magic is evident in the very fabric of the mythical land of Prydain. Powerful wizards are able to harness the magic in Prydain's atmosphere, an oracular pig can foretell the future, and people try to use magical objects to manipulate their destinies. However, in White's *Charlotte's Web* (1952), the only hint of magic is the ability of the barnyard animals to think and speak like humans. In fact, magic is the only one of the six motifs that appears in the book.

2. *Other worlds (secondary worlds).* In much of fantasy, a special geography or universe is established, a place wherein magic may freely operate. Sometimes these worlds are, as in the fairy tales, simply long, long ago. Alexander's Prydain is just this sort of place, almost recognizable as the world we know, but governed by a different set of rules.

   Authors employ two common methods of incorporating a secondary world into their stories. The first and most common is simply setting the entire tale in an imaginary place, as with the lands of Prydain (*The Book of Three* by Lloyd Alexander, 1964) and Middle Earth (*The Hobbit* by J. R. R. Tolkien, 1937). The second method takes characters from our primary world into a secondary world through some sort of portal. Classic examples include the tornado whisking Dorothy to the land of Oz (*The Wonderful Wizard of Oz* by L. Frank Baum, 1900), the Pevensie children's passage through the wardrobe into Narnia (*The Lion, the Witch and the Wardrobe* by C. S. Lewis, 1950), and Wendy and her siblings' magic flight to Neverland (*Peter Pan* by J. M. Barrie, 1906). Yet another example is when Harry Potter walks through a solid barrier onto Platform Nine and Three-Quarters, thus entering the magical world of Hogwarts School (*Harry Potter and the Sorcerer's Stone* by J. K. Rowling, 1998).

3. *Good versus evil.* The ancient, archetypal theme of good versus evil is what myth is all about, and modern fantasy stories often have a strong mythological base. "Fantasies are concerned with how good and evil manifest themselves in individuals" (Madsen, 1976, p. 49). This basic theme, of course, gives rise to the conflict in a story, and, once again, without conflict there is no story. Fantasy readers usually have no trouble aligning characters on the sides of light or dark, as fantasy characters typically are not fence-sitters.

4. *Heroism.* Natalie Babbitt (1987), drawing on the writings of mythologist Joseph Campbell (1968), explains that the hero's quest will always follow an age-old pattern that is the backbone of many of today's fantasy stories. This "hero's round" is a circular journey, ending where it began. It is a time-honored template for various types of stories, though the hero's quest originated in traditional fantasy. The following six elements, drawn from Babbitt (1987), most commonly structure the hero's quest:

   - *The hero is called to adventure by some sort of herald.* Taran in Alexander's Prydain Chronicles (see Alexander, 1964) is lured to adventure by Hen Wen, a magical pig whom he follows on a wild chase much the same way Alice follows the white rabbit (*Alice's Adventures in Wonderland*). Heralds from other stories include Gandalf (*The Hobbit*), Toto (*The Wonderful Wizard of Oz*), Mr. Tumnus (*The Lion, the Witch and the Wardrobe*), and Hagrid (*Harry Potter and the Sorcerer's Stone*).

   - *The hero crosses the threshold into the other world or into a place that is no longer safe and secure.* The hero leaves a place of relative safety and enters a world of danger. Sometimes he or she passes from the familiar modern world into a forbidding secondary world, as when the children pass through the magical wardrobe into the land of Narnia (*The Lion, the Witch and the Wardrobe*) or when Dorothy is whisked from Kansas to Oz (*The Wonderful Wizard of Oz*). In some stories, the hero already lives in an imaginary kingdom, as Bilbo Baggins does in *The Hobbit,* and is compelled to leave hearth and home to undertake a perilous journey.

   - *The hero must survive various trials in the new environment.* Heroes often face both physical hardship and emotional setbacks. They may suffer the misery of long treks through bitter winter weather or the pain of having dear friends relinquish their lives for a noble cause. They likely will be driven to examine their own hearts. The quest becomes the hero's refining fire.

   - *The hero is assisted by a protective figure.* Protective figures provide a sense of security in a tension-filled world. Older, wiser, and sometimes more powerful, the protective figure may serve as the hero's mentor. Readers will identify Dallben (The Prydain Chronicles); Gandalf (*The Hobbit*); Glinda, the Good Witch of the North (*The Wonderful Wizard of Oz*); Aslan (*The Lion, the Witch and the Wardrobe*); and Professor Dumbledore (*Harry Potter and the Sorcerer's Stone*) as protective figures.

   - *The hero matures, becoming a "whole person."* Did Edmund change in *The Lion, the Witch and the Wardrobe?* How about Dorothy in *The Wonderful Wizard of Oz?* Both of these characters matured significantly during the course of their quests. Taran from the Prydain books grows from a foolish boy to a man worthy of ascending to the High Kingship of Prydain. The hero motif involves the age-old rite-of-passage theme, wherein the young are initiated into the ranks of adulthood.

- *The hero returns home.* This step completes the hero's round. In each Prydain book, Taran returns to his home on Dallben's farm, and then symbolically finds "home" when he discovers his true destiny in the final book, *The High King.* In the high fantasy novels discussed in this section, all the young heroes return home as their quests draw to an end.

5. *Special character types.* Fantasies may include characters who come from either our legendary past or an author's vivid imagination. These characters are rarely typical humans. Characters from our legendary past are those from traditional tales: fairies, pixies, giants, wicked witches, ogres, vampires, wizards, dwarves, elves, and so on. Some special character types created in recent years by fantasy authors have become almost as well-known, such as Tolkien's hobbits, which appear in *The Hobbit* and the Lord of the Rings trilogy.

6. *Fantastic objects.* Characters in fantasy stories often employ magical props in accomplishing their heroic or evil deeds. These objects—such as magic cloaks, swords, staffs, cauldrons, mirrors—are imbued with power. Some well-known props are Dorothy's silver slippers (*The Wonderful Wizard of Oz*), the White Witch's wand (*The Lion, the Witch and the Wardrobe*), the dreadful ring that falls into Bilbo's hands (*The Hobbit*), and Harry Potter's flying broom, the Nimbus Two Thousand (*Harry Potter and the Sorcerer's Stone*).

Some books operate strongly in only one of these six motifs, such as *The Wind in the Willows* by Kenneth Grahame (1908) and White's *Charlotte's Web* (1952), where talking animals qualify as magic. *Tuck Everlasting* (Babbitt, 1975) arguably incorporates four of the six motifs: magic, good versus evil, the hero's round, and fantastic objects. Baum's *The Wonderful Wizard of Oz* operates in all six of the motifs and is thus classified as a high fantasy.

SCIENCE FICTION

Science fiction generally appears in chapters about modern fantasy. However, it differs from the stories described to this point. "Science fiction differs from fantasy not in subject matter but in aim, and its unique aim is to suggest real hypotheses about mankind's future or about the nature of the universe" (Engdahl, 1971, p. 450). Science fiction also concerns the way in which scientific possibilities might affect societies of human or alien beings, or both. Therefore, it is sometimes called *futuristic fiction.* This combination of scientific fact and scientific possibility is evident in such works as Nancy Farmer's *The Ear, the Eye, and the Arm* (1994). Farmer starts with facts about the devastation of nuclear accidents and goes on to offer a view of how a society thus affected might look in the 22nd century. Then she extrapolates scientific facts about the unusual effects radiation might have on human beings by creating three characters whose mutations have given them abnormal capabilities.

Futuristic fiction sometimes focuses on dystopia—an imaginary place where people live dehumanized and often fearful lives. Examples include the Newbery-winning *The Giver* (Lowry, 1993), the story of a community of people largely devoid of human emotion, and *City of Ember* (De Prau, 2003), which tells of a town exisitng in perpetual darkness where food supplies and fuel for providing electricity are dwindling.

There is a brand of science fiction, however, that would be better labeled *science fantasy*. These stories play loosely with scientific fact, and the plots are often mixed with magical occurrences. The original *Star Wars* films are examples of science fantasy and even incorporate the six fantasy motifs. The Animorphs, a paperback series by K. A. Applegate, is another example of science fantasy. Several young people are endowed by a dying, benevolent alien with the power to "morph" into various animals in order to fight against an invasion of evil alien beings.

The magic of fantasy cannot be explained; it is just *there,* without source or reason. But the magic of true science fiction is rooted more firmly in scientific fact. Because "Cinderella" is fantasy, the fairy godmother simply has the power to turn the pumpkin into a coach. If it were science fiction, she would zap the pumpkin with a molecular rearranger (Alexander, 1973).

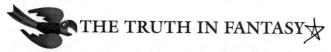

THE TRUTH IN FANTASY

Some adults dismiss all fantasy—traditional fantasy, modern fantasy, even science fiction—as peripheral fluff. It is simply too whimsical for those who want reading for young people to be grounded firmly in reality. Yet these adults miss the point that good fantasy actually tells the truth about life. It clarifies the human condition and captures the essence of our deepest emotions, dreams, hopes, and fears. If fantasy does not do these things, it fails.

Fantasy casts light on the realities of life much as a metaphor illustrates truth in general communication. On the evening news and in daily papers, fantasy language in the form of metaphor is common. Consider the italicized parts of the following: "County medics *see light at the end of the tunnel.*" "Lawmakers *torpedo* peace plan." "During the inquiry, the congressman *played his cards close to his vest.*" How can news writers get away with such wild statements when no tunnel was anywhere near the county medics, the lawmakers did not use a torpedo on the peace plan, and no cards were evident at the congressional inquiry? Because metaphor is an acceptable way of enhancing communication. In its broad definition, metaphor is figurative language and strengthens writing in at least three ways:

1. Metaphor speeds understanding. Metaphor makes the abstract become concrete by introducing an image, resulting in quicker comprehension of a situation. "County medics are confident their current troubles will be resolved in

the near future" describes the situation adequately, but using the metaphor of the tunnel introduces the idea more quickly and with more power.

2. Metaphor creates interest. No one misunderstands "Lawmakers vote against peace plan," but "Lawmakers torpedo peace plan" is richer and more interesting. The image of a *torpedo* makes the action more deliberate and more vigorous.

3. Metaphor adds emotional appeal. With the additional layer of meaning introduced by metaphor, the message goes beyond the intellect to act on the emotions. Without the metaphor, we know the congressman involved in the inquiry was secretive and careful in his responses. The metaphor stirs the emotions with suggestions of "game playing," "calculating," and "intense personal interest."

Yet metaphor is more than the sum of these parts. It simply involves the reader more with the story or message, allowing for quicker learning, more precise understanding, and longer retention because of the image. And fantasy, which is a large, worked-out metaphor, illuminates the truths about life in the same way. Children can read directly about friendship, sacrifice, selfishness, the fear of death, and death itself, but the insight is somehow more meaningful when shown metaphorically through the lives of Wilbur the pig, Templeton the rat, and Charlotte the spider in *Charlotte's Web* (White, 1952). Because Charlotte is a spider, she can embody all selflessness without losing credibility. On the other hand, if she were a character in realistic fiction dedicated completely to doing good and had no flaw or foible, she would not be believable.

Compared with fantasy, straightforward informational writing does not create the same emotional impact when dealing with topics such as the need for death. Although direct arguments certainly can be made—everyone has a time and season that must end; the earth would fill if death were to cease; living forever would hold unforeseen difficulties—such intellectual points do not convince the emotions that death ultimately is desirable. This issue is hard to explore even in realistic fiction. No human can honestly present the alternate view because all people from this world, including those in realistic fiction, are destined to die. Yet the fantasy story of Winnie Foster and the Tuck family in *Tuck Everlasting* (Babbitt, 1975) allows probing of this difficult concept. By listening to a family who has lost the ability to age or die, new light is shed on the appropriateness of an eventual death. Understanding the place of death, one of real life's greatest fears and challenges, is seen most clearly in the metaphor of fantasy.

The power of fantasy is reflected in the fact that many of the classic children's stories, those that have withstood the test of time, are fantasies: *Peter Pan* (Barrie, 1906), *Winnie-the-Pooh* (Milne, 1926), *The Wonderful Wizard of Oz* (Baum, 1900), *The Wind in the Willows* (Grahame, 1908), and *Mary Poppins* (Travers, 1934). Certainly, good fantasy stories speak clearly and convincingly about real life, as author Lloyd Alexander observed (1968b, p. 386): "I suppose you might define realism as fantasy pretending to be true; and fantasy as reality pretending to be a dream."

FIGURE 10–1
Notable authors of modern fantasy.

Listed after each name is the type of fantasy story for which each author is best known.

Alexander, Lloyd: *High fantasy.*
Barron, T. A.: *High fantasy.*
Bellairs, John: *Supernatural.*
Cooper, Susan: *High fantasy.*
Christopher, John: *Science fiction.*
Dahl, Roald: *Peculiar characters/preposterous situations.*
Dickinson, Peter: *Science fiction; high fantasy.*
Duncan, Lois: *Supernatural.*
Engdahl, Sylvia Louise: *Science fiction.*
Farmer, Nancy: *Science fiction.*
Funke, Cornelia: *Magical powers.*
Hahn, Mary Downing: *Supernatural.*
Hoover, H. M.: *Science fiction.*
Hughes, Monica: *Science fiction.*
Hunter, Mollie: *Magical powers; supernatural.*

Jacques, Brian: *Animal fantasy.*
King-Smith, Dick: *Animal fantasy.*
L'Engle, Madeleine: *Science fantasy.*
Le Guin, Ursula: *High fantasy; science fiction.*
Lewis, C. S.: *High fantasy.*
McKinley, Robin: *High fantasy.*
Nix, Garth: *High Fantasy.*
Pullman, Philip: *High fantasy.*
Rowling, J. K.: *Magical powers; high fantasy.*
Van Allsburg, Chris: *Peculiar characters/preposterous situations; magical powers.*
White, E. B.: *Animal fantasy.*
Wright, Betty Ren: *Supernatural.*
Yolen, Jane: *High fantasy; literary folktales and fairy tales.*

MODERN FANTASY READING LIST

TEN OF OUR FAVORITES

Alexander, Lloyd. 1964. *The Book of Three*. Holt. In the first book of The Prydain Chronicles, Taran, Assistant Pig Keeper at Caer Dallben, searches for the oracular pig Hen Wen while the forces of evil gather. (See the other four books in The Prydain Chronicles.)

Babbitt, Natalie. 1975. *Tuck Everlasting*. Farrar. The Tuck family is confronted with an agonizing situation when they discover that a 10-year-old girl and a malicious stranger now share their secret about the water from a spring that prevents people from ever growing any older.

Christopher, John. 1967. *The White Mountains*. Macmillan. (Science fiction.) A young boy and his companions make a perilous journey toward an outpost of freedom, where they hope to escape from the ruling tripod creatures who "cap" adult human beings with implanted metal skull plates that turn them into docile, obedient servants. (See the other three books in the White Mountains series.)

Cooper, Susan. 1966. *Over Sea, Under Stone*. Harcourt. Three children on a holiday in Cornwall find an ancient manuscript that sends them on a dangerous quest for a grail that would reveal the true story of King Arthur. (See the other four books in the Dark Is Rising series.)

Engdahl, Sylvia Louise. 1970 (reissued 2001). *Enchantress from the Stars*. Walker. (Science fiction.) When young Elana unexpectedly joins the team leaving the spaceship to study the planet Andrecia, she becomes an integral part of an adventure involving three very different civilizations, each one centered on the third planet from the star in its own solar system. A Newberry Honor book.

Hale, Shannon. 2003. *The Goose Girl*. Bloomsbury. On her way to marry a prince she's never met, Princess Anidori is betrayed by her guards and her lady-in-waiting and must become a goose girl to survive until she can reveal her true identity and reclaim the crown that is rightfully hers.

Hunter, Mollie. 1975. *A Stranger Came Ashore*. Harper. Twelve-year-old Robbie becomes convinced that the stranger befriended by his family is one of the Selkie Folk and tries to get help against his magical powers from the local wizard.

McKinley, Robin. 1978. *Beauty: A Retelling of the Story of Beauty and the Beast*. Harper. Kind Beauty grows to love the Beast, at whose castle she is compelled to stay. Through her love, she releases him from the spell that had turned him from a handsome prince into an ugly creature.

Pattou, Edith. 2003. *East*. Harcourt. A young woman journeys to a distant castle on the back of a great white bear who is the victim of a cruel enchantment.

White, E. B. 1952. *Charlotte's Web*. Harper. Wilbur the pig discovers that he is destined to be the farmer's Christmas dinner and is desolate until his spider friend, Charlotte, decides to help him. A Newbery Honor Book.

OTHERS WE LIKE

Alexander, Lloyd. 1997. *The Iron Ring*. Dutton.

Armstrong, Alan W. 2005. *Whittington*. Illustrated by S. D. Schindler. Random House.

Balliett, Blue. 2006. *The Wright 3*. Illustrated by Brett Helquist. Scholastic. (Also see *Chasing Vermeer*.)

Banks, Lynne Reid. 1981. *The Indian in the Cupboard*. Doubleday. (See others in the Indian in the Cupboard series.)

Barron, T. A. 2000. *The Wings of Merlin*. Philomel. (See others in the Merlin series.)

Bellairs, John. 1973. *The House with a Clock in Its Walls*. Dial. (See others in the Lewis Barnavelt series, also written by Brad Strickland after Bellairs's death.)

Billingsley, Franny. 1999. *The Folk Keeper*. Atheneum.

Conrad, Pam. 1990. *Stonewords*. Harper.

Constable, Kate. 2003. *The Waterless Sea*. Arthur A. Levine Books (Scholastic). (See others in The Chanters of Tremaris Trilogy.)

Cornish, D. M. 2006. *The Monster Blood Tattoo, Book One: Founding*. Putnam.

Dahl, Roald. 1988. *Matilda*. Viking Kestrel.

DiCamillo, Kate. 2006. *The Miraculous Journey of Edward Tulane*. Illustrated by Bagram Ibatoulline. Candlewick.

DePrau, Jeanne. 2006. *The Prophet of Yonwood*. Random House. (See others in The Books of Ember series.)

Dickinson, Peter. 1989. *Eva*. Delacorte. (Science fiction.)

Duncan, Lois. 1976. *Summer of Fear*. Little, Brown.

Farmer, Nancy. 2002. *The House of the Scorpion*. Richard Jackson Books (Atheneum). (Science fiction.)

Fletcher, Susan. 1989. *Dragon's Milk*. Atheneum. (See others in the Dragon Chronicles series.)

Hahn, Mary Downing. 1986. *Wait Till Helen Comes: A Ghost Story*. Houghton Mifflin.

Jacques, Brian. 1987. *Redwall*. Philomel. (See others in the Redwall series.)

L'Engle, Madeleine. 1962. *A Wrinkle in Time*. Farrar. (See others in the Time series.)

Le Guin, Ursula K. 1968. *A Wizard of Earthsea*. Parnassus. (See others in the Earthsea series.)

Levitin, Sonia. 2005. *The Goodness Gene*. Dutton. (Science fiction.)

Lewis, C. S. 1950. *The Lion, the Witch and the Wardrobe*. Macmillan. (See the other six books in the Narnia series.)

Lowry, Lois. 1993. *The Giver*. Houghton. (Science fiction.)

Nix, Garth. 2001. *Lirael*. Harper. (See other titles in the trilogy.)

Norton, Mary. 1953. *The Borrowers*. Harcourt. (See others in the Borrowers series.)

O'Brien, Robert C. 1971. *Mrs. Frisby and the Rats of NIMH*. Atheneum. (Science fiction.)

O'Brien, Robert C. 1975. *Z for Zachariah*. Atheneum. (Science fiction.)

Pullman, Philip. 1995. *The Golden Compass*. Knopf. (See others in the His Dark Materials series.)

Rowling, J. K. 1998. *Harry Potter and the Sorcerer's Stone*. Scholastic. (See the others in the Harry Potter series.)

Schsterman, Neal. 2004. *The Schwa Was Here*. Dutton.

Springer, Nancy. 2001. *I Am Morgan le Fay: A Tale from Camelot*. Philomel.

Tunnell, Michael O. 2004. *Wishing Moon*. Dutton. (Also see *Moon Without Magic*.)

Vande Velde, Vivian. 2002. *Heir Apparent*. Harcourt.

Yolen, Jane. 1982. *Dragon's Blood*. Delacorte. (See others in the Dragon trilogy.)

EASIER TO READ

Brooks, Walter R. 1932. (reissued 1997). *Freddy the Detective*. Overlook Press. (See others in the Freddy the Pig series.)

Brown, Jeff. 2003. *Stanley, Flat Again* Illustrated by Steve Björkman. Harper. (Also see *Flat Stanley* and others in the Stanley series.)

Cameron, Ann. 2002. *Gloria Rising*. Illustrated by Lis Toft. Farrar.

Catling, Patrick. 1979. (1952). *The Chocolate Touch*. Morrow.

Cleary, Beverly. 1965. *The Mouse and the Motorcycle*. Morrow. (Also see *Runaway Ralph*.)

Cooper, Susan. 2005. *The Magician's Boy*. Illustrated by Serena Riglietti. McElderry Books.

Coville, Bruce. 2005. *The Weeping Werewolf*. Illustrated by Katherine Coville. Simon & Schuster.

Fleischman, Sid. 1992. *Here Comes McBroom*. Greenwillow. (See others in the McBroom series.)

Griffin, Adele. 2001. *Witch Twins*. Hyperion.

Howe, Deborah, and James Howe. 1983. *Bunnicula*. Atheneum. (See others in the Bunnicula series.)

King-Smith, Dick. 1985. *Babe: The Gallant Pig*. Crown.

Krulik, Nancy. 2006. *Witch Switch!* Grosset & Dunlap. (See others in the Katie Kazoo series.)

Scieszka, Jon. 2005. *Oh Say, I Can't See*. Illustrated by Adam McCauley. Viking. (See others in the Time Warp Trio series.)

Wright, Betty Ren. 1998. *The Ghost in Room 11*. Holiday House.

PICTURE BOOKS

Agee, Jon. 2001. *Milo's Hat Trick*. Hyperion.

Alexander, Lloyd. 2005. *Dream-of-Jade: The Emperor's Cat*. Illustrated by D. Brent Burkett. Cricket Books.

Bannerman, Helen. 2003. *The Story of Little Black Sambo*. Illustrated by Christopher Bing. Handprint.

Cronin, Doreen. 2000. *Click, Clack, Moo: Cows That Type*. Illustrated by Betsy Lewin. Simon & Schuster.

DiTerlizzi, Tony. 2002. *The Spider and the Fly*. Simon & Schuster.

Henkes, Kevin. 2000. *Wemberly Worried*. Greenwillow.

Kellogg, Steven. 1977. *The Mysterious Tadpole*. Dial.

Meddaugh, Susan. 1992. *Martha Speaks*. Houghton. (See others in the Martha series.)

Peet, Bill. 1977. *Big Bad Bruce*. Houghton.

Rosenberg, Liz. 1993. *Monster Mama*. Illustrated by Stephen Gammell. Putnam.

Small, David. 1986. *Imogene's Antlers*. Crown.

Steig, William. 1990. *Shrek!* Farrar.

Stockton, Frank. 1887 (2003). *The Bee-Man of Orn*. Illustrated by P. J. Lynch. Candlewick.

Van Allsburg, Chris. 1979. *The Garden of Abdul Gasazi*. Houghton.

Van Allsburg, Chris. 2002. *Zathura*. Houghton Mifflin.

Wiesner, David. 1999. *Sector 7*. Clarion.

Wiesner, David. 2006. *Flotsam*. Clarion.

Yolen, Jane. 1989. *Dove Isabeau*. Illustrated by Dennis Nolan. Harcourt.

For details about books listed here and for a more complete list of modern fantasy titles, consult the Children's Literature Database: A Resource for Teachers, Parents, and Media Specialists CD *that accompanies this text.*

REFERENCES

Alexander, Lloyd. (1964). *The book of three*. New York: Holt.

Alexander, Lloyd. (1965, April). The flat-heeled muse. *The Horn Book, 41*, 141–146.

Alexander, Lloyd. (1968a). *The high king*. New York: Holt.

Alexander, Lloyd. (1968b, August). Wishful thinking—or hopeful dreaming. *The Horn Book, 44*, 382–390.

Alexander, Lloyd. (1973). Letter to Shelton L. Root, Jr., 20 February.

Almond, David. (1999). *Skellig*. New York: Delacorte.

Augarde, Steve. 2004. *The various.* New York: David Fickling Books/Random House.

Babbitt, Natalie. (1975). *Tuck everlasting.* New York: Farrar, Straus & Giroux.

Babbitt, Natalie. (1987, October). Fantasy and the classic hero. *School Library Journal, 34,* 25–29.

Barrie, J. M. (1906). *Peter Pan.* New York: Scribner's.

Baum, L. Frank. (1900). *The wonderful wizard of Oz.* New York: G. M. Hill.

Campbell, Joseph. (1968). *The hero with a thousand faces* (2nd ed.). Princeton, NJ: Princeton University Press.

Carroll, Lewis. (1865). *Alice's adventures in Wonderland.* London: Macmillan.

Catling, Patrick. (1979). *The chocolate touch.* New York: William Morrow.

Collodi, Carlo. (1904). *Pinocchio.* Boston: Ginn.

Colwell, Elizabeth. (1968, January). An oral tradition and an oral art: Folk literature. *Top of the News, 24,* 174–180.

Conrad, Pam. (1990). *Stonewords.* New York: HarperCollins.

Cooper, Susan. (1999). *King of shadows.* New York: McElderry.

DePrau, Jeanne. (2003). *City of Ember.* New York: Random House.

Engdahl, Sylvia Louise. (1971, October). The changing role of science fiction in children's literature. *The Horn Book, 47,* 449–455.

Farmer, Nancy. (1994). *The ear, the eye, and the arm.* New York: Orchard.

Grahame, Kenneth. (1908). *The wind in the willows.* London: Methuen.

Hahn, Mary Downing. (1985). *Wait till Helen comes: A ghost story.* New York: Houghton Mifflin.

Hoeye, Michael. (2004). *No time like show time.* New York: Putnam.

Jacques, Brian. (1987). *Redwall.* New York: Philomel.

Lewis, C. S. (1950). *The Lion, the witch and the wardrobe.* New York: Macmillan.

Lowry, Lois. (1993). *The giver.* New York: Houghton Mifflin.

Madsen, Linda Lee. (1976). Fantasy in children's literature: A generic study. Master's thesis, Utah State University.

Milne, A. A. (1926). *Winnie-the-Pooh.* New York: Dutton.

Norton, Mary. (1953). *The borrowers.* New York: Harcourt Brace.

Pearce, Philippa. (1958). *Tom's midnight garden.* New York: Lippincott.

Pullman, Philip. (2000). *The amber spyglass.* New York: Scholastic.

Rowling, J. K. (1998). *Harry Potter and the sorcerer's stone.* New York: Scholastic.

Rowling, J. K. (2005). *Harry Potter and the half-blood prince.* New York: Scholastic.

Scieszka, Jon. (1989). *The true story of the 3 little pigs!* Illustrated by Lane Smith. New York: Viking.

Stanley, Diane. (1997). *Rumpelstiltskin's daughter.* New York: Morrow.

Tolkien, J. R. R. (1937). *The hobbit.* London: G. Allen & Unwin.

Travers, P. L. (1934). *Mary Poppins.* London: G. Howe.

Waugh, Sylvia. (1994). *The Mennyms.* New York: Greenwillow.

White, E. B. (1952). *Charlotte's web.* New York: HarperCollins.

Chapter 11

Contemporary Realistic Fiction

Contemporary realistic fiction tells a story that never happened but *could* have happened. The events and characters of contemporary realistic fiction flow from the author's imagination, just as they do in fantasy. Unlike fantasy, which includes at least one element not found in this world, everything in contemporary realistic fiction is possible on planet Earth.

IMPORTANCE OF STORY

W. Somerset Maugham once said, "There are three rules for writing a good novel. Unfortunately, no one knows what they are" (Stephens, 1990). While the exact recipe for solid writing does not exist—if it did, anyone privy to the formula could predictably crank out an award winner—all readers recognize one unfailing earmark of a good novel: It must tell a satisfying story. Every memorable work of fiction presents a conflict or problem that affects human beings, and how this obstacle is overcome *is* the story. Writers of contemporary realistic fiction often draw on their own backgrounds or observe life around them to tell their stories.

IDENTIFYING WITH CONTEMPORARY REALISTIC FICTION

Of all the genres in children's literature, contemporary realistic fiction is the most popular. People are interested in their own lives, and this genre is about "my life." This is my world. This is how I live. This story is about a girl like me. Because the characters in contemporary realistic fiction are similar to people in my town, I get to know them quickly and feel as if I've known them a long time. The main character in particular becomes a kindred spirit. She experiences the same disappointments and hopes, rejections and joys as the reader, who is amazed and thrilled to find someone who sees the world through similar glasses. Certainly, the reader can connect with the lives of those from the past and also with fantasy characters, but something about the immediacy of here and now seems to pack an additional emotional punch.

Almost all readers want to find at least an occasional title that reflects and confirms their lives. The lack of books dealing with specific cultures can draw protest from members of a group who desire to read about something close to home. Because realistic fiction helps confirm our own membership in the human race, children's publishers and authors continue to represent the spectrum of minorities present in the United States—racial groups, religions, stories from specific regions of the country—but not all bases have yet been covered. For instance, the half-million people in the United States who are Deaf (capitalized to indicate they belong to the Deaf culture, not just that they do not hear) are represented at the time of this writing in seven picture storybooks currently in print in the United States. A scattering of informational picture books is available, detailing facts about sign language and what life is like for the nonhearing, but being represented by so few picture storybooks leaves the Deaf without the confirmation of their lives in stories about "someone like me."

The lack of such books also means that others have less opportunity to get to know and understand the Deaf. While my life is being supported and confirmed by titles dealing with "my world," these same books can be enlightening to others. "My world" is a limited concept for all of us. No matter where I live or what my life is like, my peers across the aisle, across town, and across the country are going through experiences I do not have. If I live with both my parents, I do not understand what my classmate Paul is going through now that his father has moved out and he is alone with his mother. But Beverly Cleary's *Dear Mr. Henshaw* (1983) shows me a divorced home and gives me some understanding of a boy who lives in my world but is experiencing it differently. If I live in rural Maine, I benefit by reading about kids in inner-city Chicago, and vice versa. In this genre are the experiences in my world that I do not yet have—books dealing with specific regions, cultures, nationalities, minorities, and subgroups that provide an expanded understanding of "my world."

The importance of identifying with one's own life is a reason children's books have children as the protagonists. The age of the main character is approximately the age of the reader. For this reason, *The Endless Steppe* (1968), Esther Hautzig's memoir about her childhood in World War II Poland and Russia, eventually was published as a children's book even though she did not have a child audience in mind when she wrote it. Because the main character is a young girl, its market and audience are the same—young readers. The rule of thumb is that children will read about characters who are slightly older than they are, but are hesitant about reading books with characters who are younger.

A small but important type of contemporary realistic fiction does not fit the pattern of having children as the main characters, but these books still offer enough humor, adventure, or entertainment to draw young readers. Examples are Peggy Parish's Amelia Bedelia stories about the maid who takes too literally her employer's instructions (told to "ice the cake," she puts ice cubes on its top and sticks the cake in the freezer); Cynthia Rylant's books presenting the day-to-day adventures of an old man and his cat, Mr. Putter and Tabby; and Carol Otis Hurst's picture book about her rock-collecting father, called *Rocks in His Head* (2001). Sometimes the main character isn't even human, as in Sheila Burnford's *The Incredible Journey* (1961), the story of two dogs and a cat as they travel 250 miles through the Canadian wilderness to reach their home.

Familiarity helps explain why many children who have not yet discovered the pleasure of books often find their first successful reading experiences with contemporary realistic fiction. Trying out a new book is a risk for the reader, and those not steeped in personal reading are less likely to take big chances. Contemporary realistic fiction offers less of a gamble because the book contains elements familiar to the reader. Much of the groundwork already exists for a relationship, or even a friendship, to develop between child and character.

CONTEMPORARY REALISTIC FICTION AND SOCIETY

Contemporary realism reflects society and the child's place in it. Contemporary novels written in the 1920s provide a snapshot of the American scene during that time, and novels written and set in the 1990s do the same. The view of life in a realistic story reflects societal mores and attitudes of the time in which the tale is set. In books written around the time of World War I, for example, a pregnant woman would be identified as being "in a delicate condition," if she were identified at all. The word *pregnant* was rarely used in daily conversation and, consequently, rarely found in print. Life in the early 1900s definitely had pregnancies and other realities of human existence, including crime, great injustice, and pockets of ugliness, but these aspects of life were not a part of books written for children because social attitudes dictated that they were unsuitable for children, and therefore they were unavailable to young readers.

Until the mid-1960s, the world in children's books typically was presented without negative or earthy aspects. Geoffrey Trease (1983) lists some of the generally accepted restrictions that applied to the writing of children's books before 1960: no budding love affairs, no liquor, no supernatural phenomena, no undermining of authority, no parents with serious human weaknesses, no realistic working-class speech (including the mildest cursing). But then the face of American society took on a new look because of upheavals such as the civil rights movement, the Vietnam war, and large cracks appearing in the traditional family structure. The effects were so widespread that children no longer could be kept in the dark (if they truly ever were). Evidence of the changes appeared on the front pages of newspapers, harsh realities were broadcast into the living rooms of the world on television newscasts, and no neighborhood was free from divorce.

FIGURE 11–1

Notable authors of contemporary realistic fiction.

Blume, Judy: *Teen and preteen problem novels.*

Byars, Betsy: *Preteen problem novels.*

Danziger, Paula: *Primary and middle grade humor.*

Cleary, Beverly: *Primary and middle grade humor.*

Creech, Sharon: *Middle grade problem novels.*

George, Jean Craighead: *Ecological fiction.*

Giff, Patricia Reilly: *Primary and middle grade humor; problem novels.*

Hamilton, Virginia: *African American experience.*

Henry, Marguerite: *Horse stories.*

Hobbs, Will: *Outdoor adventure stories.*

Holt, Kimberly: *Preteen problem novels.*

Konigsburg, Elaine L.: *Humorous childhood experiences; problem novels.*

Lowry, Lois: *Teen and preteen problem novels; middle grade humor.*

Myers, Walter Dean: *African American experience.*

Naylor, Phyllis R.: *Mysteries; adolescent humor; animal stories.*

Paterson, Katherine: *Teen and preteen problem novels.*

Paulsen, Gary: *Survival and adventure fiction.*

Sachar, Louis: *Middle grade humor.*

Spinelli, Jerry: *Teen and preteen problem novels.*

Voigt, Cynthia: *Teen and preteen problem novels.*

Woodsen, Jacqueline: *African American experience.*

Yep, Laurence: *Chinese American experience.*

A new attitude accompanied this shift toward facing problems previously ignored: Children were viewed as citizens with rights beyond those granted by their parents. Some voices called for children to have full access to information, and young people achieved a new prominence in society. Following tradition, contemporary realistic fiction chronicled the current scene, and the child as a full-rights citizen began to appear in books for young readers.

Contemporary realistic fiction is most often the genre in which the taboos of literature are tested. Changes in the content of children's literature typically appear first in this genre and then spread to others. Louise Fitzhugh's *Harriet the Spy* was a pivotal book when it appeared in 1964. It told about a nontraditional girl who dressed in a sweatshirt, spied on neighbors, was neglected by her well-to-do parents, and underwent psychotherapy. All of these elements signaled a shift in the acceptable literary content of the early 1960s, which featured children in protected and positive situations.

Controversy over the realities in these and other books spread widely. These changes, beginning in the 1960s and flourishing in the 1970s, came to be called *new realism* (see Chapter 5). The harsher parts of life simply had not been given center stage in books for young readers until then. When the taboos lifted, new books spewed forth problems and realities previously unseen in children's publishing. Topics such as death, divorce, drugs, abuse, profanity, nontraditional lifestyles, and single-parent families not only were mentioned in the books, but also became major themes.

Society continued to change. A new generation of problems popped up in headlines and public consciousness, such as inner-city survival, teen suicide, gang life, AIDS, random shootings, anorexia nervosa, white supremacy, and terrorism. As those issues took root in society, they sprouted in contemporary books for children, and that cycle continues as ever-newer concerns surface in both society and writing for young readers.

Because of the immediacy of the problems in realistic fiction, it traditionally has been the genre that attracts the most controversy. When a book deals with the issue of cocaine in a modern middle school, the emotional impact of the problem tends to be stronger than in a story treating the consequences of opium addiction in 18th-century China. Society was also affected drastically by drugs 200 years ago, but the middle school setting is closer to home both emotionally and physically. That books for children acknowledge such problems is seen as relevant and helpful by some people and abhorred as too stark and unnecessary by others, and thus the debate begins. (For more on controversy and censorship, see Chapter 16.)

COMMON CATEGORIES OF CONTEMPORARY REALISTIC FICTION

Children do not ask a librarian, "Do you have another good book of contemporary realistic fiction?" But a child will zero in on a particular type of book found within that genre, wanting another good title about animals. Or sports. Or survival. Or a good humorous book. Stories in these areas have proven appeal, and teachers who wish to help the variety of students in an average classroom find books of interest would do well to become familiar with some titles from each of the popular reading categories in contemporary realistic fiction: survival and adventure, animals, humor, mysteries, problem novels, series books, and sports. It is important to remember, however, that these categories are neither rigid nor exclusive. A single title may fall into more than one category, such as a sports book that is also humorous.

ANIMALS. A mainstay of contemporary realistic fiction is the animal story. The bond between humans and animals is as satisfying as it is ancient, and stories about that relationship continue to reward readers. Marguerite Henry wrote more than 50 stories about animals, beginning at age 11 with a tale about a collie and a group of children that she sold to a magazine for $12 (Murray, 1997). She wrote about dogs, cats, foxes, birds, and even a burro, but she always came back to horses, winning Newbery Honor Medals for *Justin Morgan Had a Horse* (1945) and *Misty of Chincoteague* (1947) before receiving the Newbery Medal for *King of the Wind* (1948), the story of how an Arabian stallion was brought to England and became one of the founding sires of the Thoroughbred breed. Also, many of K. M. Peyton's books are about children and their horses, such as *Poor Badger* (1992) and *Blind Beauty* (2001).

Famous and readable dog books from the past include titles by Albert Payson Terhune such as *Lad, a Dog* (1926), the incomparable *Lassie, Come Home* by Eric Knight (1940), and the guaranteed-to-make-you-cry *Where the Red Fern Grows* by Wilson Rawls (1961). Some newer dog books worth reading are Phyllis Naylor's Newbery-award-winning *Shiloh* (1991), where a boy rescues an abused beagle and finds the courage to confront its owner, and *Because of Winn-Dixie* by Kate DiCamillo (2000), a Newbery Medal book that shows the delight of a young girl finding a stray dog.

HUMOR.   It is impossible to have too many humor books in a classroom or school library. Books that make people laugh appeal to a broad range of students, plus books with healthy doses of humor are often short, an additional attraction for the hard-to-convince. Beverly Cleary's Ramona books continue to find readers in each new generation of elementary students, and Gordon Korman's long string of humorous novels such as *No More Dead Dogs* (2000) are especially popular with boys. Daniel Pinkwater is famous for his peculiar characters and funny situations in both picture books (*The Wuggie Norpel Story*, 1980) and novels (*Yo-Yo Man*, 2006). *Dilly for President* by Cynthia Copeland (2004) is a humorous graphic novel about a girl's campaign to be president of her fourth-grade class. In addition to humorous picture books and novels, teachers should also remember the irresistible pull of riddle and joke books on young readers.

MYSTERIES.   Mysteries have been at the top of children's preference lists since the 1920s, regardless of the children's sex, ethnicity, or IQ (Haynes, 1988; Tomlinson & Tunnell, 1994). Because most everyone likes mysteries, choosing one as a read-aloud at the beginning of a school year will almost guarantee a teacher will have a captive audience.

Like many of these categories, mysteries are not always contemporary realistic fiction. For instance, some of Betty Ren Wright's books (*The Dollhouse Murders*, 1983; *Moonlight Man*, 2000; *Crandall's Castle*, 2003) have contemporary settings and deal with contemporary problems, but the mystery often revolves around a supernatural occurrence. In the same way, Pullman's (1985) *Ruby in the Smoke* and Dowell's (2000) *Dovey Coe* are mysteries of another genre—historical fiction, set in 1872 and 1928, respectively. However, Wendelin Van Draanen's Sammy Keyes mysteries (*Sammy Keyes and the Hotel Thief*, 1998; *Sammy Keyes and the Hollywood Mummy*, 2001; *Sammy Keyes and the Dead Giveaway*, 2005) are pure contemporary realistic fiction.

USING THE CHILDREN'S LITERATURE DATABASE

Be sure the CD database is installed on your hard drive. Go to the Book List in the left navigation bar on the Home screen. Select New Search, and then click on Run Search. Enter "Dogs" in the Keyword Search field. Check the boxes Title, Topics, and Description. Click Run Search. When the search is complete, click on Constrain This List; then click Run Search. Check the CRF box (for contemporary realistic fiction) within Genre. Click Run Search. When this search is complete, click on Constrain This List and Run Search again; then check the PB box (for picture books) in Genre. Click Run Search. You now have a list of contemporary realistic fiction picture books about dogs. To save this list for future use, click on Save This List as Set in the top navigation bar. Give your saved set a name (in the pop-up window), and click Submit.

PROBLEM NOVELS.   The problem novel was born early in the age of new realism, when taboo topics about the problems of growing up became acceptable fare for juvenile books. Most of the topics focus on coping with problems of the human condition, including physical and mental disabilities, mental illness, death, peer-group pressure, bigotry, divorce, sibling rivalry, and loneliness—to name but a few.

In other contemporary realistic fiction categories, characters may also face personal problems, but their problems are not the major thrust of the story. For example, in Wright's *The Dollhouse Murders,* Amy struggles with the love/hate feelings she has for her mentally challenged sister. Nevertheless, the ghostly mystery of the dollhouse and the long-ago murders of her grandparents take center stage. In a modern problem novel, the problem will control the plot, as in Ann Martin's (2003) *A Corner of the Universe,* wherein the challenges of dealing with a mentally challenged relative is not upstaged by other elements of the plot.

SERIES BOOKS.   Books in series vary greatly in quality. Some find acceptance in the literary mainstream, like Lois Lowry's Anastasia Krupnik stories and Phyllis Reynolds Naylor's titles about Alice. These books have a memorable main character, appear first in hardcover, and evolve into a series as the character experiences more adventures. At the other end of the series spectrum are the books viewed unfavorably by literary critics. Most are mass-market paperbacks, which seldom appear first as hardbacks and tend to be written according to a formula with predictable plots, relatively flat characters, and a writing style that leans toward the unimaginative (Tunnell & Jacobs, 2005).

Nevertheless, whatever the content or quality, series books are important to literacy development because of two proven characteristics: comfort and story. First, series are comfortable because they are familiar and predictable. Readers know the characters—after the first book, they become friends—plus readers can make successful guesses about what is going to happen. Second, readers know that they are getting a real story with a clear problem and a satisfying solution. "Young readers frequently complain about the difficulty of getting started in a new book. In a familiar series, this difficulty is averted. This 'instant start' instead of frustration plays a large role in luring that student into regular reading" (Ross, 1995).

Some old series of realistic fiction are still popular, most notably The Hardy Boys and Nancy Drew, which have been reissued in paperback. Since then, other series have captured thousands of devoted readers. Examples include Junie B. Jones (Barbara Park), Adventures of the Bailey School Kids (Debbie Daly and Marsha Thornton Jones), The Baby-Sitters Club (Ann Martin), Hoofbeats (Kathleen Duey), and A Series of Unfortunate Events (Lemony Snicket). Even the early grades have series, such as The Kids of Polk Street School (Patricia Reilly Giff), and The Pee-Wee Scouts (Judy Delton). Older, action-seeking readers will be rewarded with the James Bond–like adventures of 14-year-old Alex Rider (*Eagle Strike,* 2004) by Anthony Horowitz and the brother-sister espionage team in Gordon Korman's On the Run series beginning with *Chasing the Falconers* (2005). Of course, not all series books are strictly contemporary realism. For example, The Magic Tree House (Mary Pope Osborne), the Katie Kazoo books (Nancy Krulik), and Dragonslayers' Academy (Kate McMullan) are modern fantasy.

Whatever the genre, readers tend to immerse themselves in a particular series only until they reach a self-determined level of saturation or until they finish all the titles. As much as some teachers and librarians believe the weaker of the series books are somehow bad for a reader's literary health, if not their overall character, no evidence exists to indicate that those who have indulged, even to extremes, tend to come to a bad end. However, the jury seems still to be out on romance books. Romance series appear under dozens of different imprints and names, each with its own label that usually identifies the degree of sexual specificity. Young readers of romance stories often make the easy transition to the endless number of romance books for adults.

SPORTS.   Stories including sports as part of the plot were once considered the reading domain of boys, but since Title IX, legislating more equitable funding of women's sport programs, girls seem to have an increased interest in sports-themed books. In fact, since the 1970s, an increasing number of titles focus on female athletes. One of the early novels featured Zan Hagen and tells of the problems she faces when trying to play on the boys' basketball team (*Zanballer;* Knudsen, 1972). Zan appears in several other novels: *Zanbanger* (1977), when she stands up to her school principal and leads her dance class onto the athletic field to form a girls' football team; *Zanboomer* (1978), wherein she dislocates her shoulder playing baseball and takes up cross-country running; and *Zan Hagen's Marathon* (1984), about Zan's goal to run in the first Olympic women's marathon in the Los Angeles Games of 1984. More recently, Dori Hillestad Butler has written *Sliding into Home* (2003) about 13-year-old Joelle, a star baseball player who moves to a new town without girls' teams. Bucking local opposition, she organizes an all-girl baseball league.

Any young reader interested in sports will likely stumble onto Matt Christopher's books. Whether the sport is football or ice hockey, soccer or snowboarding, he has titles to offer. Other well-known sports writers include Alfred Slote (*The Trading Game,* 1990 [baseball]), John Ritter (*Under the Baseball Moon,* 2006), Thomas Dygard (*Running Wild,* 1996 [football]), and Carl Deuker (*Night Hoops,* 2000 [basketball]). Dan Gutman's Baseball Card Adventures meld fantasy, historical fiction, and contemporary realistic fiction as 13-year-old Joe travels back in time to the days of famous ball players. Titles include *Honus and Me* (1997), *Babe and Me* (2000), and *Abner and Me* (2005). Not many sports titles make the Newbery list, but Bruce Brooks won a Newbery Honor Medal for his basketball story, *The Moves Makes the Man* (1984).

SURVIVAL AND ADVENTURE.   Stories of survival and adventure are most often set in the wilderness. Classic novels of this type include the Newbery Honor books *My Side of the Mountain* (George, 1959), *Hatchet* (Paulsen, 1987), and the Newbery-winning *Holes* (Sachar, 1998). Characters sometimes are faced with urban survival, as well. In Felice Holman's *Slake's Limbo* (1974), 13-year-old Aremis Slake, hounded by his fears and misfortunes, flees into New York City's subway tunnels. There he manages to survive, never again—he believes—to emerge above ground.

Often adventure stories combine survival with discovery, such as in Michael Morpurgo's *Kensuke's Kingdom* (2003), wherein the young protagonist is swept off his family's yacht and washes up on a desert island. Adventure comes when he discovers an old Japanese soldier stranded there more than four decades following World War II. Other tales of adventure involve a trek or a quest, as in Will Hobbs's *The Big Wander* (1992), where Clay searches the rugged Southwest canyon country for his lost uncle, or *Crossing the Wire* (2006), the story of young Victor Flores's journey north and his eventual attempt at crossing the Arizona border into the United States. But no matter the reason for the adventure, the draw for young readers is the excitement and danger offered by this type of story.

The offerings of contemporary realistic fiction are as wide as life, helping explore today's people, problems, and places. In this popular genre young readers can find their own lives, recognize friends, and meet strangers who can show them different ways of living and thinking. Whether the appeal of a book lies in a skillful re-creation of current lifestyles or a comfortable pattern found in a series, the best of contemporary realistic fiction examines human beings facing and overcoming the challenges of living in today's world.

CONTEMPORARY REALISTIC FICTION READING LIST

TEN OF OUR FAVORITES

DiCamillo, Kate. 2000. *Because of Winn-Dixie*. Candlewick. Ten-year-old India Opal Buloni describes her first summer in the town of Naomi, Florida, and all the good things that happen to her because of her big ugly dog, Winn-Dixie. A Newbery Honor Book.

Hunt, Irene. 1976. *Lottery Rose*. Scribner's. A young victim of child abuse gradually overcomes his fears and suspicions when placed in a home with other boys.

Konigsburg, E. L. 1967. *From the Mixed-Up Files of Mrs. Basil E. Frankweiler*. Atheneum. Twelve-year-old Claudia is tired of her life of responsibility, so she and her little brother run away from home and hide in the Metropolitan Museum of Art. Winner of the Newbery Medal.

Martin, Ann. 2002. *A Corner of the Universe*. Scholastic. The summer that Hattie turns 12, she meets the childlike uncle she never knew and becomes friends with a girl who works at the carnival that comes to Hattie's small town. A Newbery Honor Book.

Paterson, Katherine. 1978. *The Great Gilly Hopkins*. Crowell. An 11-year-old foster child tries to cope with her longings and fears as she schemes against everyone who tries to be friendly. A Newbery Honor Book.

Paulsen, Gary. 1987. *Hatchet*. Bradbury. After a plane crash, 13-year-old Brian spends 54 days in the wilderness, learning to survive with only the aid of a hatchet given him by his mother and learning also to survive his parents' divorce. A Newbery Honor Book.

Rawls, Wilson. 1961. *Where the Red Fern Grows*. Doubleday. A young boy living in the Ozarks achieves his heart's desire when he becomes the owner of two redbone hounds and teaches them to be hunters.

Robinson, Barbara. 1972. *The Best Christmas Pageant Ever*. Harper. The six mean Herdman kids lie, steal, smoke cigars (even the girls), and then become involved in the community Christmas pageant.

Sachar, Louis. 1998. *Holes*. Farrar. As further evidence of his family's bad fortune, which they attribute to a curse on a distant relative, Stanley Yelnats is sent to a hellish correctional camp in the Texas desert where he finds his first real friend, a treasure, and a new sense of himself. Winner of the Newbery Medal.

Spinelli, Jerry. 1990. *Maniac Magee*. Little, Brown. After his parents die, Jeffrey Lionel Magee's life becomes legendary, as he accomplishes athletic and other feats that awe his contemporaries. At the same time he searches in anguish for a place to call home. Winner of the Newbery Medal.

OTHERS WE LIKE

ANIMALS

Cleary, Beverly. 1991. *Strider*. Morrow.

Henry, Marguerite. 1990. (1947). *King of the Wind*. Macmillan.

Kjelgaard, Jim. 1945. *Big Red*. Holiday House.

Morpurgo, Michael. 2006. *The Amazing Story of Adolphus Tips*. Scholastic.

Mowat, Farley. 1962. *Owls in the Family*. Little, Brown.

Naylor, Phyllis R. 1991. *Shiloh*. Atheneum. (See the other Shiloh titles.)

North, Sterling. 1963. *Rascal*. Dutton.

Staples, Suzanne Fisher. 2003. *The Green Dog*. Farrar.

Wallace, Bill. 2004. *No Dogs Allowed!* Holiday House.

HUMOR

Blume, Judy. 1972. *Tales of a Fourth Grade Nothing*. Dutton.

Cleary, Beverly. 1968. *Ramona the Pest*. Morrow. (See others in the Ramona series.)

Clements, Andrew. 1996. *Frindle*. Simon & Schuster.

Gutman, Dan. 2004. *The Million Dollar Strike*. Hyperion.

Korman, Gordon. 1991. *I Want to Go Home*. Scholastic.

Lowry, Lois. 1985. *Anastasia Krupnik*. Houghton. (See others in the Anastasia Krupnik series.)

Maguire, Gregory. 2005. *One Final Firecracker*. Clarion. (See others in the Hamlet Chronicles series.)

Naylor, Phyllis Reynolds. 1989. *Alice in Rapture, Sort Of*. Atheneum. (See others in the Alice series.)

Paulsen, Gary. 2004. *Molly McGinty Has a Really Good Day*. Wendy Lamb (Random House).

See also riddle books and collections of jokes on the children's shelves at libraries and bookstores.

MYSTERIES

Alphin, Elaine Marie. 2000. *Counterfeit Son*. Harcourt.

Balliett, Blue. 2004. *Chasing Vermeer*. Illustrated by Brett Helquist. Scholastic.

Broach, Elise. 2005. *Shakespeare's Secret*. Holt.

Duncan, Lois. 1973. *I Know What You Did Last Summer*. Little, Brown.

Horowitz, Anthony. 2006. *Ark Angel*. Philomel. (See others in the Alex Rider series.)

Nixon, Joan Lowry. 1986. *The Other Side of Dark*. Delacorte.

Raskin, Ellen. 1978. *The Westing Game*. Dutton.

Smith, John D. 2005. *The Boys of San Joaquin*. Richard Jackson (Atheneum).

Smith, Roland. 2001. *Zach's Lie*. Hyperion.

Van Draanen, Wendelin. 2005. *Sammy Keyes and the Dead Giveaway*. Knopf. (See others in the Sammy Keyes series.)

Wright, Betty Ren. 1983. *The Dollhouse Murders*. Holiday.

PROBLEM NOVELS/FAMILY STORIES

Bauer, Joan. 2000. *Hope Was Here*. Putnam.

Birdsall, Jeanne. 2005. *The Penderwicks*. Knopf.

Blume, Judy. 1970. *Are You There God? It's Me, Margaret*. Bradbury.

Byars, Betsy. 1977. *The Pinballs*. Harper.

Holt, Kimberly Willis. 1998. *My Louisiana Sky*. Holt.

Lowry, Lois. 1977. *A Summer to Die*. Houghton Mifflin.

Philbrick, Rodman. 1993. *Freak the Mighty*. Scholastic.

Salisbury, Graham. 2001. *Lord of the Deep*. Delacorte.

Slepian, Jan. 1990. *Risk N' Roses*. Philomel.

Spinelli, Jerry. 2000. *Stargirl*. Knopf.

Whelan, Gloria. 2000. *Homeless Bird*. HarperCollins.

Wiles, Deborah. 2005. *Each Little Bird That Sings*. Harcourt.

Williams, Carol Lynch. 1997. *The True Colors of Caitlynne Jackson*. Delacorte.

SPORTS

Brooks, Bruce. 1984. *The Moves Make the Man*. Harper.

Christopher, Matt. 1988. *Tackle Without a Team*. Little, Brown.

Dygard, Thomas. 1993. *Game Plan*. Morrow.

Hughes, Dean. 1996. *Team Picture*. Atheneum.

Ritter, John. 2006. *Under the Baseball Moon*. Philomel.

Roberts, Kristi. 2005. *My 13th Season*. Holt.

Slote, Alfred. 1973. *Hang Tough, Paul Mather*. Harper.

Slote, Alfred. 1990. *The Trading Game*. Harper.

Spinelli, Jerry. 1996. *Crash*. Knopf.

Wallace, Rich. 2006. *Dunk Under Pressure*. Viking. (Also see others in the Winning Season series.)

SURVIVAL

Cross, Gillian. 2004. *Dark Ground*. Dutton.

George, Jean Craighead. 1972. *Julie of the Wolves*. Harper. (Also see the other "Julie" books.)

Hobbs, Will. 1996. *Far North*. Morrow.

Holman, Felice. 1974. *Slake's Limbo*. Scribner.

Korman, Gordon. 2001. *Shipwreck (Island, Book 1)*. Scholastic. (See others in the Island series.)

Neale, Jonathan, 2004. *Himalaya*. Houghton Mifflin.

O'Dell, Scott. 1960. *Island of the Blue Dolphins*. Houghton Mifflin.

Paulsen, Gary. 1997. *Tucket's Ride*. Delacorte.

Sperry, Armstrong. 1940. *Call It Courage*. Macmillan.

White, Robb. 1972. *Deathwatch*. Doubleday.

EASIER TO READ

Bulla, Clyde Robert. 1975. *Shoeshine Girl*. Crowell. (Problem.)

Byars, Betsy. 2004. *Little Horse on His Own*. Illustrated by David McPhail. Holt. (Animals.)

Christopher, Matt. 1993. *The Dog That Stole Home*. Little, Brown. (Sports; Animals.)

Cleary, Beverly. 1990. *Muggie Maggie*. Morrow. (Problem humor.)

Clements, Andrew. 2001. *Jake Drake, Bully Buster*. Simon. (Humor.)

Dahl, Roald. 1992. *The Vicar of Nibbleswicke*. Viking. (Humor.)

Giff, Patricia Reilly. 1996. *Good Luck, Ronald Morgan*. Viking. (Humor. See others in the Ronald Morgan series.)

Joosse, Barbara M. 2006. *Dead Guys Talk*. Clarion. (Mystery.)

Napoli, Donna Jo, and Robert Furrow. 2006. *Sly the Sleuth and the Sports Mysteries*. Dial. (Sports, mystery.)

Park, Barbara. 2006. *Junie B., First Grader: Aloha-ha-ha!* Illustrated by Denise Brunkus. Random. (Humor. See others in the Junie B. Jones series.)

Peck, Robert Newton. 1974. *Soup*. Knopf. (Humor.)

Smith, Doris Buchanan. 1973. *A Taste of Blackberries*. Crowell. (Problem.)

Sobol, Donald. 1963. *Encyclopedia Brown, Boy Detective*. Nelson. (Mystery. See others in the Encyclopedia Brown series.)

Stevenson, James. 1995. *The Bones in the Cliff*. Greenwillow. (Mystery.)

Wright, Betty Ren. 2006. *Princess for a Week*. Holiday House. (Mystery.)

PICTURE BOOKS

Baylor, Byrd. 1994. *The Table Where Rich People Sit*. Illustrated by Peter Parnall. Scribner's.

Beaumont, Karen. 2005. *I Ain't Gonna Paint No More*. Illustrated by David Catrow. Harcourt.

Bunting, Eve. 1994. *Smoky Night*. Illustrated by David Diaz. Harcourt.

Bunting, Eve. 2000. *The Memory String*. Illustrated by Ted Rand. Clarion.

dePaola, Tomie. 1973. *Nana Upstairs & Nana Downstairs*. Viking.

Hutchins, Pat. 2003. *There's Only One of Me!* Greenwillow.

Juster, Norton. 2005. *The Hello, Goodbye Window*. Illustrated by Chris Raschka. Hyperion.

Polacco, Patricia. 1998. *Thank You, Mr. Falker*. Philomel.

Rosen, Michael. 2005. *Michael Rosen's Sad Book*. Illustrated by Quentin Blake. Candlewick.

Say, Allen. 1997. *Allison*. Houghton Mifflin.

Schertle, Alice. 1995. *Down the Road*. Illustrated by E. B. Lewis. Browndeer/Harcourt.

Seeber, Dorothea. 2000. *A Pup Just for Me: A Boy Just for Me*. Illustrated by Ed Young. Philomel.

Viorst, Judith. 1995. *Alexander, Who's Not (Do You Hear Me? I Mean It!) Going to Move*. Illustrated by Robin Preiss Glasser. Atheneum.

Woodsen, Jacqueline. 2001. *The Other Side*. Illustrated by E. B. Lewis. Putnam.

For details about the books listed here and for a more complete list of contemporary realistic fiction titles, consult the Children's Literature Database: A Resource for Teachers, Parents, and Media Specialists CD *that accompanies this text.*

REFERENCES

Brooks, Bruce. (1984). *The moves makes the man*. New York: Harper.

Burnford, Sheila. (1961). *The incredible journey*. Boston: Little, Brown.

Butler, Dori Hillestad. (2003). *Sliding into home*. Atlanta, GA: Peachtree.

Cleary, Beverly. (1983). *Dear Mr. Henshaw*. New York: Morrow.

Copeland, Cynthia. (2004). *Dilly for president*. Brookfield, CT: Millbrook.

Deuker, Carl. (2000). *Night hoops*. Boston: Houghton Mifflin.

DiCamillo, Kate. (2000). *Because of Winn-Dixie*. Cambridge, MA: Candlewick.

Dowell, Francie O'Roark. (2000). *Dovey Coe*. New York: Atheneum.

Dygard, Thomas. (1996). *Running wild*. New York: Morrow.

George, Jean Craighead. (1959). *My side of the mountain*. New York: Dutton.

Gutman, Dan. (1997). *Honus and me*. New York: Avon.

Gutman, Dan. (2000). *Babe and me*. New York: Avon.

Gutman, Dan. (2005). *Abner and me*. New York: Harper.

Fitzhugh, Louise. (1964). *Harriet the spy*. New York: Harper.

Hautzig, Esther. (1968). *The endless steppe*. New York: Crowell.

Haynes, Carol. (1988). The explanatory power of content for identifying children's literature preferences. Doctoral dissertation, Northern Illinois University, DeKalb, IL.

Henry, Marguerite. (1945). *Justin Morgan had a horse*. Chicago: Wilcox & Follett.

Henry, Marguerite. (1947). *Misty of Chincoteague*. Chicago: Rand McNally.

Henry, Marguerite. (1948). *King of the wind*. Chicago: Rand McNally.

Hobbs, Will. (1992). *The big wander*. New York: Atheneum.

Hobbs, Will, (2006). *Crossing the wire*. New York: HarperCollins.

Holman, Felice. (1974). *Slake's limbo*. New York: Scribner.

Horowitz, Anthony. (2004). *Eagle strike*. New York: Philomel.

Hurst, Carol Otis. (2001). *Rocks in his head*. New York: HarperCollins.

Knight, Eric. (1940). *Lassie, come home*. Chicago: John C. Winston.

Korman, Gordon. (2000). *No more dead dogs*. New York: Hyperion.

Korman, Gordon. (2005). *Chasing the falconers*. New York: Scholastic.

Knudsen, R. R. (1972). *Zanballer*. New York: Delacorte.

Knudsen, R. R. (1977). *Zanbanger*. New York: Harper.

Knudsen, R. R. (1978). *Zanboomer*. New York: Harper.

Knudsen, R. R. (1984). *Zan Hagen's Marathon*. New York: Farrar, Straus & Giroux.

Martin, Ann. (2003). *A corner of the universe*. New York: Scholastic.

Morpurgo, Michael. (2003). *Kensuke's kingdom*. New York: Scholastic.

Murray, J. (1997, December 15). "Marguerite Henry—(1902–1997)." *Publishers Weekly*, 27.

Naylor, Phyllis Reynolds. (1991). *Shiloh*. New York: Atheneum.

Paulsen, Gary. (1987). *Hatchet*. New York: Viking.

Peyton, K. M. (1992). *Poor Badger*. New York: Delacorte.

Peyton, K. M. (2001). *Blind Beauty*. New York: Dutton.

Pinkwater, Daniel. (1980). *The Wuggie Norpel story*. New York: Four Winds Press.

Pinkwater, Daniel. (2006). *Yo-yo man*. New York: Harper.

Pullman, Philip. (1985). *Ruby in the smoke*. New York: Random House.

Rawls, Wilson. (1961). *Where the red fern grows*. New York: Doubleday.

Ritter, John. (2006). *Under the baseball moon*. New York: Philomel.

Ross, C. S. (1995). "If They Read Nancy Drew, So What?": Series Book Readers Talk Back. *Library and Information Science Research, 17*, 201–236.

Sachar, Louis. (1998). *Holes*. New York: Farrar, Straus & Giroux.

Slote, Alfred. (1990). *The trading game*. New York: Lippincott.

Stephens, Meic. (1990). *A dictionary of literary quotations*. London: Routledge.

Terhune, Albert Payton. (1926). *Lad, a dog*. New York: Dutton.

Tomlinson, Carl M., & Tunnell, Michael O. (1994). Children's supernatural stories: Popular but persecuted. In John S. Simmons (Ed.), *Censorship: A Threat to Reading, Learning, Thinking* (pp. 107–114). Newark, DE: International Reading Association.

Trease, Geoffrey. (1983, Autumn). Fifty years on: A writer looks back. *Children's Literature in Education, 14*(3), 21–28.

Tunnell, Michael O., & Jacobs, James S. (2005, September 1). Writers & readers: Series fiction and young readers. *Booklist, 102*(2), 64–65.

Van Draanen, Wendelin. (1998). *Sammy Keyes and the hotel thief*. New York: Random House.

Van Draanen, Wendelin. (2001). *Sammy Keyes and the Hollywood mummy*. New York: Random House.

Van Draanen. Wendelin. (2005). *Sammy Keyes and the dead giveaway*. New York: Random House.

Wright, Betty Ren. (1983). *The dollhouse murders*. New York: Holiday House.

Wright, Betty Ren. (2000). *Moonlight man*. New York: Scholastic.

Wright, Betty Ren. (2003). *Crandall's castle*. New York: Holiday House.

Chapter **12**

Historical Fiction

Primary-grade curricula typically have not included the formal study of history because concepts of time develop slowly in children. How can youngsters to whom next week seems like an eternity, or who ask if grandpa was around when the Pilgrims arrived, possibly gain an appreciation of their historical heritage? However, we have learned that teaching history through narrative, or story, can provide "a temporal scaffolding for historical understanding that is accessible even to quite young children" (Downey & Levstik, 1988, p. 338).

Humans tend to think in terms of narrative structures or story grammars, which basically involve characters formulating goals and then solving problems in order to achieve their goals. Children and adults are more likely to process and remember historical information when it comes in the form of a good story (Armbruster & Anderson, 1984; *Curriculum Review,* 2005; Hidi, Baird, & Hildyard, 1982; Jones, Coombs, & McKinney, 1994; McGowan & Guzzetti, 1991). Therefore, teachers who share and encourage the reading of historical picture books and novels likely are helping students learn historical facts, but more importantly are helping them see history as a vital and meaningful subject. Historical fiction can breathe life into what students may have considered irrelevant and dull, thus allowing them to see that their *present* is part of a *living past,* that people as real as themselves struggled with problems similar to their own, and that today's way of life is a result of what these people did in finding solutions.

HISTORY TEXTBOOKS VERSUS HISTORY TRADE BOOKS

History textbooks are *not* effective in helping children make meaningful, personal connections with the past. Studies report that students at all grade levels name social studies (history) as their most boring class and point to their textbooks as one of the major reasons (Fischer, 1997; Sewall, 1988). As far back as 1893, the National Education

Association declared, "When the facts are chosen with as little discrimination as in many school [history] textbooks, when they are mere lists of lifeless dates, details of military movements . . . [t]hey are repellent" (Ravitch, 1985, p. 13).

The criticism from historians and educators today has not lessened (American Textbook Council, 2006; Loewen, 1995; Paxton, 1999). "[History] textbooks have relied more and more on broken text and pictorial flash to hold student interest. Efforts to render textbooks 'readable'—at least by the standards of readability formulas—have contributed to their arid prose" (Sewall, 1988, p. 554). A report issued by the American Textbook Council indicates that "the most troubling writing and content are to be found among leading elementary-level social studies textbooks" (Sewall, 2000, p. 12). The report also points out that the most basic change in the books, beginning in the 1990s, has been "the loss of text"—there is considerably less print but more illustrations (Sewall, 2000, p. 5).

> Too many topics are covered superficially. Textbooks have trouble building bridges from one subject to another. Language is often choppy, stilted, and impersonal. It is a difficult style to read, understand, or remember. (Sewall, 2000, p. 5)

History Textbooks Cover Too Much

History texts' biggest problems stem from the need to cover so much material that they cannot do justice to many important events, people, and concepts. For instance, Columbus is allowed only seven short paragraphs (about 400 words) in Houghton Mifflin's fifth-grade history text (Berson, 2005). In spite of longer coverage for some topics, including Columbus, Macmillan/McGraw-Hill's fifth-grade book (Banks et al., 2005) only gives the Holocaust three short paragraphs (about 150 words), Operation Desert Storm one paragraph (about 130 words), and the Monroe Doctrine six sentences (about 90 words). Couple these short offerings with "arid prose," and you often have a formidable product that separates young readers from "the story of ourselves" (Freedman, 1993, p. 41).

The People Are Missing!

If history is indeed the story of ourselves, then another weakness of history textbooks is glaringly evident: The people are missing! The best one-word definition of history is, in fact, "people." Without human beings, whose emotions and actions influence the times, there is no history. Ask anyone who has had a memorable history class to describe why it was good, and the reasons always include a focus on people, whether prominent or ordinary.

Jean Fritz (1982), in her autobiographical novel *Homesick*, recalls her first school experience with American history texts:

> Miss Crofts put a bunch of history books on the first desk of each row so they could be passed back, student to student. I was glad to see that we'd be studying the history

of Pennsylvania. Since both my mother's and father's families had helped settle Washington County, I was interested to know how they and the other pioneers had fared. Opening the book to the first chapter, "From Forest to Farmland," I skimmed through the pages but I couldn't find any mention of people at all. There was talk about dates and square miles and cultivation and population growth and immigration and the Western movement, but it was as if the forest had lain down and given way to farmland without anyone being brave or scared or tired or sad, without babies being born, without people dying. Well, I thought, maybe that would come later. (p. 153)

But it never did.

Not only are people missing in history texts, but so are varying historical perspectives. "To present history in simple, one sided—almost moralistic—terms, is to teach nothing worth learning and to falsify the past in a way that provides worse than no help in understanding the present or in meeting the future" (Collier, 1976, p. 138).

Indeed, history textbooks approach topics from single perspectives; they have space to do little else (Burstein & Hutton, 2005; Foster, Morris, & Davis, 1996; Tunnell & Ammon, 1996). For instance, the American Revolution typically has been reported from the Whig perspective, which depicts "simple, freedom-loving farmers marching in a crusade to fulfill God's plan for a rationally ordered society based on the principles of liberty and equality" (Collier, 1976, p. 133). There are other points of view, however, such as the Imperialist view, which draws attention to the British perspective, and the Progressive view, which promotes economic reasons for the war above ideological or religious reasons. By the same token, Columbus is presented in elementary-school textbooks mostly from a Eurocentric perspective. Of course, the Native Americans have a defensible point of view that deglorifies Columbus, but this perspective is covertly censored (Shannon, 1989) from textbook pages simply by not being mentioned.

Historical Fiction: Presenting Multiple Perspectives

"When a textbook is used as the only source of information, students tend to accept the author's statements without question" (Holmes & Ammon, 1985, p. 366). But, once again, history never has a single side to its story, and children's literature in the form of historical fiction (and historical nonfiction) is more likely to invite "the reader to enter into a historical discussion that involves making judgments about issues of morality. . . . What was it like to be a person here? What was the nature of good and evil in that time and place, and with whom shall my sympathies lie?" (Levstik, 1989, p. 137).

This sort of critical thinking about the story of ourselves involves examining conflicting viewpoints and making personal judgments. For example, several pieces of historical fiction for young readers approach the American Revolution from differing perspectives, books such as Esther Forbes's *Johnny Tremain* (1943), a Whig

FIGURE 12–1
Notable authors of historical fiction.

Avi: *American history.*
Beatty, Patricia, and John Beatty: *American Civil War and westward expansion.*
Bruchac, Joseph: *Native American history.*
Collier, James Lincoln, and Christopher Collier: *American Revolution.*
Haugaard, Erik Christian: *European history.*
Hunter, Mollie: *British history.*
Lasky, Kathryn: *American history.*
Lester, Julius: *African American history.*
Meyer, Carolyn: *European history.*

O'Dell, Scott: *Native American history; American West.*
Orlev, Uri: *Holocaust.*
Park, Linda Sue: *Korean history.*
Rinaldi, Ann: *American history.*
Speare, Elizabeth George: *Colonial America.*
Sutcliff, Rosemary: *Early history of Britain.*
Taylor, Mildred: *African American history.*
Uchida, Yoshiko: *Japanese American history.*
Wilder, Laura Ingalls: *Westward expansion.*
Yep, Laurence: *Chinese American history.*

treatment of the Revolution; James and Christopher Collier's *My Brother Sam Is Dead* (1974), a combination of Whig and Progressive treatments; Avi's *The Fighting Ground* (1984), wherein a boy changes from a flaming Patriot to wondering which side (if any) he is on; Scott O'Dell's *Sarah Bishop* (1980), told through the eyes of a girl from a Loyalist, or Tory, family who is brutalized by the war; and the Colliers' *Jump Ship to Freedom* (1981), an African American perspective of the Revolution that tells of broken promises of liberty and justice for all. Read in combination, these titles provide the fodder for discussing, debating, and questioning the human motives behind the historical facts. Plus, historical fiction can be an engaging reading experience, which is perhaps the most important reason to involve its use in the classroom.

 ## WHAT MAKES GOOD HISTORICAL FICTION?

Historical fiction must, of course, be set in the past. The main characters generally are fictional, though often they rub shoulders with historically prominent people. Sometimes the story's focus is not on events in history, but rather on a wholly imaginary plot that is accurately set in a particular period and place from the past. An example is Wilson Rawls's immortal dog story, *Where the Red Fern Grows* (1961), which is set in the Ozarks of Oklahoma in the 1920s. *Where the Red Fern Grows* is perhaps more a dog story than a historical novel. At other times, a story's plot involves the protagonist in famous historical events, such as the fictional Johnny Tremain's involvement in the Boston Tea Party and the battles of Lexington and Concord (Forbes, 1943). Sometimes it is difficult to decide whether certain books are contemporary or historical. Often the determining factor is the age of the reader; the Gulf War in 1991 may be contemporary for adult readers but ancient history to a fifth grader.

Historical fiction is judged by the same criteria as any other piece of fiction: strength of character development, credibility of plot, quality of writing style, definition of setting, handling of theme. However, some considerations are peculiar to the genre.

History Should Not Be Sugarcoated

When dealing with historical events, it is important to deal plainly with the truth. Several decades ago, unsettling truths were avoided or even revised in books written for children. The age of new realism in children's literature, which started in the mid-1960s, launched a trend that dictated more honesty in the writing of realistic fiction. Topics that mostly had been avoided or handled gingerly began to appear more frequently and with increased frankness, such as the Japanese American internment camps in the United States during World War II (*Journey to Topaz* by Yoshiko Uchida, 1971), the horrors of slavery (*Nightjohn* by Gary Paulsen, 1993), and the brutality of the Holocaust (*The Devil's Arithmetic* by Jane Yolen, 1988).

Kathryn Lasky (1990) explains that an author of historical fiction has the responsibility to preserve what she calls "the fabric of time" by remaining faithful to the historical context in which a story is set. Lasky (1983) confronted the difficulty some readers have with that honesty after publication of her book *Beyond the Divide*. In her research she learned that women in the old West were constant targets of crime. They often were left alone and were vulnerable to rape and murder. And if they were raped, the women generally were ostracized, as happened with Serena Billings in *Beyond the Divide*. Lasky received a letter from an adult reader who was angry not so much because Serena was raped, but because she was ostracized. The reader said, "[This] account did not set a good example for coping with the hurt and trauma that accompanies rape or for teaching young readers how they might cope with it" (Lasky, 1990, p. 164). Lasky responded by saying, "As a writer of historical fiction, I have an obligation to remain faithful, to remain accountable in my story telling, to the manners and mores and the practices of the period" (1990, p. 165).

Indeed, much of our history is unsavory. But the lessons history has to teach us will go unlearned if we are forever softening the factual account. Understanding and being sickened by Serena's treatment help us become more aware of righting the mistakes of the past. In the immortal words of George Santayana, "Those who cannot remember the past are condemned to repeat it."

Historical Accuracy Is Required

Because historical fiction is rooted in history, an infrastructure of accurate historical facts is necessary. When events are documented, they must not be altered. However, when fictionalizing history, authors may take some liberties. For example, they may create dialogue for famous individuals (but should not put words into their mouths that don't fit with their known attitudes and personalities) or may patch in an invented character. To serve the purpose of storytelling, for instance, Esther Forbes (1943) created conversations between Johnny Tremain and many of the well-known Sons of Liberty. What Paul Revere said to Johnny is certainly not factual, although it reflects what Forbes knew about Revere's attitudes and personal life. The fictional Johnny serves as a vehicle to unite in an efficient way the major people and the complex events of the Boston Revolt, pulling fragmented occurrences together into a cohesive story. On the other hand, if Forbes had invented a surprise appearance of George Washington at the Boston Tea Party for dramatic effect, the reworking of the facts would have strained the story's historical credibility.

The Historical Period Should Come to Life

A historical period is brought to life when the author re-creates the physical environment, patterns of daily living, and spirit of the times. What was it like to live from day to day in Boston in 1775? Or London in 1215? What did a servant eat? What diseases were feared? Who went to school and who didn't? Mollie Hunter (1976, p. 43), winner of Britain's Carnegie Award for her historical novel *The Stronghold* (1974), feels that this sort of realism can best be communicated in writing when authors have come to know the place and time so well that they "could walk undetected in the past," waking in the morning to know the sort of bed they'd be sleeping in or reaching in their pockets to grasp familiar coins. Creating this atmosphere in a novel also depends on avoiding modern terms. Joan Blos (1985), author of the Newbery Award–winning *A Gathering of Days* (1979), points out that authors of historical novels struggle with the compromises that must be made in maintaining strict historical validity, and that sometimes the rules require bending to make a story readable. An overabundance of archaic speech in a story of the Middle Ages may derail a young reader. However, she says, "historical material and thought lack validity if expressed in modern phrases, idioms, or linguistic rhythms," as in this example relating to the American Revolution: "Peering out of her bedroom window, Deeny saw bunches of Hessians heading for the green" (1985, p. 39). "Bunches" to describe groups of people is an informal, modern use of the word that is out of place in a colonial American setting. Another example is found in *Tiger* (Stone, 2005), the first novel in a martial arts series set in 17th-century China. It is historically jarring to hear the young protagonists addressing one another with the phrase, "Hey, guys."

Re-creating the spirit of the times may be the most important and most difficult challenge an author faces. To understand the motivating factors that led individuals or groups of people to make decisions that altered the patterns of life or the course of political history is not a simple affair. What stirred the winds of change or suppressed them? The spirit of the times fueled the American rebellion against the Crown in the 1770s or encouraged the acceptance of slavery in the 1850s, but not everyone was moved by the spirit in the same way. Some colonists resisted the American Revolution, and some Southerners operated stations on the Underground

Railroad. Yet the varying perspectives that often lead to the conflicts that initiate change, both in the past and today, are the very sort of spirit that should permeate good historical stories.

The History Usually Is Revealed through the Eyes of a Young Protagonist

Although young main characters seem a requirement for most children's fiction, historical novels have an especially pressing need for them. Because young readers are accosted with a study of history that generally ignores the people who aren't historically famous—people like themselves—almost no children are ever mentioned. Therefore, the gap between themselves and the dusty past widens. A young protagonist who is inserted into the tumultuous times of the Boston Revolt or the difficult period of the Great Depression allows young readers to experience history through the senses of someone who views life in a similar way—as a child.

Jane Yolen (1989) tells of being invited to talk to a group of eighth graders about the Holocaust. Horrified, the students asked her if she made "all that stuff up." The realities of Europe in the 1930s and 1940s were so far outside their realms of experience that they thought this story of such massive human suffering was a joke. People couldn't do such things to one another. Yolen's answer to this problem is found in her novel *The Devil's Arithmetic* (1988), which uses a fantasy technique to transport a 14-year-old American Jewish girl of the 1980s back to World War II Poland. As a youngster disconnected with her own past, Hannah is allowed to experience personally the spirit of the times and ask questions such as "How could you be so dumb as to believe those Nazis when they say you are only being resettled?" Yolen (1989) explains,

> Children are mired in the present. . . . [So, by] taking a child out of that *today* in a novel, [with] a child protagonist that the reader identifies fully with, and throwing the child backwards or forwards in time, the reader too is thrown into the slipstream of yesterday or tomorrow. The reader becomes part of that "living and continuous process," forced to acknowledge that we *are* our past just as we *are* our future. (p. 248)

Whether bringing a modern child back in time or creating a young protagonist who is born to that time, authors of historical fiction thereby are able to give their young audience a sense of connecting with the past.

USING THE CHILDREN'S LITERATURE DATABASE

Be sure the CD database is installed on your hard drive. Click on Search Query Builder in the left navigation bar on the Home screen. Type "World War II" in the Keyword Search field. Check the boxes Title, Topics, and Description. Click Run Search. When the search is complete, click on Save This List as Set in the top navigation bar. Give your saved set a name (in the pop-up window), and click Submit. From the Saved Set Detail screen, click on the Open Set in Book List button in the top navigation bar. Select Extend This List from the book list, and then click on Run Search. Enter "Holocaust; Jews" in the Keyword Search field, and be sure to check the Any button. Check the boxes Title, Topics, and Description. Click Run Search. Click on Save This List as Set in the top navigation bar. Give your saved set a name (in the pop-up window), and click Submit. The result of the books that now appear in the book list are a combination of the first search for World War II books and the second search for Holocaust; Jews, without repeated titles.

Avoid Too Much Attention to Historical Detail

Telling a good story is still the essence of historical fiction. Although authors may be tempted to cram in as many details from their historical research as possible, including too much historical detail may make the writing laborious and destroy the sense of story. Joan Blos (1985) notes two common ways an author may give in to this temptation. First, "the overstuffed sentence" (or paragraph or chapter) is loaded with far too many intrusive clauses of historical explanation:

> Zeke was eager to get to the corner. He wanted to be certain that when the procession came by he could see President Abraham Lincoln who, with his running mate, Senator Hannibal Hamlin of Maine . . . (p. 38)

Second, "the privy observed" involves a character who launches into inappropriate descriptions. Blos explains that a good test is to ask whether a contemporary character would carry on about a similar detail and gives this example:

> Sam's mother adjusted one of the four round dials that adorned the front of the white enamelled stove, turning it from High to Simmer, and waiting a minute to be sure that the heat had been reduced. (pp. 38–39)

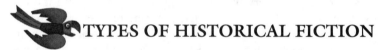

TYPES OF HISTORICAL FICTION

Historical fiction generally falls into five categories.

1. A STORY OF HISTORICAL EVENTS HAPPENING BEFORE THE LIFE OF THE AUTHOR. Most historical stories are of the type that are set completely in the past, in a period the author has not personally experienced. This means that the author relies completely on historical research rather than personal experience in creating the story. An example of this common variety of historical novel is Linda Sue Park's Newbery Award–winning tale set in 12th-century Korea, *A Single Shard* (2001).

2. A CONTEMPORARY NOVEL THAT BECOMES HISTORICAL FICTION WITH THE PASSAGE OF TIME. When Marie McSwigan (1942) wrote *Snow Treasure* during World War II, it was a contemporary novel based on the heroic true story of Norwegian children who smuggled gold bullion past Nazi guards in broad daylight on their sleds. They hid the gold in a snow cave, from which it was later secreted away by the British. Every one of today's schoolchildren and virtually all of their teachers were not yet born when this event occurred. *Snow Treasure* is now most firmly in the realm of historical fiction.

3. AUTHORS CHRONICLE THEIR OWN LIFE STORIES IN A FICTIONAL FORMAT. Another variety of historical fiction is unusual because the author recounts episodes from his or her own life. In other words, the story is a fictionalized account of the time period and events experienced by the author, but often written about years later. The Little House books (for example, *The Little House in the Big Woods,* 1932; *Little House on the Prairie,* 1935) by Laura Ingalls Wilder are books of this type.

4. THE PROTAGONIST TRAVELS BACK INTO HISTORY.   Time travel, a feature of fantasy rather than realism, has been used as a mechanism to transport contemporary characters into the past and then later return them to their own time. Everything else in this type of historical novel conforms to the realistic nature of the genre. As mentioned earlier, Jane Yolen's *The Devil's Arithmetic* (1988) is an example of this type.

5. A NOVEL SPECULATES ABOUT ALTERNATIVE HISTORICAL OUTCOMES.   Authors sometimes create "what if" stories about history. For example, Gary Blackwood's *Year of the Hangman* (2002) postulates about the state of affairs had the American colonists lost the Revolutionary War. George Washington is in prison and other patriots, such as Benjamin Franklin, are hiding in the French-controlled territory around New Orleans. This type of story accentuates the tenuous turning points that could have easily changed the course of events.

REVIEWING THE VALUES OF HISTORICAL FICTION

Historical fiction at its best is a good story and can be enjoyed as a read-aloud at home or school or as an exciting individual reading experience. Young readers may be influenced in developing lifelong positive reading behaviors by the power of story found in historical novels and picture books. Of course, historical fiction can quicken dry historical facts and breathe life into the people and events of the past. It may aid young children in developing a sense of time and of how they fit into the scheme of history. Indeed, children may connect, often for the first time, with their own heritage by reading "the story of ourselves" as offered in historical fiction. Plus, they will be better prepared to face their futures. As Winston Churchill once said, "The farther backward you can look, the farther forward you can see."

HISTORICAL FICTION READING LIST

TEN OF OUR FAVORITES

Banks, Lynne Reid. 2005. *Tiger, Tiger*. Delacorte. Two tiger cub brothers are taken from the jungle to ancient Rome, where one becomes the pampered pet of Caesar's daughter and the other becomes a man-eating "entertainment act" at the Colosseum.

Conrad, Pam. 1985. *Prairie Songs*. Harper. Louisa's life in a loving pioneer family on the Nebraska prairie is altered by the arrival of a new doctor and his beautiful, tragically frail wife.

Fleischman, Paul. 1993. *Bull Run*. Harper. Northerners, southerners, generals, couriers, dreaming boys, and worried sisters describe the glory, the horror, the thrill, and the disillusionment of the first land battle of the Civil War.

Fletcher, Susan. 1998. *Shadow Spinner*. Atheneum. When Marjan, a 13-year-old crippled girl, joins the Sultan's harem in ancient Persia, she gathers for Shahrazad the stories that will save the queen's life.

McCaffrey, Anne. 1996. *Black Horses for the King*. Harcourt. Galwyn, son of a Roman Celt, escapes from his tyrannical uncle and joins Lord Artos, later known as King Arthur, using his talent with languages and his way with horses to help secure and care for the Libyan horses that Artos hopes to use in battle against the Saxons.

Speare, Elizabeth George. 1958. *The Witch of Blackbird Pond*. Houghton Mifflin. In 1687 in Connecticut, Kit Tyler—who feels out of place in the Puritan household of her aunt and befriends an old woman the community thinks is a witch—suddenly finds herself standing trial for witchcraft. Winner of the Newbery Medal.

Sutcliff, Rosemary. 1995. (Originally published 1955). *The Outcast*. Farrar, Straus. Exiled from his ancient British tribe, Beric is captured by the Romans and forced into slavery, but harbors the hope of escaping to return to his homeland.

Taylor, Mildred. 1976. *Roll of Thunder, Hear My Cry*. Dial. A black family living in the South during the 1930s is faced with discrimination. Because the family owns its own land and is uncharacteristically independent for the era, they have an unusually difficult time living with such prejudice. Winner of the Newbery Medal.

Watkins, Yoko Kawashima. 1986. *So Far from the Bamboo Grove*. Lothrop. A young Japanese girl, her older sister, and her mother struggle to escape the dangers of an angry Korea as World War II ends.

Yolen, Jane. 1988. *The Devil's Arithmetic*. Viking Penguin. Hannah resents the traditions of her Jewish heritage until time travel places her in the middle of a small Jewish village in Nazi-occupied Poland.

OTHERS WE LIKE

Armstrong, William. 1971. *Sour Land*. Harper.

Avi. 2006. *Crispin: At the Edge of the World*. Hyperion.

Bauer, Marion Dane. 2003. *Land of the Buffalo Bones: The Diary of Mary Elizabeth Rodgers, an English Girl in Minnesota*. Scholastic. (See other titles in the Dear America series.)

Cannon, A. E. 2002. *Charlotte's Rose*. Wendy Lamb Books (Random House).

Collier, James Lincoln, and Christopher Collier. 1974. *My Brother Sam Is Dead*. Four Winds.

Crowe, Chris. 2002. *Mississippi Trial, 1955*. Phyllis Fogleman (Penguin Group USA).

Erdrich, Louise. 2005. *The Game of Silence*. HarperCollins.

Fletcher, Susan. 2006. *Alphabet of Dreams*. Atheneum.

Forbes, Esther. 1943. *Johnny Tremain*. Houghton Mifflin.

Fox, Paula. 1973. *The Slave Dancer*. Bradbury.

Greene, Bette. 1973. *The Summer of My German Soldier*. Dial.

Hunt, Irene. 1964. *Across Five Aprils*. Follett.

Hunter, Mollie. 1998. *The King's Swift Rider: A Novel on Robert the Bruce*. HarperCollins.

Ibbotsen, Eva. 2004. *The Star of Kazan*. Dutton.

Lasky, Kathryn. 1983. *Beyond the Divide*. Macmillan.

Lasky, Kathryn. 1994. *Beyond the Burning Time*. Scholastic (Blue Sky).

Lester, Julius. 2005. *Day of Tears: A Novel in Dialogue*. Hyperion.

Lowry, Lois. 1989. *Number the Stars*. Houghton Mifflin.

McGraw, Eloise. 1961. *The Golden Goblet*. Coward.

Meyer, Carolyn. 2005. *Patience, Princess Catherine*. Harcourt.

Morpurgo, Michael. 2003. *Kensuke's Kingdom*. Scholastic.

O'Dell, Scott. 1986. *Streams to the River, River to the Sea: A Novel of Sacagawea*. Houghton Mifflin.

Orlev, Uri. 1984. *The Island on Bird Street*. Houghton Mifflin.

Park, Linda Sue. 2001. *A Single Shard*. Clarion.

Paulsen, Gary. 1993. *Nightjohn*. Delacorte.

Pullman, Philip. 1988. *The Ruby in the Smoke*. Knopf.

Richter, Hans Peter. 1970. *Friedrich*. Holt.

Speare, Elizabeth George. 1961. *The Bronze Bow*. Houghton Mifflin.

Taylor, Theodore. 1969. *The Cay*. Doubleday.

Uchida, Yoshiko. 1971. *Journey to Topaz*. Creative Arts.

Yep, Laurence. 1977. *Dragonwings*. Harper.

EASIER TO READ

Avi. 1979. *Night Journeys*. Morrow.

Bishop, Claire Huchet. 1990. (1952). *Twenty and Ten*. Scholastic.

Bulla, Clyde Robert. 1956. *The Sword in the Tree*. Crowell.

Coerr, Eleanor. 2002. (1977). *Sadako and the Thousand Paper Cranes*. Putnam.

Gardiner, John. 1980. *Stone Fox*. Crowell.

Giblin, James Cross. 2006. *The Boy Who Saved Cleveland*. Holt.

MacLachlan, Patricia. 1985. *Sarah, Plain and Tall*. Harper.

McKissack, Patricia C. 2006. *Away West*. Illustrated by Gordon C. James. Viking. (See others in the Scraps of Time series.)

McSwigan, Marie. 1942. *Snow Treasure*. Dutton.

Nixon, Joan Lowery. 2000. *Aggie's Home*. Delacorte. (See other titles in the Orphan Train Children series.)

Turner, Ann. 1985. *Dakota Dugout*. Illustrated by Ronald Himler. Macmillan.

Wilder, Laura Ingalls. 1932. *Little House in the Big Woods*. Harper.

Wyeth, Sharon. 2003. *Message in the Sky, Corey's Underground Railroad Diary*. Scholastic. (See other titles in the My America series.)

PICTURE BOOKS

Bruchac, Joseph. 2000. *Squanto's Journey*. Illustrated by Greg Shed. Harcourt.

Bunting, Eve. 1990. *The Wall*. Illustrated by Ronald Himler. Houghton Mifflin.

Goble, Paul. 1987. *Death of the Iron Horse*. Bradbury.

Hest, Amy. 1997. *When Jessie Came Across the Sea*. Illustrated by P. J. Lynch. Candlewick.

Lasky, Kathryn. 1997. *Marven of the Great North Woods*. Illustrated by Kevin Hawkes. Harcourt.

Lorbiecki, Marybeth. 2006. *Jackie's Bat*. Illustrated by Brian Pinkney. Simon & Schuster.

Mochizuki, Ken. 1997. *Passage to Freedom: The Sugihara Story*. Illustrated by Dom Lee. Lee & Low.

Polacco, Patricia. 1994. *Pink and Say*. Philomel.

Provensen, Alice. 2005. *Klondike Gold*. Simon & Schuster.

Ryan, Pam Muñoz. 1999. *Amelia and Eleanor Go for a Ride*. Scholastic.

Say, Allen. 2002. *Home of the Brave*. Houghton Mifflin.

Thayer, Ernest Lawrence. 2000. *Casey at the Bat: A Ballad of the Republic Sung in the Year 1888*. Illustrated by Christopher Bing. Handprint.

Tsuchiya, Yukio. 1988. *Faithful Elephants: A True Story of Animals, People and War*. Illustrated by Ted Lewin. Houghton Mifflin.

Tunnell, Michael O. 1997. *Mailing May*. Illustrated by Ted Rand. Greenwillow.

Wiles, Deborah. 2001. *Freedom Summer*. Illustrated by Jerome Lagarrigue. Atheneum.

Winter, Jeanette. 1988. *Follow the Drinking Gourd*. Knopf.

Woodson, Jacqueline. 2005. *Show Way*. Illustrated by Hudson Talbot. Putnam.

Yin. 2001. *Coolies*. Illustrated by Chris K. Soentpiet. Philomel.

Yolen, Jane. 1992. *Encounter*. Illustrated by David Shannon. Harcourt.

For details about books listed here and for a more complete list of historical fiction titles, consult the Children's Literature Database: A Resource for Teachers, Parents, and Media Specialists CD *that accompanies this text.*

REFERENCES

American Textbook Council. (2006, May 23). Homepage. Available online at: http://historytextbooks.org.

Armbruster, Bonnie B., & Anderson, Thomas H. (1984). Structures for explanation in history textbooks, or what if Governor Stanford missed the spike and hit the rail? In Richard C. Anderson, Jean Osborn, & Robert J. Tierney (Eds.), *Learning to read in American schools*. Hillsdale, NJ: Erlbaum.

Avi. (1984). *The fighting ground*. Philadelphia: Lippincott.

Banks, James A., Boehm, Richards G., Colleary, Kevin P., Contreras, Gloria Goodwin, A. Lin, McFarland, Mary A., & Parker, Walter C. (2005). *Our nation*. New York: Macmillan/McGraw Hill.

Berson, Michael J. (Ed.). (2005). *Harcourt horizons: United States history*. Orlando, FL: Harcourt.

Blackwood, Gary. (2002). *Year of the hangman*. New York: Dutton.

Blos, Joan. (1979). *A gathering of days*. New York: Scribner's.

Blos, Joan. (1985, November). The overstuffed sentence and other means for assessing historical fiction for children. *School Library Journal*, 38–39.

Burstein, Joyce, & Hutton, Lisa. (2005, September/October). Planning and teaching with multiple perspectives. *Social Studies and the Young Learner, 18*(1), 15–17.

Collier, Christopher. (1976, April). Johnny and Sam: Old and new approaches to the American Revolution. *The Horn Book, 52*, 132–138.

Collier, James Lincoln, & Collier, Christopher. (1974). *My brother Sam is dead*. New York: Four Winds.

Collier, James Lincoln, & Collier, Christopher. (1981). *Jump ship to freedom*. New York: Delacorte.

Curriculum Review. (2005, November). Bringing ancient history back to life: An interview with Nancy Toff. *Curriculum Review, 45*(3), 14–15.

Downey, Mathew T., & Levstik, Linda S. (1988, September). Teaching and learning history: The research base. *Social Education,* 336–342.

Fischer, B. (Ed.). (1997, November). The bottom line. *NEA Today, 16*(4), 9.

Forbes, Esther. (1943). *Johnny Tremain.* New York: Houghton Mifflin.

Foster, Stuart, Morris, J. W., & Davis, O. L. (1996, Summer). Prospects for teaching historical analysis and interpretation: National curriculum standards for history meet current history textbooks. *Journal of Curriculum and Supervision, 11*(4), 367–385.

Freedman, Russell. (1993). Bring 'em back alive. In M. O. Tunnell & R. Ammon (Eds.), *The story of ourselves: Teaching history through children's literature.* Portsmouth, NH: Heinemann.

Fritz, Jean. (1982). *Homesick: My own story.* New York: Putnam.

Hidi, Suzanne, Baird, W., & Hildyard, Angela. (1982). That's important but is it interesting? Two factors in text processing. In August Flammer & Walter Kintsch (Eds.), *Discourse processing.* Amsterdam: Elsevier-North Holland.

Holmes, Betty, & Ammon, Richard. (1985, May/June). Teaching content with trade books: A strategy. *Childhood Education, 61*(5), 366–370.

Hunter, Mollie. (1974). *The stronghold.* New York: Harper.

Hunter, Mollie. (1976). Shoulder in the sky. In *Talent is not enough.* New York: Harper.

Jones, H. Jon, Coombs, William T., & McKinney, Warren C. (1994, Winter). A themed literature unit versus a textbook: a comparison of the effects on content acquisition and attitudes in elementary social studies. *Reading Research and Instruction, 34,* 85–96.

Lasky, Kathryn. (1983). *Beyond the divide.* New York: Macmillan.

Lasky, Kathryn. (1990, Summer). The fiction of history: Or, what did Miss Kitty really do? *The New Advocate, 3*(3), 157–166.

Levstik, Linda. (1989). A gift of time: Children's historical fiction. In Janet Hickman & Bernice Cullinan (Eds.), *Children's literature in the classroom: Weaving Charlotte's web.* Needham Heights, MA: Christopher-Gordon.

Loewen, James. (1995, January). By the book. *The American School Board Journal, 182*(1), 24–27.

McGowan, Tom, & Guzzetti, Barbara. (1991, January/February). Promoting social studies understanding through literature-based instruction. *The Social Studies, 82*(1), 16–21.

McSwigan, Marie. (1942). *Snow treasure.* New York: Dutton.

O'Dell, Scott. (1980). *Sarah Bishop.* New York: Houghton Mifflin.

Park, Linda Sue. (2001). *A single shard.* New York: Clarion.

Paulsen, Gary. (1993). *Nightjohn.* New York: Delacorte.

Paxton, Richard J. (1999, Fall). A deafening silence: History textbooks and the students who read them. *Review of Educational Research, 69*(3), 315–339.

Ravitch, D. (1985, Spring). The precarious state of history. *American Educator, 9*(4), 11–17.

Rawls, Wilson. (1961). *Where the red fern grows.* Garden City, NY: Doubleday.

Sewall, Gilbert T. (1988, April). American history textbooks: Where do we go from here? *Phi Delta Kappan,* 553–558.

Sewall, Gilbert T. (2000). *History textbooks at the new century: A report of the American textbook council.* New York: American Textbook Council. (ERIC document No. ED 441 731).

Shannon, Patrick. (1989, Spring). Overt and covert censorship of children's books. *The New Advocate, 2*(2), 97–104.

Stone, Jeff. (2005). *Tiger.* New York: Random House.

Tunnell, Michael O., & Ammon, Richard. (1996, April/May). The story of ourselves: Fostering new perspectives. *Social Education, 60*(4), 212–215.

Uchida, Yoshiko. (1971). *Journey to Topaz.* Berkeley, CA: Creative Arts.

Wilder, Laura Ingalls. (1932). *Little house in the big woods.* New York: Harper.

Wilder, Laura Ingalls. (1935). *Little house on the prairie.* New York: Harper.

Yolen, Jane. (1988). *The devil's arithmetic.* New York: Viking Penguin.

Yolen, Jane. (1989, March). An experiential act. *Language Arts, 66*(3), 246–251.

Chapter 13

Biography

"**D**ear Mr. Freedman," a young boy wrote in a letter, "I read your biography of Abraham Lincoln and liked it very much. Did you take the photographs yourself?" (Freedman, 1993a, p. 41). Russell Freedman, whose book *Lincoln: A Photobiography* (1987) won the Newbery Medal, explains that this fan letter expresses the highest praise a biographer can receive:

> Did you take the pictures yourself? he asks. That youngster came away from my book with the feeling that Abraham Lincoln was a real person who must have lived the day before yesterday. That's exactly the response I'm aiming for. After all, the goal of any biographer, any historian, is to make the past seem real, to breathe life and meaning into people and events that are dead and gone. (1993a, p. 41)

Of course, not all biographies are historical. Contemporary individuals are the topics of biographies and certainly autobiographies. Yet, the goal of the biographer ought to be the same—"to breathe life and meaning into people and events" (Freedman, 1993a, p. 41).

The word *biography* renders its own definition: *bio* = life, *graphy* = writing. This specialized variety of nonfiction writing focuses on the lives of human beings, usually people who are famous.

 USING THE CHILDREN'S LITERATURE DATABASE

Be sure the CD database is installed on your hard drive. Click on Search Query Builder in the left navigation bar on the Home screen. Enter "Abraham Lincoln" in the Keyword Search field. Check the All button and the boxes Title, Topics, and Description. Next, check B and PB (for biography and picture books) for Genre. Then click on Run Search. You now have a list of picture book biographies about Abraham Lincoln. To save this list for future use, click on Save This List as Set in the top navigation bar. Give your saved set a name (in the pop-up window), and click Submit.

 ## TYPICAL PERSONALITIES IN BIOGRAPHIES

Because famous personalities typically are the focus of adult as well as juvenile biographies, it is easy to organize biographies by either the careers of the individuals or some other factor responsible for their fame.

SCIENTISTS AND INVENTORS. Perhaps Thomas Alva Edison is the most popular inventor in juvenile biographies. Other scientists and inventors popular in juvenile biographies include Albert Einstein, Stephen Hawking, George Washington Carver, the Wright Brothers, Madame Curie, and Alexander Graham Bell.

POLITICAL LEADERS. The category of political leaders includes presidents and senators as well as kings, queens, and other monarchs. The publishing of this type of biography can be influenced by current elections, coups, or other swings in power. On the eve of a presidential election, especially when no incumbent is running, some publishers will have biographies of both candidates ready for printing. When the results are announced, the winner's biography goes into production and the loser's into the recycling bin.

There is fierce competition in the arena of current juvenile biographies. Of course, subjects like Abraham Lincoln are standard and lasting fare, as exemplified by Russell Freedman's *Lincoln: A Photobiography* (1987), Carl Sandburg's *Abe Lincoln Grows Up* (1928), and many, many other biographies written about Lincoln over the years.

ARTISTS, MUSICIANS, ACTORS, AUTHORS, AND OTHER PEOPLE FROM THE ARTS. The category of people in the arts also has a trendy facet. For example, many musicians and actors popular with young people do not really measure up over time and are soon forgotten, such as the rock group The Strawberry Alarm Clock from the 1960s. Yet, there is a market for quickly done, heavily illustrated with photographs, and reasonably brief biographies of figures in our popular culture. On the other hand, Mozart, the Beatles, and Glenn Miller are musicians who seem to warrant and get serious attention by biographers. Artists and authors are subjects that are less trendy for children. In fact, prior to the 1980s few biographies of authors were written for young readers. Now, many children's and young adult writers are filling the gap by publishing their autobiographies.

SPORTS PERSONALITIES. A few sports figures, such as Babe Ruth, Jim Thorpe, Jackie Robinson, and Babe Didrickson Zaharias, have withstood the test of time and appear in serious biographies for young readers. Others may be well remembered in years to come, and yet others will be forgotten except by the baseball, football, or basketball aficionado. Again, a trendy element exists in sports biography, almost to the point of dominating the subject. Watch for the slick, photograph-laden biographies that immediately appear after each Olympics, such as those for the reigning women's gymnast or figure skater.

EXPLORERS AND ADVENTURERS. Men and women who takes risks to push back the frontiers of science and geography make for interesting reading. Historical figures who line up nicely with the social studies curriculum show up often in biographies for young readers. For example, a spate of Christopher Columbus biographies appeared during the quincentennial commemoration of his monumental voyage. They provided broad coverage and varied perspectives on the motives for and impact of Columbus's mission. For example, Milton Meltzer's *Columbus and the World Around Him* (1990) was frank, perhaps even critical, about Columbus's shortcomings, and Kathy Pelta's *Discovering Christopher Columbus: How History Is Invented* (1991), though more complimentary, examined how historian biases and the infusion of myth into history have slanted Columbus's story. New titles continue to appear, such as *Columbus: Explorer of the New World* (2001) by Peter Chrisp and *You Wouldn't Want to Sail with Christopher Columbus* (2004) by Fiona MacDonald.

Some intrepid individuals, despite the fact that they aren't common topics in elementary social studies, nevertheless capture young readers' imaginations. Amelia Earhart is an example. Authors continue to write about her, and young readers, especially girls, continue to find this female aviation pioneer fascinating. Titles about Earhart include Corinne Szabo's *Sky Pioneer: A Photobiography of Amelia Earhart* (1997), Pam Muñoz Ryan's *Amelia and Eleanor Go for a Ride* (1999), and Kay Winters's *And Fly She Did!: The Amazing Childhood Adventures of Amelia Earhart* (2005).

Often we think of explorers as being from the past. Of course, our modern astronauts and oceanographers are no less intrepid in pushing back the remaining frontiers and are worthy subjects of current biographies.

HUMANITARIANS. Jane Addams, Albert Schweitzer, Florence Nightingale, and Mother Teresa may be interesting subjects for young readers because of their daring and selfless deeds. The heroic qualities of humanitarians add special appeal to their stories.

PEOPLE WHO OVERCOME TREMENDOUS ODDS. Biographies of people who overcome tremendous odds focus on a different sort of heroism. Many biographies have been published about Helen Keller (including her own autobiography), and her story of struggling to overcome nearly insurmountable physical difficulties continues to be popular reading for children and young adults.

VILLAINS. Is there a place among children's biographies for history's truly wicked? Certainly, most biographies capture the lives of people who have admirable qualities. However, villains' stories provide a contrast and a warning—and are generally interesting. Adolf Hitler is one of the villains many young readers find most horrific and yet fascinating, as portrayed in the biography *The Life and Death of Adolf Hitler* by James Cross Giblin (2002).

OTHER INTERESTING PEOPLE. A trend in juvenile biography is to write about today's ordinary people who have interesting lifestyles, occupations, or experiences. Examples are Molly Bang's *Nobody in Particular: One Woman's Fight to Save the Bays* (2000), the story of a female shrimper's attempt to stop a chemical company from polluting a bay in east Texas, and Kathryn Lasky's *Vision of Beauty: The Story of Sarah Breedlove Walker* (2000), a book about an impoverished black woman who made a fortune creating beauty and hair-care products for African Americans. This category also includes books about lesser-known personalities from history, such as *Charlotte Forten: A Black Teacher in the Civil War* (Burchard, 1995). Other examples are Don Brown's *Uncommon Traveler: Mary Kingsley in Africa* (2000), the biography of a self-educated 19th-century English woman who traveled alone through West Africa to

learn about its people, and Uri Shulevitz's *The Travels of Benjamin of Tudela: Through Three Continents in the Twelfth Century* (2005), the story of a Jewish man who embarked on a 14-year journey through Italy, Greece, Palestine, Persia, China, and Egypt. Books like these give children the sense that everyone, not just the big names from history, has a story and can make a contribution.

TYPES OF BIOGRAPHIES

Until the age of new realism began to change the face of children's books in the 1960s (see Chapter 5), juvenile biographies generally were fictionalized, sometimes at the expense of honesty and accuracy. Many publishers, librarians, and educators felt that children would not read a biography unless it looked and read like a novel. *Fictionalized biographies* are less common today. Instead, fictional treatments of a real person's life are generally classified as historical fiction. However, a personal narrative—an individual's own, slightly fictionalized story—is still considered a biography. Personal narratives are written in narrative or story form rather than in pure expository or nonfiction form. An example is *Upon the Head of the Goat* (1981), Aranka Siegal's powerful autobiographical story of her family's Holocaust ordeal.

The *authentic biography,* written as true nonfiction, is today's trend in biographies for young readers. Although crafted in expository form rather than narrative (as with novels), authentic biographies can be as vigorous and entertaining as good fiction. Milton Meltzer, known for his biographies and informational books about history and social change, says, "I think I've used almost every technique fiction writers call on (except to invent the facts) in order to draw readers in, deepen their feeling for people whose lives may be remote from their own, and enrich their understanding of forces that shape the outcome of all our lives" (quoted in Donelson & Nilsen 1989, p. 259).

Note the stylistic flair Russell Freedman gives to these paragraphs in his biography of Lincoln:

> Today it's hard to imagine Lincoln as he really was. And he never cared to reveal much about himself. In company he was witty and talkative, but he rarely betrayed his inner feelings. According to William Herndon, his law partner, he was "the most secretive—reticent—shut-mouthed man that ever lived."
>
> In his own time, Lincoln was never fully understood even by his closest friends. Since then . . . he has become as much a legend as a flesh-and-blood human being. While the legend is based on truth, it is only partly true. And it hides the man behind it like a disguise. (1987, p. 2)

The viewpoints in biographies also vary greatly. Subjectivity can't be avoided totally because authors are humans. For example, if an author is a Holocaust survivor, writing an objective biography of Adolf Hitler would be difficult. Or, a civil rights activist might have trouble writing an honest biography about Martin Luther King, Jr., an account that would show King's weak points as well as his strong ones. As Newbery-winning author James Daugherty (1972) once said, "When you're writing biography, you're also writing autobiography." In other words, how biographers feel about their subjects affects, at least subtly, how they portray them.

The scope of a biography is often dictated by format, age of intended readers, and purpose, as indicated by the categories that follow.

AUTOBIOGRAPHIES.   When people write about their own lives, the problem with objectivity just mentioned is even more acute. However, autobiography provides the unique viewpoint of self-revelation. What writing about oneself loses in objectivity it gains in wholeness. No one has as complete a view of a life as the one who lives it. Biographers who write of others' lives can never get inside their subjects' heads and hearts, although this distance may allow for a more balanced and objective view.

This category of children's biography historically had few contributors because most famous individuals write their personal stories for an adult audience. Then in the 1980s and 1990s, publishers began to encourage children's authors and illustrators to write autobiographies for young readers. Children are interested in the people who create their books, and this effort proved successful. Notable examples of author/illustrator autobiographies for children include the Newbery Honor book *Homesick, My Own Story* (1982) by Jean Fritz, the Caldecott Honor book *Bill Peet: An Autobiography* (1989), and the Pura Belpré Award-winner, *Under the Royal Palms* (1998) by Alma Flor Ada.

PICTURE BOOK BIOGRAPHIES.   Picture book biographies, usually intended for very young readers, are brief and heavily illustrated. Generally 32 pages, the standard length for picture books, such biographies provide an overview, focusing on the highlights of a subject's life. A picture book biography series by David Adler is an example of the authentic biographies in this category. Titles include *A Picture Book of Anne Frank* (1993), *A Picture Book of Sacagawea* (2000), and *A Picture Book of John Hancock* (2006). Picture book biographies for more sophisticated readers (upper elementary, junior high school) include books created by Diane Stanley. Her titles, such as *The Bard of Avon: The Story of William Shakespeare* (1993), *Cleopatra* (1994), *Michelangelo* (2000), and *Saladin: Noble Prince of Islam* (2002), have more text and are enjoyed by children in the middle and upper grades.

SIMPLIFIED BIOGRAPHIES.   Simplified biographies are aimed at newly independent readers and appear as picture books or as chapter books, typically with frequent illustrations. Examples include two series published by Grosset and Dunlap: the Who Was books (*Who Was Charles Darwin?* by Deborah Hopkinson, 2005) and the Smart About Art books about well-known artists (*Pierre-Auguste Renoir: Paintings That Smile* by True Kelley, 2005). Jean Fritz's popular biographies of American Revolutionary War personalities are included in this category. Though heavily illustrated, these books emphasize text rather than illustration as Fritz recounts in lively prose the stories of the lives of Paul Revere, Samuel Adams, John Hancock, Benjamin Franklin, Patrick Henry, and King George III.

COMPLETE BIOGRAPHIES.   Although complete biographies may be in simplified, picture book, or lengthy chapter book format, their purpose is to span the entire life of a subject. Russell Freedman's biographies are excellent examples and include four that appear on the Newbery list: *Lincoln: A Photobiography* (1987), *The Wright Brothers: How They Invented the Airplane* (1991), *Eleanor Roosevelt: A Life of Discovery* (1993b), and *The Voice That Challenged a Nation: Marian Anderson and the Struggle for Equal Rights* (2004). Another of the finest biographers for young readers is Jean Fritz. Besides the shorter books about American Revolutionary War personalities mentioned earlier, she has longer titles, such as *Bully for You, Teddy Roosevelt!* (1991), *Harriet Beecher Stowe and the Beecher Preachers* (1994), *Why Not, Lafayette?* (1999), and so on. Recent titles by James Cross Giblin are also noteworthy, including *Charles Lindbergh: A Human Hero* (1997) and *Good Brother, Bad Brother: The Story of Edwin Booth and John Wilkes Booth* (2005).

PARTIAL BIOGRAPHIES.   Partial biographies have a more focused purpose than do complete biographies. They cover only a segment of the subject's life, as in Sandburg's *Abe Lincoln Grows Up* (1928), which deals only with Lincoln's childhood, or Golenbock's *Teammates* (1990), which focuses on the years that Jackie Robinson and Pee Wee Reese worked together to break the color barrier in major league baseball. Another notable title is Robert Coles's *The Story of Ruby Bridges* (1995), which deals with several months in the life of the 6-year-old African American girl confronted by the hostility of white parents trying to keep her out of Frantz Elementary School in New Orleans in 1960.

COLLECTIVE BIOGRAPHIES.   Collective biographies contain a number of short biographical pieces about subjects who have a common trait—for example, Kathleen Krull's books about presidents (*Lives of the Presidents,* 1998), musicians (*Lives of the Musicians,* 1993), sports heroes (*Lives of the Athletes,* 1997), and so on. Some collective biographies feature popular current personalities, such as professional athletes, actors, or rock stars. Although this sort of offering may not be well written, the interest level for many young readers is high. A recent trend has provided excellent material for young readers in the form of picture book collective biographies, such as *So You Want to Be an Explorer* (St. George, 2005), which compares the lives a variety of these adventurers.

JUDGING BIOGRAPHIES FOR YOUNG READERS

Because biography is a brand of nonfiction, good biographies exhibit certain characteristics that vary from those in fiction. Naturally, the need for authenticity cannot be ignored. First, and most basic, the facts in a biography must be accurate. Often biographers acknowledge their sources of information somewhere in their books as a way of letting their readers know that plenty of research went into their writing. Also, authors of authentic biographies must take care with the use of direct quotation. Jean Fritz (1988) makes it clear that she does "not use quotation marks unless I have a source" (p. 759). For instance, in *Can't You Make Them Behave, King George?*, George's mother is quoted as saying, "Stand up straight, George. Kings don't slouch" (1977, p. 8). Although these words may sound fabricated, Fritz found them in *King George III* by John Brooke (1972). Of course, fictionalized biographies take greater liberties with the words spoken by the characters, which is why they often are classified as historical fiction today.

However, authenticity has its less exacting side. As mentioned earlier, it is impossible for biographers to be totally objective. Their personal perspectives will always color the ways in which they present their subjects. Interpretation of events must be based soundly in fact, but, once again, there is always more than one side to a story. On the other hand, a biographer ought to avoid making blatant personal judgments and should allow the actions and words of the subject to speak for themselves. For example, Jean Fritz presents Christopher Columbus as a rather arrogant, egotistical individual in her brief biography *Where Do You Think You're Going, Christopher Columbus?* (1980). However, she does not state, "Christopher Columbus was a self-absorbed egomaniac." Instead, she allows the reader to come to that conclusion through Columbus's words and deeds, as when he robbed Rodrigo of the promised prize for spotting land first. "Columbus said no, he had, himself, sighted land when he'd seen a light at ten o'clock. How could it be otherwise? Surely God, who had gone to so much trouble to bring him here, meant him to have the honor" (Fritz, 1980, p. 30).

One of the shortcomings of some juvenile biographies is that they glorify their subjects, turning them into idols or making them larger than life. This is another form of stereotyping that alienates readers from the subject of a biography instead of helping them know that person as a real human being. To present a balanced view means looking at the blemishes as well as the strong points. Instead of conveying the message, for instance, that Abraham Lincoln was born virtually perfect, a more positive and effective message for young readers is that Lincoln had many of the same human weaknesses as the rest of us, but he was able to rise above them to do great things.

FIGURE 13–1
Notable biographers.

Adler, David: *Picture book and simplified biographies.*	Krull, Kathleen: *Collective biographies.*
Fisher, Leonard Everett: *Picture book biographies.*	Marrin, Albert: *Biographies for middle school and junior high school readers.*
Fleming, Candace: *Complete biographies.*	Meltzer, Milton: *Biographies and social histories.*
Freedman, Russell: *Photobiographies.*	Severance, John: *Complete biographies.*
Fritz, Jean: *American history biographies.*	St. George, Judith: *Picture book biographes.*
Giblin, James Cross: *Picture book and complete biographies; social histories.*	Stanley, Diane: *Picture book biographies for older readers.*

Freedman's biography of Lincoln provides a nice blend of blemishes and strong points. We see a Lincoln who was self-effacing, who stood bravely to sign the Emancipation Proclamation (though it was popular with nearly no other politicians), and who wrote the Gettysburg Address. But we also see the Lincoln whose law office was a colossal mess, who argued with his wife ("When Mary lost her temper, the neighbors would hear her furious explosions of anger." [Freedman, 1987, p. 41]), and who suffered from severe depression for much of his life. We like this Lincoln better than the one on a pedestal because we recognize him as one of us. Note how human and vulnerable Lincoln appears when forced to end his courtship of Mary Todd:

> Early in 1841, Lincoln broke off the engagement. He had known bouts of depression before, but now he plunged into the worst emotional crisis of his life. For a week, he refused to leave his room. People around town said that he had thrown "two cat fits and a duck fit." He had gone "crazy for a week or two." To his law partner Stuart, who was serving a term in Congress, Lincoln wrote: "I am the most miserable man living. If what I feel were equally distributed to the whole human family, there would not be one cheerful face on earth." (Freedman, 1987, pp. 31–32)

Biographies should, of course, conform to the standards of good writing. Facts are not enough; those may be obtained from an encyclopedia or biographical dictionary. Biographies must engage young readers with fresh prose and riveting perspective, bringing the subjects to life.

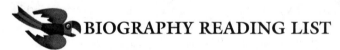

BIOGRAPHY READING LIST

TEN OF OUR FAVORITES

Fleming, Candace. 2005. *Our Eleanor: A Scrapbook Look at Eleanor Roosevelt's Remarkable Life.* Atheneum. With photographs on every page and special attention given to each important person, place, and project, this biography provides a portrait of a remarkable life.

Freedman, Russell. 1987. *Lincoln: A Photobiography.* Clarion. Photographs and text trace the life of the Civil War president. Winner of the Newbery Medal.

Freedman, Russell. 2004. *The Voice That Challenged a Nation: Marian Anderson and the Struggle for Equal Rights.* Clarion. Marian Anderson was a world-renowned African American opera star by the mid-1930s, but she was often denied the right to perform in her own country because of her race—including at Constitution Hall, Washington, D.C.'s largest and finest auditorium. Winner of a Newbery Honor Medal.

Fritz, Jean. 1973. *And Then What Happened, Paul Revere?* Illustrated by Margot Tomes. Coward. A short, illustrated biography of this American Revolution hero. (See the other titles in Fritz's series about personalities from the American Revolution: *Can't You Make Them Behave, King George?*; *What's the Big Idea, Ben Franklin?*; *Where Was Patrick Henry on the 29th of May?*; *Why Don't You Get a Horse, Sam Adams?*; *Will You Sign Here, John Hancock?*)

Fritz, Jean. 1995. *You Want Women to Vote, Lizzie Stanton?* Putnam. A biography of Elizabeth Cady Stanton, who believed in equality for everyone. In the late 19th century, she spent her time and energy traveling around the United States to promote women's right to vote.

Giblin, James Cross. 2005. *Good Brother, Bad Brother: The Story of Edwin Booth and John Wilkes Booth*. Clarion. Brothers John and Edwin Booth became two of America's finest stage actors, but their opposite political loyalties during the Civil War led them to dramatically different fates.

Hoose, Phillip. 2001. *We Were There, Too!: Young People in U.S. History*. Farrar. (Collective biography.) Biographies of dozens of young people who made a mark in history, including explorers, planters, spies, cowpunchers, sweatshop workers, and civil rights workers.

Krull, Kathleen. 2000. *Lives of Extraordinary Women: Rulers, Rebels (and What the Neighbors Thought)*. Harcourt. (Collective biography.) Focuses on the human sides of 20 of history's most influential women: queens, warriors, prime ministers, first ladies, and revolutionary leaders. (See others in Krull's *Lives of . . .* series.)

Peet, Bill. 1989. *Bill Peet: An Autobiography*. Houghton Mifflin. (Autobiography.) The well-known author and illustrator relates the story of his life and work, including his years at Disney Studios. A Caldecott Honor Book.

Stanley, Diane. 1997. *Michelangelo*. Harper. (Picture book.) A biography of the Renaissance sculptor, painter, architect, and poet, well-known for his work on the Sistine Chapel and St. Peter's Cathedral in Rome.

OTHERS WE LIKE

Ada, Alma Flor. 1998. *Under the Royal Palms*. Atheneum. (Autobiography.)

Bitton-Jackson, Livia. 1997. *I Have Lived a Thousand Years: Growing Up in the Holocaust*. Simon. (Autobiography/personal narrative.)

Fleming, Candace. 2003. *Ben Franklin's Almanac: Being a True Account of the Good Gentleman's Life*. Atheneum.

Freedman, Russell. 1990. *Franklin Delano Roosevelt*. Clarion.

Freedman, Russell. 1999. *Babe Didrikson Zaharias: The Making of a Champion*. Clarion.

Fritz, Jean. 1994. *Harriet Beecher Stowe and the Beecher Preachers*. Putnam.

Giblin, James Cross. 2002. *The Life and Death of Adolf Hitler*. New York: Clarion.

Golenbock, Peter. 1990. *Teammates*. Illustrated by Paul Bacon. Harcourt. (Picture book biography.)

Jiang, Ji Li. 1997. *Red Scarf Girl: A Memoir of the Cultural Revolution*. Harper.

Krull, Kathleen. 2004. *The Boy on Fairfield Street: How Ted Geisel Grew Up to Become Dr. Seuss*. Illustrated by Steve Johnson and Lou Fancher. Random House.

Lewis, J. Patrick. 2005. *Heroes and She-Roes: Poems of Amazing and Everyday Heroes*. Illustrated by Jim Cooke. Dial. (Picture book; collective biography.)

Marrin, Albert. 2001. *George Washington and the Founding of a Nation*. Dutton.

Meltzer, Milton. 1990. *Columbus and the World Around Him*. Watts.

Parks, Rosa (with Jim Haskins). 1992. *Rosa Parks: My Story*. Dial. (Autobiography.)

Partridge, Elizabeth. 2005. *John Lennon: All I Want Is the Truth*. Viking.

Paulsen, Gary. 1990. *Woodsong*. Bradbury. (Autobiography.)

Reef, Catherine. 2001. *Sigmund Freud: Pioneer of the Mind*. Clarion.

Severance, John. 1999. *Einstein: Visionary Scientist*. Clarion.

St. George, Judith. 2000. *So You Want to Be President?* Illustrated by David Small. Philomel. (Caldecott winner; see also *So You Want to Be an Inventor* [2002]) and *So You Want to Be an Explorer* [2005]; collective biography; picture book.)

Stanley, Diane. 2002. *Saladin: Noble Prince of Islam*. Harper. (Picture book biography.)

Szabo, Corinne. 1997. *Sky Pioneer: A Photobiography of Amelia Earhart*. National Geographic.

Uchida, Yoshiko. 1991. *The Invisible Thread*. Messner. (Autobiography.)

COLLECTIVE BIOGRAPHIES

Buller, Jon, et al. 2005. *Smart About the First Ladies*. Grosset & Dunlap. (See others in the Smart About . . . series.)

Colman, Penny. 2006. *Adventurous Women: Eight True Stories About Women Who Made a Difference*. Holt.

Dendy, Leslie. 2005. *Guinea Pig Scientists: Bold Self-Experimenters in Science and Medicine*. Holt.

Fradin, Dennis. 2003. *The Signers: The 56 Stories Behind the Declaration of Independence*. Illustrated by Michael McCurdy. Walker.

Freedman, Russell. 1987. *Indian Chiefs*. Holiday House.

Glass, Andrew. 2001. *Mountain Men: True Grit and Tall Tales*. Doubleday. (Picture book.)

Harness, Cheryl. 2001. *Remember the Ladies: 100 Great American Women*. Harper. (Picture book.)

Krull, Kathleen. 1999. *They Saw the Future: Oracles, Psychics, Scientists, Great Thinkers, and Pretty Good Guessers*. Atheneum.

Leiner, Katherine. 1996. *First Children: Growing Up in the White House*. Tambourine.

Lester, Julius. 2001. *The Blues Singers: Ten Who Rocked the World*. Illustrated by Lisa Cohen. Hyperion. (Picture book.)

Meltzer, Milton. 2002. *Ten Kings: And the Worlds They Ruled*. Illustrated by Behanne Andersen. Dutton. (See also *Ten Queens: Portraits of Women of Power* [1998].)

Parker, Nancy Winslow. 2001. *Land Ho! Fifty Glorious Years in the Age of Exploration*. Harper. (Picture book.)

Pinkney, Andrea Davis. 2000. *Let It Shine: Stories of Black Women Freedom Fighters*. Illustrated by Stephen Alcorn. Harcourt.

Provensen, Alice. 1995. *My Fellow Americans: A Family Album*. Browndeer/Harcourt. (Picture book.)

EASIER TO READ

dePaola, Tomie. 2006. *I'm Still Scared*. Putnam. (Autobiography.) (See other titles in the 26 Fairmount Avenue series.)

Edwards, Roberta. 2006. *Who Was King Tut?* Illustrated by True Kelley. Grosset & Dunlap. (See other titles in the *Who Was . . .* series.)

Freedman, Russell. 1997. *Out of Darkness: The Story of Louis Braille*. Clarion.

Kelley, True. 2005. *Pierre Auguste Renoir: Paintings That Smile*. Grosset & Dunlap. (See other titles in the Smart About Art series.)

Kimmel, Elizabeth Cody. 2003. *As Far as the Eye Can Reach: Lewis and Clark's Westward Quest*. Random House.

Kramer, S. A. 1995. *Ty Cobb: Bad Boy of Baseball*. Random House.

Kraske, Robert. 2005. *Marooned: The Strange but True Adventures of Alexander Selkirk, the Real Robinson Crusoe*. Illustrated by Robert Andrew Parker. Clarion.

Mayo, Margaret. 2000. *Brother Sun, Sister Moon: The Life and Stories of St. Francis*. Little, Brown.

Meaderis, Angela Shelf. 1994. *Little Louis and the Jazz Band*. Lodestar/Dutton.

Osborne, Mary Pope. 1987. *The Story of Christopher Columbus, Admiral of the Ocean Sea*. Dell. (See other books in the Dell Yearling Biography series.)

Stanley, George. 2006. *Dwight D. Eisenhower: Young Military Leader*. Aladdin. (See other titles in the Childhood of Famous Americans series.)

PICTURE BOOKS

Adler, David A. 2003. *A Picture Book of Lewis and Clark*. Holiday House. (See the other titles in Adler's Picture Book of . . . series.)

Adler, David. 2005. *Joe Louis: America's Fighter*. Illustrated by Terry Widener. Harocurt.

Bridges, Ruby. 1999. *Through My Eyes*. Scholastic. (Autobiography.)

Burleigh, Robert. 2004. *Seurat and La Grande Jatte: Connecting the Dots*. Abrams.

Corey, Shana. 2000. *You Forgot Your Skirt, Amelia Bloomer!* Illustrated by Chesley McLaren. Scholastic.

Darrow, Sharon. 2003. *Through the Tempests Dark and Wild: A Story of Mary Shelley, Creator of Frankenstein*. Illustrated by Angela Barrett. Candlewick.

Demi. 2001. *Gandhi*. McElderry.

Fisher, Leonard Everett. 1999. *Alexander Graham Bell*. Atheneum.

Giblin, James Cross. 2000. *The Amazing Life of Benjamin Franklin*. Scholastic.

Hurst, Carol Otis. 2001. *Rocks in His Head*. Illustrated by James Stevenson. Greenwillow.

Keating, Frank. 2002. *Will Rogers: An American Legend*. Illustrated by Mike Wimmer. Harcourt.

Kerley, Barbara. 2001. *The Dinosaurs of Waterhouse Hawkins*. Illustrated by Brian Selznick. Scholastic.

Krull, Kathleen. 2005. *Houdini: World's Greatest Mystery Man and Escape King*. Illustrated by Eric Velasquez. Walker.

Lasky, Kathryn. 1994. *The Librarian Who Measured the Earth*. Illustrated by Kevin Hawkes. Little, Brown.

McCully, Emily Arnold. 2006. *Marvelous Mattie: How Margaret E. Knight Became an Inventor*. Farrar.

Shulevitz, Uri. 2005. *The Travels of Benjamin of Tudela: Through Three Continents in the Twelfth Century*. Farrar.

Sis, Peter. 2003. *The Tree of Life: A Book Depicting the Life of Charles Darwin: Naturalist, Geologist & Thinker*. Farrar.

St. George, Judith. 2004. *You're on Your Way, Teddy Roosevelt.* Illustrated by Matt Faulkner. Philomel.

Steig, William. 2003. *When Everybody Wore a Hat.* Harper. (Autobiography.)

Stanley, Diane. 1998. *Joan of Arc.* Morrow.

For details about books listed here and for a more complete list of biography titles, consult the Children's Literature Database: A Resource for Teachers, Parents, and Media Specialists CD *that accompanies this text.*

REFERENCES

Ada, Alma Flor. (1998). *Under the royal palms.* New York: Ahteneum.

Adler, David A. (1993). *A picture book of Anne Frank.* New York: Holiday House.

Adler, David A. (2000). *A picture book of Sacagawea.* New York: Holiday House.

Adler, David, & Adler, Michael S. (2006). *A picture book of John Hancock.* New York: Holiday House.

Bang, Molly. (2000). *Nobody in particular: One woman's fight to save the bays.* New York: Holt.

Brooke, John. (1972). *King George III.* New York: McGraw-Hill.

Brown, Don. (2000). *Uncommon traveler: Mary Kingsley in Africa.* New York: Houghton.

Burchard, Peter. (1995). *Charlotte Forten: A black teacher in the Civil War.* New York: Crown.

Chrisp, Peter. (2001). *Columbus: Explorer of the New World.* New York: Dorling Kindersley.

Coles, Robert. (1995). *The story of Ruby Bridges.* Illustrated by George Cephas Ford. New York: Scholastic.

Daugherty, James. (1972). *James Daugherty.* [Videocassette.] Weston, CT: Weston Woods.

Donelson, K. L., & Nilsen. A.P. (1989). *Literature for today's young adults.* Glenview, IL: Scott, Foresman.

Freedman, Russell. (1987). *Lincoln: A photobiography.* New York: Clarion.

Freedman, Russell. (1991). *The Wright Brothers: How they invented the airplane.* New York: Holiday House.

Freedman, Russell. (1993a). Bring 'em back alive. In Michael O. Tunnell & Richard Ammon (Eds.), *The story of ourselves: Teaching history through children's literature.* Portsmouth, NH: Heinemann.

Freedman, Russell. (1993b). *Eleanor Roosevelt: A life of discovery.* New York: Clarion.

Freedman, Russell. (2004). *The voice that challenged the nation: Marian Anderson and the struggle for equal rights.* New York: Clarion.

Fritz, Jean. (1977). *Can't you make them behave, King George?* New York: Coward, McCann & Geoghegan.

Fritz, Jean. (1980). *Where do you think you're going, Christopher Columbus?* New York: Putnam.

Fritz, Jean. (1982). *Homesick: My own story.* New York: Putnam.

Fritz, Jean. (1988, November/December). Biography: Readability plus responsibility. *The Horn Book, 64,* (6), 759–760.

Fritz, Jean. (1991). *Bully for you, Teddy Roosevelt!* New York: Putnam.

Fritz, Jean. (1994). *Harriet Beecher Stowe and the Beecher preachers.* New York: Putnam.

Fritz, Jean. (1999). *Why not, Lafayette?* New York: Putnam.

Giblin, James Cross. (1997). *Charles Lindbergh: A human hero.* New York: Clarion.

Giblin, James Cross. (2002). *The life and death of Adolf Hitler.* New York: Clarion.

Giblin, James Cross. (2005). *Good brother, bad brother: The story of Edwin Booth and John Wilkes Booth.* New York: Clarion.

Golenbock, Peter. (1990). *Teammates.* Illustrated by Paul Bacon. New York: Harcourt Brace.

Hopkinson, Deborah. (2005). *Who was Charles Darwin?* New York: Grosset & Dunlap.

Kelley, True. (2005). *Pierre-Auguste Renoir: Paintings that smile.* New York: Grosset & Dunlap.

Krull, Kathleen. (1993). *Lives of the musicians: Good times, bad times (and what the neighbors thought).* Illustrated by Kathryn Hewitt. New York: Harcourt.

Krull, Kathleen. (1997). *Lives of the athletes: Thrills, spills (and what the neighbors thought).* Illustrated by Kathryn Hewitt. New York: Harcourt.

Krull, Kathleen. (1998). *Lives of the presidents: Fame, shame (and what the neighbors thought).* Illustrated by Kathryn Hewitt. New York: Harcourt.

Lasky, Kathryn. (2000). *Vision of beauty: The story of Sarah Breedlove Walker.* Illustrated by Nneka Bennett. Cambridge, MA: Candlewick.

MacDonald, Fiona. (2004). *You wouldn't want to sail with Christopher Columbus: Uncharted waters you'd rather not cross.* Canbury, CT: Franklin Watts.

Meltzer, Milton. (1990). *Columbus and the world around him.* New York: Watts.

Peet, Bill. (1989). *Bill Peet: An autobiography.* New York: Houghton Mifflin.

Pelta, Kathy. (1991). *Discovering Christopher Columbus: How history is invented.* Minneapolis: Lerner.

Ryan, Pam Muñoz. (1999). *Amelia and Eleanor go for a ride.* New York: Scholastic.

Sandburg, Carl. (1928). *Abe Lincoln grows up.* New York: Harcourt Brace.

Shulevitz, Uri. (2005). *The travels of Benjamin of Tudela: Through three continents in the twelfth century.* New York: Farrar, Straus and Giroux.

Siegal, Aranka. (1981). *Upon the head of the goat.* New York: Farrar, Straus & Giroux.

St. George, Judith. (2005). *So you want to be an explorer.* Illustrated by David Small. New York: Philomel.

Stanley, Diane. 2000. *Michelangelo.* New York: HarperCollins.

Stanley, Diane. 2002. *Saladin: Noble prince of Islam.* New York: HarperCollins.

Stanley, Diane, & Vennema, Peter. (1993). *The bard of Avon: The story of William Shakespeare.* Illustrated by Diane Stanley. New York: William Morrow.

Stanley, Diane, & Vennema, Peter. (1994). *Cleopatra.* Illustrated by Diane Stanley. New York: William Morrow.

Szabo, Corinne. (1997). *Sky pioneer: A photobiography of Amelia Earhart.* Washington, DC: National Geographic.

Winters, Kay. (2005). *And fly she did!: The amazing childhood adventures of Amelia Earhart.* Washington, DC: National Geographic.

Chapter 14

Informational Books

Informational books are nonfiction and present current and accurate knowledge about something found in our universe. The information in them is verifiable, which is the key word in defining an informational book. Everything in an informational book can be verified or documented in published sources such as books or magazines, in original sources such as letters and journals, or from firsthand, observable facts.

Fiction, on the other hand, tells a story found primarily in the author's head. Its purpose is not to present information, but to engage readers in a tale of characters experiencing the ups and downs of life. Fiction may be a total invention springing completely from the writer's imagination, but it also may contain information from the world. If fiction does have verifiable information (the appearance of downtown Seattle, the workings of nuclear submarines, the particulars of a legal process), that information must be accurate, but it is always secondary to the story. Narrative writing—the form of language used to tell a story—is used for fiction. Expository writing—the form of language that explains and conveys information—is generally used for creating nonfiction.

THE PURPOSE OF INFORMATIONAL BOOKS

The writer of fiction and the writer of nonfiction approach their tasks from different viewpoints. Fiction writers create their stories; nonfiction authors report on the real world.

> With fiction, you start with the embryo and build a person's life. You begin with "What if?" and create a whole world. You work from the inside out. With nonfiction, you start with a complete life—or an invention, or a historical event, or an animal— and take it apart layer by layer to find out what made it happen or what makes it work.

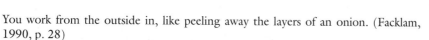

You work from the outside in, like peeling away the layers of an onion. (Facklam, 1990, p. 28)

Nonfiction books for children are divided into two main categories, biography (see Chapter 13) and informational books. The Dewey Decimal System, still used in most children's libraries, organizes all knowledge into 10 major categories, each labeled with a number from 000 to 999. Fiction is in the 800s. The rest of the numbers designate nonfiction. The content of this genre is endless: everything about history, animals, space, technology, geography, music, sports, religion, jokes, folktales, geology, cooking, and so on, until all topics and subjects known to humankind are listed.

Traditionally, students choose nonfiction for personal reading with far less frequency than fiction. But if the content of this genre truly includes everything in this interesting and vibrant cosmos, why don't they flock to informational books? At least three factors may help explain their largely negative responses.

1. *Informational books traditionally are not used for pleasure reading.* When a baby is born, parents who have learned that books can stimulate the intellect of their child and provide bonding experiences begin reading almost immediately to their newborn. Because of the high cost of picture books, they learn early to use the local library, where appropriate titles have been collected and placed on shelves labeled something like "First Books," "Beginning Books," or "Easy Reading."

   What is the subject matter of these hundreds of books read for pleasure? Almost without exception, they come from the Dewey Decimal System 800s: fiction. All those desirable skills, attitudes, and memories that come from early reading typically are associated with fiction. Reading nonfiction aloud for pleasure generally does not happen.

2. *Children's visits to the informational section of the library often are not by choice.* Although some elementary school children discover that reading nonfiction is pleasurable, many of them go to the informational section only when they have been assigned a report. Most children want to find their information as quickly and with as little pain as possible, remembering to change a word in each paragraph so it doesn't have to be put in quotation marks. They often do not come away from writing a report with a conviction that informational reading is personally rewarding.

3. *Informational books have a reputation for being boring.* To many college students, the benefit of reading a nonfiction book is to save money on sleeping pills. A lingering impression is that informational books are crammed with facts, have a few stiff drawings or utilitarian photographs, and look more like old textbooks than anything else. It is true that informational books published years ago generally had less appeal than do those of today, but even then, notable exceptions delighted and rewarded readers. The good news is that a major transformation has occurred during the past 25 years. Attractive and appealing informational

books are no longer the exception. In the past quarter-century, no other genre in children's literature has made such dramatic advances in gaining readers' attention.

For 30 years we have asked college students majoring in elementary education for their immediate personal reaction to the term *informational books*. Only a few students in three decades have identified nonfiction as desirable or interesting. Most have responded negatively. Author Margery Facklam says many adults share this view. "Nonfiction is utilitarian—like underwear and hot water heaters—the kinds of things you *have* to buy when you'd really like caviar and cruisers. Libraries have to buy nonfiction so kids can write reports" (Facklam, 1990, p. 27).

However, the purpose of an informational book in a school library is not merely to present data for writing reports but to stir a reader's interest in a particular subject. Of course, when a reader already has developed an interest in something, virtually any book with new information about that topic will be appealing. If Frank loves motorcycles, he will embrace almost any book about motorcycles. But if the reader knows nothing about a particular subject, the book must create an interest. For example, the title of *What You Never Knew About Tubs, Toilets, and Showers* by Patricia Lauber (2001) immediately captures a reader's attention. Then the book itself fuels the reader's initial interest with fascinating facts about the history of personal hygiene and a lively writing style.

As with *What You Never Knew About Tubs, Toilets, and Showers,* the appeal of a book to the average reader generally is not the topic, but how it is handled. In the right hands, any topic is potentially exciting. (The converse is also true: In the wrong hands, any topic can be deadly dull.) Fiction and nonfiction have much in common on this point. Skilled writers, regardless of genre, create interest by the smooth and artistic ways they shape their books.

The writer of compelling nonfiction does not simply collect and display facts, but weaves information and details into a vision that reveals the subject in a way that readers find irresistible. How do adults recognize nonfiction books that are likely to spark curiosity in elementary students? We can tell the potential of an informational book by picking it up and thumbing through it for no more than three minutes. If we are not "caught" before the time is up, the book ordinarily is not one that will grab younger readers who are unfamiliar with the topic. Usually the "catching" comes during the first minute and generally for one of the following five reasons: (1) attractive design; (2) compelling details; (3) fascinating comparisons; (4) unusual subjects or viewpoints; and (5) personalized content.

USING THE CHILDREN'S LITERATURE DATABASE

Be sure the CD database is installed on your hard drive. Click on Search Query Builder in the left navigation bar on the Home screen. Enter "Weather" in the Keyword Search field. Check the Any button. Next, check the boxes Title, Topics, and Description. Check the INF box (for informational) for Genre. Then click on Run Search. When the search is complete, click on Extend This List, and then click Run Search. Enter "Science Projects; Experiments" in the Keyword Search field. Check the All button, and check the boxes Title, Topics, and Description. Click on Run Search. You now have a list of science experiment books about weather. To save this list for future use, click on the Save Displayed List as Set button in the upper left portion of the screen. Give your saved set a name (in the pop-up window), and click Submit.

FINDING GOOD INFORMATIONAL BOOKS

Attractive Design

Conventional wisdom cautions against making a hasty decision about books: "Don't judge a book by its cover." Yet, children pass over books that appear boring or unrewarding. Beverly Kobrin's motto is, "Say NO to ugly books" (Kobrin, 1988, p. 59). An informational book may have solid and thoughtful content, but if it does not look interesting, it seldom gets the chance to work on a child unless someone else points out the strengths.

In years past, nonfiction books looked more like textbooks than they do today. Books for older children were built of substantial chapters with information that seemed to drone on and on. Thinner informational picture books were brief and predictable. Although the content in earlier informational books was largely accurate and dependable, usually it did little to awaken interest or stir the imagination.

Currently, informational books for children are designed to catch the eye. Careful attention is given to making both the cover and the contents visually appealing. The increased use of illustrations and photographs has resulted in many new titles appearing in picture book format—large, slender volumes that skillfully mix text and illustration to make the content appealing. No longer the exclusive property of the very young, many contemporary picture books are geared for children in upper elementary grades, and even beyond, by presenting more sophisticated views of the subject matter and dealing with it in depth.

One successful approach to informational books was developed in the late 1970s when Usborne Books in England targeted older readers as an appropriate audience for picture books. In Usborne picture books, content is divided into short, distinct topics, each with its own focus or viewpoint treated fully on one double-page spread. Their appeal is evident in one of the first Usborne books available in North America, *The Instant Answer Book of Countries* (Warrender, 1978), which presents information about the world. One double-page subject is weather: hot spots, cold spots, most rain, highest and lowest places. Turn the page and find a new point of focus, such as transportation: the country with the largest airline, most miles of roads, fewest cars, smallest street, and broadest highway. Every two-page spread can be read independently. The text is nonsequential, appearing in bite-size clusters near each illustration rather than in full paragraphs in columns. This format invites browsing and satisfies the reader, who can begin anywhere on the page and read as little or as much as desired—finishing only one sentence, skipping randomly throughout, or consuming the entire book.

Other publishers have adopted and sometimes extended this concept. Dorling Kindersley, another British publisher (known as DK Publishing in the United States and now a part of Penguin Group [USA]), kept the double-page spread but uses photographs almost exclusively, varies the layout, and adds more white space. The photographs of each item, trimmed at the borders like paper-doll cutouts, are placed on a white background that highlights them dramatically. In addition, Dorling Kindersley created a number of distinct series, such as general information, art, science, and nature for younger readers.

With the right format and layout, books written even for the very young can capture the attention of adults. *Color Zoo* (Ehlert, 1989) is a book of shapes aimed at preschoolers—one shape cut from the center of each heavy page. By overlaying three shapes at a time, Ehlert creates the face of an animal, which changes to a new shape and a different animal as each page is lifted. Keeping the same set of eyes, the lion (turn page) becomes a mouse, which (turn page) becomes a fox. The young reader practices not only identifying the shapes, but also seeing how different animal faces contain those shapes.

Compelling Details

Information becomes interesting when details are included. Details in nonfiction make the difference between showing and telling, just as they do in fiction, but in nonfiction that difference often accounts for a reader's becoming interested in a new subject or ignoring it. Without sufficient details, it is difficult for the reader to be involved in a subject and experience a kinship with it. Details come in a variety of types, including quotations, anecdotes, and little-known facts.

QUOTATIONS.   *The Boys' War* (Murphy, 1990) focuses on the Civil War from the viewpoint of boys age 16 and younger who served in that conflict (estimated between 250,000 and 420,000). Imagining the glory of battle, young soldiers found instead fear and disillusionment, resulting in their loss of innocence, as illustrated in a letter written by Private Henry Graves:

> I saw a body of a man killed the previous day this morning and a horrible sight it was. Such sights do not effect [sic] me as they once did. I can not describe the change nor do I know when it took effect, yet I know that there is a change for I look on the carcass of a man with pretty much the same feeling as I would do were it a horse or dog. (p. 75)

The words of the young soldier put a face on the weariness and desensitization mentioned in a less descriptive way by the author.

Some informational books have no author's narrative, using only quoted material. Jill Krementz brings insight to young readers by interviewing children and teenagers who have experienced major challenges in their lives: adoption, a parent's death, divorce, or a life-threatening disease. In *How It Feels When Parents Divorce,* many children express the wish that their parents will marry each other again. One 16-year-old did not harbor that hope:

> When my parents were first getting divorced they used to have the most terrible fights on the phone which I can still remember vividly—they would have these violent conversations which were mostly about money. So, one thing you can be sure of is that I was never one of those "divorced kids" who kept hoping their parents would get back together, because when I saw the way they fought, I was just glad there was a phone line separating them. I didn't even want them in the same house. (Krementz, 1984, p. 99)

ANECDOTES.   Anecdotes come from a person who has firsthand experience. During the 1800s in the American South, by law slaves were kept illiterate and consequently did not keep many written records. Despite that law, some did learn to read and write, as did many blacks who were free. In Milton Meltzer's *The Black Americans: A History in Their Own Words* (1984), we read the words of Solomon Northrup, a free black man who was kidnapped in New York and taken to New Orleans, where he was sold on the auction block. Other blacks were auctioned the same day, including a woman named Eliza who had two children. One, the boy, was purchased separately.

> She kept on begging and beseeching them, most piteously, not to separate the three. Over and over again she told them how she loved her boy. A great many times she repeated her former promises—how very faithful and obedient she would be; how hard she would labor day and night, to the last moment of her life; if he would only buy them all together. But it was of no avail; the man could not afford it. The bargain was agreed upon, and Randall must go alone. Then Eliza ran to him; embraced him passionately; kissed him again and again; told him to remember her—all the while her tears falling in the boy's face like rain. . . .
>   The planter from Baton Rouge, with his new purchase, was ready to depart.
>   "Don't cry, mama. I will be a good boy. Don't cry," said Randall, looking back, as they passed out the door.
>   What has become of the lad, God knows. It was a mournful scene indeed. I would have cried myself if I had dared. (pp. 49–50)

The human drama in this heartbreaking scene, which must have been repeated thousands of times, has greater impact because it is recounted by one who was there.

LITTLE-KNOWN FACTS.   Little-known facts hold elements of both mystery and discovery. They create an image that both stirs up interest and provides a starting point for greater understanding. For example, *Stephen Biesty's Cross-Sections: Man of War* (Platt, 1993) explores the little-known facts of life aboard a British warship during the Napoleonic era, when sailing ships ruled the world's oceans. Men on these vessels were at sea for long periods. With no refrigeration, the kinds of food were limited—salt pork, dried peas, salt beef, oatmeal, beer in sealed barrels, and hard, moldy cheese. Fresh bread was out of the question, but each ship had a store of unleavened bread called hardtack, which was something like very thick crackers. Unfortunately, weevils and black-headed maggots liked hardtack, too, and sailors inadvertently chewed them up in their bites of the hard biscuits. The sailors found "black-headed maggots were fat and cold, but not bitter . . . like weevils" (p. 12). Weevils were impossible to dislodge, but the cook knew how to get rid of the black-headed maggots. He placed a raw fish on a plate on top of the hardtack. When it was completely covered with maggots, he threw the fish into the sea, replacing it as necessary until no more maggots appeared. The hardtack then was easier to eat. These little-known facts help take the reader into the life of an early sailor, providing a platform for expanded learning.

The human face of the Holocaust is presented in *Smoke and Ashes* (Rogasky, 2002). Not only does Rogasky present a broad view of treatment of the Jews by the Nazis, but she also offers unusual insights and explanations, such as how German children were taught to view Jews. The caption next to the photograph of a board game reads:

> Children were taught from the earliest years to stay away from "the evil Jew." Here is a popular children's game called "Get the Jews Out!" By throwing dice, the winner manages to get six Jews out of their homes and businesses—the circles—and on the road to Palestine. The game sold over a million copies in 1938, when Nazi policy was to force Jews to emigrate. (Rogasky, 2002, p. 12)

Little-known facts create interest in familiar topics as well as in new ones. *Amazing Mammals,* for example, describes a fox's unusual hearing. "A fox's ears are so sensitive it can hear a worm wriggling on the other side of a field" (Parsons, 1990, p. 15). In the same volume, the sloth's lack of cleanliness is shown to have some merit. "Sloths don't clean their fur. After a while it grows a greenish scum and moths and beetles come to live in it. This is a good disguise—it makes the sloth look like a bunch of leaves" (p. 18).

A regular sprinkling of little-known facts spices up the classroom by introducing students to new areas of knowledge, giving them things to think about, laying a groundwork for wanting further information, and reminding everyone just how broad and interesting this world is.

Fascinating Comparisons

Human beings do not communicate well in the abstract or the complex. When we talk about any abstract or complex concept—kindness, the plight of endangered species, divorce, war, digestion, enormous numbers—we understand much more quickly and clearly when comparisons bring the fuzzy areas into sharp focus. Fascinating comparisons create instant and powerful images, working in much the same manner as metaphor or simile.

Seymour Simon, a former science teacher who has written more than 100 informational books for young readers, frequently uses comparisons to clarify his content. In *Saturn,* he mentions that the ringed planet is much larger than Earth. How much larger? "If Saturn were hollow, about 750 planet Earths could fit inside" (1985, p. 5). Made of gases, Saturn is also lighter than Earth. How much lighter? "If you could find an ocean large enough, Saturn would float on the water" (p. 5). Large figures do not communicate well to the young mind; comparisons make the information instantly clear.

Large numbers can be the focus of an entire book. In *How Much Is a Million?* David Schwartz (1985) uses comparisons to give readers a grasp of how the numbers million, billion, and trillion differ from each other by comparing how long it takes to count to each. To count to a million, saying each number completely and going nonstop, would take 23 days. To reach a billion would consume 95 years, and counting to a trillion over 200,000 years.

Fascinating comparisons can be found in the illustrations as well as the text. In *Incredible Comparisons,* Russell Ash (1996) looks at 23 separate topics, including the universe, disasters, animal speed, the human body, and big buildings. In addition to showing differences in the text (the same volume of stone found in the Great Pyramid would build 40 Empire State Buildings), he includes 15 buildings in a line, each drawn to scale, so the reader can see the relative size of some of the world's most famous structures. The Leaning Tower of Pisa, for example, reaches about halfway up the Statue of Liberty.

The digestive process becomes clearer in Linda Allison's *Blood and Guts* (1976) by using a comparison. After food leaves the stomach as "a mashed-up, milky liquid," it goes into the small intestine,

> a long, curly tube with a shaggy lining. It is equipped with its own set of digestive juices for final food breakdown. The walls of this tube hug and push the food along in an action called peristalsis (perry STAL sis).
>
> Peristalsis puts the squeeze on food muscles in the intestinal wall. They contract and relax, forcing the food around and through. It's the same way you might squeeze a tube of toothpaste. (p. 76)

The wonder of food moving through intestines becomes clearer by comparing the process to that of toothpaste moving through a tube.

Unusual Subjects or Viewpoints

Some subjects are so unusual that they offer appeal simply by being presented. Often the title of the book treating an unusual subject or viewpoint is enough to entice readers to pick it up.

> *Kids Shenanigans: Great Things to Do That Mom and Dad Will Just Barely Approve Of* (Klutz Press Editors, 1992)
> *The Secret Life of School Supplies* (Cobb, 1981)
> *Gold: The True Story of Why People Search for It, Mine It, Trade It, Steal It, Mint It, Hoard It, Shape It, Wear It, Fight and Kill for It* (Meltzer, 1993a)
> *I Wonder What's Under There?: A Brief History of Underwear* (Lattimore, 1998)

Books on unusual subjects generally appeal to a wide range of readers. *Arms and Armor* (Byam, 2000) is a picture book study of selected weapons and of protection against weapons that humans have developed since earliest times. The photographs and text are simple enough to appeal to children in the middle grades and complete enough to satisfy adults. Stone axes are no surprise, nor are the variety of swords and knives used throughout history. But Byam presents some unusual inventions we have used, and continue to use, to hurt each other. The African throwing knife from Zaire is an odd arrangement of sharp edges and five irregularly placed points with one handle. "When thrown, the knife turns around its center of gravity so that it will inflict a wound on an opponent whatever its point of impact" (Byam, 2000, p. 22). Another unusual weapon is the Apache pistol used around 1900 in Paris. It has a six-shot cylinder but no barrel, so it was accurate only at point-blank range. Instead of a barrel, it sports a folding dagger ideal for stabbing, and the pistol grip is a set of brass knuckles—three weapons in one.

The unusual topic allows books written for an adult audience to find their place in the elementary classroom. *Alaska Bear Tales* (Kaniut, 1983) is a collection of more than 100 encounters between bears and humans in Alaska that have been taken from magazines, newspapers, and personal interviews. The variety is enormous—in length, humor, violence, and tension. In these encounters some people were killed, some maimed, and some left unscathed, with the same true for the bears. For example:

> One of the most unusual bear escapes and deaths I've heard about took place near Wainwright. A woman was walking along the beach across the bay from Wainwright. She was gathering coal when she saw a bear approaching. She searched her brain for some means of escape, realizing that she couldn't outrun Nanook. It seemed futile, and as the bear shuffled up to her, it opened its mouth just inches from her. As a last resort, she shoved her fur-mittened fist down its throat and withdrew her arm before it could bite her, leaving the mitten in its throat. The bear instantly started choking, and forgot about its victim. Within minutes it lay suffocated at her feet. (p. 219)

And that is the only incident of a mitten-killed brown bear on record.

Another adult author also successful with children is David Feldman, who asks questions and finds answers about why the world is as it is. His series of 11 books (for example, *How Do Astronauts Scratch an Itch?* [1996]) explores what he calls "imponderables," and during the exploring, teaches children as a by-product how to observe, question, and discover. For example:

- Why do some ice cubes come out cloudy and others come out clear?
- Why don't birds tip over when they sleep on a telephone wire?
- How does the Campbell Soup Company determine which letters to put in their alphabet soup? Is there an equal number of each letter? Or are the letters randomly inserted in the can?
- Why don't crickets get chapped legs from rubbing their legs together? If crickets' legs are naturally lubricated, how do they make that sound?
- What flavor is bubble gum supposed to be? Why is bubble gum usually pink?
- Why do we have to close our eyes when we sneeze?

Personalized Content

A good informational book is not a bucket of facts but a personal tour of a subject. The format and design, the details, the comparisons, and even the topics reflect the individuality of the author and illustrator. What we have not mentioned is that authors of good informational books teach the same way good classroom teachers teach: They examine a subject, think about things, make discoveries, and then share a personal view of what they have learned. Skilled authors of informational books personalize content using the techniques already described, but they also may provide readers with a new perspective on old subjects and may take readers along on an eyewitness journey.

NEW PERSPECTIVE.   When subjects have been around a while, particularly as a part of the curriculum, they sometimes take on a familiarity that produces yawns. Quality informational books prove those prejudices groundless, reminding us it is never the subject that is dull but the presentation. For instance, the eight parts of speech are still taught in most classrooms, although learning about them generally does not rivet students to their seats. Ruth Heller has created a number of picture books to introduce and define the parts of speech in polished meter and stunning illustrations. The following text is found on the first 10 pages of *A Cache of Jewels and Other Collective Nouns* (Heller, 1987):

A word that means a collection of things,
like a
CACHE
of jewels
for the crowns of kings. . .

or a BATCH of bread all warm and brown,
is always called a COLLECTIVE NOUN.

a SCHOOL of fish

a GAM of whales

a FLEET of ships
with
purple sails . . .*

In *Round Buildings, Square Buildings, & Buildings That Wiggle Like a Fish*, Philip Isaacson (2001) looks at dozens of structures, including the Brooklyn Bridge. After a brief discussion of the French and Egyptian influences in its stone towers, he mentions the thin cables that support the road and how he sees those massive towers and spidery cables contrasting and interacting with each other.

> Most bridges are made of concrete and steel and tell us about the power of engineering. The Brooklyn Bridge is not like them; it tells us about the shapes of grand old buildings. It will always be a wonder because of a friendly game it seems to play. Its designers wove webs of light wires and cables and hung them from the towers to hold the bridge's roadways and paths. The fat towers make the webs look silky, and the silky webs make the towers seem even heavier than they are. This game of tag will go on forever. (p. 14)

FIRST-PERSON ACCOUNTS.   Another form of personalized content is the first-person account. When the author actually experiences something and then writes about it, the resulting book often has the feel of a personal tour. It is not a recounting of information, but an experience that reader and author seem to discover together. For instance, we watch Bianca Lavies as she tries to improve the soil in her home garden by making a compost pile. But what is garbage to Bianca Lavies becomes a banquet for a host of organisms from microscopic bacteria to earthworms and snails, an army of new guests she photographs and describes in *Compost Critters* (1993). The human element and progressive changes she witnesses in her compost pile personalize the way nature creates rich soil.

The same power of personal story is in *My Season with Penguins: An Antarctic Journal* (Webb, 2000). In journal format, Sophie Webb combines both the scientific and artistic viewpoint in her account of why scientists want to research penguins and

---

*From *A Cache of Jewels and Other Collective Nouns* by Ruth Heller. Copyright © 1987 by Grosset & Dunlap. Reprinted by permission of the publisher.

The interplay of towers and cables adds to the beauty of the Brooklyn Bridge.

From *Round Building, Square Buildings, & Buildings That Wiggle Like a Fish* by Philip M. Isaacson. Copyright © 2001 by Philip M. Isaacson. Used by permission of Alfred A. Knopf, an imprint of Random House Children's Books, a division of Random House, Inc.

is candid about the messy and smelly work of studying animals. With her attention to detail and humor, the result is a personal journey for the reader that ends up being much more than a compilation of information.

Informational books reach out and grab readers for a number of reasons, but these five elements—attractive design, compelling details, fascinating comparisons, unusual subjects or viewpoints, and personalized content—are often at the heart of a good book's appeal.

 ## ACCURACY

The basis of all informational books is accuracy. The books exist to introduce the reader to the world or to present something particular about it, so the content must be factual and dependable. Anything that might lead a young reader to assume inaccuracies about factual information is to be avoided. This includes anthropomorphism (giving animals and objects human motives) and mixing fact and fiction, such as inserting an imagined story of a boy who survives the destruction of Pompeii in the midst of an informational book on the subject.

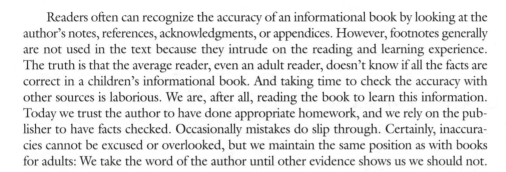

Readers often can recognize the accuracy of an informational book by looking at the author's notes, references, acknowledgments, or appendices. However, footnotes generally are not used in the text because they intrude on the reading and learning experience. The truth is that the average reader, even an adult reader, doesn't know if all the facts are correct in a children's informational book. And taking time to check the accuracy with other sources is laborious. We are, after all, reading the book to learn this information. Today we trust the author to have done appropriate homework, and we rely on the publisher to have facts checked. Occasionally mistakes do slip through. Certainly, inaccuracies cannot be excused or overlooked, but we maintain the same position as with books for adults: We take the word of the author until other evidence shows us we should not.

TYPES OF INFORMATIONAL BOOKS

Informational books fall into recognizable categories that are generally determined by format. The following formats make up the typical nonfiction book categories: traditional chapter books, informational picture books, activity books (craft, how-to, experiment), journals and interviews, photo essays, pop-ups, reference books, and series.

TRADITIONAL CHAPTER BOOK FORMAT.   The bulk of children's informational books introduce or explain one subject in a traditional chapter book format. The depth of detail may vary depending on the age of the target audience or the length of the book. For example, an accounting of the Shackleton expedition to Antarctica is treated in 48 pages in Connie and Peter Roop's *Escape from the Ice* (2001). The same topic spans 134 pages in Jennifer Armstrong's *Orbis Pictus* Award-winner, *Shipwreck at the Bottom of the World* (1998).

Traditional nonfiction chapter books may be a general survey of an enormous topic, such as Mary Pope Osborne's (1996) *One World, Many Religions,* an overview of our varied faiths. Or this type of informational book may focus on a narrower topic, such as *Children of the Dust Bowl: The True Story of the School at Weedpatch Camp* (Stanley, 1992), another *Orbis Pictus* winner, a social history which documents the plight of migrant workers who came to California during the Depression.

All topics, whether presented in broad strokes or examined under a magnifying glass, are fair game for traditional nonfiction chapter books. Examples include plagues (*When Plague Strikes: The Black Death, Smallpox, AIDS* by James Cross Giblin, 1995), prehistoric cave paintings (*Painters of the Caves* by Patricia Lauber, 1998), superstitions (*Cross Your Fingers, Spit in Your Hat: Superstitions and Other Beliefs* by Alvin Schwartz, 1974), and outer space (*Don't Know Much About Space* by Kenneth C. Davis, 2001).

INFORMATIONAL PICTURE BOOKS.   Informational picture books serve the same purposes as informational chapter books. They are to present accurate and appealing content aimed at awakening an interest in the reader. The difference lies only in the format: usually taller, thinner, and more heavily illustrated than chapter books. In recent years the informational picture book has become commonplace, with many being created for readers in the upper elementary grades as well as in middle school and junior high.

FIGURE 14–1

Notable authors and illustrators of informational books.

Aliki: *Informational picture books for younger readers.*

Ancona, George: *Photographer and author of photoessays.*

Arnosky, Jim: *Illustrator and author of nature books.*

Bartoletti, Susan Campbell: *Social histories.*

Blumberg, Rhoda: *History—transcontinental railroad, California gold rush, Louisiana Purchase, Commodore Perry in Japan.*

Cobb, Vicki: *Hands-on science books.*

Cole, Joanna: *Science topics, notably the Magic School Bus series.*

Curlee, Lynn: *Author and illustrator of picture books about famous structures.*

Fisher, Leonard Everett: *Illustrator and author of books on a variety of topics—architecture, historical figures and events, social history.*

Freedman, Russell: *Social histories.*

Gibbons, Gail: *Informational picture books for preschool and primary grades on a vast variety of topics.*

Giblin, James Cross: *Informational chapter books about unique subjects—scarecrows; histories of chairs, windows, and eating utensils; plagues; Rosetta Stone; chimney sweeps.*

Heller, Ruth: *Illustrator and author of brilliantly colored picture books about the individual parts of speech and about plants and animals.*

Jenkins, Steven: *Picture books about animals and nature.*

Lasky, Kathryn, and Christopher Knight: *Wife (author) and husband (photographer) team; photoessays, primarily about nature topics.*

Lauber, Patricia: *Physical and natural science topics.*

Markle, Sandra: *Natural science, math, and computer books.*

McKissack, Patricia, and Fredrick McKissack: *Primarily African American history.*

Meltzer, Milton: *Social histories; known particularly for presenting history using the words of the people who lived through it.*

Micklethwait, Lucy: *Picture books about fine art.*

Murphy, James: *U.S. social histories— immigrant train, Chicago fire, Civil War.*

Pringle, Laurence: *Natural and physical science books.*

Schwartz, Alvin: *Specialist in American folk culture; collects superstitions, legends, true stories, scary stories, tongue twisters.*

Simon, Seymour: *Physical and natural science topics.*

Swanson, Diane: *Natural science topics, particularly animals.*

Tang, Greg: *Picture books about mathematics.*

The informational picture book presents an idea in sufficient depth to pique curiosity, as well as increase understanding. These books can treat large topics, such as the entire history of the earth from the present to 4,600,000 years ago (*A Journey Through Time* [Wood, 2001]) as well as smaller subjects such as the discovery and restoration of the 7,500 terra-cotta soldiers and horses sculpted 2,500 years ago in China (*The Emperor's Silent Army* [O'Connor, 2002]).

Many of the categories of informational picture books are the same as those found in Chapter 7. Concept books are simplified picture books that present basic knowledge about a single topic in a way both understandable and interesting for a small child. Baby board books may also deal with informational content and treat it with even more simplicity than concept books. Beginning reader titles are the same shape and style for both fiction and nonfiction and can explore a surprising range of topics. Engineered books reflect innovative ways in which to visualize a topic, such as the opportunity to manipulate a paper pop-up catapult in a book about medieval warfare or to lift the layers of an Egyptian mummy's wrappings.

ACTIVITY BOOKS. Activity books include any books that invite the reader to engage in a specific activity beyond their reading. Classic types of activity books include science experiments; how-to, craft, and cookbooks; and art activities, such as Joan Irvine's *Easy-Make Pop-Ups* (2005). By following clear directions, children are able to create more than 30 three-dimensional pop-ups for cards, toys, or gifts. In *Egyptian Symbols* (Larson, 2000), young readers learn about hieroglyphics as they use the book and 29 rubber stamps to write their own names and construct messages. Today's offerings in activity books seem practically unlimited.

CONCEPT BOOKS. Usually, the first type of informational book a child sees is a concept book (discussed at length in Chapter 7), a simplified picture book that presents basic knowledge about one topic in a way both understandable and interesting for a small child learning about the world. Concept books often invite the young reader to engage in some activity to reinforce the idea being presented, such as picking out which object is small and which is large in Margaret Miller's *Big and Little* (1998) or identifying the circles and squares from familiar surroundings in Tana Hoban's *So Many Circles, So Many Squares* (1998).

JOURNALS AND INTERVIEWS. Journals and interviews are the two most common kinds of books based on primary sources. *I, Columbus: My Journal 1492–3* (Roop & Roop, 1990) offers edited but accurate selections from the log of Columbus's first voyage. Milton Meltzer uses journals from more than one person to paint a specific picture of an era or event. *Voices from the Civil War* (Meltzer, 1989) is a mosaic created from the journals of those who participated in or were affected by America's bloodiest conflict. Interviews, like journals, offer information directly to the reader with only a minimum of author manipulation.

PHOTO ESSAYS. Photo essays employ photographs in a journalistic fashion to capture emotion and to verify information. Photographs accompany the text on almost every page in a photo essay. For example, in the Newbery Honor book *Volcano: The Eruption and Healing of Mount St. Helens* (Lauber, 1986), the story of the devastating eruption of the mountain and its recovery from fire, ash, and shifted landmass is documented in stunning photos. But the pictures do more than merely illustrate; they create in the reader a sense of the massive devastation and then kindle emotions associated with recovery as they show nature healing itself. The photographs in Seymour Simon's *Animals Nobody Loves* (2001) show why the subjects of this book have a hard time finding friends. The crocodile is shown with mouth wide open and appears to be nothing but rows of crooked teeth. The vulture, with its huge bill and ugly, hairless head, is pulling on the skin of a carcass. All the photographs clearly display the unappealing characteristics of the uncuddly and unlovable members of the animal world.

POP-UPS.   Once pop-up books were largely for entertainment, but today a number of excellent informational books appear in pop-up format. *Nature's Deadly Creatures* (Jones, 1992) features a cobra with a flickering tongue that jumps off the page. Scorpion, black widow, and gila monster all appear in three dimensions along with fold-out information and photos. *The Amazing Pop-Up Geography Book* (Petty & Maizels, 2001) uses hidden doors, sliding boats, and pop-up mountains to present facts about the earth. Ron Van der Meer's series of seven pop-up titles presents overviews of a variety of subjects: art, music, architecture, the brain, math, rock music, and Earth (*The Architecture Pack* [Van der Meer & Sudjic], 1997; *Music Pack,* 1994; and so on). Sailing ships, castles, the universe, and modes of transportation are a few other subjects that are treated seriously in this format.

REFERENCE BOOKS.   Encyclopedias, encyclopedic overviews of specific subjects, dictionaries, and atlases are examples of reference books. Although some children may spend time browsing in reference books or occasionally reading them from beginning to end, young readers generally go to reference books for isolated bits of knowledge. The current trend to make reference books attractive and readable adds a new dimension: reference books as recreational reading. DK Publishing and Scholastic are two publishers that produce a number of interesting and readable reference books.

SERIES.   School libraries traditionally have informational books in series, partly because subject areas studied in school provide ready-made topics. For example, elementary schools frequently have a series of books about the United States, one title per state, which students use mostly for doing reports. Although the information in traditional series is generally acceptable, their appeal is usually low. Often information is neatly stacked in unexciting lines of text that do little to reach out to the reader.

Fortunately, some series have been conceived and executed by those who go beyond simply listing information to seeing inside it. Their views are accurate, and the books convey excitement about the topics. Some examples of series that readers find interesting are listed at the end of this chapter.

As never before, informational books provide sources for appealing, accurate, and practical classroom use. Evidence that these books are finding their place in the world of children's literature includes the establishment of two awards exclusively for nonfiction books: the *Orbis Pictus* Award given by the National Council of Teachers of English, and the Robert F. Sibert Award presented by the American Library Association. These awards underscore what teachers and children have already discovered about today's informational books: they not only teach us about the world, but they also make pleasurable reading.

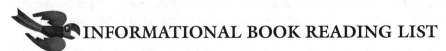

INFORMATIONAL BOOK READING LIST

TEN OF OUR FAVORITES

Armstrong, Jennifer. 1998. *Shipwreck at the Bottom of the World: The Extraordinary True Story of Shackleton and the* Endurance. Crown. Describes the events of the 1914 Shackleton Antarctic

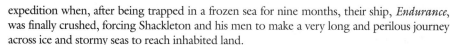

expedition when, after being trapped in a frozen sea for nine months, their ship, *Endurance*, was finally crushed, forcing Shackleton and his men to make a very long and perilous journey across ice and stormy seas to reach inhabited land.

Bartoletti, Susan Campbell. 2005. *Hitler Youth: Growing Up in Hitler's Shadow*. Scholastic. Bartoletti explores how Hitler gained the loyalty, trust, and passion of so many of Germany's young people and includes telling interviews with surviving Hitler Youth members. A Newberry Honor book.

Freedman, Russell. 2005. *Children of the Great Depression*. Clarion. Along with photographs by famous photographers of the depression era, Freeman's overview clearly covers the causes of the Great Depression, schooling, work life, migrant work, the lives of children who rode the rails, entertainment, and so on.

Fritz, Jean. 2001. *Leonardo's Horse*. Illustrated by Hudson Talbot. Putnam. Leonardo da Vinci sculpted in clay a horse two-and-a-half stories high with plans to cast it in bronze. He never completed the project, but Charles Dent, a 20th-century airline pilot who loved art, fulfilled Leonardo's dream almost 500 years later.

Jenkins, Steve. 2004. *Actual Size*. Houghton Mifflin. Discusses and gives examples of the size and weight of various animals and parts of animals.

Micklethwait, Lucy. 1993. *A Child's Book of Art: Great Pictures, First Words*. Famous paintings are used to introduce basic concepts (seasons, weather, opposites, colors, counting, etc.) to young children.

Murphy, Jim. 1990. *The Boys' War*. Clarion. Documents the lives of the young boys who actually fought in the American Civil War. Illustrated with archival photographs.

Sabuda, Robert, and Matthew Reinhart. 2005. *Dinosaurs: Encyclopedia Prehistorica*. Candlewick. Full of fascinating facts and lighthearted good humor, this breathtaking pop-up book includes fascinating, up-to-the-minute information about popular dinosaurs as well as many lesser-known varieties.

Schwartz, Alvin. 1974. *Cross Your Fingers, Spit in Your Hat: Superstitions and Other Beliefs*. Lippincott. Superstitions collected into 23 categories, such as love and marriage, money, ailments, travel, weather, school, and death.

Stanley, Jerry. 1992. *Children of the Dust Bowl: The True Story of the School at Weedpatch Camp*. Crown. Describes the plight of the migrant workers who traveled from the Dust Bowl to California during the Depression and were forced to live in a federal labor camp. Focuses on the marvelous school that was built for their children.

OTHERS WE LIKE

Allison, Linda. 1976. *Blood and Guts*. Little, Brown. (See others in the Brown Paper School Book series.)

Ambrose, Stephen. 2001. *The Good Fight: How World War II Was Won*. Atheneum.

Ardley, Neil. 1995. *A Young Person's Guide to Music*. Dorling Kindersley.

Bachrach, Susan D. 2000. *The Nazi Olympics: Berlin 1936*. Little, Brown.

Blumberg, Rhoda. 1985. *Commodore Perry in the Land of the Shogun*. Lothrop.

Cobb, Vickie, and Kathy Darling. 1980. *Bet You Can't: Science Impossibilities to Fool You*. Lothrop. (See the companion volume, *Bet You Can*.)

Cohn, Amy L., compiler. 1993. *From Sea to Shining Sea: A Treasury of American Folklore and Folk Songs*. Illustrated by 11 Caldecott Medal and 4 Caldecott Honor Book artists. Scholastic.

Crowe, Chris. 2003. *Getting Away with Murder: The True Story of the Emmett Till Case*. Phyllis Fogelman/Penguin.

Dash, Joan. 2000. *The Longitude Prize*. Farrar.

Davis, Kenneth C. 2003. *Don't Know Much About American History*. Harper. (See others in the Don't Know Much About . . . series.)

Fleischman, John. 2002. *Phineas Gage: A Gruesome but True Story About Brain Science*. Houghton Mifflin.

Freedman, Russell. 2006. *Freedom Walkers: The Story of the Montgomery Bus Boycott*. Holiday House.

Fritz, Jean. 2004. *The Lost Colony of Roanoke*. Illustrated by Hudson Talbott. Putnam.

Giblin, James Cross. 1990. *The Riddle of the Rosetta Stone*. Crowell.

Henderson, Douglas. 2000. *Asteroid Impact*. Dial.

Isaacson, Philip M. 1988. (reissued 2001). *Round Buildings, Square Buildings, & Buildings That Wiggle Like a Fish*. Knopf.

Jackson, Donna M. 1996. *The Bone Detectives: How Forensic Anthropologists Solve Crimes and Uncover Mysteries of the Dead*. Photographs by Charlie Fellenbaum. Little, Brown.

Jones, Charlotte Foltz. 1996. *Accidents May Happen: Fifty Inventions Discovered by Mistake*. Delacorte.

Lefkowitz, Arthur S. 2006. *Bushnell's Submarine: The Best Kept Secret of the Revolutionary War*. Scholastic.

Marrin, Albert. 2002. *Dr. Jenner and the Speckled Monster: The Search for the Small Pox Vaccine*. Dutton.

Macaulay, David. 1998. *The New Way Things Work*. Houghton.

McKissack, Patricia, and Fredrick L. McKissack. 1994. *Christmas in the Big House, Christmas in the Quarters*. Illustrated by John Thompson. Scholastic.

Meltzer, Milton. 1993. *Gold: The True Story of Why People Search for It, Mine It, Trade It, Steal It, Mint It, Hoard It, Shape It, Wear It, Fight and Kill for It*. Harper.

Pascoe, Elaine. 2005. *Fooled You: Fakes and Hoaxes Through the Years*. Illustrated by Laurie Keller. Holt.

Platt, Richard. 1993. *Stephen Biesty's Cross-Sections: Man of War*. Dorling Kindersley.

Rogasky, Barbara. 1988. (reissued 2002). *Smoke and Ashes*. Holiday House.

Rubin, Susan Goldman. 2001. *There Goes the Neighborhood: Ten Buildings People Loved to Hate*. Holiday House.

Sandler, Martin W. 2005. *America Through the Lens: Photographers Who Changed the Nation*. Holt.

Sayre, Henry. 2004. *Cave Paintings to Picasso: The Inside Scoop on 50 Art Masterpieces*. Chronicle.

Schwartz, Alvin. 1981. *Scary Stories to Tell in the Dark*. Harper.

Simon, Seymour. 1979. *Pets in a Jar*. Puffin.

Swanson, Diane. 1994. *Safari Beneath the Sea: The Wonder World of the North Pacific Coast*. Photographs by the Royal British Columbia Museum. Sierra Club.

Tunnell, Michael O., and George W. Chilcoat. 1996. *The Children of Topaz: The Story of a Japanese-American Internment Camp Based on a Classroom Diary.* Holiday House.

Walker, Barbara M. 1995. *The Little House Cookbook: Frontier Foods from Laura Ingalls Wilder's Classic Stories.* Illustrated by Garth Williams. Harper.

Walker, Sally M. 2005. *Secrets of a Civil War Submarine.* Carolrhoda.

EASIER TO READ

Altman, Joyce. 2001. *Lunch at the Zoo: What Zoo Animals Eat and Why.* Illustrated by Rick Chrustowski. Holt.

Bare, Colleen Stanley. 1989. *Never Kiss an Alligator.* Dutton.

Fritz, Jean. 1987. *Shh! We're Writing the Constitution.* Illustrated by Tomie dePaola. Putnam.

George, Jean Craighead. 2000. *How to Talk to Your Dog.* Illustrated by Sue Truesdell. Harper.

George, Jean Craighead. 2002. *Summer Moon.* Harper. (See others in the Seasons of the Moon series.)

Getz, David. 1994. *Frozen Man.* Illustrated by Peter McCarty. Holt.

Getz, David. 2000. *Purple Death.* Illustrated by Peter McCarty. Holt.

Grover, Wayne. 1993. *Dolphin Adventure.* Greenwillow.

Lavies, Bianca. 1993. *Compost Critters.* Dutton.

Markle, Sandra. 2000. *Outside and Inside Dinosaurs.* Atheneum.

Osborne, Mary Pope, and Natalie Pope Boyce. 2006. *Ancient Rome and Pompeii.* Illustrated by Sal Murdocca. Random House. (See others in the Magic Tree House Research Guide series.)

Simon, Seymour. 2006. *Emergency Vehicles.* SeaStar. (See others in the SeeMore Reader series.)

Singer, Marilyn. 2000. *A Dog's Gotta Do What a Dog's Gotta Do: Dogs at Work.* Holt.

Snedden, Robert. 1996. *Yuck! A Big Book of Little Horrors—Micromarvels in, on, and around You!* Simon.

Sobol, Donald J., and Rose Sobol. 1991. *Encyclopedia Brown's Book of Strange but True Crimes.* Illustrated by John Zielinski. Scholastic.

Trumble, Kelly. 1996. *Cat Mummies.* Illustrated by Laszlo Kubinyi. Clarion.

PICTURE BOOKS

Aliki. 1979. *Mummies Made in Egypt.* Harper.

Ammon, Richard. 2004. *Valley Forge.* Illustrated by Bill Farnsworth. Holiday House.

Appelbaum, Diana. 1993. *Giants in the Land.* Illustrated by Michael McCurdy. Houghton.

Burleigh, Robert. 1991. *Flight: The Journey of Charles Lindbergh.* Illustrated by Mike Wimmer. Philomel.

Celenza, Anna Harwell. 2006. *Gershwin's Rhapsody in Blue.* Illustrated by Joann E. Kitchel. Charlesbridge.

Collard, Sneed B. 2005. *One Night in the Coral Sea.* Illustrated by Robin Brickman. Charlesbridge.

Curlee, Lynn. 2007. *Skyscrapers* . Atheneum. (See also Curlee's other picture books about various famous structures.)

Giblin, James Cross. 2004. *Secrets of the Sphinx.* Illustrated by Bagram Ibatoulline. Scholastic.

Heller, Ruth. 1998. *Fantastic! Wow! And Unreal!: A Book About Interjections and Conjunctions.* Grosset & Dunlap. (See others in Heller's English grammar picture book series.)

Hooper, Meredith. 2001. *Who Built the Pyramid?* Illustrated by Robin Heighway-Bury. Candlewick.

Hopkinson, Deborah. 2006. *Sky Boys: How They Built the Empire State Building.* Illustrated by James E. Ransome. Schwartz & Wade.

Kudlinski, Kathleen V. 2005. *Boy, Were We Wrong About Dinosaurs!* Illustrated by S. D. Schindler. Dutton.

Macaulay, David. 2003. *Mosque.* Houghton. (See also the other Macaulay picture books about architecture, such as *Castle, Cathedral,* and *Pyramid.*)

Prince, April Jones. 2005. *Twenty-One Elephants.* Illustrated by François. Houghton Mifflin.

Schwartz, David. 1985. *How Much Is a Million?* Illustrated by Steven Kellogg. Lothrop.

Simon, Seymour. 2007. *Lungs.* Smithsonian/Collins.

Spier, Peter. 1980. *People.* Doubleday.

Sturges, Philemon. 2000. *Sacred Places.* Illustrated by Giles Laroche. Putnam.

Swain, Ruth Freeman. 2003. *How Sweet It Is (and Was): The History of Candy.* Illustrated by John O'Brien. Holiday House.

Tang, Greg. 2005. *Math Potatoes: Mind-Stretching Brain Food.* Illustrated by Harry Briggs. Scholastic.

Weitzman, Jacqueline Preiss. 2002. *You Can't Take a Balloon into the Museum of Fine Arts.* Illustrated by Robin Preiss Glasser. Dial. (See others in the You Can't Take a Balloon . . . series.)

For details about books listed here and for a more complete list of informational book titles, consult the Children's Literature Database: A Resource for Teachers, Parents, and Media Specialists CD *that accompanies this text.*

REFERENCES

Allison, Linda. (1976). *Blood and guts.* Boston: Little, Brown.

Armstrong, Jennifer. (1998). *Shipwreck at the bottom of the world: The extraordinary true story of Shackleton and the* Endurance. New York: Crown.

Ash, Russell. (1996). *Incredible comparisons.* New York: DK Publishing.

Byam, Michelle. (2000). *Arms and armor.* New York: Knopf.

Cobb, Vicki. (1981). *The secret life of school supplies.* Philadelphia: Lippincott.

Davis, Kenneth C. (2001). *Don't know much about space.* New York: HarperCollins.

Ehlert, Lois. (1989). *Color zoo.* New York: Lippincott.

Facklam, Margery. (1990). Writing nonfiction. Speech given at the Highlights Writer's Conference, Chautauqua, New York, 12 July.

Feldman, David. (1996). *How do astronauts scratch an itch?* New York: Putnam.

Giblin, James Cross. (1995). *When plague strikes: The black death, smallpox, AIDS.* New York: HarperCollins.

Heller, Ruth. (1987). *A cache of jewels and other collective nouns.* New York: Grosset & Dunlap.

Hoban, Tana. (1998). *So many circles, so many squares.* New York: Greenwillow.

Hoose, Phillip. (2001). *We were there, too!: Young people in U.S. history.* New York: Farrar.

Irvine, Joan. (2005). *Easy-to-make pop-ups*. New York: Dover.

Isaacson, Philip M. (2001). *Round buildings, square buildings, & buildings that wiggle like a fish*. New York: Knopf.

Jones, Frances. (1992). *Nature's deadly creatures*. New York: Dial.

Kaniut, Larry. (1983). *Alaska bear tales*. Anchorage, AK: Alaska Northwest.

Klutz Press Editors. (1992). *Kids shenanigans: Great things to do that Mom and Dad will just barely approve of*. Palo Alto, Calif.: Klutz Press.

Kobrin, Beverly. (1988). *Eyeopeners!* New York: Viking.

Krementz, Jill. (1984). *How it feels when parents divorce*. New York: Knopf.

Larson, Jennifer. (2000). *Egyptian symbols*. San Francisco: Chronicle.

Lattimore, Deborah. (1998). *I wonder what's under there?: A brief history of underwear*. San Diego: Harcourt.

Lauber, Patricia. (1986). *Volcano: The eruption and healing of Mount St. Helens*. New York: Bradbury.

Lauber, Patricia. (1998). *Painters of the caves*. Washington, DC: National Geographic Society.

Lauber, Patricia. (2001). *What you never knew about tubs, toilets, and showers*. New York: Simon & Schuster.

Lavies, Bianca. (1993). *Compost critters*. New York: Dutton.

Meltzer, Milton. (1984). *The black Americans: A history in their own words*. New York: Crowell.

Meltzer, Milton. (1989). *Voices from the Civil War*. New York: Crowell.

Meltzer, Milton. (1993a). *Gold: The true story of why people search for it, mine it, trade it, steal it, mint it, hoard it, shape it, wear it, fight and kill for it*. New York: HarperCollins.

Miller, Margaret. (1998). *Big and little*. New York: Greenwillow.

Murphy, Jim. (1990). *The boys' war*. New York: Clarion.

O'Conner, Jane. (2002). *The emperor's silent army*. New York: Viking.

Osborne, Mary Pope. (1996). *One world, many religions: The ways we worship*. New York: Knopf.

Parsons, Alexandra. (1990). *Amazing mammals*. New York: Dorling Kindersley.

Petty, Kate, & Maizels, Jennie. (2001). *The amazing pop-up geography book*. New York: Dutton.

Platt, Richard. (1993). *Stephen Biesty's cross-sections: Man of war*. New York: Dorling Kindersley.

Rogasky, Barbara. (2002). *Smoke and ashes*. New York: Holiday House.

Roop, Connie, & Roop, Peter. (2001). *Escape from the ice: Shackleton and the* Endurance. Illustrated by Bob Doucet. New York: Scholastic.

Roop, Peter, & Roop, Connie. (1990). *I, Columbus: My journal, 1492–3*. New York: Walker.

Schwartz, Alvin. (1974). *Cross your fingers, spit in your hat: Superstitions and other beliefs*. Philadelphia: Lippincott.

Schwartz, David. (1985). *How much is a million?* New York: Lothrop.

Simon, Seymour. (1985). *Saturn*. New York: Morrow.

Simon, Seymour. (2001). *Animals nobody loves*. New York: SeaStar.

Stanley, Jerry. (1992). *Children of the Dust Bowl: The true story of the school at Weedpatch Camp*. New York: Crown.

Van der Meer, Ron. (1994). *Music pack*. New York: Knopf.

Van der Meer, Ron, & Sudjic, Deyan. (1997). *The architecture pack*. New York: Knopf.

Warrender, Annabel. (1978). *The instant answer book of countries*. London: Usborne.

Webb, Sophie. (2000). *My season with penguins: An Antarctic journal*. New York: Harper.

Wood, Selina. (2001). *A journey through time*. New York: DK Publishing.

Chapter 15

Multicultural and International Books

Multicultural and international books offer positive experiences to young readers in at least three ways. Books about specific cultures and nations can

- foster an awareness, understanding, and appreciation of people who seem at first glance different from the reader.
- present a positive and reassuring representation of a reader's own cultural group.
- introduce readers to the literary traditions of different world cultures or cultural groups within a specific nation.

Well-written books that express multicultural themes or are international in their origins may have a profound effect on readers, prompting a global outlook as well as an understanding that members of the human family have more similarities than differences.

MULTICULTURAL LITERATURE

Today, we have a growing awareness and concern to include all cultures and nationalities as equal members of the world's family. "Parallel cultures" (Cai & Bishop, 1994) is the term sometimes used to describe the goal of according "equal status" to all of the world's populations. However, we are far from achieving this ideal. Well-written multicultural (diverse culture) children's books may serve to help our new generations see people living in far-flung parts of the globe or even in their own city from this perspective.

Multicultural literature has often been equated with books about people of color, especially within the United States and Canada: African Americans, Native Americans, Asian Americans, Latinas/Latinos. However, this definition is far too narrow. Our diverse population includes a variety of cultural groups that often cross color lines, such as religious groups. Jews, Catholics, Muslims, Mormons, and Amish all have their own subcultures and often have been misunderstood and even persecuted for their beliefs. Books can promote understanding among religious factions. For example, many Jewish students have expressed both interest and pleasure in reading Barbara Robinson's *The Best Christmas Pageant Ever* (1972). Some students said they had always wondered about the Christian Christmas tradition of the pageant, and Robinson's book made understandable what was strange to them—the story helped bridge a cultural gap. Individuals with intellectual or physical challenges also deserve books that represent them in honest, positive ways. For instance, some deaf individuals consider themselves part of the Deaf culture and are concerned about how the rest of society misunderstands them.

The labels and terms we use to talk about diverse cultures are sometimes self-created and sometimes created by external forces, such as government agencies. As cultural groups continue clarifying their status and worth, they create new terms and labels to identify themselves. Therefore, it may be difficult to keep up with the currently acceptable words to describe or identify cultures. In this chapter, we have tried to employ the terms that are most prevalent in the current literature.

The Need for Multicultural Books

Xenophobia, the mistrust or fear of people who are strangers or foreigners, is in part responsible for our worldwide inability to live together in peace. Parents and society may purposely or inadvertently program children to mistrust, fear, or even hate certain groups of people who are unlike them. Teaching children at an early age "about the [positive] differences and similarities between people will not singularly ensure a more gentle and tolerant society, but might act as a prerequisite to one" (Sobol, 1990, p. 30). Candy Dawson Boyd (1990) makes it clear that we cannot begin too early to give our children a multicultural perspective:

> We know that there's a substantial body of research on the development of racial consciousness begun in 1929, and what does it tell us? It tells us that children develop negative attitudes towards other people as they take on the culture of their parents. It tells us that by age three, racial awareness is evident. *Three*. And that by age ten, racial attitudes have crystallized.

Yet children in early adolescence "are not too old for significant attitudinal change. Counteraction is therefore possible . . . " (Sonnenschein, 1988, p. 265).

Literature can be one of the most powerful tools for combating the ignorance that breeds xenophobic behavior. "For decades experienced educators have reported success stories about using children's literature to broaden attitudes toward people from a variety of cultures" (Hansen-Krening 1992, p. 126). Rudine Sims Bishop, who has long been a champion of the well-written multicultural book, believes that "literature is one of the most powerful components of a multicultural education curriculum, the underlying purpose of which is to help make the society a more equitable one" (Bishop, 1992, p. 40). In support of this view, she quotes James Baldwin: "Literature is indispensable to the world. . . . The world changes according to the way people see it, and if you alter, even by a millimeter, the way a person looks at reality, then you can

change it" (Sims, 1982, p. 1). Indeed, studies have indicated that students' prejudices have been reduced because of their involvement with good multicultural books (Darigan, 1991; Pate, 1988).

Certainly, children of minority cultural groups need books that bolster self-esteem and pride in their heritage (Nieto, 2000). And children of all groups, especially majority children, need books that sensitize them to people from cultural groups different from their own. By the same token, "white people, as the majority in U.S. society, seldom think of themselves as *ethnic*—a term they reserve for the other, more easily identifiable groups. Nevertheless . . . we are all ethnic, whether we choose to identify ourselves in this way or not" (Nieto, 2000, p. 26).

Judging Multicultural Literature

As with all books, multicultural books ought to measure up to the criteria used to judge literature in general (see Chapters 2 to 4). However, additional criteria focusing on multicultural themes and content are also necessary to consider.

Racial or cultural stereotyping must be avoided. Stereotypes are alienating because they perpetuate a simplified, biased, and often negative view of groups of people: All African Americans are poor, all Mexicans are lazy, all Asians are secretive and sly, all Jews are born entrepreneurs, all white Americans are arrogant and loud. Though common elements often link the lives and daily practices of members of a cultural group, it is important to communicate that every group is made up of individuals who have their own sets of personal values, attitudes, and beliefs. Books written for children need to represent characters who are members of cultural minorities as true individuals and must present a positive image. However, this still leaves room for showing both positive and negative behaviors in minority-group as well as majority-group characters. For instance, in the Newbery-winning novel *Roll of Thunder, Hear My Cry,* a story of racial prejudice in Mississippi of the 1930s, Mildred Taylor (1976) creates African American characters who represent a broad spectrum of human characteristics. Cassie Logan is proud and honorable, though a bit stubborn. T. J. is weak and dishonest. By the same token, Taylor does not make all whites racial bigots.

Cultural details need to be represented accurately in literature. These may include the use of dialects or idioms; descriptions of ethnic foods, customs, and clothing; and information about religious beliefs and practices. Of course, sensitivity to subcultures within a group is also important. For example, customs vary among the different factions of Judaism; Hasidic Jews are strictly orthodox, as evidenced by dress codes and other identifiable practices, but Reform Jews are much less bound by religious law. In the same way, customs and lifestyles vary greatly among the many Native American tribes.

"Cultural authenticity," a sensitive issue in children's literature today, means that those from within a culture feel that a book has accurately and honestly reflected their experiences and viewpoints. We acknowledge that the idea of "cultural authenticity" is debatable. Some say that people within a "culture" vary widely in innumerable ways, making the rigid definition of their culture impossible. However, many people feel that books representing a specific cultural group should not be written by someone who is an outsider. For instance, the Newbery-winning novel *Sounder* by William Armstrong (1969) portrays the lives of a poor family of African American sharecroppers. Armstrong is not African American, and critics charge that there is no way he could understand the nuances of living in this culture. "Someone who does not share the specifics of a culture remains an outsider, no matter how astute a student or how well-meaning their intentions" (Wilson, 1990, p. A25). Some critics even maintain that many multicultural books written by outsiders provide a distorted view because the author is biased or culturally prejudiced.

At the same time, others believe that if outsiders make concentrated efforts not only to understand but also to inhabit a different cultural world, then they may indeed be able to write with accurate voice. Of course, some rare authors seem to have a particular gift for "imagining others' lives" (Horn, 1993, p. 78). For instance, Miriam Horn (1993) makes a case for Eudora Welty's uncanny ability:

> "Miss Eudora" could . . . enter into the stolid, exhausted body of an old black woman or let loose with a bluesy tale as full of tumbles and howls as a Fats Waller jam. Before she was 30, she could feel the frantic loneliness of a middle-aged traveling salesman. . . . She could even, on the hot night in 1963 that civil-rights leader Medgar Evers was killed, transform her own soft, lilting voice into the bitter ranting of a hate-filled assassin. Of the story she wrote that night in the voice of the murderer she says: "You have to give any human being the right to have you use your imagination about them." (p. 78)

Whoever the author, it is of great importance to have books for young readers that are culturally accurate.

Awareness about the types of multicultural books that exist may be helpful in judging and selecting books for libraries and classrooms. Certainly, they include folktales, biographies, historical novels, informational books, fantasy, picture books, and contemporary realistic novels. However, Rudine Sims Bishop (Bishop, 1992) suggests that in addition there are three general categories of books about people of color: neutral, generic, and specific. In many instances, these categories can also be applied to other cultural groups.

Culturally neutral children's books include characters from cultural minorities but are essentially about other topics. Bishop says that this variety is made up mostly of picture books and gives the example of a book about medical examinations wherein "a Japanese-American child might be shown visiting the doctor, who might be an African-American female" (1992, p. 46). Neutral books randomly place multicultural faces among the pages in order to make a statement about the value of diversity.

Generic books focus on characters representing a cultural group, but few specific details are included that aid in developing a cultural persona. Instead, the characters are functioning in the books as regular people existing in a large common culture, such as American culture. A classic example is the Caldecott-winning *The Snowy Day* by Ezra Jack

USING THE CHILDREN'S LITERATURE DATABASE

Be sure the CD database is installed on your hard drive. Click on Search Query Builder in the left navigation bar on the Home screen. Enter "India" in the Keyword Search field. Check the All button. Next, check the boxes Title, Topics, and Description. Then click on Run Search. You now have a list of books that in some manner deal with East Indian culture. To save this list for future use, click on the Save Displayed List as Set button in the upper left portion of the screen. Give your saved set a name (in the pop-up window), and click Submit.

Keats (1962), which features an African American family living in an inner city. The book shows a black child enjoying newly fallen snow, just as any child might. Although this book is noted as one of the first picture books to have an African American child as a protagonist, some critics feel that the child's mother is presented as a stereotypical black woman—the large, loving Negro mammy image. Although this variety of multicultural book contains little culturally specific material, readers concerned about multicultural issues still scrutinize these books hoping to find characters with realistic, nonstereotypical qualities.

Culturally specific children's books incorporate specific cultural details that help define characters. Cultural themes are evident, if not prevailing, in fictional plots or nonfiction content. Of course, in picture books the artwork expresses many of these cultural details. In this category of multicultural literature cultural accuracy is particularly important. The recommended reading list at the conclusion of this chapter is organized by cultural divisions and presents books considered by many to be both quality literature and "culturally authentic."

The Growth of Multicultural Literature

Children's books in the past generally treated minority groups badly or ignored them completely. However, when African American author Arna Bontemps (1948) won a Newbery Honor Award in 1949 for *Story of the Negro* and became the first African American to appear on the Newbery list, he ushered in the real beginnings of change for all cultural groups. Though few other minority authors or illustrators appeared on award lists during the next two decades, more of their work was being produced. Also, books by majority-culture authors that presented less stereotypical images of minority cultures appeared and received awards: *Song of the Swallows* by Leo Politi (1949) won the Caldecott Award in 1950 and was the first Caldecott winner with a Latino protagonist. Then *Amos Fortune, Free Man* by Elizabeth Yates (1950; African American protagonist), *Secret of the Andes* by Ann Nolan Clark (1952; Native American protagonist), and . . . *And Now Miguel* by Joseph Krumgold (1953; Latino protagonist) each won the Newbery Award. *The Snowy Day* by Ezra Jack Keats won the Caldecott in 1963 (African American protagonist).

As the civil rights movement gained momentum in the 1960s, awareness of and sensitivity toward minorities increased. In 1965, the literary world was awakened by the publication of a startling article titled "The All White World of Children's Books." Printed in the *Saturday Review* and written by Nancy Larrick, this article reported that almost no African Americans appeared in any of America's children's books. The publishing and library worlds took notice, and efforts to include more African Americans in children's books eventually blossomed to include other racial minorities, people with physical and mental disadvantages, and other groups.

In 1966, the Council on Interracial Books for Children (CIBC) was founded. Its publication pointed to racial stereotypes still appearing in children's books, and its efforts with publishers helped promote and get into print the works of authors and illustrators of color, particularly African Americans. In fact, for a number of years the CIBC sponsored an annual contest for unpublished writers and illustrators of color and saw to it that the winners' works were published. The authors and illustrators who were given their start by the CIBC are some of the best known today in the world of multicultural children's literature: African American authors Mildred Taylor and Walter Dean Myers, Native American author Virginia Driving Hawk Sneve, and Asian American writers Ai-Ling Louie and Minfong Ho.

In 1969, the American Library Association (ALA) established the Coretta Scott King Award to recognize the distinguished work of African American writers and illustrators. Soon after, in 1974, the National Council for the Social Studies created the Carter G. Woodson Award for the most distinguished children's books that treat topics related to ethnic minorities and race relations.

As books by minority authors and about diverse cultures began to receive more attention, writers and illustrators of color also began to receive the major U.S. literature awards. In 1975, Virginia Hamilton won the Newbery Award for *M. C. Higgins, the Great* (1974), the first African American to be so honored. The next year, Leo Dillon became the first African American to win the Caldecott Medal, an award he shared with his wife, Diane, for their illustrations in *Why Mosquitoes Buzz in People's Ears,* written by Verna Aardema (1975). More recently, Christopher Paul Curtis (1999) was awarded the 2000 Newbery Medal for *Bud, Not Buddy.*

In 1990, Ed Young became the first Chinese American to win the Caldecott Medal (*Lon Po Po: A Red Riding Hood Story from China,* 1989), and in 1994, Allen Say was the first Japanese American to win the award (*Grandfather's Journey,* 1993). It was not until 1995 that a person of Latina/Latino background was awarded one of the ALA's major children's book prizes. David Diaz won the Caldecott for his illustrations in *Smoky Night,* written by Eve Bunting (1994). Since that time, the ALA has established the Pura Belpré Award (1996) to honor the work of Latina/Latino writers and illustrators. In 2002, Linda Sue Park, who is Korean American, was awarded the Newbery Medal for *A Single Shard* (2001), and in 2005, Cynthia Kadohata, who is Japanese American, won the Newbery for *Kira-Kira* (2004).

Since the 1960s, more authors from minority cultural and racial groups have been writing for children and appear consistently on best-books lists and awards lists. Still, there is much room for growth in this area of publishing. More minority titles and writers are needed, particularly Latina/Latino and Native American, and books representing the intellectually and physically disabled cultures.

# INTERNATIONAL BOOKS

Just as multicultural books dealing with North American societies assist in creating a bridge of understanding, international books can help children gain an appreciation and understanding of global societies. The history and culture of other countries as well as their literary traditions are illuminated through books that have their origins outside North America.

The most common international books in the United States and Canada are English-language titles written and published in other English-speaking countries, such as the United Kingdom, Australia, and New Zealand. Because these books need

no translation, they can be acquired and marketed readily by U.S. and Canadian publishers. (See Appendix D for the names of foreign English-language book awards.)

Although translated books are less plentiful in North America, this area of publishing is growing. These foreign-language books were originally written and printed in other countries. U.S. and Canadian companies acquire the rights to publish them, and they are translated into English. A very limited number of foreign-language children's books from other countries are released in North America in untranslated form.

One consideration when judging translated books is the quality of the translation. Though the flavor of the country needs to be retained, the English text must be fluent and readable, yet not too Americanized. Often a few foreign words and phrases can provide readers a feel for the culture and language, but too many may be troublesome for children.

There is an ever increasing exchange of children's books among countries, but most of the international books published in the United States and Canada come from Europe. Each year since 1966, publishers from around the world have attended an international children's book fair in Bologna, Italy, where they share their books with one another and work out agreements for publishing them in other countries.

Since World War II, a number of organizations, publications, and awards have been established to promote the idea of an international world of children's books. In 1949, the International Youth Library was founded in Munich, Germany. It has become a world center for the study of children's literature. In 1953, the International Board on Books for Young People (IBBY) was established, and soon after, in 1956, this organization created the first international children's book award. The Hans Christian Andersen Medal is given every two years to an author whose lifetime contribution to the world of children's literature is considered outstanding. In 1966, a separate award for illustration was added to the Hans Christian Andersen Medal, and IBBY also began publishing *Bookbird,* a journal linking those interested in international children's books. In 1968 in the United States, the ALA first presented the Mildred Batchelder Award to the U.S. publisher of the most noteworthy translated children's book of the year.

With the increased emphasis on well-written multicultural and international children's books, teachers and parents have an additional means by which they may help children avoid the pitfalls of ignorance that breed intolerance, hatred, and conflict. In an atomic age, we certainly cannot afford the increasingly deadly outcomes sparked by xenophobic behaviors.

MULTICULTURAL BOOKS READING LIST

Many fine multicultural and international titles, indeed many of our favorites, have been included in the other reading lists in this book. For the most part, they have not been repeated here.

AFRICAN AMERICAN

Bolten, Tonya. 2003. *Wake Up Our Souls: A Celebration of Black American Artists.* Abrams.

Clifton, Catherine, ed. 1998. *I, Too, Sing America.* Illustrated by Stephen Alcorn. Houghton.

Cline-Ransome, Lesa. 2000. *Satchel Paige*. Illustrated by James Ransome. Simon & Schuster.

Curtis, Christopher Paul. 1995. *The Watsons Go to Birmingham—1963*. Delacorte.

Draper, Sharon M. 1997. *Forged by Fire*. Atheneum.

Giovanni, Nikki. 2005. *Rosa*. Illustrated by Bryan Collier. Holt.

Hamilton, Virginia. 1995. *Her Stories: African American Folktales, Fairy Tales, and True Tales*. Illustrated by Leo Dillon and Diane Dillon. Blue Sky/Scholastic.

Haskins, James. 2006. *John Lewis in the Lead: A Story of the Civil Rights Movement*. Lee & Low.

Hopkinson, Deborah. 1999. *A Band of Angels: A Story Inspired by the Jubilee Singers*. Illustrated by Raúl Colón. Atheneum.

Howard, Elizabeth Fitzgerald. 2000. *Virgie Goes to School with Us Boys*. Illustrated by E. B. Lewis. Simon & Schuster.

Johnson, Angela. 2002. *Looking for Red*. Simon & Schuster.

Johnson, Angela. 2004. *A Sweet Smell of Roses*. Illustrated by Eric Velasquez. Simon & Schuster.

Lester, Julius. 2005. *The Old African*. Illustrated by Jerry Pinkney. Dial.

Lorbiecki, Marybeth. 2006. *Jackie's Bat*. Illustrated by Brian Pinkney. Simon & Schuster.

McKissack, Patricia C., and Fredrick L. McKissack. 2003. *Days of Jubilee: The End of Slavery in the United States*. Scholastic.

Meltzer, Milton. 1984. *The Black Americans: A History in Their Own Words, 1619–1983*. Crowell.

Myers, Walter Dean. 1999. *Monster*. HarperCollins.

Nelson, Marilyn. 2005. *A Wreath for Emmett Till*. Illustrated by Philippe Lardy. Houghton Mifflin.

Taylor, Mildred. 1990. *Road to Memphis*. Dial.

Woodson, Jacqueline. 2001. *Other Side*. Illustrated by E. B. Lewis. Putnam.

Woodson, Jacqueline. 2003. *Locomotion*. Putnam.

ASIAN AMERICAN

Choi, Sook Nyul. 1997. *Yunmi and Halmoni's Trip*. Houghton.

Ho, Minfong. 2003. *The Stone Goddess*. Orchard.

Kadohata, Cynthia. 2004. *Kira-Kira*. Atheneum.

Lee, Milly. 2006. *Landed*. Illustrated by Yangsook Choi. Farrar, Straus & Giroux.

Lord, Bette Bao. 1984. *In the Year of the Boar and Jackie Robinson*. Harper.

Mochizuki, Ken. 1993. *Baseball Saved Us*. Illustrated by Dom Lee. Lee & Low.

Mochizuki, Ken. 1997. *Passage to Freedom: The Sugihara Story*. Illustrated by Dom Lee. Lee & Low.

Morey, Janet Nomura, and Wendy Dunn. 1992. *Famous Asian Americans*. Dutton.

Mori, Kyoko. 2000. *Stone Field, True Arrow*. Metropolitan.

Park, Linda Sue. 2005. *Project Mulberry: A Novel*. Clarion.

Salisbury, Graham. 1994. *Under the Blood-Red Sun*. Delacorte.

Say, Allen. 1993. *Grandfather's Journey*. Houghton Mifflin.

Say, Allen. 2004. *Music for Alice*. Houghton Mifflin.

Uchida, Yoshiko. 1981. *A Jar of Dreams*. McElderry.

Wong, Janet. 2000. *The Trip Back Home*. Illustrated by Bo Jia. Harcourt.

Yee, Paul. 1990. *Tales from Gold Mountain: Stories of the Chinese in the New World*. Macmillan.

Yep, Laurence. 1977. *Child of the Owl*. Harper.

Yep. Laurence. 2006. *The Earth Dragon Awakes: The San Francisco Earthquake of 1906*. HarperCollins.

Young, Ed. 2006. *My Mei Mei*. Philomel.

HISPANIC AMERICAN (LATINO)

Ancona, George, Alma Flor Ada, and F. Isabel Campoy. 2005. *Mi Musica/My Music*. Children's Press.

Bernier-Grand, Carmen T. 2004. *César: !Sí Puede! = Yes, We Can*. Illustrated by David Diaz. Marshall Cavendish.

Buss, Fran Leeper. 1991. *Journey of the Sparrows*. Lodestar.

Canales, Viola. 2005. *The Tequila Worm*. Wendy Lamb/Random House.

Carlson, Lori M., ed. 2005. *Red Hot Salsa: Bilingual Poems on Being Young and Latino in the United States*. Holt.

Cofer, Judith Ortiz. 1995. *An Island Like You: Stories of the Barrio*. Orchard.

Delacre, Lulu. 2000. *Salsa Stories*. Scholastic.

Dorros, Arthur. 1991. *Abuela*. Illustrated by Elisa Kleven. Dutton.

Garza, Xavier. 2005. *Lucha Libre: The Man in the Silver Mask: A Bilingual Cuento*. Cinco Puntos Press.

Jiménez, Francisco. 1999. *The Circuit: Stories from the Life of a Migrant Child*. Houghton Mifflin.

Krumgold, Joseph. 1953. *. . . And Now Miguel*. Crowell.

Martinez, Floyd. 1997. *Spirits of the High Mesa*. Arte Público Press.

Martinez, Victor. 1996. *Parrot in the Oven: Mi Vida: A Novel*. Harper.

Ryan, Pam Muñoz. 2000. *Esperanza Rising*. Scholastic.

Ryan, Pam Muñoz. 2004. *Becoming Naomi León*. Scholastic.

Soto, Gary. 2000. *Chato and the Party Animals*. Illustrated by Susan Guevara. Putnam.

Soto, Gary. 2005. *Help Wanted: Stories*. Harcourt.

Soto, Gary. 2005. *Neighborhood Odes*. Illustrated by David Diaz. Harcourt.

NATIVE AMERICAN

Begay, Shonto. 1992. *Ma'ii and Cousin Horned Toad: A Traditional Navajo Story*. Scholastic.

Begay, Shonto. 1995. *Navajo: Visions and Voices Across the Mesa*. Scholastic.

Bierhorst, John. 1987. *Doctor Coyote: Native American Aesop's Fables*. Illustrated by Wendy Watson. Macmillan.

Bruchac, Joseph. 2002. *Navajo Long Walk: The Tragic Story of a Proud People's Forced March from Their Homeland*. Illustrated by Shonto Begay. National Geographic Society.

Bruchac, Joseph. 2005. *Code Talker: A Novel About the Navajo Marines of World War Two*. Dial.

Bruchac, Joseph. 2006. *The Return of Skeleton Man*. Illustration by Sally Wern Comport. HarperCollins.

Cohen, Carol. 1988. *The Mud Pony*. Illustrated by Shonto Begay. Scholastic.

Dorris, Michael. 1996. *Sees Behind Trees*. Hyperion.

Ekoomiak, Normee. 1988. *Arctic Memories*. Holt.

Erdrich, Louise. 2005. *The Game of Silence*. HarperCollins. (Sequel to *The Birchbark House*.)

Freedman, Russell. 1992. *Indian Winter*. Illustrated by Karl Bodmer. Holiday House.

Goble, Paul. 2002. *Mystic Horse*. HarperCollins.

Goble, Paul. 2005. *All Our Relatives: Traditional Native American Thoughts About Nature*. World Wisdom.

Highwater, Jamake. 1977. *Anpao: An American Indian Odyssey*. Lippincott.

Maher, Ramona. 2003. *Alice Yazzie's Year*. Illustrated by Shonto Begay. Tricycle Press.

O'Dell, Scott. 1970. *Sing Down the Moon*. Houghton Mifflin.

Sneve, Virginia Driving Hawk, ed. 1989. *Dancing Teepees: Poems of American Indian Youth*. Illustrated by Stephen Gammell. Holiday House.

Sneve, Virginia Driving Hawk. 2005. *Bad River Boys: A Meeting of the Lakota Sioux with Lewis and Clark*. Illustrated by Bill Farnsworth. Holiday House.

Viola, Herman J. 1998. *It Is a Good Day to Die: Indian Eyewitnesses Tell the Story of the Battle of the Little Bighorn*. Crown.

RELIGIOUS CULTURES

Ammon, Richard. 2000. *An Amish Year*. Illustrated by Pamela Patrick. Atheneum. (Christian–Amish.)

Bakhtiar, Laleh. 2004. *Muhammad*. Illustrated by Demi. Diane Publishing. (Islam.)

Cormier, Robert. 1990. *Other Bells for Us to Ring*. Delacorte. (Christian–Catholic.)

Demi. 1997. *Buddha Stories*. Holt. (Buddhist.)

Demi. 1998. *The Dalai Lama*. Holt. (Buddhist.)

Feiler, Bruce. 2004. *Walking the Bible: An Illustrated Journey for Kids Through the Greatest Stories Ever Told*. HarperCollins. (Judeo-Christian.)

Genari, Anita. 1996. *Out of the Ark: Stories from the World's Religions*. Illustrated by Jackie Morris. Harcourt. (Various religions.)

Ghazi, Sumaib Hamib. 1996. *Ramadan*. Illustrated by Omar Rauuan. Holiday House. (Islam.)

Haddix, Margaret. 1997. *Leaving Fishers*. Simon. (Religious cults—Christian.)

Heuston, Kimberley. 2002. *The Shakeress*. Front Street. (Shakers, Mormons.)

Highwater, Jamake. 1994. *Rama: A Legend*. Holt. (Hindu.)

Kimmel, Eric. 2004. *Hayyim's Ghost*. Illustrated by Ari Binus. Pitspopany Press. (Jewish.)

Kimmel, Eric. 2004. *Wonders and Miracle: A Passover Companion: Illustrated with Art Spanning Three Thousand Years*. Scholastic. (Jewish.)

Litchman, Kristin Embry. 1998. *All Is Well*. Delacorte. (Christian—Mormon.)

Oppenheim, Shulamith Levey. 1994. *Iblis: An Islamic Tale*. Illustrated by Ed Young. Harcourt. (Islam.)

Osborne, Mary Pope. 1996. *One World, Many Religions: The Ways We Worship*. Knopf. (Various religions.)

Rocklin, Joanne. 1999. *Strudel Stories*. Delacorte. (Jewish.)

Rylant, Cynthia. 1986. *A Fine White Dust*. Bradbury. (Christian–Protestant.)

Sturges, Philemon. 2000. *Sacred Places*. Illustrated by Giles Laroche. Putnam. (Various religions.)

CULTURES OF THE PHYSICALLY AND MENTALLY CHALLENGED

Bloor, Edward. 1997. *Tangerine*. Harcourt. (Blindness.)

Choldenko, Gennifer. 2004. *Al Capone Does My Shirts*. Putnam. (Autism.)

Ferris, Jean. 2001. *Of Sound Mind*. Farrar. (Deafness.)

Fraustino, Lisa Rowe. 2001. *The Hickory Chair*. Illustrated by Benny Andrews. Scholastic. (Blindness.)

Gantos, Jack. 2000. *Joey Pigza Loses Control*. Farrar. (Attention-deficit hyperactivity disorder.)

Gernis, Meg. 2000. *ABC for You and Me*. Photographs by Shirley Leamon Green. Albert Whitman. (Down syndrome.)

Maguire, Gregory. 1994. *Missing Sisters*. McElderry. (Physical disabilities.)

Martin, Ann M. 2002. *A Corner of the Universe*. Scholastic. (Autism/mental disorders.)

McKenzie, Ellen Kindt. 1990. *Stargone John*. Illustrated by William Low. Holt. (Emotional disabilities.)

McMahon, Patricia. 2000. *Dancing Wheels*. Photographs by John Godt. Houghton Mifflin. (Physical disabilities.)

Millman, Isaac. 2000. *Moses Goes to School*. Farrar. (Deafness.)

Morpurgo, Michael. 1996. *The Ghost of Grania O'Malley*. Viking. (Cerebral palsy.)

Rottman, S.L. 1999. *Head Above Water*. Peachtree. (Down syndrome.)

St. George, Judith. 1992. *Dear Dr. Bell . . . Your Friend, Helen Keller*. Putnam. (Deafness, blindness.)

Sullivan, George. 2000. *Helen Keller*. Scholastic. (Deafness, blindness.)

Uhlberg, Myron. 2005. *Dad, Jackie, and Me*. Illustrated by Colin Bootman. Peachtreee. (Deafness.)

White, Ruth. 2000. *Memories of Summer*. Farrar. (Mental illness.)

Winkler, Henry, and Lin Oliver. 2006. *My Dog's a Scaredy-cat: A Halloween Tail*. Grosset & Dunlap. (See others in the Hank Zipzer series.) (Dyslexia.)

Wolff, Virginia Euwer. 1988. *Probably Still Nick Swansen*. Holt. (Mentally challenged.)

# INTERNATIONAL BOOKS READING LIST

ENGLISH-LANGUAGE BOOKS

Aiken, Joan. 2007. *Bridle the Wind*. Harcourt. (U.K.)

Almond, David. 2006. *Clay*. Delacorte. (U.K.)

Fine, Anne. 2002. *Up on Cloud Nine*. Delacorte. (U.K.)

Fox, Mem. 1987. *Possum Magic*. Illustrated by Terry Denton. Harcourt. (Australia.)

Fox, Mem. 2006. *Particular Cow*. Illustrated by Tricia Tusa. Harcourt. (Australia.)

Hughes, Monica. 2000. *Storm Warning*. Harper. (Canada.)

Ibbotson, Eva. 2004. *The Star of Kazan*. Dutton. (U.K.)

Lunn, Janet. 1997. *The Hollow Tree*. Knopf. (Canada.)

Mahy, Margaret. 2006. *Down the Back of the Chair*. Illustrated by Polly Dunbar. Clarion. (New Zealand.)

Naidoo, Beverly. 1997. *No Turning Back*. Harper. (South Africa.)

Nicholson, William. 2001. *Slaves of the Mastery*. Hyperion. (U.K.)

Nix, Garth. 1995. *Abhorsen*. EOS/Harper. (Australia.)

Nix, Garth. 2005. *Drowned Wednesday*. Scholatic. (See others in The Keys of the Kingdom series.) (Australia.)

Park, Ruth. 1980. *Playing Beatie Bow*. Macmillan. (Australia.)

Pullman, Philip. 2005. *The Scarecrow and His Servant*. Illustrated by Peter Bailey. (U.K.)

Sutcliff, Rosemary. 1993. *Black Ships Before Troy*. Illustrated by Alan Lee. Delacorte. (U.K.)

Valgardson, W. D. 1995. *Winter Rescue*. Illustrated by Ange Zhang. McElderry. (Canada.)

Waugh, Sylvia. 2004. *Who Goes Home?* Delacorte. (U.K.)

Westall, Robert. 1997. *Time of Fire*. Scholastic. (U.K.)

TRANSLATED BOOKS

Björk, Christina. 1999. *Vendela in Venice*. Illustrated by Inga-Karin Eriksson. R & S Books. (Sweden.)

Bredsdorff, Bodil. 2004. *The Crow-Girl: The Children of Crow Cove*. Farrar. (Danish.)

Carmi, Daniella. 2000. *Samir and Yonatan*. Scholastic. (Israel.)

Chotjewitz, David. 2004. *Daniel Half Human: And the Good Nazi*. Richard Jackson/Atheneum. (Germany.)

de Beers, Hans. 2001. *Alexander the Great*. North-South. (Switzerland.)

Duquennoy, Jacques. 1999. *Operation Ghost*. Harcourt. (France.)

Funke, Cornelia. 2005. *Inkspell*. New York: Chicken House/Scholastic. (Germany.)

Gaarder, Jostein. 1996. *The Solitaire Mystery*. Illustrated by Hilde Kramer. Farrar. (Norway.)

Gallaz, Christophe. 1985. *Rose Blanche*. Illustrated by Roberto Innocenti. Creative Education. (France.)

Goscinny, René. 2005. *Nicholas*. Illustrated by Jean-Jacques Sempé. Phaidon Press. (France.)

Gündisch, Karin. 2001. *How I Became an American*. Cricket Books. (Germany.)

Heine, Helme. 1998. *The Boxer and the Princess*. McElderry. (Germany.)

Ho, Minfong. 1996. *Maples in the Mist: Children's Poems from the Tang Dynasty*. Illustrated by Jean and Mou-sien Tseng. Lothrop. (China.)

Holub, Josef. 2005. *An Innocent Soldier*. Arthur Levine/Scholastic. (Germany.)

Lindgren, Astrid. 1983. *Ronia, the Robber's Daughter*. Viking. (Sweden.)

Llorente, Molina. 1993. *The Apprentice*. Farrar. (Spain.)

Maruki, Toshi. 1982. *Hiroshima No Pika*. Lothrop. (Japan.)

Orlev, Uri. 1991. *The Man from the Other Side*. Houghton Mifflin. (Israel.)

Orlev, Uri. 2003. *Run, Boy, Run*. Houghton Mifflin. (Israel.)

Reuter, Bjarne. 1994. *The Boys from St. Petri*. Dutton. (Denmark.)

Richter, Hans Peter. 1972. *I Was There*. Holt. (Germany.)

Stolz, Joëlle. 2004. *The Shadows of Ghadames*. Delacorte. (France.)

Yumoto, Kazumi. 2002. *The Letters*. Farrar. (Japan.)

For details about books listed here and for a more complete list of multicultural and international titles, consult the Children's Literature Database: A Resource for Teachers, Parents, and Media Specialists CD *that accompanies this text.*

REFERENCES

Aardema, Verna. (1975). *Why mosquitoes buzz in people's ears*. New York: Dial.

Armstrong, William. (1969). *Sounder*. New York: Harper & Row.

Bishop, Rudine Sims. (1992). Multicultural literature for children: Making informed choices. In Violet J. Harris (Ed.), *Teaching multicultural literature in grades K–8*. Norwood, MA: Christopher-Gordon.

Bontemps, Arna. (1948). *Story of the negro*. New York: Knopf.

Boyd, Candy Dawson. (1990). Presentation given at the American Bookseller's Association Convention and Trade Exhibit, Las Vegas, Nevada, 5 June [cassette recording].

Bunting, Eve. (1994). *Smoky night*. New York: Harcourt.

Cai, Mingshui, & Sims Bishop, Rudine. (1994). Multicultural literature for children: Towards a clarification of the concept. In Anne Haas Dyson & Celia Genishi (Eds.), *The need for story: Cultural diversity in classroom and community* (pp. 57–71). Urbana, IL: National Council of Teachers of English.

Clark, Ann Nolan. (1952). *Secret of the Andes*. New York: Viking.

Curtis, Christopher Paul. (1999). *Bud, not Buddy*. New York: Delacorte.

Darigan, Daniel. (1991). The effects of teachers reading aloud on elementary children's attitudes toward African Americans. Dissertation, University of Oregon, Eugene.

Hamilton, Virginia. (1974). *M. C. Higgins, the great*. New York: Macmillan.

Hansen-Krening, Nancy. (1992, October). Authors of color: A multicultural perspective. *Journal of Reading, 36*(2), 124–129.

Horn, Miriam. (1993). Imagining other's lives. *U.S. News and World Report, 114*(6), 78–81.

Kadohata, Cynthia. (2004). *Kira-Kira*. New York: Atheneum.

Keats, Ezra Jack. (1962). *The snowy day*. New York: Viking.

Krumgold, Joseph. (1953). *. . . And now Miguel*. New York: Crowell.

Larrick, Nancy. (1965, September 11). The all white world of children's books. *Saturday Review,* pp. 63–65, 84–85.

Nieto, Sonia. (2000). *Affirming diversity* (3rd ed.). White Plains, NY: Longman.

Park, Linda Sue. (2001). *A single shard*. New York: Clarion.

Pate, Glenn S. (1988, April/May). Research on reducing prejudice. *Social Education, 52*(4), 287–291.

Politi, Leo. (1949). *Song of the swallows*. New York: Scribner.

Robinson, Barbara. (1972). *The best christmas pageant ever*. New York: Harper & Row.

Say, Allen. (1993). *Grandfather's journey*. New York: Houghton Mifflin.

Sims, Rudine. (1982). *Shadow and substance: Afro-American experience in contemporary children's fiction*. Urbana, IL: National Council of Teachers of English.

Sobol, Thomas. (1990, November). Understanding diversity. *Educational Leadership, 48*(3), 27–30.

Sonnenschein, Frances M. (1988). Countering prejudiced beliefs and behaviors: The role of the social
studies professional. *Social Education, 52*(4),
264–266.

Taylor, Mildred. (1976). *Roll of thunder, hear my cry.*
New York: Dial.

Wilson, August. (1990, September 26). I want a black
director. *New York Times,* p. A25.

Yates, Elizabeth. (1950). *Amos Fortune, free man.*
New York: Dutton.

Young, Ed. (1989). *Lon Po Po: A Red Riding Hood
story from China.* New York: Philomel.

Chapter 16

Controversial Books

Books are dangerous. They can undermine morals, fuel revolutions, and indoctrinate our children. Hitler certainly believed in the power of print and saw to it that publications challenging Nazi policy or written by anyone he deemed an enemy of the state (which, of course, included all books by Jewish authors) were banned, or worse, burned. No doubt there are books that we as individuals would find offensive or that would challenge our way of thinking and make us uncomfortable. But danger exists far less in these books than in the people who would usurp the power and authority to decide for the rest of us what is fit to be read.

THE FIRST AMENDMENT

Our First Amendment rights are under constant attack by those who consider paramount their personal agendas, sets of standards, or brands of special interest. The more radical or fanatical the group objecting to certain printed materials—and extremists come from both the political right and the political left—the more control they seek over individual freedom of choice. Give fanatics the power, and they will decide for us what is best, as Hitler so self-righteously did for his people. Supreme Court Justice William Brennan eloquently expressed this idea when he said, concerning the censorship case *Texas* v. *Johnson,* "If there is a bedrock principle underlying the First Amendment, it is that the Government may not prohibit the expression of an idea simply because society finds the idea itself offensive or disagreeable" (American Library Association, 1998).

This is not to say that individuals should not have the right to make decisions about the personal acceptability of books. We have not only the right but also the responsibility to make choices for ourselves and to help our children make wise choices. And if we find a book particularly

---

USING THE CHILDREN'S LITERATURE DATABASE

On the Internet, type in the address for banned books—http://www.ala.org/bbooks/challeng.html. Go to one of the lists of banned books. Select five children's titles, noting the reason they were banned. Go to the database. Locate two of the five books and see if the reason they were banned is evident in the Topic or Description fields.

offensive or dangerous, we should express that opinion without seeking to destroy the book.

In today's diverse society, what may seem clearly offensive to one group of people may be viewed as beautiful and uplifting by another. An example of this dichotomy occurred not long ago in Rockford, Illinois. Parents of a particular religious sect felt that reading Greek myths in the public schools was an evil practice. Believing strongly in the truth of their Christian convictions, they considered the Greek myths pagan theology that threatened to undermine the faith of their children. Of course, many others, Christians and non-Christians alike, viewed the Greek myths as remarkable literature that illuminates the history of our world and fosters an understanding of cultures unlike our own. The controversy in Illinois is, unfortunately, not an isolated incident of this sort of censorship aimed at public schools and libraries.

Predictable and Unpredictable Controversy

We do not wish to give the impression that any and all books should be available without considering the ages of the children or the prevailing community standards. For example, in virtually every community excessively pornographic books are unacceptable materials for school and public libraries and even for bookstores. We use the term *excessively* because even pornography does not seem to have clearly defined borders. Some adults consider Judy Blume's *Are You There God? It's Me, Margaret* (1970) to be a form of pornography because it includes sexual topics. Others would consider laughable the labeling of this book as pornographic. Nonetheless, a fine line often must be trod by school librarians and teachers when it comes to preserving intellectual freedoms and students' right to read. In some instances, certain titles are kept in closed areas to be circulated only with parental permission. Sex education books often are kept on these restricted shelves, especially in elementary schools.

As school and library personnel know, sex and bad language in books for young readers predictably generate controversy anywhere in the country. Other topics may be volatile in particular communities, such as violence, the occult, racism, or religion; but sex and bad language in children's books seem to alienate adults generally. For example, Katherine Paterson's Newbery Honor Book, *The Great Gilly Hopkins* (1978), has a number of potentially controversial elements. Gilly racially slanders her black teacher. She steals without conscience from the blind man next door, who is also black. She is cruel to her foster brother. Yet, as Paterson (1989) explains, the vast amount of mail she has received from adults complains only about the so-called rough language Gilly uses in the story. When it comes to children's reading, adults seem particularly sensitive to this issue.

Because controversies about sexual content or bad language in books are predictable, teachers and librarians know that if they use certain books they must be prepared to weather the inevitable storm of complaints. Unpredictable controversies, on the other hand, take educators by surprise. They can feel extremely vulnerable and even defenseless against unexpected censorship attacks for which they have prepared neither intellectually nor emotionally. Here are several surprising examples of unpredictable controversy occurring within the last few decades:

- The 1970 Caldecott winner, William Steig's *Sylvester and the Magic Pebble* (1969), seemed an innocuous animal fantasy until someone pointed out that the policemen in the book were depicted as pigs. The book was published during the era of Vietnam War protests, when police officers often were branded as "pigs" by demonstrators. "No wonder that the children and some adults have no respect for the law enforcement officer . . . we demand the book be removed," said the International Conference of Police Associations (Harvey, 1971).

- A public librarian reported an objection about a children's Halloween book raised by a woman who claimed to be a witch. She "felt the book was anti-witch and presented an unfair and unfavorable picture" (Chu, 1982, p. 7).

- A poem in Shel Silverstein's popular collection *A Light in the Attic* (1981) tells of a girl who tries to make a milkshake by shaking a cow and is accompanied by a pen-and-ink drawing that shows her in action. The Eagle Forum, a politically conservative organization, charged that the illustration was "an example of subliminal suggestion of 'sex with animals'" (Haferd, 1988).

- Dr. Seuss (1971) found his book, *The Lorax*, in hot water in Laytonville, California, a single-industry lumber town. *The Lorax* tells of a "little creature who loses his forest home when greedy Once-lers cut down all the Truffula trees." Residents saw this as "a flagrant attack on the livelihood" of the town and on the lumber industry in general and demanded that the book be removed from the second-grade required reading list (Arias & McNeil, 1989).

- The Newbery Award–winning book *Bridge to Terabithia* by Katherine Paterson (1977) consistently shows up on the American Library Association's yearly banned-books list. Not surprisingly, many complaints center on the theme of death or the use of bad language, but one complaint (American Library Association, 1998) accused the book of creating "an elaborate fantasy world that might lead to confusion."

- Ed Young's 1993 Caldecott Honor Book, *Seven Blind Mice* (1992), is a variant of the story of the three blind men and the elephant. Each mouse, a different and brilliant color, incorrectly identifies the object (elephant) it encounters until the white mouse solves the riddle. A host of critics surfaced, complaining that representing the white mouse as the "savior" perpetuates the racist viewpoint of white supremacy.

- BBC News (2001) reported "a bonfire of Harry Potter books" in Alamogordo, New Mexico, started by the congregation of the Christ Community Church. About the book burning, Pastor Jack Brock said, "Behind that innocent face [Harry Potter] is the power of satanic darkness. Harry Potter is the devil and he is destroying people."

Intellectual Freedom and Individual Choice

Controversy about children's books may spring from anywhere, and the challenge may be about almost anything. Often the prevailing social and political climate will determine what is controversial at a given point in time. So, how should we as teachers and school librarians proceed in our selection and use of books? First, we need to affirm our personal commitment to individual choice by examining how we view books. If we see them strictly as mirrors that must reflect our particular mores, lifestyles, or standards, then our problem is a difficult one. Whose standards or beliefs are the books to model? The answer could mean the difference between Greek myths or no Greek myths. If, instead, we view books as windows to the world, we have determined that literature is designed to celebrate diversity and that we accept the risks that may accompany such a stance.

The diagram in Figure 16–1 shows an expanding circle encompassing ever-increasing numbers of the population some hope to control when it comes to books. However, attempting to exert control over the reading choices of others is myopic. As we move outward through the concentric circles in the diagram, it is less probable that the manner in which a book affects us will be the same for other individuals. For example, one who decides a book containing sexual indiscretions should be universally abhorred might be surprised to know the story convinces a teenager across town that sexual abstinence until marriage is the best choice for him.

The smallest circle is self. No one would disagree that we each have the responsibility to decide what we personally will or will not read and, as the circle widens, that parents have the right to at least influence the reading of their minor-aged children. It is the people who view books strictly as mirrors who more likely will choose to operate in the expanded circles of control by seeking to censor reading materials in their

FIGURE 16–1
Circles of control.

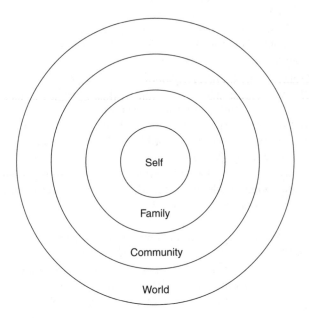

community or, if they only had the power, in the entire world. The International Conference of Police Associations wished to exercise this sort of far-reaching control by demanding that *Sylvester and the Magic Pebble* (Steig, 1969) be removed from all libraries.

Professional organizations such as the American Library Association (ALA), the International Reading Association (IRA), and the National Council of Teachers of English (NCTE) have adopted statements of philosophy concerning intellectual freedom and our right to read. Organizations that actually assist teachers and librarians who need help in fighting censorship attacks include the ALA's Freedom to Read Foundation (phone: 800-545-2433, ext. 4226; http://www.ftrf.org), the National Coalition Against Censorship (phone: 212-807-6222; http://www.ncac.org), and People for the American Way (phone: 800-326-7329; http://www.pfaw.org). But even with this sort of support network, teachers and librarians may wish to exercise some caution, especially in selecting books to read aloud to children or to be required classroom reading. Therefore, a few touchstones may help us decide about potentially controversial books.

CAREFULLY CONSIDER ASSIGNED BOOKS.   There is a difference between a book that is assigned reading and a book that is merely available on school or classroom library shelves. When a title is compulsory reading for students, book watchdogs are more strident. Teachers should consider carefully whether a book they plan to assign is one they would be willing to defend.

RECOGNIZE THAT POSITIVE LEARNING CAN COME FROM NEGATIVE PORTRAYALS.   It is not unusual for books with negative content to be dismissed out of hand. For example, some adults do not want their children reading a novel that involves drug abuse, because they feel it may plant a suggestion that could lead to trouble. However, if the story illustrates the negative consequences of drug abuse, the book actually may be desirable. That drug use appears in a book does not automatically condemn the title; its presence may serve positive ends.

Even religious literature includes negative episodes for positive purposes. In the Bible, King David's story involves lust, adultery, deceit, and even murder in an illustration of how indulgence and becoming self-serving can lead to undesirable ends.

Avoiding the harsh and often unsavory realities of life does not make them go away. In fact, a child may be more susceptible to the effects of controversial material by being totally unprepared. As Jane Smiley (1994) said, "A child who is protected from all controversial ideas . . . is as vulnerable as a child who is protected from every germ. The infection, when it comes, and it will come, may overwhelm the system, be that the immune system or the belief system."

JUDGE BOOKS HOLISTICALLY.   It is impossible and unfair to judge a book simply by the subject. All books that deal with sexual topics or contain swear words are not automatically bad. Nor are they automatically good. The way in which these subjects are presented makes the difference. If uncomfortable subject matter offers insight, helps develop attitudes and skills for dealing successfully with life, and fosters resolution or hope, the book

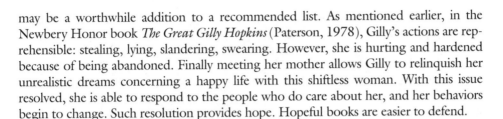

may be a worthwhile addition to a recommended list. As mentioned earlier, in the Newbery Honor book *The Great Gilly Hopkins* (Paterson, 1978), Gilly's actions are reprehensible: stealing, lying, slandering, swearing. However, she is hurting and hardened because of being abandoned. Finally meeting her mother allows Gilly to relinquish her unrealistic dreams concerning a happy life with this shiftless woman. With this issue resolved, she is able to respond to the people who do care about her, and her behaviors begin to change. Such resolution provides hope. Hopeful books are easier to defend.

DETERMINE WHEN A BOOK IS DEVELOPMENTALLY APPROPRIATE FOR CHILDREN. Some exposure to life's harshness can prepare children for difficult times; too much exposure can traumatize them. With literature we hope to sensitize children to important issues of the human experience. If details are too explicit, however, children may be traumatized instead of sensitized. The age of the children can make a difference—what may be appropriate for 12-year-olds may not be appropriate for 8-year-olds. Also, individual differences in children of the same age can be significant. Adults need to know both the books and the children to make this judgment call.

An example of a book that sensitizes most 11-year-olds to an issue without an excess of raw detail is Paula Fox's Newbery winner *The Slave Dancer* (1973). She goes just far enough in this story of the American slave trade to show people's inhumanity without becoming too explicit. By comparison, the adult book *Roots* by Alex Haley (1976), published three years earlier, covers the same basic material in far more complete and explicit detail.

However, former school librarian and current children's book author Cynthia DeFelice (2002) wonders if we shouldn't trust children more than we often do. She remembers the powerful experience she had reading *To Kill a Mockingbird* (Lee, 1960) when she was in fifth grade.

> My parents had given it to me, but when I brought it out at school, I was told I had to bring in a note from my parents saying it was okay. As I reread the book . . . [recently], part of me kept thinking, "This would never be given to a fifth grade child today and what a shame."
>
> I thank my parents for having faith that I would be able to take the events of that story, the discussions of rape, the racial and class conflicts, the sometimes cruel actions and crude personalities of the diverse characters, and see them through the eyes of young Scout Finch and come to understand them along with her. (DeFelice, 2002, p. 18)

HANDLING BOOK CHALLENGES

Because controversy about books is so unpredictable, almost any book sitting on the library shelf or being shared in the classroom might be challenged by parents and other adults. Therefore, we may find ourselves defending our choice of books. If a parent comes in to complain, remember that reaching an understanding is possible and even probable. Sometimes the problem may be a simple misunderstanding that can be cleared up once teacher and parent communicate. For example, parents may hear about a troublesome book but then discover they have been misinformed. However,

if a serious challenge surfaces, teachers and librarians need to have a plan in place to control a potentially explosive situation.

The first rule of thumb when materials are challenged is to deal with *only* one book at a time. Allowing complainants to challenge several books at once or all books by one author makes for an unmanageable situation. To keep things under control, each library system, school, or school district must have policies and procedures to govern censorship cases. Consider the following three guidelines for handling book challenges: (1) materials selection policy, (2) grievance procedure, (3) steps to reduce emotional tension.

Materials Selection Policy

A selection policy will guide the process of choosing books and other media for libraries and classroom use. Often, guidelines and procedures outlined in a selection policy will include the ALA's Library Bill of Rights or other "right to read" statements that confirm the institution's support of the First Amendment and intellectual freedom. Also, selection policies will suggest the use of nationally recognized review journals in helping to make selections. Generally, a selection committee with teacher representatives from various grade levels or disciplines, and sometimes with parent representatives, is named to make final selection recommendations. Policy statements also may specify the standards of all materials used in a school setting, even personal books that a teacher may bring to read to students.

Grievance Procedure

Each library system, school, or school district must have a formal grievance procedure in place, either as a section of the materials selection policy or as a separate document. This procedure dictates the process by which an individual may request that the library or school reconsider a book. It always includes a formal complaint form that must be filled out and signed by the complainant. A sample form is shown in Figure 16–2. With no signature, the school or library does not need to consider the challenge to the book. However, if the form is filed, the grievance procedure dictates further action by the library system or school district. Generally, a committee, which may be the same as the selection committee, is convened to consider the complaint. It is wise to include community representation. The recommendation of the committee is then forwarded to the school or library board, which makes the final decision. It is possible that the censors might take their case to the court system if they are not pleased with a board's decision. However, the fact that the complaint was given a fair and careful hearing can only strengthen a school's or library system's case.

Steps to Reduce Emotional Tension

With policies in place, teachers and librarians can breathe easier. Still, when the time comes to face someone who is challenging a book, two other guidelines are helpful.

FIGURE 16–2

Example of citizen's request for reconsideration of a book.

Citizen's Request for Reconsideration of a Book

Paperback _____

Hardcover _____

Author _____

Title _____

Publisher (if known) _____

Request initiated by _____

Telephone _____ Address _____

City _____ Zip Code _____

Complainant represents:

_____ Himself/herself

_____ Organization (Name) _____

_____ Other group (Identify) _____

1. To what in the book do you object? (Please be specific; cite pages.) _____
_____
_____

2. What do you feel might be the result of reading this book? _____
_____
_____

3. For what age group would you recommend this book? _____
_____
_____

4. Is there anything positive about this book? _____
_____
_____

5. Did you read the entire book? _____ What parts? _____
_____
_____

6. Are you aware of the judgment of this book by literary critics? _____
_____
_____

7. What would you like the library/school to do about this book?

_____ Withdraw it.

_____ Return it to the selection committee/department for reconsideration.

_____ Do not assign or lend it to my child.

_____ Other. (Please explain.) _____
_____

8. In its place, what book would you recommend that would convey as valuable a picture and perspective of the subject treated? _____
_____
_____

_____   _____

Signature of Complainant   Date

First, we must make a supreme effort to keep conversation with an upset parent or library patron on a rational rather than an emotional level. First, *listen to the complaint* without overreacting. This may not be as easy as it sounds, for often teachers and librarians feel attacked and their natural response is to be defensive. If angry words rule, however, chances are the book will not be as big an issue as the escalating distaste for one another. So, we need to hold our tongues and listen, which allows us to determine if the complaint is a product of a misunderstanding or if we need to channel the complainant peacefully into the formal grievance procedure.

Along with listening calmly to the complaint, we also ought to *get someone else to listen:* another librarian, the teacher from across the hall, the principal. Having someone else present helps keep everyone honest and serves to reduce tension. People are always more careful with their words when others are there to hear. If the complainant remains unsatisfied, the next step is to have that person *fill out the request to reconsider a book* (Figure 16–2) and begin the formal grievance procedure.

Of the top 10 challenged titles of 2004, 8 were young adult or children's books. Also, of the top 10 most challenged authors of 2004, 9 were young adult or children's writers (American Library Association, 2005). These figures are indicative of the particular attention adult censors give to children's books. As we have seen earlier in this chapter, these challenges are spawned by a vast variety of special interests that may or may not represent mainstream thought. And even if mainstream opinion is supported by a successful censorship attempt, then certain voices from our pluralistic society will be silenced. Ultimately, those of us who love books and cherish the right to choose must actively stand on the side of individual choice and intellectual freedom.

REFERENCES

American Library Association. (1998, March 10). Internet Web site: Office on Intellectual Freedom (http://www.ala.org/oif.html); Challenged and Banned Books (http://www.ala.org/bbooks/challeng.html).

American Library Association. (2005, February 10). Internet Web site: Office of Intellectual Freedom (http://www.ala.org/oif.html); Challenged and Banned Books (http://www.ala.org/bbooks/challeng.html).

Arias, Ron, & McNeil, Liz. (1989, October 23). A boy sides with Dr. Seuss, and puts a town at loggerheads. *People Weekly, 32*(17), 67–68.

BBC News. (2001, December 31). "Satanic" Harry Potter books burnt. Internet website: http://news.bbc.co.uk/hi/english/entertainment/arts/newsid_1735000/1735623.stm.

Blume, Judy. (1970). *Are you there God? It's me, Margaret.* New York: Bradbury.

Chu, Nancy. (1982, March). Some thoughts concerning censorship. *The Dragon Lode, 3*(2), 6–10.

DeFelice, Cynthia. (2002). Untitled, unpublished speech presented at the Brigham Young University Symposium on Books for Young Readers, Provo, Utah, 19 July.

Fox, Paula. (1973). *The slave dancer.* Scarsdale, NY: Bradbury Press.

Haferd, Laura. (1988, April 23). Activist leads fight against "subliminals." *Akron (Ohio) Beacon Journal,* April 23.

Haley, Alex. (1976). *Roots.* New York: Doubleday.

Harvey, James S. (1971, March). *Newsletter on intellectual freedom,* 44–45.

Lee, Harper. (1960). *To kill a mockingbird.* New York: Lippincott.

Paterson, Katherine. (1977). *Bridge to Terabithia.* New York: Crowell.

Paterson, Katherine. (1978). *The great Gilly Hopkins.* New York: Crowell.

Paterson, Katherine. (1989, Winter). Tale of a reluctant dragon. *The New Advocate, 2*(1), 1–8.

Seuss, Dr. (1971). *The lorax.* New York: Random House.

Silverstein, Shel. (1981). *A light in the attic.* New York: Harper & Row.

Smiley, Jane. (1994, February 15). Censorship in a world of fantasy. *Chicago Tribune,* Section 1, p. 19.

Steig, William. (1969). *Sylvester and the magic pebble.* New York: Windmill/Simon & Schuster.

Young, Ed. (1992). *Seven blind mice.* New York: Philomel.

Chapter 17

Motivating Students to Read

When T. H. Bell served as U.S. Secretary of Education, he traveled the country observing schools to find ways to make them better. His experiences led him to identify three areas where change must take place if education is to improve (Bell, 1982). "The first," he said, "is student motivation." He explained that nothing of any consequence is learned without the consent and involvement of the learner. Students have to *want* to know something in order to acquire it genuinely rather than temporarily, say, to pass a test. If teachers are to make a difference in current educational practice, they must pay more attention to students' attitudes. He then identified the second area as "student motivation." And the third area of needed change: "Student motivation." In short, he said nothing is as important in improving schools as motivating students.

But in practice, motivation in educational circles often means carefully planning an activity so the students appear to choose it when actually the whole thing is the teacher's idea. That definition comes closer to manipulation. Genuine motivation is a personal decision and comes from the heart.

There is never a guarantee that a teacher's most sincere efforts will motivate anyone. The best we can do is offer such efforts, sincerely and continually, and hope that students will resonate with what they see and hear. However, teachers must *be* readers before they can motivate children to *become* readers. If the adults in children's lives love to read—and model that enthusiasm—they are then the bedrock of successful literacy education. Indeed, Perez (1986, p. 9) tells us that nothing in the entire school has a greater impact on convincing children that books are worthwhile than teachers' reading habits.

> . . . teachers have a choice in motivating children to become lifelong readers. They can either preach on the joys of reading, or they can model for the youngsters what a reader who enjoys reading does. And what teachers do ultimately will depend on how much they truly believe in the importance of reading. (Perez, 1986, p. 11)

Figure 17–1 provides a quiz that will help you determine how positive a reading model you are for your students; in addition, it offers ways to become a stronger model by suggesting some ways to improve.

FIGURE 17–1
Reading model self-assessment for teachers.

How Good a Reading Model Am I?

Personal Model

1. I read in a book for personal pleasure at least two different days per week.　Yes　　No
2. Two of my favorite authors for children are _____.
3. One of my favorite illustrators of children's books is _____.
4 The title of a picture book published during the past 3 years is _____.
5. The title of a children's chapter book published during the past 3 years is _____.
6. I have a personal library of more than 40 children's trade books.　Yes　　No
7. The book I am going to read next is _____.
8. During the past 3 months, I found myself showing an interesting book to someone else or mentioning it in conversation. The title is _____.
9. My favorite genre or type of books is _____.
10. Two of my favorite authors for adults are _____.

Classroom Model

1. At least twice weekly I engage in personal reading where my students can see me with a book.　Yes　　No
2. My students can identify at least one type of book I like or dislike.　Yes　　No
3. I have a growing classroom library of trade books.　Yes　　No
4. I introduce or "book talk" books with my students at least twice a week.　Yes　　No
5. I read aloud a picture book or from a chapter book to my class at least once every day.　Yes　　No
6. I read aloud something other than books to my class daily.　Yes　　No
7. Sustained silent reading (SSR) is a part of our daily schedule.　Yes　　No
8. I always read in my own book during SSR.　Yes　　No
9. I require my children to read regularly on their own outside of class.　Yes　　No
10. I run a regular book club program or encourage children to buy books, and help make that possible.　Yes　　No

Scoring

Personal Model. Each question counts 2 points.

1. Yes = 2 points. If teachers aren't reading, they can't deliver an honest love of books to students.
2. 1 point for each author. Teachers who read children's books will respond more to some authors than others and need to recognize they have favorites.
3. 2 points for completion. Even die-hard upper elementary teachers need to be familiar with picture books.
4. 2 points for completion. If a teacher knows only old books, chances for reaching children are more limited.
5. 2 points for completion. See number 4.

(continued)

FIGURE 17–1

Continued

6. One point for every 20 children's trade books you own (2 points maximum).
7. 2 points for completion. If you don't have an idea of what to read next, chances are you're not reading much.
8. 2 points for completion. If teachers never talk about the books they read, their influence will be limited.
9. 2 points for completion. Identifying a favorite type of book or genre is important self-knowledge.
10. 1 point for each author. Teachers who are readers generally will have a broader interest than just children's books.

Classroom Model. Each "yes" response receives 2 points.

1. Yes = 2 points. Adults who are most successful in turning children into readers do not hide their own reading. This is as true at home as in the classroom. One of our graduate students read regularly, yet none of her four children valued books. Further conversation revealed she read only in the bathtub and in bed after the children were asleep. Because she never talked to them or in front of them about her reading, they had no idea at all she liked books.
2. Yes = 2 points. If you emphasize personal reading with children, they need to learn about your personal reading, which includes the types of books you like and those that are not as appealing to you. Children deserve a teacher with identified favorites.
3. Yes = 2 points. We have a difficult time convincing children that books are worthwhile if none are at hand.
4. Yes = 2 points. Sharing titles consistently will give children needed and welcome ideas of what to read next as well as draw attention to the pleasure and importance of reading.
5. Yes = 2 points. Hearing books read aloud is the most important classroom activity for turning children into readers.
6. Yes = 2 points. The more we immerse students in "real" reading (see Chapter 1), the better chance we have that they will become readers.
7. Yes = 2 points. SSR is the second most important classroom activity for turning children into readers.
8. Yes = 2 points. The key to a successful SSR program is seeing the teacher read.
9. Yes = 2 points. This is the most important out-of-class activity for turning children into readers.
10. Yes = 2 points. Book ownership is a mark of a truly literate person.

Each quiz has a maximum of 20 points. Scores and ratings for each quiz, and both combined, are as follows:

Personal or Classroom Score	Total Score	Rating
16–20	32–40	Stupendous. You're a fine model.
12–15	24–31	Very good. You're better than most.
8–11	16–23	Okay, but you need work.
4–7	8–15	Weak. Quick—get books into your life.
0–3	0–7	Don't have children or teach school just yet.

HELPING STUDENTS FIND THE BOOKS THEY LIKE

Perhaps the most common way to motivate a child to read is to identify the child's interests and then locate books on those subjects. Although this method largely works well, it has two drawbacks: (1) In a regular library, all the books on a favorite topic are soon exhausted, so the teacher still needs to know how to get children interested in other subjects. More important, (2) some children do not know what they are interested in and tend to fall between the cracks. Unfortunately, such children usually are the ones who need books the most. Teachers can help create the desire to read in both types of students—those who would benefit from expanding their areas of interest and those who have none—when they introduce and read from a variety of children's books they personally like.

Choosing personal favorites to recommend to children is at least as successful as any other way of selecting titles. No source or method is foolproof. Even picking books exclusively from lists of award winners such as the Caldecott and Newbery carries no guarantee children will respond positively to them. When teachers introduce and read from books they genuinely like, students are more likely to be motivated for two reasons:

1. Those books generally are better books. They usually are more solidly crafted and contain more levels on which children can make connections.
2. When teachers recommend books that are personally meaningful, a genuine and irresistible enthusiasm accompanies their words. When people talk about books they like, those who listen often are influenced by their sincerity and conviction.

Nothing we offer children is more important than an adult who reads. Children end up doing what we do, not what we say, and all the admonitions about the importance of reading in their lives fall on deaf ears if they view us as people who do not take our own advice. When we speak from experience, however, our words are more honest and persuasive. We can't convince children of the beauty of mathematics unless that vision comes from our own hearts and minds. We can't paint a believable picture of how appealing life in the desert is unless we have lived there and loved it. And we largely waste our time singing the virtues of reading when the last time we read a book was five years ago.

LEARNING FROM MOTIVATED READERS

A group of college-age Americans was living in Germany, trying to learn German but making slow progress. An old hand offered a piece of advice that made an enormous difference: "If you want to speak like the Germans, listen to the way Germans speak." Embarrassingly simple and obvious, it changed the course of their learning, which until then had been too formal and academic.

We adapt that advice for this chapter: "If we want students to be motivated readers, look at how motivated readers read." Teachers sometimes believe that students need careful preparation to read a book or that they have to be bribed or prodded into reading. Yet some children jump right into books, reading without the benefit of preparatory steps or the intervention of either a carrot or a stick. Two principles underlie the motivation of these eager readers: (1) Reading is personal. (2) Reading is a natural process. The following common characteristics of motivated readers reflect these two principles:

1. Motivated readers read not for others, but for their own purposes. They read what is important to them and know that real reading is not done to answer someone else's questions or fill out a worksheet.
2. Motivated readers have personal and identifiable likes and dislikes in books: subject matter, authors, illustrators, formats, styles, and so on.
3. Motivated readers feel rewarded during the reading process. They find immediate pleasure in the book and don't read because they will need the information next year.
4. Motivated readers do not feel trapped by a book. They can put it down without guilt when it no longer meets their needs.
5. Motivated readers are not hesitant about passing judgment on a book. They have their own viewpoints and do not apologize for them.
6. Motivated readers read at their own rate. They skip, scan, linger, and reread as necessary or desirable.
7. Motivated readers don't feel obligated to remember everything they read. They find reading worthwhile even if they can't recall every concept or idea, and they allow themselves to skip over words they don't know as long as they understand the idea or story.
8. Motivated readers read broadly, narrowly, or in between, depending on how they feel.
9. Motivated readers develop a personal attachment to books they like.
10. Motivated readers find time to read regularly.

Motivated readers don't look over their shoulders as they read. They are in charge. We adults shouldn't get excited when they put down books without finishing them, when they devour what we think are worthless books, when their taste does not reflect our own, or when they read very narrowly.

Yet teachers with the best of intentions can interfere with motivated readers. Often the most difficult hurdle is simply getting out of their way. Whatever an adult does that keeps the child from becoming involved with the book is something to be avoided. It is easy to spot mind-numbing exercises that treat the book as merely a repository of facts to be mined, and those practices should be avoided.

Yet even the right principles can be followed with too much fervor, as is evident in the following two examples.

Rose Napoli is an experienced, dedicated teacher who became enthusiastic about trade books and their classroom use during a summer institute. She returned to her teaching inflamed with ideas about allowing students to choose their own books, providing time for them to read, and initiating discussions based on their personal responses. The trouble was that her enthusiasm had become so strong, she simply overpowered the children. She jumped immediately into questions about their involvement with the stories and so peppered them with requests for their feelings that even those children who initially responded began to keep quiet. Only when she began to let students talk from their own perspectives, and sincerely listened to them, did the children start to respond honestly. In time, the simplistic but honest comments became more complex and perceptive, and Rose eventually found the kind of student involvement she earlier had tried to force (Calkins, 1994, pp. 243–249).

Gordon Whiting, a professor at Brigham Young University, prided himself on allowing his 9-year-old daughter adequate rein in selecting the books she would read. He was pleased to see her choose The Little House series and was not bothered when she finished them all and began immediately to reread the seven titles in the slipcase. She read them a third time, then a fourth. When she began a fifth reading, he wondered if she wouldn't be served better by reading something else but said nothing. As she started the sixth time, he had to hold his tongue. When she picked up the first book to begin a seventh reading, he could keep his peace no longer. He did not forbid her to read them again but insisted she read one different book before returning to the series. Result? She quit reading altogether. Chances are good that she would have moved to other titles in her own time, but clearly she was getting something from the series that caused her to read the books again and again. We simply don't know what goes on in the heads of children when they are immersed in a book. If they are to become motivated readers, we must allow them to be in charge.

GETTING STUDENTS QUICKLY INTO BOOKS

We learn a useful lesson about reading from TV. Why do people watch it so much? Because it is so good? No, because watching TV is so easy. It is in a central place in the home, highly visible, and simple to use. If the TV were stored in a basement closet, we might bring it out on weekends, but would likely find something else to do instead of hauling it upstairs every time we wanted to see a program.

When we make reading easier, we find more children reading. We need to make books as accessible as TV—a part of the decor, visible, and within easy reach. We need to use them. Have them handy. Hold them up. Read passages. Get students to see what is inside. We need to handle children and books like we handle children and basketball: Provide them a hoop and a ball and let them play. No need to recite the history of the game, learn about the manufacturing of basketballs, or study the specifications of different backboards. Give them the ball, and let them on the court. (Not that a little discussion during reading can't give added depth to the experience, just as wise coaching can improve the play on a basketball court.) An interesting book does not need elaborate introductions or preparations any more than an appealing movie needs a narrator to set the stage for the viewer. We open the cover and read.

READING INCENTIVE PROGRAMS

To focus on individual reading in the classroom and inspire students to spend time with books, teachers sometimes use an incentive program to introduce children to books and get them involved in reading. Reading incentive programs are of two types: teacher generated and commercially prepared.

Teacher-generated reading incentive programs generally use a chart or other visual record to keep track of each child's reading. Often thematic, the chart may be called "Shoot for the Moon," with a rocket ship for each child lined up at the bottom and a moon at the top. For every book read, the rocket ship advances an inch. Or paper ice cream cones may line the back wall. Every time a child reads a book, the title is written on a paper scoop of ice cream and placed on the cone. When every cone has 10 scoops, the class has an ice cream party.

Commercially prepared reading incentive programs are available to schools and school districts. While the particulars differ among commercial programs, they usually give point values to books, which can then be redeemed for prizes or used as goals for grading. To be sure that children read the books, a quick evaluation is included as a part of the program, usually a multiple-choice quiz that requires the child to score within a certain range to get credit for reading the book, often giving more points for a higher score.

Both kinds of programs—teacher-prepared and commercial—have the potential to be helpful or harmful. They are helpful if they actually aid a child in finding and getting involved with a book. Sometimes the boost offered by a program will jump start a reader by encouraging that first step, and, once into a book, the child may turn into a genuinely engaged reader. Yet teachers need to be cautious about incentive programs. Some research shows that extrinsic rewards actually can hinder the development of intrinsic motivation to read (Krashen, 2004; Lepper, Greene, & Nisbett, 1973). Yet other research reports that extrinsic rewards do not necessarily have a negative impact on intrinsic motivation to read, at least in the areas of attitude, time on task, and performance (Cameron & Pierce, 1994). Teachers need to be aware, however, that when they offer a prize as a reward for reading, they must be able to determine when the prize overshadows the book. Teachers should ask, "How can I know if the student is reading for the prize or for the love of the book?" If they are not sure of the answer, then they should examine the situation more closely to determine whether the reward is getting in the way. If the reading never becomes as important as the prize, then the incentive program is no longer a friend, but has become the enemy. If teachers are sure students are motivated primarily by the books, then nothing is wrong with getting an ice cream cone or collecting points. But one reward, and one reward only, keeps people reading over time: the reading itself. Over the long haul, people turn to books because the books are worthwhile, not because they are the means to treats or grades.

An example of an incentive program going awry was given by a university student who told about the contest sponsored by his school when he was in the third grade. Whoever read the most books over 3 months would win a bicycle. This student burned with the idea of owning that bike and read during every free moment at school and home. He read more than any of the fourth, fifth, or sixth graders. And he won the bicycle. During the schoolwide assembly when the principal presented him with the prize, his fine example was held up to the rest of the students as stellar and enviable. Finishing the story, the student said, "Since winning the bike, I have not read one book except those required by my classes." The reading champion of the school never was a reader. To win a bicycle, he simply engaged in a competitive activity involving books.

One problem with the moon shot and the ice cream cones is that these programs tend not to help those who need help most. Often the charts show a few rockets still on the launching pad or some cones without scoops of ice cream. These belong to the children in every class who need books the most. They do not read easily, are not doing well in school, and receive little or no encouragement at home. And because they are not doing well at school, the chart meant to inspire instead can condemn, revealing at a glance the names of those children who are behind.

At the other end of the spectrum is the handful of achievers whose rockets take off in a blinding blast. They shoot to the moon, continue beyond the mark to the top of the wall, and then make a turn at the ceiling toward the opposite wall. These competitive types can't stand to lose. Like the boy who won the bike, their compulsion to win often overshadows the pleasures of reading, and they tend to zoom through book after book at home with thoughts like "I'll beat that Ruthie! I'll bet I'm reading more pages tonight than she is." As if possessed, these readers exhibit the same drive whether the contest is skipping rope or gathering leaves. Born to win, they sail through stacks of books with little benefit.

Some concerns also accompany the commercial incentive programs adopted on a district or school basis. Students who read for points are interested only in books approved by the program. Many terrific books are not a part of the program, but students skip over them because they do not count in the point total. Since passing the program's test on each book is the mark of a successful reader, some students find other ways to answer the questions, such as viewing a movie based on the book. An additional problem is that the tests themselves are not always accurate. Matthew, a sixth grader uninterested in books, found a title that captivated him. He stayed up several nights in a row to finish it, but when he took the commercial test (for the book Accelerated Reader), he failed. The fact is, in order to make such tests discriminating, the questions are often so nitpicky or confusing as to be both meaningless to the reader and useless for evaluation. For example, we took the Accelerated Reader 10-question quiz for *Tuck Everlasting* (Babbitt, 1975), a book each of us had read at least a dozen times. When we scored 80 percent, we tried again, discussing each test item as we proceeded. Still, we were only able to score 90 percent. It was not that we were unprepared. We simply could not figure out what two of the questions were really asking. If two adults who were very familiar with the book were stymied by some of the test items, what would fifth graders feel? In fact, author Susan Fletcher took the Accelerated Reader test for her own book, *Dragon's Milk* (1989) and scored only 90 percent (Fletcher, 2006).

While concerns exist with individual reading incentive programs, group motivation and group record keeping are another matter. The teacher who requires students to keep records of their personal reading can tally each week's reading and then display the increasing total, perhaps in a thermometer where the temperature rises with continued reading or simply in a growing line that snakes around the top of the classroom walls. These visual summaries provide bragging rights to everyone in the class, as opposed to the individual successes offered by the rocketship or ice cream charts. When a goal is reached, everyone participates in the victory, even those kids who have read few or no books. No one but the teacher is aware of the amount each child reads, so no additional stigma is placed on those who are not performing. The teacher now has the opportunity to work individually with those students who need extra time and attention.

ORGANIZING THE CLASSROOM TO GET CHILDREN INTO BOOKS

Teachers who desire to make reading a natural part of the educational landscape will want to plan so that books fit smoothly and easily into the school day and their students' lives. Six areas to consider when organizing the ideal reading classroom are teacher example, providing books, making time, creating a reading atmosphere, working with parents, and choosing meaningful activities.

First: Set an Example

In motivating children to read, the most important element is a teacher who reads. The power of a teacher's example, as described earlier in this chapter and covered more thoroughly in Chapter 18, appears here as a reminder. "The key to developing a personal love of books is a teacher who communicates enthusiasm and an appreciation of literature through his attitudes and examples" (Wilson & Hall, 1972, p. 341).

Second: Provide Books

The love of reading cannot be taught generally; it depends on contact with specific titles, certain subjects, and particular authors. To catch students, an enormously wide variety of books of different formats and levels of difficulty needs to be available in the elementary classroom. All grades need fiction, nonfiction, and poetry. Every lower grade needs some chapter books. Every upper grade needs some picture books. The most sincere and devoted intentions to help children become readers turn to dust if books are not handy for teachers to read aloud and introduce to the class and for students to pick over for silent reading time. (Appendix A suggests specific ways to acquire books and build a classroom library. Appendix B lists some appealing magazines.)

Third: Make Time for Books

Put books on the agenda. If reading for its own sake does not appear on the daily schedule, the message to students is clear: "We do not value personal reading in this classroom." Four useful ways to structure time for books are (1) reading aloud, (2) silent reading, (3) introducing books to children, and (4) going to the library.

Make time to read aloud.   Good experiences with reading aloud don't just happen. They occur when certain principles are followed.

1. Reading aloud at the same time every day has a number of advantages over working it in when convenient. Having a scheduled time:
   - assures the teacher and the class that the reading will happen.
   - legitimizes the activity by making it a regular part of the school day.
   - allows the students to anticipate the experience.
2. Teachers should honestly like the books they read aloud. The difference in reading a book aloud only because it is handy and reading a book aloud because it is loved is enormous.
3. Don't read unfamiliar books aloud. The temptation is great to discover the contents of a book along with the class, but too many drawbacks can occur:
   - The teacher may not like the book.
   - The book may have unpleasant surprises—words the teacher is not comfortable saying aloud, a character with negative traits who shares a name with a child in the class, or something in the plot that is inappropriate.
   - The teacher can't dramatize or emphasize highlights because they are unknown ahead of time.
   - Most important, the teacher's enthusiasm for the story will likely be weak because the adult is learning at the same time as the children.
4. Teachers should do the oral reading themselves. Even if a child is skilled enough to read the book aloud, teacher participation carries a message: Our teacher *wants* to be a part of this activity; it must be important. In addition, students get to see a teacher's personal involvement in books that, over time, generally will include both laughter and tears. Children benefit from much more than the story when an adult reads aloud.
5. Don't expect all students to like every book. Tell the class, "We will read many books in class this year. No one will like them all, but I expect everyone will find some they do like."
6. Establish rules for read-aloud time. Some teachers allow students to draw; others don't. Some are not concerned when children fall asleep; others are. If anything bothers a teacher, it must be fixed, or the distraction will weaken the reading experience.

Make time for silent reading.   Students need time at school to read books of their own choosing (Krashen, 2004). Commonly called SSR (*s*ustained *s*ilent *r*eading), DEAR (*d*rop *e*verything *a*nd *r*ead), or SQUIRT (*s*tudents' *qu*iet *un*interrupted *r*eading *t*ime), this portion of the daily schedule is reserved for personal reading. The rules are easy: For the allotted time, everyone reads—including the teacher. SSR is not an automatic success. To make it work, these are the essentials:

- The teacher reads during SSR. When a number of SSR programs were evaluated, findings indicated the program failed when the teacher did not participate (Jensen & Jensen, 2002; McCracken & McCracken, 1978). If the teacher does not read, the message to the students is clear: "This is only a school assignment, important for you but not for me." One of the best parts about SSR is the time it provides the teacher to catch up on new children's books, but the teacher's reading does not have to be limited to titles appropriate for children. Anything personally interesting is fair game. However, when a student recommends a book and the teacher actually reads it, the positive results are overwhelming.

- If someone starts a book and loses interest, finishing it is not required.
- The teacher makes no assignments for the books read during SSR. Students may choose to use a book they read during SSR for an assigned activity, but they are not required to formally report the reading of SSR books.
- The teacher should anticipate possible distractions or interruptions, and let students know what to do about them. Fine-tuning the activity is inevitable—no one can consider every possible difficulty beforehand—but being clear on as many points as possible makes for a smoother reading time. For example:
  - What does a student do who finishes a book in the middle of a reading period? (Students should be sure to have at least one additional book in their desks, particularly when they are getting to the end of the one they're reading.)
  - Do children have to stay in their seats during the entire reading time? (Some teachers have trained students to get up quietly and find another book; others do not allow them to wander about for any reason.)
  - What happens if a student took the book home last night and forgot to bring it back today? (A box or plastic carton of short books or magazines might be available so that appealing reading material is not difficult to locate.)
  - What if a student has a pressing question during SSR? (It can wait until the reading period is over. This time is also for the teacher, who does not want to be interrupted.)

MAKE TIME TO INTRODUCE BOOKS TO CHILDREN.   Simply releasing children into a world filled with books does not make them readers. If they have no interest in books, no reading habit, and nothing they are looking for, children can easily ignore a wealth of superb titles. It is up to the teacher to bridge the gap between book and child, and one successful way is for the teacher to introduce new titles to the students.

There are many ways to introduce books. Holding up the book so students can see what it looks like while telling them something about it is all that is necessary. Teachers are most successful when introducing books they have read and liked, but it is possible to introduce books the teacher does not yet know. Reading the blurb on the back of paperbacks or on the inside flap of hardcovers usually provides enough information to present the book to the class. In addition, teachers may want to tune in a book-introduction program such as *Reading Rainbow*.

A book-introduction time should be on the daily schedule, but the number of books shown to students can vary. For the first week or two of the school year, you may want to introduce as many as five or more per day to ensure that enough books have been presented to get the students started. After that, a book or two every day is fine. The point is to provide students with some titles they can look forward to trying out.

MAKE TIME FOR GOING TO THE LIBRARY.   If the elementary school has a library, teachers should plan to get their children there regularly. Some teachers elect not to sign up the entire class, but after a few introductory visits make a schedule for students so they may use the library singly or in pairs before and after school, at lunch, or during the school day. If you visit as a class, always stay in the library and circulate among the students, helping them find good books. The more titles they know and the more excitement generated for books, the more successful the library visit will be.

Even with your presence in the library, be prepared to have students wander aimlessly and create small disturbances. Giving them specific directions before entering can help eliminate trouble and streamline the process. These three directions from a teacher to the students work as well as any:

1. *Try 'em on*. Your job is to find books that fit you. One way to pick a good chapter book is to turn somewhere near the middle and start reading. If you read two or three pages and find the story interesting, this could be a good choice.
2. *Check 'em out*. Check out the books that appeal to you.
3. *Read 'em*. Sit down and read your books until we all are ready to go back to class.

Fourth: Create a Reading Atmosphere

A classroom where reading is valued has an atmosphere that says books are important. That message may be delivered in a number of ways:

- Make the emotional climate safe but exciting. Students' reactions to books are accepted and not belittled. Teachers hope students will catch their enthusiasm for books without expecting the children to mirror their reading preferences.
- Promote the idea of a community of readers. Focus on developing a group attitude that reading is a pleasurable way of making discoveries about the world. Everyone in the community will have the chance to select reading materials that reflect personal choices and interests.
- Liven up the room. Ask for old displays or posters from bookstores. Tack up children's drawings inspired by books. Display books or book jackets. Write publishers for free, attractive materials—posters, postcards, bookmarks—to decorate the walls. (Check publisher offerings in the *CBC Features* brochure from the Children's Book Council, mentioned in Appendix B.)
- Keep the classroom library visible, not behind locked cabinet doors. Have books become a part of the classroom's interior decoration scheme.
- As your personality and classroom space permit, allow students to do their free reading in places other than at their desks. You may want a reading center—a place designated for pleasure reading that may have pillows, a comfortable chair or couch, or other homey furnishings. But make sure everyone gets to use the reading center. If it becomes the domain of those who finish their work first, those who need it most never get the chance.
- Connect students and authors. Children are curious about the people who write their books. The literary atmosphere in a classroom can be enlivened by

encouraging young readers to contact authors through each writer's personal Web site. The e-mail address usually available at the site allows students to write to their favorite author. If a writer doesn't have a Web address, young readers can write letters to the author in care of the publisher. Publishers' addresses are available on the Web or often can be found on the back of a book's title page.

Fifth: Work with Parents

Except for the often painfully polite back-to-school evenings, parents and teachers usually have contact only when there is trouble. As a result, teachers and parents have a natural hesitancy to communicate, much to the delight of many children who prefer keeping their two worlds separate. The teacher who decides to bridge this traditional gap between school and home can do so with relative ease and much positive effect on children and their reading.

Teachers need to initiate the contact, either through a letter or a meeting with each child's parents. To gain support for your approach to reading, that contact should deal with two points: letting parents know about your emphasis on personal reading and requesting their support in helping it work.

COMMUNICATE WITH PARENTS.   You should communicate to the parents the benefits of regular, yearlong reading for their child, both in school and at home. Include your own views on the advantages of daily reading, and you could also cite research that supports those ideas (see Chapter 18).

REQUEST PARENTAL SUPPORT.   You should request parental support for each child's personal reading at home. Parents can help their child in the following ways:

- Encourage the child to read regularly at home. Setting aside a certain time is helpful. (If you require children to read daily outside of school, mention that and ask for parental support.)
- Talk with the child about the books being read.
- Read with and to the child.
- Buy books for birthdays and holidays, and allow the child to buy from school-sponsored book clubs when possible.
- Help the child create a place in the bedroom to keep personal books.
- Read where the child can see you.
- Periodically tell the child about what you are reading.
- Volunteer to come to the classroom and assist children with their reading.

Sixth: Choose Meaningful Activities and Assignments

The purpose of having children engage in an activity after reading a book is to enhance their experience, not to check their reading or evaluate their comprehension. Chapter 18 describes activities, but the idea is noted here as one of the six areas to consider when planning instruction to highlight reading.

Children's Literature Database
A Resource for Teachers, Parents, and Media Specialists

The Children's Literature Database identifies more than 20,000 books for young readers selected from myriad award-winning books, "best book" compilations, lists of classics, and our own reading experiences. The emphasis has been on choosing and categorizing high-quality literature for pre-K through eighth graders; however, many books also are appropriate for ninth to twelfth graders. You can keep the database dynamic, adding your own favorite books and new award-winning titles. You are limited only by the capacities of your own hard drive.

As you use the database, go to the User Guide for detailed information about its functions and navigation. The Children's Literature Database allows you to:

- find books quickly in a database of more than 20,000 titles
- view a complete record of information for any book on the database
- sort and create book lists by title, author, illustrator, grade level, awards, and six other criteria
- create lists of books using key words
- trim or constrain a list by searching with more specific terms
- print selected books in a brief list or as complete records
- annotate books of interest with your own comments
- add your own books to the database, without limit
- find websites for all award-winning books to determine criteria for winners and updates

This CD will be an invaluable tool for you. Any time you need a reading list catered to one child, a group of related books for students at different developmental levels, or a set of titles appropriate to connect to a unit of study, you will find what you need on this CD.

Getting Started

Begin by loading the database onto your MAC or PC hard drive. Once the database has been installed, click on the Tunnell_Jacobs icon, which provides a shortcut to open the database on your desktop. The program will display this splash screen.

The splash screen contains a sidebar navigator that allows you to move from section to section with icons for Book List, Saved Sets, Search Query Builder, Awards, Resources, User Guide, and Home.

Book List is the listing of more than 20,000 children's literature titles, which presents itself in two formats: list and detail. Click on the column head to sort the book list by a particular field. The listing can be sorted by Title, Genre, Grade Level, Topics, Author, Illustrator, Year, and Publisher. All eight columns are sortable. When you click on any book record, it will open up in Book Detail format, which

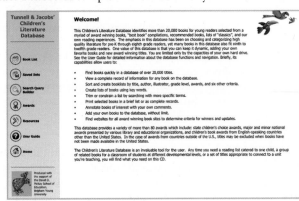

shows all of the information about a particular book in a single screen. The Book List can be expanded by adding your own books and personal comments, reminders, ratings, or any other detail.

To display detailed information about a single book, click on the title of the work that is underlined on the Book List page. A record display window will appear, Book Detail, which contains complete information about the book. By clicking on the View as List icon at the top of your navigation bar, you will be returned to the complete book list view.

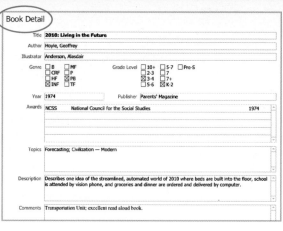

Navigation Bar

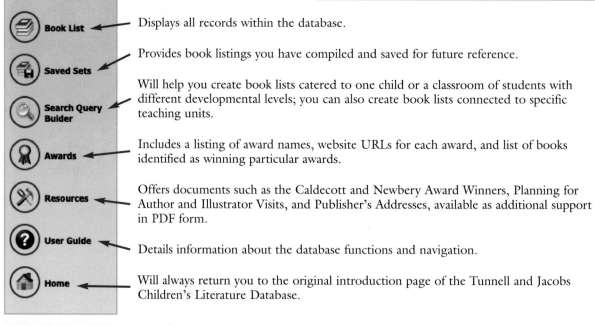

Book List — Displays all records within the database.

Saved Sets — Provides book listings you have compiled and saved for future reference.

Search Query Builder — Will help you create book lists catered to one child or a classroom of students with different developmental levels; you can also create book lists connected to specific teaching units.

Awards — Includes a listing of award names, website URLs for each award, and list of books identified as winning particular awards.

Resources — Offers documents such as the Caldecott and Newbery Award Winners, Planning for Author and Illustrator Visits, and Publisher's Addresses, available as additional support in PDF form.

User Guide — Details information about the database functions and navigation.

Home — Will always return you to the original introduction page of the Tunnell and Jacobs Children's Literature Database.

Save This List as Set   Add Book   Print   Help   Home

- Save This List as Set will allow you to save book listings that were created to accommodate particular students.
- Add Book allows you to create a new book record.
- Print allows you to print listings from the database.
- User Guide provides you with detailed information about the database functions and navigation.
- Home will return you to the original introduction page.

Using the Database

To create your own book lists, click on the Screen Query Builder icon. The Keyword Search field allows you to type in any word or phrase, such as *boats, airplanes,* and *trains,* in your search for books. Clicking the All icon will return records with all of the words typed into the Keyword Search field; clicking the Any icon will return records with any of the words typed into the Keyword Search field.

To narrow your book list, the Keyword Search will allow you to search by Title, Topic, and/or Description. Click on one or more of the clickboxes that identify these fields. In addition, you may search for these books by Year, Awards, Genre, Grade Level, Author, Illustrator, Publisher, and Comments. There are 11 searchable fields for each title in the database:

Title: Shown as it appears on the book's cover.

Author: The author, reteller, or editor of each book in the database.

Illustrator: The artist or photographer who created the book's illustrations.

Publisher: The company that published the book.

Year: The year the book was published.

Genre: The type of book by content or form:
- B   Biography
- CRF Contemporary Realistic Fiction
- HF   Historical Fiction
- INF   Informational Book
- MF   Modern Fantasy
- P   Poetry
- PB   Picture Book
- TF   Traditional Fantasy

Topic: Identifies significant topics addressed within the book.

Grade Level: An approximate grade level assigned to each title. More than one level listed below can be used when appropriate—even the inclusion of all nine when a book appeals to all ages and grade levels.
- Pre-S
- K-2
- 2-3
- 3-4
- 5-6
- 5-7
- 7
- 7+
- 10+

Awards: The awards the book received. Thirty-six national awards and "best books" are indexed, as are 45 state awards.

Description: A short summary or annotation of the book.

Comments: A blank field for comments or notes added by the user.

To save your search criteria for future reference, click on the Print This Screen icon at the top of the Search Query Builder. If you do not elect to save these criteria by printing out what you have searched, you will lose this data.

Extending or Constraining Current Book Lists

Once a book list has been assembled according to your parameters, click in the search drop-down box to choose New Search, Extend This List, or Constrain This List.

To extend a book list from your Search Query, click Extend This List at the top of the navigation bar and then click Run Search. The Search Query Builder screen will come up; make changes as necessary to your search so that it will include a broader listing. Books from your extended search will be added to your current book list.

To constrain your book list, narrow the list of books in your current book list by adding more specific information in the Constrain This List search. You can also Omit books from your list before saving it as a set. Remember that Omit does not delete books from the database, but only from the current set presented on the screen.

Saving a Search or a Set

If you want to save found sets of titles for later reference—for example, a set of books defined using the key words "Civil War,"—you would click on the Save This List icon in the top navigation bar. A window will appear that contains a field in which you can enter a name for the list or set you wish to save (e.g., Civil War).

Retrieve saved sets by clicking on the Saved Sets icon on your navigation bar to see a list of your recorded sets and searches. Once you have opened a saved set, click on the Open Set in Book List icon at the top of your navigation bar so that you can view, modify, or print your book listing.

Adding Comments and Records

You can make the Children's Literature Database even more useful by adding reminders, ratings, additional book details, and so on. Use this field to identify commented books in a later search. To add a comment, select a single record from the Book List and click in the Comments field, add your text, and it is automatically saved.

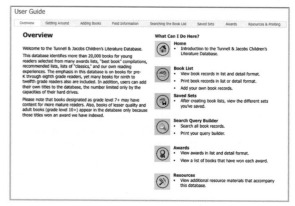

Add your own books to the database by clicking on the Add Book icon at the top of your navigation bar. A blank version of the book detail screen will appear. Fill in information about the new book in any or all of the fields. To add an author or illustrator name, click on the Add Author or Add Illustrator icon. A pop-up window will appear. Type in the first name, middle name (if available), and last name. Click Submit in the top navigation bar to add the name to the book detail screen.

To indicate any awards a new book has won, click on the Add Award icon. Select an award from the drop-down list and indicate the year in which the book won the award. Click Submit in the top navigation bar to add any of the awards to the book detail screen. If a book has won an award other than what is offered in the award list, note this information in the Description or Comments section. New books are automatically saved as they are added.

User Guide

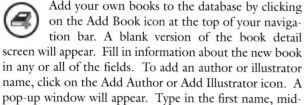

The User Guide icon is on the left and the top navigation bars. You can quickly access a set of screens that will explain the database functions:

- Overview
- Getting Around
- Adding Books
- Field Information
- Searching the Book List
- Saved Sets
- Awards
- Resources & Printing

This easy-to-navigate User Guide will be invaluable to you as you explore the many uses for this CD.

Database compiled by Michael O. Tunnell and James S. Jacobs, with Megan Tanner, Michelle Groesbeck, Rebecca Maxfield, Rosemary Groesbeck, Nicole Swain, and Catherine Verhaaren.

The Authors gratefully acknowledge and thank the David O. McKay School of Education, Brigham Young University, for the financial and professional support that enabled the development of this database.

Remember that not every book a child reads must result in a written report or other learning activity. In fact, most personal reading experiences should not be coupled with an assignment. But when a learning activity does center upon literature, children should be able to select from a variety of titles.

The ideas in this chapter come from years of classroom experience, both ours and others'. Unfortunately, following them to the letter will not guarantee that every child will become a reader. No reading approach, person, or program has a 100 percent conversion rate with children. Simply expect that in every classroom there are some tough nuts to crack who will not fall in love with books no matter what you do. Implementing these ideas, however, will increase the odds that children will read more and read better.

REFERENCES

Babbitt, Natalie. (1975). *Tuck everlasting*. New York: Farrar, Straus and Giroux.

Bell, T. H. (1982). Speech given to faculty of the College of Education at Brigham Young University, Provo, Utah, 21 October.

Calkins, Lucy McCormick. (1994). *The art of teaching writing*. Portsmouth, NH: Heinemann.

Cameron, J., & Pierce, W. D. (1994). Reinforcement, reward, and intrinsic motivation: A meta-analysis. *Review of Educational Research, 64*, 363–423.

Fletcher, Susan. (2006). Personal letter to Michael O. Tunnell (March 3).

Jensen, Terry L., & Jensen, Valerie S. (2002, Fall). Sustained silent reading and young adult short stories for high school classes. *Alan Review*.

Krashen, Stephen D. (2004). *The power of reading: Insights from the research*. Westport, CT: Libraries Unlimited.

Lepper, M. R., Greene, D., & Nisbett, R. E. (1973). Undermining children's intrinsic interest with extrinsic rewards: A test of the "overjustification" hypothesis. *Journal of Personality and Social Psychology, 28*, 129–137.

McCracken, R. A., & McCracken, M. J. (1978, January). Modeling is the key to sustained silent reading. *The Reading Teacher, 31,* 406–408.

Perez, Samuel A. (1986, October). Children see, children do: Teachers as reading models. *The Reading Teacher, 40,* 8–11.

Wilson, Robert, & Hall, Mary Ann. (1972). *Reading and the elementary school child*. New York: Van Nostrand Reinhold.

Chapter 18

Teaching with Children's Books

with Gregory Bryan, University of Manitoba

If your goal is to help children become lifelong learners, then children's literature is perhaps the most important class you will take. No discovery is more valuable to a lifelong learner than finding out there is something personally worthwhile between the covers of a book. Students who are self-motivated readers continue their education as long as they breathe. And an education is not always the same as having a diploma. Just as it is possible to gain a diploma without much education having taken place, it is also possible to become educated without formal instruction. Getting an education is a personal decision.

What distinguishes truly educated people, what identifies them and sets them apart, is that they are readers. This is true even for a school dropout who has spent 70 percent of his life in prison. When Wilbert Rideau was 18 years old, he robbed a bank, killed a teller, and was sent to the Louisiana State Prison for life. After a few angry years doing nothing beyond sitting and rebelling, Rideau picked up a book and spent a number of weeks reading it. Then he picked up another. Although he left school in eighth grade and English was his least favorite subject, soon he was reading two books a day on a variety of subjects. But he liked history best.

> "I read about Napoleon, Muhammed, Lincoln, Washington, Bolivar, Sukarno," says Rideau. "I came to realize that a lot of people had terrible beginnings, but they lifted themselves up and gave something back to the world. I read *Profiles in Courage*. I'll never forget what it said—that a man does what he must, regardless of the cost." One day a guard passed him a copy of Ayn Rand's *Atlas Shrugged*. Its message of self-reliance became Rideau's credo. "I started seeing that no matter how bad things looked, it was all on me whether I made something of myself or I died in some nameless grave." (quoted in Colt, 1993, p. 71)

What Rideau did was initiate and become editor of *The Angolite,* the convict magazine that is required reading in training classes for new correctional officers and also the first prison publication ever nominated for a National Magazine Award (an honor it has since earned six times). In addition, it is the first to win the Robert F. Kennedy

Journalism Award, a George Polk Award, and the American Bar Association Silver Gavel Award (Colt, 1993, p. 72).

# OPENING DOORS WITH BOOKS

Schools use books as tools of education, and those books fall into three distinct categories: reference, text, and trade. Each type of book is philosophically different and serves a different purpose. Reference books are those volumes a person consults for an immediate answer to a specific question, such as a dictionary, encyclopedia, atlas, or thesaurus. Textbooks are designed for use in formal instruction, presenting a dispassionate view of a subject in an organized, methodical manner. These two varieties, especially textbooks, are the books most often associated with classroom instruction, and yet students seldom choose them for personal reading.

Trade books are published for the retail market and typically are available in bookstores and libraries. They are written by authors who wish to express themselves in a way they hope will appeal to readers who seek pleasure, insight, and knowledge. However, with the exception of English teachers, educators historically have not considered trade books of much use in the classroom.

Textbooks and reference books both have an important role in education, but trade books should not be dismissed. When children are interested in what they read, and read broadly—whether fiction, nonfiction, or both—they can learn much of value from trade books. People are able to grow and develop intellectually without the carefully structured approach to learning typical of textbooks. In fact, some individuals have gained the bulk of their learning primarily from trade books, as the following examples illustrate.

- Robert Howard Allen has never seen his father. Divorced before he was born, Robert's mother left him at age 6 to be raised by his grandfather, three great-aunts, and a great-uncle, all of whom lived in the same house in rural Tennessee. After his grandfather taught him to read, Robert regularly read the Bible to a blind great-aunt. "From age seven he read thousands of books—from Donald Duck comics to Homer, James Joyce and Shakespeare. . . . He began picking up books at yard sales, and by his early 20s he had some 2000 volumes" (Whittemore, 1991, p. 4).

  Robert never went to school, not even for a day. He stayed home and helped—and read. At age 30, he easily passed a high school equivalency test, and at age 32, he showed up at Bethel College in McKenzie, Tennessee. Three years later, he graduated summa cum laude (3.92 GPA) and continued his education by enrolling in graduate school at Vanderbilt University. Having earned his Ph.D. in English, he became a visiting lecturer at Murray State College in Kentucky (Whittemore, 1991).

- Dale Wasserman makes his living writing for stage and screen. This winner of almost 50 writing awards is perhaps best known for *Man of La Mancha*. After

a five-year run on Broadway, it has remained in continuous production and currently is being performed in more than 30 languages. When Dale was 14—"undisciplined, secretive, and almost entirely unschooled"—both his parents died, and the Wasserman children were parceled out to relatives and orphanages. He lasted a month before running away, hitching a ride to Pierre, South Dakota, and in the middle of the night hopping on his first freight train. For the next five years, he rode the rails, never having a home, going to a school, or working a steady job. While crossing the country on freight trains, however, Dale did not neglect his learning. "In the library of a small town, I would select two books, slip them under my belt at the small of my back, read as I rode, and slip them back into the stacks of another library in another town far down the line, where I would 'borrow' two more. I thus acquired a substantial, if incoherent, fund of knowledge that, together with my experience, became my total education"—an education sufficient for him to become a renowned playwright (Wasserman, 2001, p. 64).

- Cushla Yeoman was born with multiple handicaps. Chromosome damage caused her spleen, kidneys, and mouth cavity to be deformed and prevented her from holding anything in her hand until she was three years old. She could not see clearly more than a foot away. Muscle spasms kept her from sleeping more than two hours a night. She was diagnosed as mentally and physically retarded, and doctors recommended that she be institutionalized.

  Cushla's parents had seen her respond to picture books they read aloud, so they kept her home and increased their reading to 14 picture books a day, week after week and month after month. By age five, Cushla was pronounced by doctors to be socially well adjusted and intellectually well above average (Butler, 1980).

The Strengths of Trade Books

People can and do acquire substantial knowledge beyond the walls of formal education when they read often and broadly. We need to recognize that books can create interest in readers, that people learn better when they are interested, and that people can learn a great deal by reading widely on their own. The purpose of both fiction and nonfiction trade books is not so much to inform, which they do very well, as it is to excite, to introduce, to let the reader in on the irresistible secrets of life on planet Earth.

Consider the following two passages that describe asteroids, one from a textbook and the other from an informational trade book.

Passage 1: Science textbook

Asteroids are rocky or metallic objects that orbit the Sun. They are too small to be considered planets. . . . Some astronomers suggest that asteroids are material that never combined to become a planet. They are found mostly in a belt between the orbits of Mars and Jupiter. They orbit the Sun just like planets. Some asteroids travel out as far as Saturn's orbit. Others have orbits that cross Earth's path.

Space probes have passed by asteroids and obtained much information. On June 2, 1997, the spacecraft NEAR encountered the asteroid Mathilde. This and other flybys by space probes are giving a good picture of the nature of these smaller members of the solar system. The spacecraft *Galileo* has already flown by the asteroids Gaspra and Ida. (Moyer et al., 2002, p. C-55)

Passage 2: Science trade book

Made of stone, or nickel and iron, or a mix of both stone and metal, asteroids are rubble from a planet that never formed. Some asteroids are less than a mile across. Some are much larger. A few are as big as very small planets.

Because of their small size, the asteroids' orbits are easily disturbed. Jupiter is an enormous planet, and its gravity can pull smaller asteroids in new directions. The gravity of larger asteroids can also tug on smaller ones that pass close by. And from time to time, asteroids can collide and be nudged into new orbits.

By such events, some asteroids can be pulled or pushed out of the asteroid belt to fall closer to the sun. They can wander in long, elliptical orbits that cross the paths of Mars and the other inner planets, including Earth. These asteroids can hit the planets— and on rare occasions they do. (Henderson, 2000, pp. 7–8)

The following points identify some of the strengths of tradebooks, as compared to textbooks. Note how these apply to the examples above.

WRITING STYLE.   Where textbooks are formal and often unappealing to the child, trade books are designed to engage the young reader. Trade book authors shape and develop their views in individualized language, allowing for a personalized explanation that often results in more meaning and perspective. Textbooks, on the other hand, tend to use a more detached and disjointed style, which can result in puzzling information like that found in the second paragraph of the textbook example. It offers precise information about space probes, including their names and the names of asteroids they pass by. Without background information or perspective, however, the reader has difficulty finding meaning in those facts. In addition, we are told that these probes have garnered "much information" and provide "a good picture of the nature of [asteroids]," but no details are shared with the reader.

VARIED FORMATS AND STRUCTURES.   Trade books come in all sizes, formats, and lengths. The illustrations in trade books are generally superior, often containing stunning artwork. Textbooks have a dense, industrial appearance and usually have less-appealing illustrations and diagrams.

MANY PERSPECTIVES.   Books are available on any subject, providing overviews as well as exhaustive treatments from a variety of viewpoints. For example, dozens of trade books about asteroids are available, rounding out reader knowledge as much as one chooses. Textbooks typically offer one perspective. Because trade books are shorter and more quickly read, one can read many trade books and get many perspectives.

RICH LANGUAGE.   Trade books are written in more interesting and engaging language. They are deliberately written to both entertain and inform. The words in trade books create images by using more precise, colorful vocabulary. The sentences are varied and read more interestingly. Trade books have the freedom and space to make meaningful comparisons and use more detail to enlarge understanding.

DEPTH OF CONTENT.   Trade books can provide the space to bring a subject to life with interesting observations and details, presenting the reader with a richer understanding of the topic. Because textbooks must cover such a large number of topics, they are unable to develop a single idea with any depth. Therefore, textbooks offer a broad and consequently more shallow view of subjects that does not allow for the kind of compelling presentation available in trade books. For example, another passage in the textbook quoted earlier simply mentions that asteroids can hit the earth. The trade book, however, chronicles the event of an asteroid's entry into atmosphere, its collision with the planet, and the blasting of a crater 25 miles deep and 100 miles across. It describes in fascinating detail the vaporization at the impact point, the earthquakes, the fires, and the debris that caused a worldwide period of intense heat followed by darkness and freezing temperatures. It is difficult to provide readers this kind of detail and insight in the limited space allowed by a textbook.

CURRENCY.   Trade books are written and published more often and more quickly than textbooks, offering the latest findings and information. In addition, most school districts can afford a new textbook for each subject only every 5 to 10 years, which is a distinct disadvantage in this information-rich age.

VOICE.   Trade books allow a personal viewpoint to emerge in the writing. Information has more power to influence others when it is presented through the strong, individual voice of a human being. Textbooks, usually written by committee, have no personal voice; their viewpoint is detached and distant. Whereas trade books often contain a strong individual voice, textbooks generally do not. In striving for objectivity, their viewpoints tend to be impersonal and bland.

REFLECT INDIVIDUAL READING ABILITIES.   Different trade books suit different levels of reading ability. A given set of classroom textbooks will be at the reading level of only a select number of students. In a typical classroom, the reading abilities of students vary widely. Because of the number and variety of trade books, students at many levels—even those with reading problems—can locate titles on any subject, books they can read, learn from, and enjoy.

TOOLS OF LIFELONG LEARNING.   Trade books are available in all libraries and bookstores. After graduation, they are the books people go to most often to learn about the world. Trade books are the stuff of "real life" reading. Textbooks are limited to formal education and can be found only in classrooms and academic bookstores. Regular bookstores have none, and libraries very few, which causes some people to ask, "If schools are to prepare children for lifelong learning, why do they rely so heavily on a tool that is not easily accessible in their actual future?"

Teachers should not think that only informational books can generate interest in school subjects. Historical fiction, for instance, sheds light on history in a way that nonfiction has difficulty duplicating. Introducing historically accurate fiction, complete with its compelling plot and well-developed characters can, as Cynthia Stokes Brown (1994) says, make history come alive by allowing children more readily to "identify . . . with heroes and heroism and . . . explore their own lives and identity, character and convictions through heroic stories" (p. 5).

RESEARCH SUPPORT FOR USING TRADE BOOKS TO TEACH READING

The idea of using children's literature for classroom instruction is not new. The research literature contains considerable and ongoing support for literature-based instructional approaches, as seen in the following historical and contemporary sampling.

In the 1960s, Cohen (1968) conducted a landmark study involving a control group of 130 second-grade students who were taught using traditional basal reader instruction. The control group was compared to the 155 children in an experimental group using a literature component along with regular instruction. The experimental treatment consisted mainly of reading aloud to children from 50 children's trade picture books—books without controlled vocabulary or fixed sentence length—and then following up with meaning-related activities. The children were encouraged to read the books anytime. Achievement tests administered in October and June demonstrated that the experimental group showed significant increases over the control group in word knowledge, reading comprehension, vocabulary, and quality of vocabulary.

In the 1970s, Fader and colleagues (Fader, Duggins, Finn, & McNeil, 1976) succeeded in raising reading achievement and developing the reading interests of students at the W. J. Maxey Boys' Training School in Whitmore Lake, Michigan. Fader's team provided hundreds of paperbacks for the W. J. Maxey students, along with the time to read them. Another midwestern boys' training school was used as a control group. Although no significant differences were found in control and experimental groups at the onset, by the end of the school year, the boys at W. J. Maxey showed significant gains over the control group on measures of self-esteem, literacy attitudes, anxiety, verbal proficiency, and reading comprehension. In some instances, the control group's scores actually decreased from the year before, while the experimental group's surged ahead, even doubling control-group scores.

In the 1980s, the popularity of literature-based instruction increased significantly. A literature-based, developmental program for first-graders called the Shared Book Experience was examined closely under the auspices of the New Zealand Department of Education. Reading skills and strategies were taught within the context of real reading experiences, using natural, whole texts. Holdaway (1982) reported that, on a variety of measures, the experimental, literature-based group of students demonstrated skills equal or superior to other experimental and control groups. So impressed was the Department of Education that it embarked on a countrywide inservice program in New Zealand and, subsequently, developmental programs, such as Shared Book Experience, took over on a national scale.

During the 1990s, Morrow (1992) investigated the impact of a literature-based program on the literacy achievement of children from U.S. minority backgrounds. One hundred and sixty-six children were randomly assigned to one control group and two experimental groups. The control group continued to receive the type of class-room reading instruction that all 166 children received before the study began. This reading instruction involved a heavy reliance on basal reading materials, including the regular use of worksheets. On the other hand, in the experimental groups, there was a reduction in the time spent working with basal materials in order that the teachers could introduce more literature-based activities, including time for independent and self-selected reading and writing, literacy centers, and teacher-guided literature activ-ities such as daily read alouds, story retelling and rewriting, and book sharing. Chil-dren in the experimental groups demonstrated significantly better performances on all of the project literacy measures, except for the standardized test, where no significant differences were evident.

Research support for literature-based instruction continues in the new millen-nium. Recent studies reflect the motivational benefit of access to books. Both Edmunds and Bauserman (2006) and Pachtman and Wilson (2006) interviewed and surveyed children with regard to motivation to read. Pachtman and Wilson reported that hav-ing lots of books in the class library was the single-most important factor influencing children's reading practices. Edmunds and Bauserman similarly found that children's motivation to read is strongly influenced by access to books.

USING TRADE BOOKS IN THE READING CURRICULUM

Given the many strengths of tradebooks, and given the research support for literature-based instruction, many teachers use trade books to augment reading instruction and provide children with authentic experiences while teaching students how to read.

Talking about Books

The most natural response to reading is talking about what one has read. Our desire to share with others information about what we read has given rise to the numerous adult book discussion groups, often called book clubs, that can now be found from coast to coast. This natural response to reading has an equally important role to play in school.

GRAND CONVERSATIONS.   For books or poems everyone has read or has had read to them, discussions can provide opportunities for meaningful responses. Peterson and Eeds (1990) call these discussions "grand conversations," which are characterized by teachers participating fully in the conversation—modeling and sharing their thought processes and personal interpretations about the story. The teacher, however, is not the central focus and needs to be careful that adult comments do not become pronouncements. Rather, the spotlight is on the book and the readers' responses, and teachers must be prepared for discussion that goes beyond their own preparation and understanding. The teacher is no longer seen as the authority possessing all the answers, but is simply a participant with the students (Eeds & Peterson, 1997; Wells, 1995). Teachers allow and encourage students to share their personal responses, providing open-ended prompts when necessary for group discussion: "What did you notice in the story?" "What do you remember from the story?" "What details in the story remind you of your own life?"

Grand conversations can also include the discussion of literary merit and technique. As long as the questions do not have a right and wrong answer—so the talk is truly a discussion—children will become involved. "What hints did the author drop to prepare us for the ending?" "Are there any facts or details in the book that let us know Josh was not to be trusted?" "Can you find an image—a picture in you mind—put there by the author that helps you to see the castle clearly?"

Teachers must be prepared for discussion that goes beyond their own preparation and understanding. In grand conversations, even a young child can notice something an experienced teacher has missed. For instance, when discussing *Sylvester and the Magic Pebble* (Steig, 1969), 6-year-old Tracy responded to an illustration showing Sylvester using the magic pebble to abruptly stop a rainstorm as ducks in the background peer skyward in confusion. Tracy shared with her teacher examples of things she thought were funny:

Tracy:	When Sylvester finds the red pebble—and the ducks are cute . . .
Teacher:	The what?
Tracy:	The ducks are cute . . .
Teacher:	The ducks *are* cute. They've got their bills up in the air like they're just enjoying the sunshine, having a grand time, uh-huh . . .
Tracy:	Or else they're thinking, "How'd that happen?"
Teacher:	How'd what happen?
Tracy:	The rain started, then stopped.
Teacher:	Yes! Of course they're thinking that!
Tracy:	They go—"It started a little while ago—what happened?" (Peterson & Eeds, 1990, pp. 17–18).

The teacher was looking at the picture but had not noticed the ducks. She was dumbfounded that a 6-year-old had picked up on a subtle point of interpretation that an adult had overlooked.

LITERATURE CIRCLES.   Literature circles (Daniels, 2002; Day, Spiegel, McLellan, & Brown, 2002) provide an opportunity for small groups of children to talk together about a text. Children ask their own questions about a book and help each other answer those questions. Time is not unstructured, however, but includes discussion on characters and events, personal experiences and observations, and even writing and the writing process.

Certain elements help foster this kind of group learning. The small groups are temporary and linked to book choice. Different groups read different books. Groups meet at scheduled and regular times. Students use written or drawn notes to guide both their reading and discussion. Topics for discussion come from the students. Group meetings are to be open, natural conversations about the book. The teacher serves as a facilitator, not as a group member or instructor. Any evaluation is by teacher observation and student self-evaluation. When the book is finished and the discussion is over, students form new groups with new books.

BOOK CLUBS.   For small groups of readers, the teacher has multiple copies of a number of books in the classroom and then tells the entire class about five or six of the titles. Each student is then allowed to choose one that sounds interesting. Those reading the same title naturally form a discussion group—a book club.

Because children read at different rates and with different intensities, one problem in choreographing small-group responses is having everyone read the same book without making it seem like work. One member of a group may finish the book overnight, while another might take a couple of weeks to get to the last page. One way to allow for this natural difference is to plan for small-group responses to take about three weeks. Let students read at their natural rates, and those who finish first can move on to other titles. Those who are moving more slowly have two weeks to complete the book, and then the group responds sometime during the third week.

To provide necessary variety, the teacher can offer the groups four or five response options for the first three-week period. Then the next time, each group may be allowed to choose from one section of the possibilities listed in Figure 18–1. The time after that, the students might come up with their own plan. The idea is that the responses are always honest and varied. And for that reason, small reading groups (book clubs) should not be in constant session, but should have liberal vacations between three-week periods.

Written and Creative Responses

Although book discussions provide for natural and authentic response to books, opportunities for written or otherwise creative responses are also important for children. Before considering specific approaches and activities, it is critical to understand the principles that lead to successful involvement with books so that meaningful responses can occur. Newbery-winning author Madeleine L'Engle (1980) outlined the main characteristic of involvement teachers want to capitalize on:

> Readers usually underestimate their own importance. If a reader cannot create a book along with the writer, the book will never come to life. Creative involvement: That's the difference between reading a book and watching TV.
>
> In watching TV, we are passive—sponges; we do nothing. In reading we must become creators, imagining the setting of the story, seeing the facial expressions, hearing the inflection of the voices. The author and reader "know" each other; they meet on the bridge of words. (pp. 37–38)

FIGURE 18–1
Death to the traditional book report.

Writing Activities

1. Rewrite part of the story, telling it from the viewpoint of a different character.
2. Write an advertisement for the book. Identify where the advertisement will be displayed.
3. Write a poem based on the book.
4. Make up riddles about the book or any parts of it.
5. Write a rebus of the book's title, a short summary, or a certain scene in the book.
6. Develop a word game based upon the book (word scramble, crossword puzzle, acrostic).
7. Write a letter to the author, particularly if you enjoyed the book or have a question. (Send the letter to the publisher of the book and it will be forwarded.)
8. Write an imaginary interview with the main character—or any character or object.
9. Make a newspaper which summarizes or presents elements from the book. Include as many regular departments of a newspaper (sports, comics, lovelorn, classified ads, business, and so on) as you desire.
10. Write your own book on the same theme, perhaps writing some and outlining the rest.
11. Rewrite a section of the book in either radio or stage script.
12. Select a passage or quotation which has special significance for you. Write it down and then tell why it is meaningful.
13. Rewrite the story or part of the story as a news article.
14. Rewrite part of the book in a different time period—space age future, cavemen days, wild West, etc.
15. Write some trivia questions to exchange with someone else.
16. Write a chapter which tells what happened before or after the book.
17. If the book were made into a movie, choose who would play the characters. (See if you can select real people familiar to your classmates.)
18. Write a letter from some character to a real or fictitious person not in the story.
19. Write the same scene from three or four different points of view.
20. Write a simplified version of the story in picture book form.
21. Write a review of the book.

Art and Craft Activities

1. Make a diorama of an important scene in the book.
2. Construct a mobile representative of the book or some part of it.
3. Draw portraits of the main character(s).
4. Draw a mural which highlights events from the book or retells the story.
5. Draw a picture in the same style as the illustrator, or using the same medium (pen and ink, collage, watercolor, etc.).
6. Cut out words from newspapers and magazines for a word collage which gives a feeling for the book.
7. Use stitching or liquid embroidery to make a wall hanging or decorate a T-shirt with art related to the story.
8. Draw a coat of arms for a character(s) and explain the significance of each symbol.
9. Draw a silhouette of a person, scene, or object from the book.
10. Design a new dust jacket for the book.

(continued)

FIGURE 18–1
Continued

11. Illustrate what you believe is the most important idea or scene from the book.
12. Make a poster advertising the book.
13. Make a time line of the important events in the book.
14. Make a roll movie of the book which can be shown on a TV set made from a box using your own illustrations, photographs, or pictures cut from magazines.
15. Retell the story using a flannel board and bits of string, yarn and felt—or create recognizable characters to use in the retelling.
16. Identify the important places in the book on a map of your own making.
17. Make paper dolls and clothes of the main character(s).
18. Make a travel poster inviting tourists to visit the setting of the book.
19. Construct a scene or character out of clay.
20. Design a costume for a character to wear.
21. Prepare and serve a food that the characters ate or which is representative of the book.

Drama, Music, and Assorted Activities

1. Make puppets—sack masks, socks, or finger—of the characters and produce a puppet show of the book.
2. Dress as a character and present some of the character's feelings, or tell about a part of the book, or summarize very briefly the story.
3. Videotape a dramatized scene from the book.
4. Write a song which tells about the book.
5. Conduct an interview between an informed moderator and character(s) . . . maybe TV news?
6. Research music from the time of the book, and find some songs the characters may have sung.
7. Pantomime a scene from the book.
8. Perform a scene from the book with one person taking all the parts.
9. Choosing a familiar tune, write lyrics which tell about the book.
10. For each character in the book, choose a musical selection which typifies that person.
11. Give a sales pitch to get listeners excited about the book.
12. Give a party for characters and their friends, or for characters from many books. Invite parents and have characters present themselves.
13. Research some real aspect of the book and present your newly found facts.
14. Bring something from home which reminds you of the book. Explain.
15. Choose a real life person who reminds you of a character in the book. Explain.
16. Select one passage which is the focal point of the book. Explain.
17. Collect and display a collage of quotes that you like from the book.
18. Make a board game using characters and elements from the book. Have pitfalls (lose a turn, etc.) and rewards (shake again, etc.) reflecting parts of the book.
19. Find other books on the same subject and set up a display with them.
20. Perform a choral reading from the book, or write something about the book to perform in a choral reading.
21. Emphasize the setting of the book using any or all of the following: a) objects, b) food, c) costumes, d) culture, e) music, f) art.

We want readers to "create a book along with the writer." We want them to live in the book—to be active in their experience and response. To keep them from being sponges, we must provide them with assignments and activities that allow the kind of reading to take place where reader and author "meet on the bridge of words."

If an activity allows and encourages readers to respond in a way that L'Engle calls "creative involvement," the assignment is generally a plus. When used with self-selected books, such an activity is helpful as long as it adheres to three principles: (1) Students choose the books they wish to respond to, (2) students choose the activities, and (3) students read most books without any obligation to respond.

Even when students are enthusiastic about a certain way of responding to books, teachers need to remember that variety is the key to keeping them involved (see Figure 18–1). No response or activity designed to involve readers with their books works for long. Students may love recording their personal thoughts in a reading journal, but if it is required for every book, the idea wears thin. As one teacher said, "What I want when they finish reading *Tuck Everlasting* is a gleam in their eyes." If assigned responses dim that gleam—like the traditional book report—they need to be rethought.

The traditional book report (focusing on elements of fiction, including plot, characters, setting, style, and theme) has done more to kill the love of reading in Americans ages 9 to 18 than any other idea to come from the schools (Root, 1975) and as an evaluative tool often tells a teacher very little. Traditional book reports are almost universally detested. Although most Americans remember writing traditional book reports in school, very few remember the task with fondness. Book reports continue to be used because some teachers demand tangible evidence that the child has read the book. Of course, it is possible for students to write reports on books they have not read. Any sixth grader can offer a variety of ways. Rent the movie. Read the front flap. Talk to someone about the book. Use someone else's old book report. Or, for the daring, invent the book—title, author, plot, characters—the entire thing. The only defense for traditional book reports is that they foster imagination by teaching kids to cheat creatively.

The response options in Figure 18–1 offer alternatives to the traditional book report. It is important to remember, however, that with the worthy and useful goal of having students respond thoughtfully to what they read, asking for a response to every book will likely backfire and turn a positive experience into a negative one. Readers do not want to respond to every book they read any more than viewers want to repond to every movie they see. Most of the books a person reads should be left alone—the reading is sufficient.

But every so often, perhaps once or twice a grading period, teachers can ask students to respond to a book they have read. Allowing the students to select the title and giving them some choice in the method of response are both essential if the response is to have any real meaning to the reader.

The variety of response options in Figure 18–1 is designed to improve and encourage reading. The more children read, the better they get at it (Cunningham & Stanovich, 1998), opening up an ever-increasing reading ability gap over their unmotivated, nonreading peers. The rich (capable and motivated readers) get richer, and the poor (struggling, unmotivated readers) get poorer (Stanovich, 1986). A highly motivated, "voracious" middle school reader might read as many as 50 million words per year, compared to an average for that age level of about 1 million words per year. The least capable and least motivated middle school readers might read just 100,000 words per year (Nagy & Anderson, 1984). Therefore, it is important that response activities serve the purpose of not only solidifying understanding but also increasing the desire for further reading.

USING TRADE BOOKS IN THE OTHER SUBJECT AREAS

Trade books, textbooks, and reference books are different from one another and should be used differently. If we ignore those differences and, say, use trade books exactly as we use texts, the trade books lose much of their power. We need to avoid using *The Very Hungry Caterpillar* (Carle, 1969) as the core of 32 separate language arts activities, or devising 19 mathematical procedures from *Frog and Toad Are Friends* (Lobel, 1970). The strength of trade books is their ability to create interest and encourage reading. Recognizing that they also can be used for instruction, we need to choose ways to preserve their ability to stimulate and engage readers and not turn the books into reading assignments with lists of questions to be answered.

One way to show students the appeal of trade books in the instructional program is for teachers to involve them in the school day. Children won't see how books from the library fit into daily instruction unless the teachers include them as a natural part of class-room learning. An easy way to bring the books into lessons is to ask the librarian for titles on the subject to be taught—for instance, magnetism. Look through the books until you find enough interesting ideas, experiments, or information for a lesson or unit, and then present it to the class, showing the books that gave you the information. Teachers' use of these books as read-alouds is particularly important in the lower grades, where children have more limited reading abilities. Middle- and upper-grade children will be able to make more of their own discoveries, as outlined in the three approaches that follow.

The Individual Reading Approach

Holmes and Ammon (1985) devised a strategy to use with an entire class, grades 3 and above, but it can be adapted for use with groups, individuals, or children in the lower grades. It is designed to be used as a series of lessons instead of one presentation, and has four steps: readiness, reading, response, and record keeping.

READINESS.   First, the teacher finds a way to activate prior knowledge of the subject, such as eliciting the facts students already know about the topic during a discussion and listing them on the chalkboard or white board. Another way to activate prior knowledge is to generate word associations as a class. The topic "dinosaurs," for instance, may elicit words like *huge, fighters,* and *extinct*. After this introduction, each student generates a personally interesting question about dinosaurs, writes it on a small piece of paper, and puts it randomly on the wall or a bulletin board. Finally, the teacher asks students if any of the questions are related. Similar questions are grouped and become a subtopic. Student groups then select a subtopic, such as "birth and death of dinosaurs," and proceed to step two.

READING.   The teacher collects dinosaur books of varied lengths and levels of difficulty. Students choose their own books and read silently, focusing on a subtopic, one of the questions within it, or reading for a general overview. After the reading, the teacher directs the class in collecting data by taking each subtopic in turn, asking for information the students found, and writing it on an overhead projector or chart. During the activity, children might present conflicting facts. This provides a chance to do what seldom happens at school—return to their sources to corroborate information. In one session, for instance, a child identified the largest dinosaur as a Brachiosaurus, whereas another said it was a Tyrannosaurus rex. A rereading showed that the Tyrannosaurus rex was the largest *meat-eating* dinosaur. If rereading offers no solution, other possibilities for clarification should be explored, such as looking at the recency of publication or consulting further sources.

RESPONSE.   Now the class is ready to summarize together the information under each subtopic, perhaps enrich their learning (more reading, a field trip, or guest lecturer), and then make their own personal responses: art projects, model construction, writing projects.

RECORD KEEPING.   During this series of lessons, students keep their own records of the books they consulted and their proposed responses in a folder where they also place a variety of pieces of evidence: snippets of work, drafts, note cards, and the like. The teacher has access to their folders for evaluation.

The Large-Group Reading Approach

Brozo and Tomlinson (1986) incorporate fiction as well as nonfiction into the content curriculum. They suggest using trade books, especially reading them aloud to the class, to introduce and extend the textbook in a four-step approach.

STEP 1. IDENTIFY SALIENT CONCEPTS.   Textbooks only hint at many important concepts that need a closer look if students are to identify and understand them. Consider the following description of Nazis and Jews in a fifth-grade textbook:

> German soldiers rounded up and transported Jews and other minorities from all over Europe to death camps called concentration camps. The Nazis killed 11 million men, women, and children at the camps. Six million of those killed were Jews. The remaining victims included Gypsies, Russians, Poles, and others. This mass murder is known as the *Holocaust,* which means total destruction. (Boehm et al., 2000)

The preceding paragraph is the entire discussion of the Holocaust in that textbook. It hints at the drama and tragedy of the Holocaust, but provides few details and little insight into this terrible event. To personalize students' understanding, the teacher needs to identify the unmentioned but important concepts that underlie the Holocaust. Asking questions such as the following can identify these salient concepts: What are the driving forces behind the events? What phenomena described in the textbook have affected ordinary people or may do so in the future? What universal patterns of behavior related to this event should be explained? Such questions lead us to pursue core elements of Nazi persecution of the Jews, such as prejudice, inhumanity, and the abuse of power.

STEP 2. IDENTIFY APPROPRIATE TRADE BOOKS TO HELP TEACH CONCEPTS.   Subject guides, such as the annual publication *Subject Guide to Children's Books in Print* (2008), help teachers find books to strengthen their collections (also consult the Children's Literature Database CD-ROM accompanying this text). The library can assist with immediate needs. Teachers naturally should read the books before using them in class, looking for captivating nonfiction and powerful fiction that breathe life into the important concepts to be learned. Take, for example, the following excerpt from *Friedrich* (Richter, 1970). The concepts of bigotry and injustice only hinted at in the textbook entry are brought to life when an attendant at a German swimming pool in 1938 discovers that a boy retrieving his clothes is a Jew.

> "Just take a look at this!" the attendant said. . . . "This is one of the Jewish identification cards. The scoundrel lied to me . . . a Jew that's what he is. A Jew in our swimming pool!" He looked disgusted. . . .
>   As if he could no longer bear to touch it, the attendant threw Friedrich's identification card and its case across the counter. "Think of it! Jewish things among the clothes of respectable human beings!" he screamed, flinging the coat hanger holding Friedrich's clothes on the ground so they scattered in all directions. (pp. 76–77)

STEP 3. TEACH.   The teacher then reads the trade book or books to the class as a schema and interest builder before getting to the overview presented in the textbook. After providing to the whole class a foundation for understanding, the teacher presents the main points from the text. The teacher also introduces additional trade books that are valuable to the students for elaboration and extension of content.

STEP 4. FOLLOW-UP.   After the content is presented and students have explored it, follow-up activities personalize and extend learning. They can be as varied as the people who create them: imagined on-the-scene descriptions of places or events, letters to historical figures, dramatizations, interviews, and debates are a few suggestions.

The Small-Group Reading Approach

Ad Spofford taught sixth grade and successfully used small groups in the teaching of subject matter. He divided the students into groups of between four and six. He then gave each group children's trade books on a common topic, making sure that there was one book less than there were members of the group. By providing fewer books than people, they had to share and work together more. He then gave the group an assignment that depended on the group's reading and compiling information from the books, such as the following: "Prepare a report for the board of directors on active volcanoes within the boundaries of the United States. They have little understanding of the number and potential threat of American volcanoes, so be sure to give background and experts' opinions on how dangerous our volcanoes are. Use visuals to help present your information."

At other times, Spofford provided the books—still one fewer than the number of group members—and asked the group to generate a response (write a report, make a video, create charts, and so on) using information in the titles on their table. They decided what to present and how to present it, but each person was required to contribute.

An additional way to generate small-group involvement with content is to use a literature circle approach, choosing books that focus on the information or issues that are important to the area being studied.

Three Principles of Using Trade Books to Teach Subject Matter

The individual, large-group, and small-group approaches are good ways to help students become involved with learning from and responding to trade books. As much as these methods help us teach with trade books, we need to remember that people were engaged readers centuries before these approaches were developed. The principles that help these methods succeed are important to recognize, for when we know what kinds of ideas help children respond to books, we can create any number of successful ways to bring person and print together. Elements of these techniques can be combined to form other strategies. A class can, for example, read a book together as a springboard to small-group work or individual study, bypassing the textbook completely.

What are the basic principles that are guideposts for success in using trade books with students? The following three seem to be important keys in any program that uses trade books to spark learning, and they can be implemented in a wide variety of ways. As long as these three principles are followed, good things will result.

1. *Students read trade books as they are meant to be read*—as windows to the world that do not cover a subject but, like peeling layers off an onion, uncover it.
2. *Teachers allow students to discover, or uncover, the information.* When the teacher knows *exactly* what the student should find in a given trade book, that book is being misused. Teachers who allow students to select their own evidence often will be pleasantly surprised at what students bring back as proof of learning, even when the assignment is fairly specific (for example, "Find evidence of how animals adapt to their environment.").
3. *Students share their discoveries and insights.* Teachers reinforce genuine learning by providing some means for the excited student to present new knowledge to an audience or make a personal response to new discoveries—through an oral

or written summary, poster, display, explanation to a small group, or a diary or story from the perspective of a character in the book.

Trade books even can be used to learn beyond the curriculum. They explore so much more of the world than is covered in traditional school subjects: child labor laws, the development of dynamite, the making of baseball bats, printing paper money, living with a terminal disease, illustrating comic books, and on and on. It is difficult to find a topic in the world that is *not* the focus of a children's book. After a brief discussion of how much interesting information exists outside school subjects, children may be assigned to find a book about something they will not learn about in school yet is appealing to them. After reading it, they should have a chance to share their new knowledge. Using trade books to learn subject matter provides children freedom to discover while still keeping them accountable.

If we want children to develop intellectually, we make the greatest strides when we concentrate on helping them become curious. A curious person is observant, is aware, asks questions, and tries to find the answers. Being curious is a mind-set and is a common denominator of those who make new discoveries and who solve problems. It is the curious who continue to learn under their own power. As Rabelais reportedly advised us, "Children are not vessels to be filled but fires to be lit." Because trade books reflect the curiosity and humanity of authors who have learned to see, and wish to share that vision, they have the spark that can light that flame.

 THE LAST WORD

It is important that teaching produces children who *can* read and *do* read. With this in mind, it is fitting that the final word goes to the author of one of the most famous of all books for children. In 1876, Mark Twain published *The Adventures of Tom Sawyer*—a book loved by young and old. As Mark Twain said, "The man who does not read good books has no advantage over the man who cannot." Trade books are some of the best materials used to help ensure that children *can* read and *do*.

REFERENCES

Boehm, Richard G., Hoone, Claudia, McGowan, Thomas M., McKinney-Browning, Mabel C., Miramontes, Ofelia B., & Porter, Priscilla H. (2000). *United States*. Orlando, FL: Harcourt Brace & Company.

Brown, Cynthia Stokes. (1994). *Connecting with the past: History workshop in the middle and high schools*. Portsmouth, NH: Heinemann.

Brozo, William G., & Tomlinson, Carl M. (1986, December). Literature: The key to lively content courses. *The Reading Teacher, 40,* 288–293.

Butler, Dorothy. (1980). *Cushla and her books*. Boston: The Horn Book.

Carle, Eric. (1969). *The very hungry caterpillar*. New York: Philomel.

Cohen, Dorothy. (1968, February). The effects of literature on vocabulary and reading achievement. *Elementary English, 45,* 209–213, 217.

Colt, George Howe. (1993, March). The most rehabilitated prisoner in America. *Life Magazine,* pp. 69–76.

Cunningham, Anne E., & Stanovich, Keith E. (1998, Spring/Summer). What reading does for the mind. *American Educator, 22,* 8–15.

Daniels, Harvey. (2002). *Literature circles, voice and choice in book clubs and reading groups.* Honesdale, PA: Stenhouse.

Day, Jeni Pollack, Spiegel, Dixie Lee, McLellan, Janet, & Brown, Valerie B. (2002). *Moving forward with literature circles.* New York: Scholastic.

Edmunds, Kathryn M., & Bauserman, Kathryn L. (2006, February). What teachers can learn about reading motivation through conversations with children. *The Reading Teacher, 59,* 414–424.

Eeds, Maryann, & Peterson, Ralph. (1997, Winter). Literature studies revisited: Some thoughts on talking with children about books. *The New Advocate, 10,* 49–59.

Fader, Daniel, Duggins, James, Finn, Tom, & McNeil, Elton. (1976). *The new hooked on books.* New York: Berkley.

Henderson, Douglas. (2000). *Asteroid impact.* New York: Dial.

Holdaway, Don. (1982, Fall). Shared book experience: Teaching reading using favorite books. *Theory into Practice, 21,* 293–300.

Holmes, Betty C., & Ammon, Richard I. (1985, May/June). Teaching content with trade books: A strategy. *Childhood Education, 61,* 366–370.

L'Engle, Madeleine. (1980). *Walking on water: Reflections on faith and art.* Wheaton, IL: H. Shaw.

Lobel, Arnold. (1970). *Frog and Toad are friends.* New York: Harper.

Morrow, Lesley Mandel. (1992, Summer). The impact of a literature-based program on literacy achievement, use of literature, and attitudes of children from minority backgrounds. *Reading Research Quarterly, 27,* 250–275.

Moyer, Richard, Daniel, Lucy, Hackett, Jay Baptiste, H. Prentice, Stryker, Pamela, & Vasquez, JoAnne. (2002). *Science.* New York: Macmillan/McGraw-Hill.

Nagy, William. E., & Anderson, Richard C. (1984, Spring). How many words are there in printed school English? *Reading Research Quarterly, 19,* 304–330.

Pachtman, Andrew B., & Wilson, Karen A. (2006, April). What do the kids think? *The Reading Teacher, 59,* 680–684.

Peterson, Ralph, & Eeds, Maryann. 1990. *Grand conversations: Literature groups in action.* Richmond Hill, Ontario: Scholastic.

Richter, Hans Peter. (1970). *Friedrich.* New York: Holt, Rinehart & Winston.

Root, Shelton L., Jr. (1975). Lecture, University of Georgia, Athens, 21 March.

Stanovich, Keith. E. (1986, Fall). Matthew effects in reading: Some consequences of individual differences in the acquisition of literacy. *Reading Research Quarterly, 21,* 360–407.

Steig, William. (1969). *Sylvester and the magic pebble.* New York: Windmill.

Subject guide to children's books in print. (2007). New York: R. R. Bowker. (Published annually.)

Wasserman, Dale. (2001, February/March). Flipping the meat train. *American Heritage,* pp. 58–66.

Wells, D. (1995). Leading grand conversations. In N. Roser & M. Martinez (Eds.). In *book talk and beyond: Children and teachers respond to literature.* Newark, DE.: International Reading Association.

Whittemore, Hank. (1991, December 22). The most precious gift. *Parade Magazine,* pp. 4–6.

Appendix **A**

Guidelines for Building a Classroom Library

Every classroom needs its own library. Even if the school has a fine offering of books in an attractive central library or media center, each classroom should have a collection of conspicuously displayed titles. Two main reasons:

1. If books are present and prominent, they can be found easily and used for sustained silent reading, for browsing, or for answering personal questions as well as questions arising from classroom discussions.
2. The presence of trade books in a classroom speaks volumes about their central place in the learning process. Simply by being there, shelves of real books—not textbooks—give evidence to the teacher's commitment to immediate and lifelong learning. If a teacher talks about the importance of reading, but only a few books are visible, the message rings hollow to young ears.

The greatest obstacle to building a classroom library is impatience. Once convinced of the value of having books close at hand, most teachers want their collections to mushroom *right now*. The enthusiasm and desire are understandable, but sometimes harmful. It simply takes time, usually years, to get the kinds and numbers of books a teacher wants. The point is to begin building the collection and learning to resist the natural feeling of discouragement because it isn't growing faster. Concentrate on two areas: finding free books and finding money to buy books. Even in tight economic times, both are possible.

 ## FREE BOOKS

With ingenuity and grit, a teacher can bring books into the classroom from a variety of sources, such as the following. Note the pluses (+) and minuses (−) of each.

SCHOOL LIBRARY.   The easiest and fastest way to get books on classroom shelves is to borrow them from the school library or media center. Regulations vary, but teachers generally can check out large numbers of books for classroom use. Some teachers do not allow these library books to go home, but others develop a checkout system.

+ Effortless way to get many books into the classroom. Good selection of titles.
− Books need to be returned to the library. Teacher is responsible for lost books.

PUBLIC LIBRARY. Another quick way to get books on the shelf is to visit the public library and borrow as many titles as allowed. Many libraries have special arrangements for classroom teachers, which often include a longer checkout time and an easier check-out system. If your town has no local library, you are likely served by some other library—in a neighboring town, a county system, a bookmobile, or the state library.

+ Wide selection of materials. Immediate availability.
− Transporting books back and forth. Teacher is responsible for lost books. Limited checkout time.

ASKING STUDENTS TO BRING BOOKS FROM HOME. Many children have books at home that are appropriate for classroom reading. Often, they are willing to share these books with others for the year. Before they bring their personal books, ask students to write their names in each book in at least two places. Tell them to leave treasured books at home be-cause they can be damaged or lost even when students take pains to treat them carefully. During the final week of the school year, these books are to be returned to their owners.

+ Less work for the teacher than any other method. Students feel ownership in their library and like to recommend their personal titles to others.
− Inevitably some books will be damaged or will disappear.

BONUS TITLES FROM BOOK CLUBS. When students order from a book club, the teacher receives points that can be used to order free books. Ordering regularly from a book club not only helps students by focusing on book reading and ownership, but also by adding substantially to the classroom library with the bonus books. Some clubs even have extra teacher catalogs offering Big Books, classroom sets, recommended packages of preselected books, or individual titles for good reading.

+ Bonus books are often attractive and always new.
− Somewhat limited selection.

BIRTHDAY BOOKS. If it is a classroom custom for parents to provide a treat on their child's birthday, the teacher can request that a book be donated to the classroom li-brary instead. Inscribing the child's name and birth date inside the front cover helps personalize the gift and make it more noteworthy. Be sure parents do not think they need to spend a great deal. Paperbacks are perfectly acceptable as birthday books. These birthday books might be placed on a special shelf.

+ Encourage parents to participate in building the library. Children leave a legacy for others.
− Can introduce a small degree of competitiveness.

LIBRARY DISCARDS.   All libraries undergo a periodic weeding process. The titles taken from the shelves are usually sold for a dollar or less. It is possible that a library will donate these discards to a school. Ask the library director.

+ Little or no cost.
− Many titles are discarded for good reasons, including excessive wear, unusual topics, and being outdated. Be selective in your choices.

RAISING MONEY FOR BOOKS

Teachers have three sources of money to buy trade books: (1) ask, (2) earn, or (3) dip into their own bank accounts. The third is the quickest but should be avoided. The first two can produce adequate funds to keep new books coming to classroom shelves, and the easier of those is simply to ask. All requests for raising money need to be cleared with the principal. Sometimes you may be unaware of conditions or rules that affect your plans. To ensure maximum success, the principal must support your efforts in soliciting funds.

In addition, when you request money to buy trade books for your classroom, you should write some kind of rationale or proposal. Ask about and follow the procedure of each particular benefactor. If a benefactor has no formal procedure, present a clear, attractive, professional-looking, but brief (one page is fine) request at the time you ask for funds. Include a specific dollar amount you are seeking, the kinds and number of books you will buy, and the benefit those books will bring to your students and teaching. Frankly, if you can't make it clear how these books will benefit your students, you don't deserve the money.

Ask for Money

THE PRINCIPAL.   Resist the urge to think asking the principal is senseless, even if the faculty was just asked to cut back on copier paper because money is tight this year. Schools are budgeted organizations and have to keep money in reserve for unforeseen problems. Usually some funds remain near the end of the fiscal year. Because budgeted monies are spent instead of returned, a worthy project has a high chance of getting funding at that time.

To increase the chance for support from the principal, acknowledge that money is short, look at the expenditures made for your classroom, and identify purchases you can do without. Perhaps you can get by without a basal workbook. Or commit to using 10 fewer reams of copier paper (and stick to that). Principals often are edgy about requests for money because so many teachers simply ask. When your idea is stated clearly in writing *and* accompanied by your willingness to cut present expenses, your chances of getting the money are greatly improved.

THE PTA (OR SIMILAR ORGANIZATIONS).   The PTA (Parent/Teacher Association) is committed to improving the school and generally hosts some kind of fundraiser as a part of its duties. Write a plan that shows how you will strengthen teaching and learning by using more trade books in the curriculum. You are likely to merit closer consideration if you propose the idea along with other teachers, showing how all of you can share or rotate the books to get maximum use from them.

LOCAL SERVICE CLUBS.   Service organizations such as Rotary, Kiwanis, Sertoma, Lions, Eagles, and B.P.O.E. (Elks) are interested in being a part of and improving the community. Requesting $200 to $300 for a specific improvement in a school is reasonable. Follow the group's specific procedures. If invited to a meeting, prepare the children so that they make the bulk of the presentation.

GRANTS.   It is surprising how many district and state grants are available. Call the school district office to ask about them, and overcome the idea that applying for grants is formidable. The applications for some educational grants can be filled out in half an hour, and the awards are significant. Teachers may also apply for special funding in areas of their interest. For instance, if you are particularly fond of social studies or feel a need to strengthen your social studies instruction, propose a plan that relies more heavily on trade books to involve students and improve their social studies learning.

Earn Money

The following all involve some kind of labor beyond a simple request.

HOST A BOOK FAIR.   Bringing tables full of new books to the school for student browsing and buying is called a book fair. Usually book fairs run a number of days and provide an easy way for students to discover and buy appealing titles. An additional advantage is that a percentage of the total sales goes to the school, generally from 20 to 40 percent. Books are available from local bookstores (it's always nice to have a local bookstore support the project and bring a salesperson), local news distributors (check the Yellow Pages under "Magazines—Distributors" and then select an adult to be in charge), and national companies. A national book fair company is Scholastic Book Fairs. Go online to *www.scholastic.com/bookfairs* to locate the nearest Scholastic Book Fair office.

ORGANIZE A FUNDRAISER.   Avoid commercial programs that prey on schools. Most people feel held hostage by children who ask them to buy overpriced jewelry or very small bars of expensive chocolate. A good fundraiser should enable the children to learn something. For example, one principal taught photography and darkroom procedures to sixth-grade students. Those children then organized a portrait program for families, set up appointments, shot the pictures, and printed and sold them. Another teacher taught students how to make salt-and-pepper centerpieces for picnic tables, which they then constructed and sold.

HAVE CHILDREN EARN MONEY FOR BOOKS.   Instead of asking children to bring money for books, contact parents and ask for support in having their child work at home doing extra chores for a standard price. All parents pay, perhaps a dollar an hour, for good, honest labor.

SET UP A STUDENT STORE.   During lunch, your class sells treats to the student body, keeping profits for books. Students help plan and conduct the daily business. Sometimes this gets approval more easily when it is for a specified period of time, say, one month.

WHERE TO BUY BOOKS

Once you have money for books, you want to spend it wisely. Following are some recommended sources, including the pluses ($+$) and minuses ($-$) of each.

Book Clubs

The two biggest clubs are the Trumpet Club, phone 800-826-0110 and online at *http://www.trumpetclub.com;* and Scholastic, phone 800-724-2424 and online at *http://teacher.scholastic.com/clubs.* Each has separate clubs according to grade levels.

- $+$ Inexpensive. Relatively quick turnaround time—maximum of 2 weeks if the order is called in or submitted online.
- $-$ Limited titles. Some books are a slightly smaller size than regular bookstore editions.

Local Bookstores

Ask about educational discounts (if you can't get at least 20%, look elsewhere). Inquire about minimum orders (some stores give no discounts on small purchases). Take the school's tax-exempt number to avoid paying sales tax.

- $+$ Immediate availability.
- $-$ Discount is small. Availability limited to stock on hand.

Local Paperback Wholesalers

Cities with populations over 100,000 are likely to have a paperback distributor. Look in the Yellow Pages under "Magazines—Distributors." Those listed generally carry a line of paperbacks, including children's books, and sell at a substantial discount to teachers who pay with a school check or purchase order. Call first for details.

- $+$ Books available today. Can do your own book club or book fair.
- $-$ Paperback wholesalers are found only in metropolitan areas. Limited to stock on hand.

Local Sources for Used Books

Some bookstores specialize in used books and have decent ones for greatly reduced prices. Thrift stores have better prices, but the pickings tend to be slimmer. Garage sales? Spotty.

+   Very inexpensive.
−   Very limited selection. Condition of books varies.

Internet Bookstores (New and Used Books)

Today, the Internet provides schools and individuals the opportunity to find any book, new or used, at discounted prices. For example, Allbookstores.com (*http://www. allbookstores.com*) speeds up the searching process for buyers by comparing the offerings and prices of the major online booksellers, such as Amazon.com, Barnes & Noble.com, Alibris, Abebooks.com, and Half.com.

+   Selection is endless. New, used, and out-of-print books are available. For orders over $25 or $50, shipping may be free.
−   Shipping for inexpensive single titles may exceed the price of the book.

Paperback Books

The Booksource (*http://booksource.com*) offers paperback titles for a 25% discount on orders of 25 books or more. Shipping is free. In addition, the Booksource offers teachers many additional services. For example, it offers selected lists for struggling readers, suggested classroom libraries by grade level, and specially created lists according to individual teacher need.

+   Wide selection (25,000 titles).
−   No discount on orders of 24 books or fewer.

Remaindered Books

When books go out of print, publishers frequently sell the remaining copies in bulk to a remainder house. These books are then available at tremendous savings, often discounted 80% from the original price. Sources for remaindered books can be found online. Two good ones are Book Closeouts (*http://www.bookcloseouts.com*) and Daedalus Books (*http://www.daedalusbooks.com*).

+   Enormous savings on new books. Will ship to private as well as institutional addresses.
−   Limited to returned and remaindered titles.

FREE (OR ALMOST FREE) BOOKS FOR STUDENTS: READING IS FUNDAMENTAL

Reading Is Fundamental (RIF) will not help build a classroom library, but it does provide books to give to students. RIF is a federally funded nonprofit organization with the goal of increasing book ownership among students, particularly those with special needs (defined as meeting 1 criterion from a list of 10, including below-average reading skills, eligibility for free or reduced-price lunch, emotionally disturbed, without access to a library, or having disabilities). When 80% of the children in a school or special school program meet 1 of the 10 criteria, RIF will give 75% of necessary funds to buy paperback books for all students in the qualifying group (25% of the money must be provided locally). RIF provides 100% of the necessary funds for children of migrant or seasonal farm workers. Deadlines for submitting applications are January 14 and October 1. Contact: Reading Is Fundamental, Inc., 1825 Connecticut Avenue, Suite 400, Washington, DC 20009. Phone toll-free: 877-RIF-READ (877-743-7323). Web site: *http://www.rif.org*. E-mail: contactus@rif.org.

USING THE CLASSROOM LIBRARY

Once a classroom has a library, the teacher has to make some decisions about its use. Should those books be limited to reading in the classroom, or can students take them home? Are they on their honor to return the books, or should there be some kind of checkout system? How many books is each child allowed to check out? How long may children keep the books? Does the teacher serve as class librarian, or can children handle the job?

Each teacher has to devise a system that is personally comfortable. One fact every teacher can count on: If children borrow books from a classroom library, some titles will be lost. Period. The only way not to lose books is to keep students from touching them. Accepting this inevitability is essential. Yet few titles are lost to calculated theft. Most missing books are due to students misplacing them or simply forgetting to return them. Some kind of system is recommended to help students remember they have a book from the classroom library. The easiest system is to have the students themselves write their names, dates, and book titles on a form attached to a clipboard or filed in a folder. As students return books, they draw lines through their names and the other information. Appointing one or more students as librarians also works well.

No matter how small the school budget, it is possible for a teacher to find free books and money for books. With perseverance and patience, any teacher can build an enviable library that will help turn kids into readers.

Appendix B

Book Selection Aids

PROFESSIONAL ORGANIZATIONS

American Library Association (ALA)

http://www.ala.org

Founded in 1876, ALA is the oldest and largest national library association in the world. It works to maintain the highest quality of library and informational services in institutions available to the public. The ALA publishes *Booklist*, one of the most respected book review journals.

- *Association for Library Service to Children (ALSC).* ALSC, a branch of the ALA, evaluates and selects print and nonprint materials to use in libraries for children. Awards sponsored by ALSC include the John Newbery and Randolph Caldecott Medals, the Mildred L. Batchelder Award, the Laura Ingalls Wilder Award, the Pura Belpré Award, and the Robert F. Sibert Award.
- *Young Adult Library Services Association (YALSA).* YALSA's special focus is on library services for older youth beyond the elementary level. Awards granted by YALSA include the Michael L. Printz Award and the Margaret A. Edwards Award.

The Children's Book Council (CBC)

http://www.cbcbooks.org

The CBC sponsors National Children's Book Week in November and Young People's Poetry Week in April. Each year the council cosponsors the selection of outstanding trade books through its participation in the following: Children's Choices (with the International Reading Association), Outstanding Science Trade Books for Children (with the National Science Teachers Association), and Notable Children's

Trade Books in the Field of Social Studies (with the National Council for the Social Studies). The CBC publishes a twice-yearly newsletter, *CBC Features*.

International Reading Association (IRA)

http://www.reading.org

The IRA seeks to improve the quality of reading instruction at all educational levels. This organization publishes *The Reading Teacher*, a journal for elementary-level teachers interested in reading education. IRA also promotes children's literature through its annual book awards (IRA Children's Book Awards) and through its cooperation with the Children's Book Council in administering Children's Choices, an annual booklist chosen by young readers.

- ***Children's Literature Special Interest Group.*** Sponsors the Notable Books for a Global Society annual book list.

National Council of Teachers of English (NCTE)

http://www.ncte.org

The NCTE works to increase the effectiveness of instruction in English language and literature. Children's literature is promoted through award programs for nonfiction writing (*Orbis Pictus* Award) and poetry (NCTE Excellence in Poetry for Children Award). NCTE publishes *Language Arts*, a journal for elementary-level teachers interested in language education.

- ***Children's Literature Assembly (CLA).*** A branch of the NCTE, the CLA publishes *The Journal of Children's Literature*. The CLA also sponsors the NCTE Notable Books in the Language Arts.

PUBLICATIONS ABOUT CHILDREN'S LITERATURE

Review Sources

Booklist

http://www.ala.org

This review journal from the American Library Association describes its purpose as "to provide a guide to current print and nonprint materials worthy of consideration for purchase by small and medium-sized public libraries and school library media centers." Printed biweekly, *Booklist* publishes annually a list of best books titled "Editor's Choice," as well as the ALA Notable Children's Books and Best Books for Young Adults.

Horn Book Magazine

http://www.hbook.com

Published six times per year, this magazine contains reviews of books, articles about literature, and interviews with authors. *Horn Book* cosponsors the Boston Globe/Horn Book Awards and publishes a list of best books called "Fanfare." The July/August issue includes the acceptance speeches for Newbery and Caldecott Awards.

Kirkus Reviews

http://www.kirkusreviews.com

Kirkus is published twice monthly. It makes an effort to review a book 2 months before the official publication date.

School Library Journal

http://www.slj.com

This monthly journal is one of the most complete providers of news, information, and reviews for librarians and media specialists. A special issue in December includes an index and a "Best Books" section.

Publishers Weekly

http://www.publishersweekly.com

In addition to weekly reviews of titles for both adults and children, *Publishers Weekly* offers spring and fall special editions on books for young readers. Regular features include interviews with authors, illustrators, and publishers.

Bibliographies

A to Zoo: Subject Access to Children's Picture Books. 2005. By Carolyn W. and John A. Lima. 7th ed. Westport, CT: Bowker-Greenwood.
   Most useful for teachers of preschool and the early grades, this source lists and cross-references thousands of picture books for children.

Adventuring with Books: A Booklist for Pre-K–Grade 6. 2002. Edited by Amy McClure and Janice Kristo. 13th ed. Urbana, IL: NCTE.
   Published by the NCTE, this bibliography includes annotated listings of fiction and nonfiction books recommended for children before and during the elementary

school years. Books are grouped according to subject matter. New editions are published periodically.

The Children's Catalog. 2006. Edited by Anne Price. 19th ed. New York: H. W. Wilson.

Published every 4 years, with annual supplements, this extensive retrospective source is arranged in sections: nonfiction, fiction, short story collections, and easy books (picture books).

Something About the Author. Farmington Hills, MI: Gale Group. (New volumes published frequently.)

Volume One of *Something About the Author* was published in 1971, and since that time nearly 200 volumes have been added. Each volume offers biographical information about and photographs of children's authors and illustrators, as well as lists of their works.

Subject Guide to Children's Books in Print. New York: R. R. Bowker. (Published annually.)

All children's books currently in print are grouped by approximately 9,000 subject categories, making this the most comprehensive subject guide available.

Other Journals

Book Links: Connecting Books, Libraries, and Classrooms

American Library Association; http://www.ala.org

Published every 2 months, this journal is designed for those interested in exploring themes with children through literature.

Bookbird: A Journal of International Children's Literature

International Board of Books for Young People (IBBY); http://www.ibby.org

United States Section (USBBY); http://www.usbby.org

Bookbird, published quarterly, contains articles examining children's book authors, illustrators, titles, and publishing trends from around the world.

CBC Features

Children's Book Council; http://www.cbcbooks.org

Often themed, *CBC Features* is a semiannual newsletter including profiles of authors written by experts in the field of children's literature and listings of free or inexpensive materials.

Journal of Children's Literature

Children's Literature Assembly of NCTE; http://www.ncte.org

The *Journal of Children's Literature* contains articles and features on all aspects of children's literature, including news and other items of interest to members.

Language Arts

National Council of Teachers of English; http://www.ncte.org

This bimonthly periodical includes themed issues on topics relating to the teaching of English and language arts as well as practical teaching ideas, reviews of children's books, and reviews of professional resources.

The Reading Teacher

International Reading Association; http://www.reading.org

The Reading Teacher focuses on the theory and practice of teaching reading skills to elementary-age children. Features include children's and professional book reviews, research reports, and practical teaching ideas. Published eight times a year.

SELECTED WEB SITES FOR FINDING BOOKS

The Library of Congress Online Catalog

http://catalog.loc.gov

This site allows users to search the entire holdings of the Library of Congress in a number of ways: by author, title, subject, notes, publisher, category, date, collection, ISBN, and Dewey Decimal or Library of Congress call number. Specialized searches are also possible. Among other possibilities, users can locate the complete output of one author (all titles appear here, even out-of-print), check the exact wording of the title, determine the correct date of publication, find out which books are on the library shelf next to a certain title, or see how many different editions of a title have been published.

BookFinder

http://www.bookfinder.com

Locating out-of-print books was a frustrating pursuit until the advent of the Internet. BookFinder brings together a worldwide inventory of millions of volumes from thousands of individual book dealers who specialize in used, hard-to-find, and rare books. Simply type in the title or author, and a list of available books appears on the screen. After looking at price and a detailed description of the condition, the user selects the desired copy and then is given all the necessary ordering information.

Amazon.com

http://www.amazon.com

This site needs no explanation. Amazon.com, the largest online bookstore, is also an exhaustive source for finding both in-print and out-of-print titles.

Appendix C

Magazines for Children

A broad variety of magazines matches the interests of almost any young reader: *Clavier's Piano Explorer* for young music lovers; *School Mates* for chess fans; *Junior Baseball* for little league baseball players; *Disney's Princess* for young fans of the animated princesses in Disney's films. Successful magazines can, and do, have circulations from 100 (*Acorn Magazine*) to 3 million (*Highlights*).

A selection of children's magazines belongs in every elementary school because magazines

- offer the latest, freshest information about many subjects.
- present a variety of viewpoints on a specific topic.
- draw the attention and interest of young readers with appealing layouts and photography.
- are not imposing, thus attracting readers who hesitate to open a book.
- support and strengthen the elementary school curriculum.

Following are magazine titles selected for their quality, energy, curricular applications, and/or general appeal. Because subscription rates frequently change, as may addresses and phone numbers, we have provided the Web site address for each magazine, which will provide the most current information.

Ask (Ages 7–10). A *Smithsonian* magazine for younger readers, *Ask* is a science and discovery magazine for elementary-age children. The magazine features the best in science, history, technology, and the arts. Young readers investigate the world with inventors, artists, thinkers, and scientists of the past and present. Web site: *http://www.cobblestonepub.com*.

Babybug (6 Months–2 Years). "A board-book magazine designed for small hands" (cardboard pages, 6 1/4 by 7 inches with rounded edges and no staples). *Babybug* contains simple stories, rhymes, and colorful pictures. Web site: *http://www.cricketmag.com*.

Boy's Life (Ages 7–17). Published by Boy Scouts of America, this magazine covers electronics, cartoon features, sports, hobbies and crafts, careers, history and science, and scouting projects and programs. Fiction is also included. Web site: *http://www.scouting.org.*

Boys' Quest (Ages 6–12). In addition to fiction and nonfiction pieces, *Boys' Quest* has many exploratory, investigative, and problem-solving pages. This publication "emphasizes wholesome, innocent, childhood interests" and is designed "to inspire boys to develop interest in reading at an early age." Web site: *http://www.boysquest.com.*

Calliope (Ages 8–15). World history and archaeology are presented to young readers through fiction and nonfiction, time lines, maps, activities, and historical photographs, demonstrating that history is a continuation of events, not a series of isolated, unrelated occurrences. Web site: *http://www.cobblestonepub.com.*

Chickadee (Ages 6–9). *Chickadee* is a science and nature magazine from Canada for younger children. Illustrated with drawings and color photographs, each issue contains a short story or poem, an easy-to-read animal story, puzzles, a science experiment, and a pull-out poster. Web site: *http://www.owlkids.com.*

Childart (6–14). Published by the International Child Art Foundation, a nonprofit organization dedicated to promoting child art and visual learning, *ChildArt* presents a broad view of the world of art. Often written from a child's perspective, the magazine looks at art history, contemporary art and artists, and the variety of forms art may assume. Children's artwork also appears in this publication. Web site: *http://www.icaf.org.*

Click (Ages 3–7). A *Smithsonian* magazine, *Click* is a science and discovery magazine for young children. Thirty-eight full-color pages are filled with exciting photographs, beautiful illustrations, and stories and articles that are both entertaining and thought provoking. Parents also get an online Parent's Companion with suggestions for things to do and books to read. Web site: *http://www.cobblestonepub.com.*

Cobblestone (Ages 8–15). American history comes alive through articles, maps, illustrations, songs, poems, puzzles, crafts, and activities. Web site: *http://www.cobblestonepub.com.*

Cousteau Kids (Ages 7–15). Published by the Cousteau Society, this magazine is packed with news and adventures from Cousteau expeditions and amazing stories about the wet and wild creatures of the sea. Web site: *http:// www.cousteaukids.org.*

Creative Kids (Ages 8–14). *Creative Kids* is a forum for children's writing. Young writers' work about almost any subject may be accepted for publication. Web site: *http://www.prufrock.com.*

Cricket (Ages 9–14). This magazine publishes quality stories, poems, and nonfiction pieces often written by well-known names in the field of children's literature. It is nicely illustrated in full color. Web site: *http://www.cricketmag.com.*

Dig (Ages 9–14). *Dig,* published with the Archaeological Institute of America, lets young people share in the thrill of archaeological discovery while learning about the cultural, scientific, and architectural traits and beliefs of different societies. Recent developments in the field of archaeology form the magazine's core subject matter. Each issue focuses on one theme, providing a broad understanding of the topic. Colorful graphics, photos, puzzles, games, and hands-on projects enhance cognitive and critical thinking skills. Web site: *http://www.cobblestonepub.com.*

Faces (Ages 8–14). This magazine explores and celebrates human diversity. The editorial staff is aided by the Anthropology Department of the American Museum of Natural History in creating a magazine that examines the lifestyles, beliefs, and customs of world cultures. Web site: *http://www.cobblestonepub.com.*

Highlights for Children (Ages 2–12). *Highlights* contains fiction, nonfiction, science projects and experiments, craft projects, games, puzzles, and hidden pictures. It emphasizes "values instead of violence" and "fun with a purpose." Web site: *http://www.highlightsforchildren.com.*

Hopscotch (Ages 6–12). *Hopscotch* is a magazine for young girls that includes articles and features, short stories, poetry, nonfiction, games, crafts, and activities. It is one of the few magazines targeted at younger girls. Web site: *http://www .hopscotchmagazine.com.*

Kids Discover (Ages 6–12). Each issue is themed, focusing on a fascinating subject that is sure to stimulate young curiosity. Illustrations, diagrams, and photographs illuminate each topic, such as the construction and use of skyscrapers. Web site: *http://kidsdiscover.com.*

Ladybug (Ages 2–6). Each issue includes songs, finger plays, poems, nursery rhymes, longer read-aloud stories illustrated by award-winning illustrators, and activities for preschool and primary grade children. *Ladybug* is designed to encourage a lifetime of reading and learning in youngsters. Web site: *http:// www.cricketmag.com.*

Muse (Ages 10+). A *Smithsonian* magazine for children, *Muse* is produced by the editors and publishers of *Cricket* magazine. It features articles covering the breadth and wonder of the Smithsonian's collections and research, including topics such as the latest technology, architecture, paleontology, music, physics, theater, math, visual arts, earth sciences, space travel, ancient and modern world history, and almost everything else in the universe. Web site: *http://www .cobblestonepub.com.*

National Geographic Kids (Ages 8–14). Designed to encourage geographic awareness in young readers, *National Geographic Kids* includes full-color pictures, short articles, far-out facts, and activities. Children who subscribe become members of the National Geographic Society. Web site: *http://www.nationalgeographic.com.*

Nickelodeon Magazine (Ages 6–14). *Nickelodeon Magazine* is a humorous publication with the same irreverent tone of the Nickelodeon cable channel. It focuses on popular culture and is formatted in a busy, energetic style. Web site: *http://www.nick.com.*

Odyssey (Ages 10–16). With a focus on physical and natural science, this magazine contains full-length articles, star charts, spectacular photographs, activities, contests, puzzles, and interviews. Web site: *http://www.cobblestonepub.com.*

Owl (Ages 9–14). *Owl* is a beautifully illustrated nature magazine from Canada. Full-color photographs and paintings illustrate an interesting assortment of articles, stories, and experiments concerning the environment. Web site: *http://www.owlkids.com.*

Ranger Rick (Ages 6–12). *Ranger Rick* contains nonfiction, fiction, jokes and riddles, crafts and activities, plays, and poetry—all focused on nature and natural history. This well-illustrated magazine comes with membership in the Ranger Rick Nature Club. Web site: *http://www.nwf.org/rangerrick*.

Skipping Stones (Ages 7–16). *Skipping Stones* is a multicultural, multilingual magazine accepting art and original writings from people of all ages and from all corners of the globe. Issues have included photos, stories, and art by children from Russia; traditional arts and crafts of East Africa; environmental games in Spanish and English; and songs from India. Web site: *http://www.skippingstones.org*.

Spider (Ages 6–9). *Spider* includes quality stories, poems, and nonfiction pieces. It is nicely illustrated in full color. Web site: *http://www.cricketmag.com*.

Sports Illustrated for Kids (Ages 8–13). This magazine focuses on sports-related subjects and introduces young readers to professional and amateur sports figures, including athletes who began their careers at young ages. Departments include sports cards, legends, puzzles, activities, and "Tips from the Pros." Web site: *http://www.sikids.com*.

Stone Soup (Ages 6–13). *Stone Soup* is a bimonthly literary magazine that publishes fiction, poetry, book reviews, and art produced by children. Web site: *http://www.stonesoup.com*.

Time for Kids (*Big Picture* Edition, Ages 3–6; *News Scoop* Edition, Grades 2–3; *World Report* Edition, Grades 4–6). *Time for Kids* is a news and nonfiction magazine that comes in three editions matched to age level. Features include articles, maps, charts, and graphs about current events; activities that build critical thinking skills; ideas for research projects and writing assignments; and a weekly teacher's guide. Web site: *http://www.timeforkids.com*.

Your Big Backyard (Ages 3–5). This magazine presents a conservation message by focusing on animals and nature. Each issue contains a "read-to-me" story and encourages language and number skills in very young children. Web site: *http://www.nwf.org/yourbigbackyard*.

Zoobooks (Ages 5–14). This magazine contains photographs, artwork, and scientific facts about wildlife and often focuses on a particular animal. Web site: *http://www.zoobooks.com*.

Appendix D

Children's Book Awards

Children's book awards have proliferated in recent years; today over 200 different awards and prizes are presented by a variety of organizations in the United States alone. The awards may be given for books of a specific genre or simply for the best of all children's books published within a given period. An award may honor a particular book or an author or illustrator for a lifetime contribution to the world of children's literature. Most children's book awards are chosen by adults, but now a growing number of children's choice book awards exist. Awards help considerably to raise public awareness about the books being published for young readers. Of course, readers are wise not to put too much faith in award-winning books. An award doesn't necessarily mean a good reading experience, but it does provide a starting place when choosing books. A complete listing of the books to which these awards were given can be found on the CD-ROM that accompanies this book.

 NATIONAL AWARDS

United States of America

JOHN NEWBERY MEDAL. Sponsored and administered by the Association for Library Service to Children, an arm of the American Library Association, the Newbery Medal is presented to the author of the most distinguished contribution to children's literature published in the United States during the preceding year. A variable number of Honor Books also may be named by the Newbery Selection Committee. Eligibility for this award is limited to U.S. citizens and residents. Named for the 18th-century British publisher, the Newbery Medal is one of the world's oldest and most prestigious children's book prizes.

 USING THE CHILDREN'S LITERATURE DATABASE

To create a list of all Newbery Honor Books, first be sure the CD database is installed on your hard drive. On the Home page of the database, click on the Awards button (located in the left navigation bar). Find the Newbery Honor Awards record on the Award List screen, and click on it. Click on Open Winners in Book List (in the top navigation bar), and a list view of all the Newbery Honor Books will appear. You can also search for award-winning books from the Search Query Builder screen.

 USING THE CHILDREN'S LITERATURE DATABASE

To find the Caldecott Honor Books for a given year, first be sure the CD database is installed on your hard drive. Click on Search Query Builder in the left navigation bar on the Home screen. Enter "2000" in the Year field (for the publication year). Choose Caldecott Honor Book from the drop-down list for Awards, and click on Run Search. The 2001 Caldecott Honor Books will appear. Remember, the 2001 Caldecotts (and Newberys) were chosen from books puiblished the year before (2000).

RANDOLPH CALDECOTT MEDAL. Sponsored and administered by the Association for Library Service to Children, an arm of the American Library Association, the Caldecott Medal is presented to the illustrator of the most distinguished picture book for children published in the United States during the preceding year. A variable number of Honor Books also may be named by the Caldecott Selection Committee. Eligibility for this award is limited to U.S. citizens and residents. Named for the 19th-century British illustrator, the Caldecott Medal is America's major picture book award.

The winners of both the Newbery and Caldecott Awards are printed on the inside of the front and back covers of this book. However, the Children's Literature Database CD-ROM accompanying this book also contains all the winners plus all the Honor Books. Use the search engine to create lists of award-winning books. You may also find complete lists of Newberys and Caldecotts at http://www.ala.org/alsc.

Canada

CANADIAN LIBRARY ASSOCIATION BOOK OF THE YEAR FOR CHILDREN AWARD. Sponsored and administered by the Canadian Library Association since 1947, the Canadian Library Association Book of the Year for Children Award is presented to the authors of the outstanding children's books published during the preceding year. Only Canadian citizens are eligible for this award.

AMELIA FRANCES HOWARD-GIBBON MEDAL. Sponsored and administered by the Canadian Library Association since 1971, the Amelia Frances Howard-Gibbon Medal is presented to the illustrator of the most outstanding artwork in a children's book published in Canada during the preceding year. Eligibility for this award is limited to citizens and residents of Canada.

United Kingdom

CARNEGIE MEDAL. Sponsored and administered since 1936 by the British Library Association, the Carnegie Medal is presented to the author of a children's book of outstanding merit, written in English and first published in the United Kingdom in the preceding year.

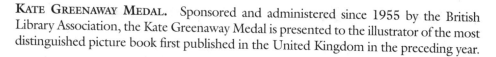

KATE GREENAWAY MEDAL.   Sponsored and administered since 1955 by the British Library Association, the Kate Greenaway Medal is presented to the illustrator of the most distinguished picture book first published in the United Kingdom in the preceding year.

Australia

CHILDREN'S BOOKS OF THE YEAR AWARDS.   The Children's Books of the Year Awards program began in 1946 under the direction of various agencies in Australia. In 1959, the administration of the award program was taken over by the Children's Book Council of Australia. Currently, four awards are given annually: the Picture Book of the Year Award, the Children's Book for Younger Readers Award, the Children's Book of the Year for Older Readers Award, and the Eve Pownall Award for Information Books. Eligibility for the awards is limited to authors and illustrators who are Australian residents or citizens.

New Zealand

RUSSELL CLARK AWARD.   The New Zealand Library and Information Association established the Russell Clark Award in 1975. It was first awarded in 1978 and is given "for the most distinguished illustrations for a children's book." The illustrator must be a citizen or resident of New Zealand. The award is given annually to a book published in the previous year.

ESTHER GLEN AWARD.   Sponsored and administered by the New Zealand Library and Information Association since 1945, the Esther Glen Award is presented to the author of the most distinguished contribution to New Zealand's literature for children published in the previous year. Eligibility for the Esther Glen Award is limited to New Zealand residents and citizens.

 AWARDS FOR A BODY OF WORK

Hans Christian Andersen Awards

Sponsored and administered by the International Board on Books for Young People, the Hans Christian Andersen Awards honor biennially one author (since 1956) and one illustrator (since 1966) for his or her entire body of work. This truly international award is chosen by a panel of judges representing several countries. The award must be given to a living author or illustrator who has made important and time-proven contributions to international children's literature. The Americans who have won the Hans Christian Andersen Award are Meindert DeJong (1962), Maurice Sendak (1970), Scott O'Dell (1972), Paula Fox (1978), Virginia Hamilton (1992), and Katherine Paterson (1998).

NCTE Award for Excellence in Poetry for Children

Sponsored and administered by the National Council of Teachers of English, the Excellence in Poetry for Children Award was given annually from 1977 to 1982, but beginning with the 1985 award, it is now presented every 3 years. The award is given to a living American poet whose body of work is considered an outstanding contribution to poetry for children ages 3 through 13. (See Chapter 8 for a listing of the winners.)

Laura Ingalls Wilder Award

Sponsored and administered by the Association for Library Service to Children, an arm of the American Library Association, the Laura Ingalls Wilder Award is presented to a U.S. author or illustrator whose body of work is deemed to have made a substantial and lasting contribution to literature for children. The Wilder Award was first given in 1954. Between 1960 and 1980, it was presented every 5 years; from 1980 to 2001, every 3 years; and since 2001, every 2 years. Winners include Laura Ingalls Wilder (1954), Clara Ingram Judson (1960), Ruth Sawyer (1965), E. B. White (1970), Beverly Cleary (1975), Theodor S. Geisel (Dr. Seuss) (1980), Maurice Sendak (1983), Jean Fritz (1986), Elizabeth George Speare (1989), Marcia Brown (1992), Virginia Hamilton (1995), Russell Freedman (1998), Milton Meltzer (2001), Eric Carle (2003), Laurence Yep (2005), and James Marshall (2007).

OTHER SELECTED AWARDS

Boston Globe/Horn Book Award

Since 1967, the *Boston Globe* and *The Horn Book Magazine*—one of America's oldest and most prestigious children's book review sources—have sponsored awards for children's book writing and illustration. As of 1976, three Boston Globe/Horn Book Awards have been presented annually: Fiction or Poetry, Nonfiction, and Picture Book.

Carter G. Woodson Award

Since 1974, the National Council for the Social Studies has sponsored awards for the most distinguished social science books for young readers that treat topics related to ethnic minorities and race relations within the United States with sensitivity and accuracy. The annual awards are given to books published in the United States in the preceding year, and since 1980, winners for both elementary and secondary school readers have been named.

Coretta Scott King Award

Since 1970, the Social Responsibilities Round Table, with the support of the American Library Association, has sponsored and administered the Coretta Scott King Award. This award commemorates the life and dreams of Dr. Martin Luther King, Jr., as well as the work of his wife, Coretta Scott King, for peace and world brotherhood. It also recognizes the creative work of African American authors. Beginning in 1974, two awards have been presented annually, one to an African American author and one to an African American illustrator whose books for young readers published in the preceding year are deemed outstanding, educational, and inspirational.

Edgar Allan Poe Award

Since 1962, the Mystery Writers of America has presented an award for the Best Juvenile Novel in the fields of mystery, suspense, crime, and intrigue. In 1989, a second category was added: Best Young Adult Novel. A ceramic bust of Edgar Allan Poe is presented to the winners in all categories, which include adult fiction and filmmaking. The Edgars are the mystery writers' equivalent of Hollywood's Oscars.

International Reading Association Children's Book Award

Since 1975, the International Reading Association has sponsored and administered an award presented to new authors of children's books. Publishers worldwide nominate books whose authors show special promise for a successful career in writing for young readers. Beginning in 1987, two awards were given annually, one for novels and another for picture books. In 1995, a third award was added for informational books. In 2002, a total of six award categories were put in place: Primary—Fiction, Primary—Nonfiction, Intermediate—Fiction, Intermediate—Nonfiction, Young Adult—Fiction, Young Adult—Nonfiction.

Jane Addams Children's Book Awards

The Jane Addams Children's Book Awards are given annually to the children's books published the preceding year that effectively promote the cause of peace, social justice, world community, and the equality of the sexes and all races as well as meet conventional standards for excellence.

The Jane Addams Children's Book Awards have been presented annually since 1953 by the Women's International League for Peace and Freedom (WILPF) and the Jane Addams Peace Association. Beginning in 1993, a Picture Book category was created.

Lee Bennett Hopkins Promising Poet Award

The Lee Bennett Hopkins Promising Poet Award, sponsored by the poet Lee Bennett Hopkins and administered by the International Reading Association, is a monetary award given every 3 years, starting in 1995, to a promising new author of children's poetry who has published no more than two poetry books.

The Michael L. Printz Award for Excellence in Young Adult Literature

Since 2000, the Michael L. Printz Award has been given for a book that exemplifies literary excellence in young adult literature. It is named for a Topeka, Kansas, school librarian who was a long-time active member of the Young Adult Library Services Association.

Mildred L. Batchelder Award

Since 1968, the Association for Library Service to Children, an arm of the American Library Association, has presented an award to an American publisher for the most outstanding children's book originally published in another country in a language other than English and subsequently translated and published in the United States during the previous year.

National Book Awards

A consortium of book publishing groups has presented the National Book Awards since 1950. The sponsors' goal was to enhance the public's awareness of exceptional books written by Americans and to increase the popularity of reading in general. The awards are given in these categories: Fiction, Nonfiction, Poetry, and Young People's Literature.

Orbis Pictus Award for Outstanding Nonfiction for Children

The *Orbis Pictus* Award has been given annually since 1990 by the National Council of Teachers of English. Only nonfiction or informational children's books published in the United States during the preceding year are considered. The selection committee chooses the most outstanding contribution by examining each candidate's "accuracy, organization, design, writing style, and usefulness for classroom teaching in grades K–8." One winner and up to five honor books are selected each year. The award is named for the book *Orbis Pictus* ("The World in Pictures"), which is considered to be the first nonfiction book created exclusively for children. This work was written and illustrated by Johann Amos Comenius in 1659.

Phoenix Award

Since 1985, the Children's Literature Association has sponsored an award for "a book for children published twenty years earlier which did not win a major award at the time of its publication but which, from the perspective of time, is deemed worthy of special recognition for its literary quality." Consideration is limited to titles published originally in English.

Pura Belpré Award

The Pura Belpré Award is cosponsored by the Association for Library Services to Children and the National Association to Promote Library Services to the Spanish Speaking, both part of the American Library Association. First presented in 1996, this award is given biennially to a writer and an illustrator who are Latino/Latina and who have produced works that best portray, affirm, and celebrate the Latino cultural experience. The Pura Belpré Award is named after the first Latina librarian from the New York Public Library.

Robert F. Sibert Informational Book Award

The Robert F. Sibert Informational Book Award, administered by the Association for Library Services to Children and first presented in 2001, is given annually to the author of the most distinguished informational book published during the preceding year. The award is named in honor of Robert F. Sibert, the long-time president of Bound to Stay Bound Books, Inc., of Jacksonville, Illinois, and is sponsored by the company.

Scott O'Dell Award for Historical Fiction

The Scott O'Dell Award, first presented in 1984, is given to the author of a distinguished work of historical fiction written for children or adolescent readers. The winning books must be written in English, published by a U.S. publisher, and set in the New World (North, Central, or South America). The award was originated and donated by the celebrated children's author Scott O'Dell and is administered and selected by an advisory board.

Theodor Seuss Geisel Award

This award is given annually (since 2006) to the author(s) and illustrator(s) of the most distinguished contribution to the body of American children's literature known as beginning reader books published in the United States during the preceding year.

STATE CHILDREN'S CHOICE AWARDS

Most U.S. states now have an organization, such as a state library or children's literature association, that sponsors a children's choice book award. Typically, schoolchildren nominate books and an adult committee narrows the list to about 10–20 titles. During the year, schools participating in the award process make the books available to children. To vote, the children must have read or had read to them a specified number of the titles. Only children may vote.

For an up-to-date list of the state children's choice book awards in the United States, access the following two websites:

McBookwords: State and Regional Book Awards—*http://www.mcelmeel.com/ curriculum/bookawards.html*

State Awards for Children's and Young Adult Books—*http://www.cynthia leitichsmith.com/lit_resources/awards/stateawards.html*

Following is a current list as of the publication date of this textbook:

Alabama	Emphasis on Reading: Children's Choice Book Award Program, since 1980 (three categories: grades K–1, 2–3, 4–6)
Alaska	See Pacific Northwest Library Association's Young Reader's Choice Award.
Arizona	Grand Canyon Readers' Awards (formerly Arizona Young Readers Award), since 1977 (four categories: picture books, intermediate, teen, nonfiction)
Arkansas	Charlie May Simon Children's Book Award, since 1971 (grades 4–6) Diamond Primary Book Award, since 1998 (grades K–3)
California	California Young Reader Medals, since 1974 (four categories: primary, intermediate, middle school/junior high, and young adult)
Colorado	Colorado Children's Book Award, since 1976 (two categories: picture book, junior novel) Blue Spruce Award, since 1985 (young adult)
Connecticut	Nutmeg Children's Book Award, since 1993 (two categories: intermediate, teen)
Delaware	Blue Hen Book Award, since 1996 (two categories: picture book, chapter book) Delaware Diamonds, since 1990 (two categories: grade K–2, 3–5)
Florida	Florida Reading Association Children's Book Award, since 1989 (grades K–2)

	Sunshine State Young Reader's Award, since 1984 (grades 3–8)
	Florida Teens Read, since 2006 (high school)
Georgia	Georgia Children's Book Award, since 1969 (grades 4–8)
	Georgia Children's Picture Storybook Award, since 1977 (grades K–4)
Hawaii	Nene Award, since 1964 (grades 4–6)
Idaho	See Pacific Northwest Library Association's Young Reader's Choice Awards.
Illinois	Rebecca Caudill Young Readers' Book Award, since 1988 (grades 4–8)
	Monarch Award, since 2003 (K–3)
	Abraham Lincoln Award, since 2005 (high school)
Indiana	Young Hoosier Award, since 1975 (three categories: picture book, intermediate, middle grades)
	Eliot Rosewater Indiana High School Book Award, since 1997 (grades 9–12)
Iowa	Iowa Children's Choice Award, since 1980 (grades 3–6)
	Iowa Teen Award, since 1985 (grades 6–9)
	Iowa High School Book Award, since 2004 (high school)
Kansas	William Allen White Children's Book Award, since 1953 (two categories: grades 3–5, 6–8)
	Heartland Award, since 1997 (young adult)
Kentucky	Kentucky Bluegrass Award, since 1983 (four categories: grades K–2, 3–5, 6–8, 9–12)
Louisiana	Louisiana Young Reader's Choice Award, since 2000 (two categories: grades 3–5, 6–8)
Maine	Maine Student Book Award, since 1989 (grades 4–8)
	Lupine Award, since 1989 (two categories: picture book, juvenile/young adult)
Maryland	Maryland Children's Book Award, since 1988 (three categories: primary, intermediate, middle school)
	Black-Eyed Susan Award, since 1992 (picture book, grades 4–12, grades 6–9)
Massachusetts	Massachusetts Children's Book Award, since 1976 (grades 4–6). An award for grades 7–9 was presented during the years 1978–1983.
Michigan	Michigan Young Readers' Awards, since 1980

	Great Lakes Great Books Awards, since 2004 (five divisions: grades K–1, 2–3, 4–5, 6–8, 9–12)
Minnesota	Maud Hart Lovelace Award, since 1980 (two categories: grades 3–5, 6–8)
Missouri	Mark Twain Award, since 1972 (grades 4–8)
	Show Me Readers Award, since 1995 (grades 1–3)
	Building Block Picture Book Award, since 1997 (grades birth–K)
	Gateway Award, since 2004 (grades 9–12)
Montana	Treasure State Award, since 1994 (grades K–3)
	Also see Pacific Northwest Library Association's Young Reader's Choice Awards.
Nebraska	Golden Sower Award since 1981 (three categories: grades K–3, 4–6, 6–9)
Nevada	Nevada Young Readers' Award, since 1988 (four categories: picture book, intermediate, young reader, young adult)
New Hampshire	Great Stone Face Award, since 1980 (grades 4–6)
	Ladybug Picture Book Award, since 2003 (picture book)
New Jersey	Garden State Children's Book Awards, since 1977 (four categories: easy to read, easy to read series, children's fiction, children's nonfiction)
	Garden State Teen Book Award, since 1995 (three categories: fiction, grades 6–8; fiction, grades 9–12; nonfiction)
New Mexico	Land of Enchantment Book Award, since 1981 (two categories: children's, young adult)
New York	Charlotte Award, since 1990 (three categories: primary, intermediate, young adult)
North Carolina	Children's Book Award, since 1992 (two categories: picture book, junior book)
North Dakota	Flicker Tale Children's Book Award, since 1978 (five categories: picture book, intermediate, juvenile, early-primary grades, upper grade level nonfiction)
Ohio	Buckeye Children's Book Awards, since 1982 (three categories: grades K–2, 3–5, 6–8)
Oklahoma	Sequoyah Children's Book Award, since 1959 (grades 3–6)
	Sequoyah Young Adult Book Award, since 1988 (grades 7–9)
Oregon	See Pacific Northwest Library Association's Young Reader's Choice Awards.

Pacific Northwest	Library Association's Young Reader's Choice Awards (Alaska, Alberta, British Columbia, Idaho, Montana, Oregon, Washington), since 1940 (three categories: junior—grades 4–6, intermediate—grades 7–9, senior—grades 10–12)
Pennsylvania	Carolyn W. Field Award, since 1984 (grades K–8)
	Keystone to Reading Book Award, since 1985 (two categories: primary, intermediate)
	Pennsylvania Young Reader's Choice Award, since 1992 (grades K–12)
Rhode Island	Rhode Island Children's Book Award, since 1991 (grades 3–6)
	Rhode Island Teen Book Award, since 2002 (young adult)
South Carolina	South Carolina Children's Book Award, since 1976 (children's division)
	South Carolina Young Adult Book Award, since 1980 (young adult division)
	South Carolina Junior Book Award, since 1993 (junior division)
	South Carolina Picture Book Award, since 2003 (picture book division)
South Dakota	Prairie Bud Children's Book Award, since 1998 (grades K–3)
	Prairie Pasque Children's Book Award, since 1987 (grades 4–6)
Tennessee	Volunteer State Book Award, since 1979 (three categories: grades K–3, 4–6, 7–12)
Texas	The Texas Bluebonnet Award, since 1981 (grades 3–6)
	Lone Star Award, since 1990 (grades 6–8)
	Tayshas Award, since 1996 (high school)
	2X2 Award, since 2001 (age 2–grade 2)
Utah	Beehive Book Awards, since 1980 (five categories: picture book—K–3, fiction—grades 3–6, informational—grades 3–6, young adult—grades 7–12, poetry—grades K–9)
Vermont	Dorothy Canfield Fisher Children's Book Award, since 1957 (grades 4–8)
	Red Clover Award, since 1996 (grades K–4)
Virginia	Virginia Readers' Choice (formerly Virginia Young Readers Program), since 1982 (four divisions: primary, elementary, middle school, high school)

Washington	Washington Children's Choice Picture Book Award, since 1982 (grades K–3)
	Sasquatch Award, since 1998 (grades 4–8)
	Evergreen Young Adult Book Award, since 1991 (middle and high school)
	Also see Pacific Northwest Library Association's Young Reader's Choice Awards.
West Virginia	West Virginia Children's Book Award, since 1985 (grades 3–6)
Wisconsin	Golden Archer Award, since 1974 (three categories: primary, intermediate, middle/junior high)
	Elizabeth Burr/ Worzalla Award (for Wisconsin artists and illustrators), since 1992 (grades K–8)
Wyoming	Indian Paintbrush Book Award, since 1986 (grades 4–6)
	Soaring Eagle Young Adult Book Award, since 1989 (grades 7–12)
	Buckaroo Book Award, since 1999 (grades K–3)

 LISTS OF THE BEST BOOKS

The American Library Association

Notable Children's Books, an annual list of outstanding children's books chosen by a committee of the Association for Library Service to Children. Available at *http://www.ala.org/alsc.*

Best Books for Young Adults, an annual list of outstanding young adult books chosen by a committee of the Young Adult Library Services Association. Available at *http://www.ala.org/yalsa.* YALSA also offers two other lists, Quick Picks for Reluctant Teenage Readers and Popular Paperbacks for Young Adult Readers.

School Library Journal

School Library Journal Best Books, an annual list of the best books reviewed in *School Library Journal.* Available at *http://www.slj.com.*

The Horn Book Magazine

Hornbook Fanfare, an annual list of recommended books chosen from among those reviewed in *The Horn Book Magazine.* Appears in the March/April issue and at *http://www.hbook.com.*

The Children's Book Council

Children's Choices. In cooperation with the International Reading Association, the Children's Book Council sponsors a project that produces an annual list of about 100 titles that 10,000 young readers from five project locations across the country have selected as their "best reads." Available at *http://www.cbcbooks.org.*

Outstanding Science Trade Books for Children. In cooperation with the National Science Teachers Association (NSTA), the CBC sponsors an annual listing of the best science trade books for young readers. Available at *http://www.cbcbooks.org.*

Notable Children's Trade Books in the Field of Social Studies. In cooperation with the National Council for the Social Studies (NCSS), the CBC sponsors an annual listing of the best social studies trade books (fiction and nonfiction) for young readers. Available at *http://www.cbcbooks.org.*

Others

There are many other annual "best books" lists prepared by a variety of organizations and individuals. Some others of note include:

- Blue Ribbons (*The Bulletin of the Center for Children's Books*)
- Books for the Teenage 2007 (New York Public Library; compiled annually)
- Children's Books 2007: One Hundred Titles for Reading and Sharing (New York Public Library; compiled annually)
- Children's Books of the Year (Children's Literature Center, Library of Congress)
- Editor's Choice (*Booklist,* American Library Association)
- *New York Times* Best Illustrated Children's Books of the Year (*New York Times Book Review Supplement*)
- Notable Books for a Global Society (International Reading Association, Children's Literature Special Interest Group)
- Notable Books in the Language Arts (National Council of Teachers of English, Children's Literature Assembly)
- Parents' Choice Awards (Parents' Choice Foundation)
- Teachers' Choices (International Reading Association)
- VOYA Nonfiction Honor List (*Voice of Youth Advocates,* Young Adult Library Services Association, American Library Association)

For complete lists of all the awards and the award-winning books, see the latest edition of *Children's Books: Awards and Prizes* published online by the Children's Book Council (*http://awardsandprizes.cbcbooks.org*).

Also, you may search and create lists of most of these award books using the Children's Literature Database CD-ROM that comes with this book. Follow the instructions found in the Database margin notes located near the beginning of this appendix to search for and list particular award-winning titles.

Appendix E

Publishing Children's Books

Children generally do not come to school knowing that books are written and illustrated by people. In their minds books simply *are,* appearing magically on library and bookstore shelves. Teachers familiar with the publishing process can round out children's perceptions by helping them see how books come to be.

Reflecting a general business trend, large corporations have been buying independent publishers, so that today most national publishing houses are owned by someone other than the company whose name appears on the book. But the business of getting a book published remains the same.

STEPS IN GETTING A FIRST BOOK PUBLISHED

Because submission procedures can vary from publisher to publisher, an aspiring author benefits from checking one of the many publishing guides, such as *Children's Writer's and Illustrator's Market,* published by Writer's Digest. Some publishers announce that they are not currently accepting picture book manuscripts, for instance. Or the hopeful author may learn that a query letter is needed before submitting anything. (A query letter is a letter sent to the publisher describing the manuscript to see whether the publisher is interested in seeing the actual work.) Then the submission process is generally as follows:

1. Author sends query letter or manuscript to a publisher. Depending on information gleaned from a publisher's guide, the would-be author sends off a query letter or the manuscript. After the final rewriting, the author of a picture book prints out a double-spaced manuscript of the complete text, and the author of a chapter book either prints out a few chapters and prepares a detailed outline of the rest or submits the entire manuscript. A cover letter of no more than one page should accompany the manuscript. It is becoming an accepted practice for authors to submit to more than one publisher at a time. Once frowned on by publishers, their acquiescence to this practice recognizes that publishers may hold onto unsolicited manuscripts for a few months to more than a year. The manuscript will be looked at by a staff member or freelance reader. If not acceptable, it is returned to the author with a rejection notice. If the first reader finds some promise in the manuscript, it is passed to another staff member and eventually to the editor, usually the fourth or fifth reader. An editor who likes the manuscript may be required to present it to the rest of the editorial staff for approval.

2. Author signs contract.   When the publisher decides to accept the manuscript, a multipage contract is sent to the author. The contract states the financial conditions as well as scores of other income-producing possibilities, such as translation into other languages; adaptation into film, stage play, or CD; paperback rights; and the right to consider for publication the author's next manuscript. Half of the advance goes to the author when the contract is signed. The editor will ask the author to make some changes, usually when the contract is signed, but sometimes as a condition of signing. The changes can be small or extensive, but almost always the author has revisions to make. The author now works on the corrections suggested by the editor, and eventually the manuscript is declared ready for publication. When the final copy is submitted, the remaining half of the advance is sent to the author.

3. Book is printed.   The publisher sees that the manuscript is edited, proofread, and polished, laying out all the plans for printing: typeface style and size, where page numbers go, placement of text with art, weight of paper, finish of paper, color of paper, style of endpapers, and so on. Because publishers do not own printing presses (too expensive), a printer is selected to produce the book according to the publisher's specifications. Unless the printer has binding facilities, the printed sheets then go to a binder to be made into books. Finished books are delivered to the warehouse.

4. Book is sold.   Marketing people at the publishing house decide how to feature the book in a catalog and whether to promote the book with a poster, display, or advertisements in book review journals. Except for sending sample copies to book reviewers, the publisher has no say in how, or even if, the book is reviewed, but author and publisher alike hope for favorable reviews to appear.

OFTEN-ASKED QUESTIONS

Where do authors get their ideas?   This is the question asked most often of authors. Like all people, they get their ideas from living and thinking. Russell Freedman visits an exhibition of old photographs and comes away with the idea for a book about immigrant children (*Immigrant Kids,* 1980). Lloyd Alexander sees in his mind an adolescent boy running up wide steps leading to an official government building in what seems to be Europe about 200 years ago. He then has to determine who this boy is, why he is hurrying, and what is going on in the world around him. After months of asking and answering his own questions, Alexander eventually fashions the idea for *The Marvelous Misadventures of Sebastian* (1970). Eric Kimmel scours collections of folktales to locate one that strikes his fancy and can be turned into the text for a picture book. Richard Peck hears a librarian say that any book with "secret" in the title won't stay on the shelf. His next book is *The Secrets of the Shopping Mall* (1979). Where authors get their ideas is as varied as human personalities and the books that line library shelves, but the common denominator is that each seems interesting or important to the writer.

What are the chances that a publisher will buy an author's first book?   About 1 manuscript of every 5,000 received will be published. But, as one publisher pointed out, "some people win the lottery." Every author was once a new author, and new authors must persevere. Madeleine L'Engle's *A Wrinkle in Time* (1962) was rejected by every publisher in New York, so she started at the top of the list again. This time Farrar, Straus and Giroux took it, and the book promptly won the Newbery Medal.

Why are most picture books 32 pages long?   Books are not printed on small pieces of paper that are then collated, but on one large sheet that is folded four times by a machine and then made into pages by trimming the folds on three sides. The most economical way to produce a short book, like a picture book, is to print only one sheet—32 book pages when folded and trimmed. (Sometimes the first and last four pages—eight total—are used as endpapers, making the book itself 24 pages.)

If the author of a picture book can't draw, how is an artist chosen to do the illustrations?   The publisher chooses the artist. Traditionally, the author has no say in who is chosen to illustrate the manuscript and gets no chance to approve the artwork. If the two had to agree, people could grow old waiting for a successful compromise. So the author is in charge of the words, the artist is given authority to interpret the story visually, and the book gets printed on time.

When an author finishes a book, how long will it take before it is on bookstore shelves?   Time varies, but 1 year is customary.

How many copies of an author's first book are printed?   The usual number printed is around 7,500 for picture books and 5,000 for novels. Considering that the population of the United States is about 300 million, that translates into one copy of a new novel for approximately every 60,000 Americans. When authors are well-known, the press run is much larger. Most initial printings for established authors are in the 20,000 to 50,000 range. A first printing of more than 100,000 copies would indicate that the author is one of a handful of the most popular writers.

What do *in print, out of stock,* and *out of print* mean?   *In print* means the book is currently available; the publisher has copies stacked in a warehouse ready to ship to bookstores and libraries when ordered. *Out of stock* means the books aren't in the warehouse but probably will be reprinted and available in the near future. *Out of print* means the book is no longer available and the publisher has no plans to reprint it.

What do *first printing, second printing,* **and** *third printing* **mean?**   The first time a book is printed is the first printing. When the first printing sells out within a reasonable time, a second lot of books is printed—a second printing. Printings are identified on the back of the title page with a row of numbers, usually 1 through 10. When the book is printed again, the 1 is removed leaving 2 as the lowest number, indicating the second printing. The next time the 3 will be the lowest, and so on.

What is a royalty?   In trade book publishing, the royalty is a percentage paid to the author for each copy sold. The standard royalty is 10% of the retail price. Royalties are calculated and checks are mailed twice a year, so an author living solely from creative works usually needs to budget well.

What is an advance?   When the publisher agrees to buy a book, the author is given an advance against royalties—good faith money that will be paid back to the publisher with future earnings from the book. Only when the advance is repaid does the author receive additional money. An advance for a first-time author of a children's picture book text is in the range of $3,500 to $6,000 (with the illustrator receiving the same), and a new novelist for children will receive from $5,000 to $10,000 for a first book. Established authors, of course, receive a much larger advance. In providing an advance, the publisher is saying, in essence, "We believe your book will sell well enough to return this investment to us." If the book does not sell enough to repay the advance, however, the author still keeps the money.

How much money do authors make?   At a 10% royalty, a $20 picture book earns $2.00 for the author. If the press run is 7,500 copies and all sell, the author will make $15,000 (7,500 multiplied by $2.00). If the picture book has both an author and an illustrator, the two share the royalty with the usual split 50/50: $7,500 each. If a first novel, on the other hand, sells for $18 with a print run of 5,000 copies, the total earnings would be $9,000 if all the books sell. Production time for a book is about a year, royalties are calculated every 6 months, and the money the book first earns repays the advance, so it is not unusual for an author to wait a year or two after publication of a book before receiving money beyond the advance. Of course, the author hopes the book will go into additional printings. For instance, *Make Way for Ducklings,* first published in 1941, was in its 67th printing when Robert McCloskey died in 2003. He must have been very satisfied when a book he created more than 60 years earlier was still being bought and read, as well as continuing to produce income.

Why do books cost so much, particularly picture books?   The $20 a consumer pays for a picture book usually is split into the categories that follow, but the percentages vary from publisher to publisher and year to year. They depend on the general health of the publishing industry and the economy. The following ballpark figures show the approximate percentages of where a book buyer's dollar goes:

50% discount to the bookseller (jobbers, chain stores, and warehouse stores receive a slightly higher discount; independent bookstores slightly lower) = $10.00, which leaves the publisher with $10.00

10% of the retail price to the author and illustrator = $2.00, which leaves the publisher with $8.00

20% for manufacturing costs (color separations, press plates, paper, printing, binding, shipping) = $4.00, which leaves the publisher with $4.00

10% for overhead (salaries, rent, office equipment, utilities, advertising, marketing, and warehousing) = $2.00, which leaves the publisher with $2.00

10% profit = $2.00 left after paying all expenses

Chapter books cost less than picture books because of the expense related to color printing. Producing full-color books requires a larger press so each sheet can printed on four separate times—one for each primary color plus black—which takes longer and demands more sophisticated technology and equipment, thus costing more. Chapter books, usually printed only in black and white, simply are cheaper to produce.

Does every book make money for the publisher? No. Much like the movie industry, some make a profit and some don't. In children's books, about 65% of the books never pay out, which means they don't make back enough money to reimburse the publisher for expenses—author's advance, some overhead costs, preparing the manuscript for printing, and paper and ink for printing. Approximately 35% of the children's books published do pay out, and they must earn enough additional money to bear the costs of those titles that do not meet their expenses. Naturally, the publisher hopes that each title will be profitable, even though two-thirds will become financial liabilities. When a book is not selling enough to meet expenses, the additional copies remaining in the warehouse often are sold in bulk to a remainder house, which pays pennies on the dollar for each hardcover book. Those remaindered books then are resold to chain stores and bookstores, where customers can buy titles for a fraction of their list price.

REFERENCES

Alexander, Lloyd. (1970). *The marvelous misadventures of Sebastian*. New York: Dutton.

Freedman, Russell. (1980). *Immigrant kids*. New York: Dutton.

L'Engle, Madeleine. (1962). *A wrinkle in time*. New York: Farrar, Straus & Giroux.

McCloskey, Robert. (1941). *Make way for ducklings*. New York: Viking.

Peck, Richard. (1979). *The secrets of the shopping mall*. New York: Delacorte.

NAME INDEX

SUBJECT INDEX